The Literature/Film Reader

Issues of Adaptation

Edited by
James M. Welsh
Peter Lev

THE SCARECROW PRESS, INC.
Lanham, Maryland • Toronto • Plymouth, UK
2007

SCARECROW PRESS, INC.

Published in the United States of America
by Scarecrow Press, Inc.
A wholly owned subsidary of
The Rowman & Littlefield Publishing Group, Inc.
4501 Forbes Boulevard, Suite 200, Lanham, Maryland 20706
www.scarecrowpress.com

Estover Road
Plymouth PL6 7PY
United Kingdom

British Library Cataloguing in Publication Information Available

Library of Congress Cataloging-in-Publication Data

The literature/film reader : issues of adaptation / edited by James M. Welsh, Peter Lev.
    p. cm.
  Includes bibliographical references and index.
  ISBN-13: 978-0-8108-5949-4 (pbk. : alk. paper)
  ISBN-10: 0-8108-5949-1 (pbk. : alk. paper)
  1. Film adaptations—History and criticism. 2. Literature and motion pictures.
I. Welsh, James Michael. II. Lev, Peter, 1948–

PN1997.85.L516 2007
791.43'6—dc22

                                                              2007009828

∞™ The paper used in this publication meets the minimum requirements of
American National Standard for Information Sciences—Permanence of
Paper for Printed Library Materials, ANSI/NISO Z39.48-1992.
Manufactured in the United States of America.

*To our friends and colleagues, early and late, whose efforts we do appreciate.
Special thanks to Tom Erskine, who first suggested we form an association
with annual meetings, and to the late William Horne,
the congenial cohost of several such meetings.*

Frankenstein

No one sits beside the prof here in the dark,
but behind me they whisper and giggle and bark
their disdain for what? The poetry, the black
and white, the naïveté of the monster, its lack
of common sense, which they possess in spades?
Aren't we, too, pieced together from open graves?

To the monster the child was like a flower,
therefore she was a flower, and since a flower
can float, so should the child. But she can't, she dies.
To the students, some thirty years younger than I,
the monster is merely dumb, the girl a splash,
like a punchline, a machine to produce laughs.

The prof packs his notes, useless, dismisses the kids,
a few linger with questions I can't rid
them of, ever—children drawn to the abyss.
A bus passes; I wave it on. What is
the night to do when its terrors shed their beauty?
I stumble home, past villagers hungry for duty.

—Tom Whalen

~

Contents

~

Acknowledgments

The Literature/Film Association (LFA) grew from the friends and contributors of *Literature/Film Quarterly* (*LFQ*), and to attempt to name them all might result in hideous and embarrassing errors of omission. But without people like Rebecca M. Pauly of West Chester University, an astute counselor to both LFA and *LFQ*, or Victoria Stiles, first treasurer of LFA (now retired from SUNY Courtland), and so many others, neither the journal nor the association could have endured. We thank all of our LFA and *LFQ* colleagues for creating and sustaining a remarkable scholarly community.

In the beginning, Tom Erskine, academic dean at Salisbury State College, could not have funded *LFQ* in 1972–1973 without the splendid administrative support of Dr. Norman C. Crawford, then president of Salisbury State. Thereafter, *LFQ* could not have survived over three decades without the continued support of later presidents Thomas A. Bellavance, K. Nelson Butler, William C. Merwin, and Janet Dudley-Eshbach, who currently heads the institution.

We owe a debt of gratitude as well to the current editors of *LFQ*, Elsie M. Walker and David T. Johnson, and their capable business manager, Brenda Grodzicki. Many English Department colleagues at Salisbury were also supportive in many ways, especially the late Francis Fleming (former chair), Bill

Zak (associate chair), Connie Richards (former chair and current associate dean), Elizabeth Curtain (current chair), and Timothy O'Rourke (current dean of the Fulton School at Salisbury). Donald M. Whaley, director of American studies at Salisbury, has been supportive in attending, organizing, and running LFA conferences. In the former Public Relations and Publications Departments of Salisbury State University, Gains Hawkins and Richard Culver helped to build public awareness of LFQ within the state of Maryland, while Carol Bloodsworth, director of publications, helped to keep publication on schedule. For two decades, Anne Welsh, who worked with Carol Bloodsworth in publications, was simply essential to the journal's continuation.

At Towson University, we thank Greg Faller and William Horne for their many contributions to LFA conferences, including creative and scholarly work but also moving furniture, as needed. Barry Moore, Jennifer Lackey, Ronald J. Matlon, Kit Spicer, Maravene Loeschke and Towson's Design Center have been very helpful and supportive as well. We also thank Yvonne Lev for so graciously lending a hand at recent LFA conferences.

Credits

Tom Whalen's poem "Frankenstein" originally appeared in LFQ 28 (3).

Brian McFarlane's "It Wasn't Like That in the Book . . ." originally appeared in LFQ 28 (3).

Thomas M. Leitch's "Literacy vs. Literature: Two Futures for Adaptation Study" originally appeared in his book *Film Adaptation and Its Discontents: From* Gone with the Wind *to* The Passion of the Christ. © 2007 The Johns Hopkins University Press. Reprinted with the permission of The Johns Hopkins University Press.

Walter C. Metz's "The Cold War's 'Undigested Apple-Dumpling': Imaging *Moby-Dick* in 1956 and 2001" originally appeared in LFQ 32 (3).

James M. Welsh's "What *Is* a 'Shakespeare Film,' Anyway?" was originally published in the *Journal of the Wooden O Symposium* 5 (2005). Reprinted with the permission of Southern Utah University Press.

Yong Li Lan's "Returning to Naples: Seeing the End in Shakespeare Film Adaptation" originally appeared in LFQ 29 (2).

A shorter version of Elsie Walker's "Pop Goes the Shakespeare: Baz Luhrmann's *William Shakespeare's Romeo + Juliet*" originally appeared in LFQ 28 (2).

J. P. Telotte's "Heinlein, Verhoven, and the Problem of the Real: *Starship Troopers*" originally appeared in *LFQ* 29 (3).

Odette Caufman-Blumenfeld's "*The Oak*: A Balancing Act from Page to Screen" originally appeared in *LFQ* 26 (4).

Joan Driscoll Lynch's "*Camille Claudel*: Biography Constructed as Melodrama" originally appeared in *LFQ* 26 (2).

Thomas M. Leitch's "Where Are We Going, Where Have We Been?" originally appeared in *LFA Newsletter* 1 (1).

Peter Lev's "The Future of Adaptation Studies" originally appeared in *LFA Newsletter* 1 (1).

~

Introduction: Issues of Screen Adaptation: What Is Truth?[1]

James M. Welsh

"'What is truth?' said jesting Pilate, and would not stay for an answer."

—Sir Francis Bacon, "Of Truth"

Overview

After a century of cinema, movies have changed substantially, both techno-logically and stylistically, but after a hundred years, mainstream cinema is still telling and retelling stories, and most of those stories are still being (or have been) appropriated from literary or dramatic sources, as much as 85 per-cent by some calculations and accounts. Adaptation has always been central to the process of filmmaking since almost the beginning and could well maintain its dominance into the cinema's second century. This collection in-vestigates the present and future of screen adaptation and of adaptation study, through essays written by the editors of *Literature/Film Quarterly* (*LFQ*) further enhanced by the work of some of that journal's most thoughtful con-tributors. The goal is to teach, by example or theory, and to explore some po-tential new avenues of discussion as well.

This collection of essays has been assembled by Jim Welsh, the cofound-ing editor of *LFQ*, and by Peter Lev, long a member of the *LFQ* editorial board. Both have also served as president of the Literature/Film Association (LFA) and are recognized senior scholars in the field of cinema studies and screen adaptation. Welsh is coeditor of *The Encyclopedia of Novels into Film* (now in its second revised edition) and of sixteen other books; Peter Lev's latest book, *The Fifties: Transforming the Screen, 1950–1959*, published in 2003, appeared as volume 7 in the prestigious Scribners History of American Cinema series. Contributors to the present volume include teacher-scholars from England, Romania, Singapore, Australia, New Zealand, and the United States; though the United States is best represented (at least quantitatively), one-third of the contributing authors are non-American.

The (Alleged) Persistence of "Fidelity"

One problem with cinema criticism and theory is that it has all too often involved a hermetic and limited society of scholars writing in codes for their mutual but limited enlightenment. *LFQ* has always reached out for a larger and more general audience. The fact that the journal has survived for more than thirty-five years is perhaps an indication that this goal has been achieved. The most basic and banal focus in evaluating adaptations is the issue of "fidelity," usually leading to the notion that "the book was better." This limited and "literal" approach is represented by bibliophiles and is the guiding principle of Robin H. Smiley's *Books into Film: The Stuff That Dreams Are Made Of* [sic] (2003), a book that was totally ignored by the cinema studies establishment. At the opposite extreme is Brian McFarlane, author of *Novel to Film: An Introduction to the Theory of Adaptation* (1996). Brian's plenary address, quizzically entitled "It Wasn't Like That in the Book . . ." and given at the University of Bath Millennium Film Conference in 1999, insists on film's creative possibilities and opens the present collection. Certainly, fidelity hovers in the background of many of the essays included here, but the anthology also presents film as having a separate identity and separate aesthetic principles, as suggested by Professor McFarlane and others. In other chapters (see e.g., Thomas M. Leitch and Walter C. Metz), intertextuality is presented as a possible alternative to fidelity criticism. One "new" focus here is the attention paid to the problem of adapting historical conflicts (such as the battle of the Alamo and the war with Mexico for Texican independence: see Frank Thompson's chapter) and the problems of adapting the lives of famous people in the genre of the biopic (see Joan Driscoll Lynch on the sculptress Camille Claudel and John C. Tibbetts on the biopic of the American composer W. C. Handy).

The Myth of the "Unfilmable"

Let's begin with the notion that everything is adaptable, that whatever exists in one medium might be adapted or translated into another, given the right imaginative initiative. Some may protest, of course, that the medium of film has its limitations, that it is epidermal, even superficial, that it cannot probe the depths of psychology or emotional consciousness. Countering these charges are the achievements of Ingmar Bergman in Sweden, of Michelangelo Antonioni in Italy, and of Yasujiro Ozu or Akira Kurosawa in Japan. Quite apart from human psychology, however, there are narrative and novelistic techniques that could be considered "unfilmable." Shades of nuance in "voice" and tone, for example, could prove problematic. The experimental prose and drama of such writers as Samuel Beckett and James Joyce would seem to pose insurmountable problems, and yet the inner monologues of *Ulysses* were filmed by director/producer Joseph Strick in 1967, and the same filmmaker adapted the interminable musings of Stephen Daedalus (as represented by Irish actor Bosco Hogan) in *A Portrait of the Artist as a Young Man*, released in 1977. Beckett himself wrote an exercise on the nature of perception in a film entitled, appropriately enough, *Film* (1965) and starring, appropriately enough, Buster Keaton. So much for conventional wisdom.

"A Cock and Bull" Digression

Take the example of Laurence Sterne's comic novel, *The Life and Opinions of Tristram Shandy, Gentleman* (1759–1767), adapted to the screen as *Tristram Shandy: A Cock and Bull Story* by writer Frank Cottrell-Boyce and director Michael Winterbottom in 2005. The book is a famously whimsical romp that turns narrative conventions upside down and delights in playing with unconventional structure. Charles McGrath describes the plot of this "unfilmable" novel as a series of "endless digressions, false starts and wheels-within-wheels. The protagonist, who is also the narrator, isn't even born until Volume III, and by the end of the book he still hasn't progressed beyond childhood, much less become an opinionated gentleman" (2006, 13). So how did Michael Winterbottom solve this problem? According to *Variety*, he did it by "cheating flagrantly" (Felperin, 2005, 63). He transformed the whimsical spirit of the novel by imagining his film as a movie being made of a movie of a book about a book. Winterbottom recognized that this "insanely digressive" novel was about 200 years ahead of its time. As one of the actors remarks, *Tristram Shandy* was a "postmodern classic which was written before there was any modernism to be 'post' about" (McGrath, 2006, 13). So was Sterne's novel "unfilmable"? Yes, certainly, in a way and to a degree. Could it be transformed in an agreeable way so as to make it *seem* "filmable"? Absolutely. Much of the adaptation is improvised by the actors Steve Coogan, who plays Tristram Shandy and Walter Shandy and an actor named Steve Coogan, and Rob Brydon, who plays Uncle Toby and an actor named Rob Brydon. Asked at a press conference whether either of them had ever read the book, Coogan said "I've read *of* it," and Brydon said "Not in the traditional sense. You know, where you go from beginning to end" (McGrath, 2006, 28). So here is an "adaptation" partly created by actors impressionistically riffing on material they have not read or encountered directly. Go figure, and ponder the future of adaptation and what the process might mean nowadays.

"In general, I'm not a fan of literary adaptations," Michael Winterbottom told *Sight and Sound* (Spencer, 2006, 14). "Usually if you're making the film of the book it's because you like the book, but that gives you all sorts of problems in trying to produce a version of it. So there's always something a bit restrictive, a bit secondhand about them. What was great here [in the case of *Tristram Shandy*] is that the book is about *not* telling the story you're supposed to be telling, so it's the perfect excuse for doing whatever you want."

Given the appetite that Hollywood and other film industries have shown and continue to show for novels, plays, biographies, histories, and other published stories, it is perhaps not surprising that the untouchable and "unfilmable" classics have been regularly touched and filmed, sometimes with good results. Consider, for example, the sprawling novels of Henry Fielding (director Tony Richardson captured the spirit of *Tom Jones* in 1963, followed by *Joseph Andrews* in 1977), William Makepeace Thackeray (*Vanity Fair* and even *Barry Lyndon* have been essayed), and Thomas Hardy (John Schlesinger's *Far from the Madding Crowd* in 1967, Roman Polanski's *Tess* in 1979, and Michael Winterbottom's *Jude* in 1996 are interesting celluloid versions). Most of the novels of Jane Austen have been filmed and refilmed, with varying degrees of success. Indeed, the Austen adaptations have become a reliably commercial enterprise, with the recent version of *Pride and Prejudice* starring Keira Knightley holding its own with the Christmas blockbusters of 2005. We might add that Austen is a special case, appealing, on the one hand, to an academic audience for her splendid wit and irony and, on the other, to a far wider readership drawn to Austen for reasons having to do with romance, courtship, and "heritage" nostalgia.

"Unmanageable" Novels: Dickens and Oliver, with a Twist

Of course, in the case of massive novels, length will almost certainly be a problem. One solution here is the "Masterpiece Theatre" television miniseries approach, applied, reasonably enough, in 2005 to the Dickens classic, *Bleak House*, originally written in twenty installments that appeared serially between 1852 and 1853 and adapted by screenwriter Andrew Davies to eight massive hours of programming. The screenwriter's credentials included the successful and popular epic 1995 miniseries treatment of Jane Austen's *Pride and Prejudice*. Arguably, television might be the best medium for assuring the "persistence of fidelity" in adapting "classic" novels. Every facial tic and verbal nuance could be captured, lovingly, in an eight-hour adaptation, every gasp, every sigh, every wink of the eye. But what about a feature film that has to be captured in less than three hours?

Roman Polanski's *Oliver Twist*, filmed in 2004 and released in 2005, may serve as a convenient demonstration here. This adaptation was not a popular success, despite Polanski's credentials and obvious talent. Even though *Oliver Twist* followed upon the tremendous success of *The Pianist* in 2002, and even though Polanski was working with much the same crew, including the playwright Ronald Harwood as screenwriter.

Published in 1837 and 1838, *Oliver Twist* was the first success of young Charles Dickens, and is second only to *Great Expectations* in terms of popularity. Oliver Twist (played by Barney Clark) is the name given to an orphan of unknown parentage, born and raised in a miserable workhouse, where he is mistreated by the parish beadle, Mr. Bumble (Jeremy Swift plays Polanski's Bumble-beadle). Oliver's story has been considerably simplified for Polanski's film, which begins with Oliver at age nine. Oliver runs away to London, where he falls in with bad company—a juvenile gang of thieves trained by Fagin (Sir Ben Kingsley), a caricatured Jewish villain—to work as a pickpocket with his more experienced colleagues, the "Artful Dodger" (Harry Eden), and Charley Bates (Lewis Chase). More dangerous than Fagin (who is somewhat humanized by Polanski's treatment though still a Dickensian caricature), however, is the ruthless burglar Bill Sikes (Jamie Foreman), a psychopath who brutalizes both his companion, Nancy (Leanne Rowe), and Oliver. The spirit of the novel is retained and the adaptation is well directed, well acted, and entirely agreeable.

According to Harwood, the "phenomenal variety of characters" found in the world of this Dickens novel had to be condensed, as well as the far-fetched complications of the subplots, particularly Oliver's relationship to the benevolent Mr. Brownlow, who rescues the boy from a life of crime.

Harwood described this simplified version as follows: "It's about a boy, a little boy, who takes charge of his own life, escapes from terrible trials and dangers, and emerges triumphant." Dickens purists should not have been offended, given the atmospheric beauty of the visualization and the integrity of the reimagined characterizations. The multilayered Dickens narrative is simplified to a story of survival in a grim and uncaring world.

It's hardly surprising that, after having adapted Thomas Hardy's *Tess of the D'Urbervilles* in 1979 (and winning three Oscars), Polanski would eventually turn his talents toward adapting Charles Dickens's first novel to cinema, even if that meant following in the wake of one of England's greatest directors, David Lean, who adapted *Oliver Twist* in 1948 with a cast that included Alex Guinness as Fagin, Robert Newton as Bill Sikes, and John Howard Davies as Oliver. Indeed, the 1948 David Lean adaptation probably still constitutes the gold standard for film adaptations of this Dickens classic. In the Lean treatment, Fagin's juvenile gang and Bill Sikes's unrelenting psychopath are presented as diametrically opposed to Mr. Brownlow's benevolence, as if representing two autonomous worlds. Lean used expressionist camera angles and lighting techniques to contrast the darkness of the underworld with the cozy whiteness of the Brownlow sequences. Polanski takes a similar approach. Mr. Brownlow's home is ordinarily bathed in sunshine and seems to be located on the bucolic edge of town, whereas the mise-en-scène is often drab and gloomy, with brown tones dominant, in the slums frequented by Fagin and his crew.

Adapting a Stereotypical Ethnic Villain

One particular challenge in this example, beyond the obvious narrative sprawl that needs to be contained, is how to adapt the character of the Jewish villain in a way that may not be utterly offensive. The David Lean adaptation was so controversial for its characterization of Fagin that, according to *Variety*, "its U.S. release was delayed for three years" (McCarthy, 2005, 62). Sir Ben Kingsley took the challenge for the Polanski adaptation and was certainly capable of doing justice to the role. Without question, Kingsley's Fagin would be familiar to anyone who had read the Dickens description: "a very shriveled old Jew, whose villainous-looking and repulsive face was obscured by a quantity of matted red hair" (quoted by Brownlow, 1996, 230).

Even so, Polanski's approach to Fagin was intended to be the opposite of the Lean/Guinness treatment, according to Todd McCarthy's evaluation for *Variety*: "Kingsley and Polanski appear most interested in attempting to humanize him, to argue that, even though he takes advantage of his boys and makes them break the law, this might be preferable to their fates if they were left to their own devices on the streets" (2005, 62). As a consequence, Kingsley's Fagin exudes "a certain feebleness and insecurity that makes him more pathetic than hateful" (McCarthy, 2005, 62). Moreover, the film ends with Oliver visiting Fagin on an errand of mercy and forgiveness before that "wretched" man's execution. Though it is certainly a challenge to rethink such a stereotyped character, this film presents Fagin as a "lovable" villain, a sorcerer whose wards are also apprentices; indeed, Kingsley saw this character as a magician.

Polanski himself, born in 1933 and about Oliver's age at the time of the Nazi invasions, could personally contextualize the Dickens story of survival. Polanski's previous film *The Pianist* was also a story of survival, though involving a much older protagonist. Polanski's *Oliver Twist* was praised by *New York Times* reviewer A. O. Scott as a "wonderful new adaptation" of Dickens (2005, B6). In his *New Yorker* review, however, Anthony Lane was offended by the anti-Semitic nastiness attached to the Dickens descriptions of Fagin, a "hideous old man [who] seemed like some loathsome reptile, engendered in the slime and darkness through which he moved: crawling forth, by night, in search of some rich offal for a meal" (2005, 107). For a director who had lost his mother to Auschwitz to even think of approaching such material, Lane implied, could be tantamount to a betrayal; but can such criticism be fairly applied to the director who made *The Pianist?* Polanski was pulled between the nastiness of Dickens's Fagin and a desire to soften the character and thus move closer to contemporary sensibilities; his "solution" (if it is that) provides one example of how adaptors respond to contradictory pressures.

A Question of Translation or Transformation?

At first, early in the eighteenth century, English novels were considered inferior to works of history and biography, even immoral, in an era when sermons were commonly published and read for enlightenment. Readers expected honesty and truth; novelists therefore disguised their fictions as fact. Samuel Richardson pretended he had found a cache of letters written by Pamela Andrews to her poor but honest parents, for example; these fabrications were embraced as truth, as was Daniel Defoe's shipwreck of a novel, *Robinson Crusoe*. Early novel readers had to be weaned away from their taste for accuracy and fidelity to the facts. Aristotle believed that art should imitate life, which is the mantra of *The Poetics*, his analysis of tragic drama. In English literature, the lines between art and life, between the fictional and the factual, began to blur first in fiction, then in theatre, as plays became increasingly realistic during the nineteenth century. The invention first of photography, then of cinematography, suggested that Aristotle's injunction might be even more demanding and that art might even *duplicate* life. But if life is merely reflected through the lens, is it art? And what of the marriage between cinematography and theatre that enabled the cinematic illusion merely to extend the theatrical illusion?

By the turn of the twentieth century, movies were "imitating" or "replicating" historical events in documentary-styled "actualities," then dramatizing stories from the Bible (e.g., *Judith of Bethulia*) or great scenes from Shakespeare or remarkable moments in literature. All of a sudden, everything was adaptable, apparently, and naïve audiences expected fidelity (in the case of literary or dramatic approaches) or authenticity (in the case of historical events, such as the Battle of the Somme during World War I). Perhaps it is pointless to demand historical, biographical, or even fictive "truths" or to worry much about the issue of "fidelity" when historical events or personages or fictional narratives are adapted to the screen. On the other hand, should not one question the accuracy of such stories or histories? Can there be—or *should* there be—any more central issue in the field of adaptation studies? Even for nonbelievers and infidels?

Some might claim that cinema inherently involves manipulation and illusion and is not really about "truth" or "reality." Others might prefer to believe that the possibility of truth in the abstract could still exist and that fidelity is not only desirable but admirable. Even that erstwhile trendy semiotician, Christian Metz, believed that "'cinematographic language' is first of all [concerned with] the literalness of a plot," as critic Robert Eberwein (1979) wrote, quoting Metz (189). In general, however, theorists cannot stand to be limited by "literal" constraints and would not therefore readily admit to being impressed by a merely "literal" adaptation.

Adapting du Maurier: Hitchcock and Selznick Court *Rebecca*

The problem will effectively be framed in an auteur context, perhaps, if we consider the example of the Daphne du Maurier novel *Rebecca*, adapted for the screen by Robert E. Sherwood and Joan Harrison. Significantly, *Rebecca* was the first film Alfred Hitchcock directed in America for producer David O. Selznick. Du Maurier, the true "auteur," was not at all pleased with the project because she did not believe Hitchcock, the developing movie "auteur," had been properly respectful in filming her first novel, *Jamaica Inn* (1939), adapted by Joan Harrison and Sidney Gilliat, with additional dialogue provided by novelist J. B. Priestley. She expected better treatment with *Rebecca*, and Selznick was determined to protect her future interests and integrity. Selznick assigned the Pulitzer Prize–winning playwright Robert Sherwood as the lead screenwriter over Hitchcock regular Joan Harrison; no doubt Sherwood's contribution (and prestige) helped to earn Selznick the Academy Award nomination.

David O. Selznick sided with the novelist and was determined to harness Hitchcock's tendency to manipulate the source novel, as he had done with *Jamaica Inn*. Selznick clearly stated his intentions in a memo dated 12 June 1939: "We bought *Rebecca*, and we intend to make *Rebecca*." Thus the battle was joined, with both Hitchcock and Selznick seeking "auteur" status. According to Tom Leitch in his *Encyclopedia of Alfred Hitchcock*, the producer and the director each had his own notion about how to proceed with this adaptation: "Selznick's allegiance [was] to an American tradition of quality based on fidelity to acknowledged literary classics and popular successes, Hitchcock's to the generic formulas that subordinated character to situation and the flair for witty visual exposition that had served him so well in England" (2002, 271). Although Selznick won this battle (in fact, the film was nominated for eleven Academy Awards and won the Best Picture Oscar), Alfred Hitchcock ultimately won the war, when the auteur theory emerged in France in the late 1950s and in America a few years later. An industry dominated by Hollywood studios was clearly in transition, as the studio era, defined by all-powerful producers like Selznick and Irving Thalberg, was drawing to a close.

Hitchcock the auteur director was not especially worried about absolute fidelity to his sources. This will be obvious if one considers the changes he made to Joseph Conrad's *The Secret Agent* as he transformed that story into *Sabotage* (1936), a film that would teach him the consequences of sacrificing an endearing character in order to maintain suspense. British writer-director Christopher Hampton would remake the Conrad story in the 1990s and be far more respectful of the source decades later in an adaptation carefully guided by notions of fidelity, but this admittedly more "faithful" treatment hardly replaces the Hitchcock classic.

Hitchcock was not destined to become famous for his adaptations, however; usually he did not assail the work of writers of the magnitude of Joseph Conrad, or the popularity of Dame Daphne du Maurier. Even so, Hitchcock did adapt all sorts of material to the screen, drama as well as fiction. His technologically daring film *Rope* (1948), for example, was adapted for Hitchcock by Hume Cronyn and Arthur Laurents from the play by Patrick Hamilton. Although not exactly a box-office success, this cult film became famous for its dramatic irony, its twisted style, and its technique (most notably for its inventive long takes). Hitchcock's later dramatic adaptation of *Dial M for Murder* (1954), adapted by Frederick Knott from his own play, proved more popular but was also famous mainly for its gimmickry, particularly its 3-D cinematography (courtesy of Robert Burks), a potentially engaging attempt to involve viewers within the mise-en-scène. Despite such innovative experiments, Hitchcock's best work was still to come. Hitchcock knew a good story but generally avoided "classic" adaptations.

If traditional Hollywood cared about issues of fidelity, it was not especially out of respect for literature or for those who created it but in order to avoid disappointing readers who knew what they wanted and expected, as demonstrated by the uninspired literalness of the first Harry Potter movies, for example. By contrast, Selznick's own *Gone with the Wind* might serve as an apt example of *inspired* literalness. As critic-reviewer Stanley Kauffmann might suggest, the more purely "literary" the achievement of the source novel, the less likely it is to be effectively or "faithfully" adapted to the screen.

Can One "Repeat the Past" or Even Hope to Recapture It?

Picture this: Jack Clayton's *The Great Gatsby* (1973), adapted to the screen by no less a talent than Francis Ford Coppola, catches the flavor, the music, the amorality of the 1920s well enough, but even though it may replicate the Zeitgeist of the "Roaring Twenties," it seriously mistakes F. Scott Fitzgerald's satire of American optimism and materialism for a romance, and it unfortunately misfires accordingly, to be partially salvaged by the casting of Mia Farrow as a luminescent Daisy Buchanan (whose voice cannot really sound "like money," though it perhaps comes close enough) and Robert Redford as gorgeous Jay Gatsby (his pink suit glowing in the dark). Though Redford may be able to wear that ridiculous pink suit, he is never entirely convincing as the bootlegger who has "business connections" with the gambler who fixed the World Series of 1919; but this was more a failure of imagination and casting than a lapse of fidelity. "Literal translations are not the faithful ones," wrote André Bazin, the guiding spirit of the French New Wave. "A character on the screen and the same character as evoked by the novelist are not identical" (1967, 127). Robert Redford is able to sanitize a role by his very presence, removing all of Jay Gatsby's rough edges and making the bitter and cynical Roy Hobbes seem absolutely heroic in Barry Levinson's adaptation of Bernard Malamud's *The Natural* (1984). That sanitized image will consequently change the nature of the character (in both instances) and the larger meaning of the story itself. While Jack Clayton and Francis Coppola's *Gatsby* merely fizzled away ever so gradually and boringly, Levinson's *The Natural* completely reversed the corrupt and corrosive conclusion of Malamud's novel in its desperate attempt to demonstrate the possibility of second chances. "Repeat the past?" Gatsby incredulously asserts to Nick Carraway, then answers himself, "Of course you can!" In fact Gatsby *couldn't* repeat the past in his own lifetime, but ten years later Redford could as Roy Hobbes in Levinson's crowd-pleasing (but outrageously distorted) adaptation of *The Natural*.

The Persistence of Fidelity, Again

Such flawed film adaptations are interesting because they at least play for high stakes. Levinson's *The Natural* has been voted the most popular sports film ever made but only because it thoroughly dismissed any notion of fidelity and turned Roy Hobbes into a Romanticized "hero." In the case of Fitzgerald's perfectly crafted story of failed Romantic optimism and aspiration brought down to earth, *Gatsby* was crippled by its misplaced fidelity to the original, but it was more a betrayal of tone than of narrative structure and development. "More important than such faithfulness," however, as André Bazin wrote, "is knowing whether the cinema can integrate the powers of the novel (let's be cautious: at least a novel of the classical kind), and whether it can, beyond the spectacle, interest us less through the representation of events than through our comprehension of them" (2002, 7).

For those who worry about the problems and the process of cinematic adaptation, Bazin's statement still resonates and questions of fidelity still linger because *any* adaptation will necessarily demonstrate what the medium of film can or cannot achieve in relation to literary sources (whether reaching for the elegance of a Marcel Proust or the vulgarity of a Mickey Spillane), depending upon the imagination of the director and screenwriter. How was the story told? How is it retold? How is it to be sold? Is point of view a particular problem because of a first-person narrator (however limited by relationship or circumstance) or a third-person omniscient narrator? Is the story completely told? If not, has it been intelligently abridged, but if so, was anything lost as a consequence? Do the characters appear much as most readers might expect? Has the story's meaning been changed and, if so, in what way or ways and to what degree? Has fidelity to tone and nuance been scrupulously observed? (Consider, for example, Francis Ford Coppola's mistitled *Bram Stoker's Dracula* [1992], which turns Lucy Westerna into a randy aristocratic tart, whose language and behavior is inappropriate by polite Victorian drawing-room standards.) Finally, has the film adaptation been true to the "spirit" of the original (subjective and problematic though such an assessment may be)? Should readers of Laurence Sterne be willing to settle for the "Cock and Bull Story" delivered by the film?

Dancing in the Dark, to the Measure of History and Art

For a final example, let's consider John Lee Hancock's *The Alamo* (2004), adapted from history, colored by myth and legend, not a "literary" challenge but a historic one because youngsters raised on this adaptation will no doubt "Remember the Alamo!" accordingly. Did screenwriters Leslie Bohem and Stephen Gaghan (better known as the writer-director of *Syriana*, one of the best films of 2005) and director John Lee Hancock get the story right? Were the characters dressed as they might have been in 1836? Was the casting "right"? Was Santa Anna, who called himself the "Napoleon of the West," as vain and as cowardly, for example, as the actor Emilio Echevarría makes him seem? Did "Jim" Bowie and "Davy" Crockett die as heroically as Jason Patric and Billy Bob Thornton represented them in the film? Does it matter? Isn't it "only a movie," as Alfred Hitchcock once advised a disturbed actress?

Well, yes, it *does* matter, we would argue (and for that reason we have included Frank Thompson's essay in the collection that follows). Historical accuracy (which is to say, historical *truth*) *should* matter, if viewers or students are to have any authentic appreciation of Texican history. A young viewer's understanding of *The Great Gatsby* or *The Natural* or Edith Wharton's *The Age of Innocence* or *The House of Mirth* or even *Gone with the Wind* will certainly be influenced by the Hollywood treatment, which ought to place a responsibility on the filmmaking team. A good adaptation doesn't necessarily have to be exactly "by the book," but many will expect it to be at least *close* to the book and not an utter betrayal. And, as the essays that follow here suggest, the "book" could be a history book or a biography, as well as a novel or play.

Celluloid is a notoriously unstable medium (literally, in terms of film preservation, for example), but it is a powerful one that makes an impact. In fact, it can be explosive. All the reading one does of Texas/Mexican history could well be obliterated by the silly icon of Fess Parker as "The King of the Wild Frontier" for an earlier generation of students raised on television images or of Billy Bob Thornton as "David" Crockett in John Lee Hancock's *The Alamo*, who might rather fiddle than fight. Likewise, students who have seen *Bram Stoker's Dracula* will have an oddly skewed impression of the relationship between Mina Murray and "Vlad" because Coppola's odd screenplay goes well beyond the novel to suggest that Mina is somehow the reincarnation of the count's wife Elizabeta, who, Coppola's newly invented prologue suggests, died of suicide in the Middle Ages while Vlad was out impaling Turks. Coppola's disappointed Vlad turns against God in this "interpretation" and is made monstrous as a consequence. Coppola's treatment builds sympathy for the monster and also builds in the means for his salvation. Presumably that was *not* what Bram Stoker had in mind.

Cinema is wonderful, and film can be entertaining, but pedagogically it needs to be approached carefully. Fidelity, accuracy, and truth are all important measuring devices that should not be utterly ignored or neglected in evaluating a film adapted from a literary or dramatic source. The whole process of adaptation is like a round or circular dance. The best stories and legends, the most popular histories and mysteries, will constantly be told and retold, setting all the Draculas to dancing in the dark as their ghastly stories are spun, or the tall tales of brave Davy Crockett and his ilk, 'til the battle's lost and won, 'til the dance is over and done. But the point is, it will never be, in cinema or in poetry.

Of course, what we have outlined here does not exactly represent a consensus, and even the contributors to this volume may not agree with such notions concerning fidelity and accuracy. The great majority of these contributors to this project would surely agree that the relationship between film and literary (or historical) sources is the basis of the field, but they have different and varied notions about the importance of fidelity. No doubt some, such as Frank Thompson or David Kranz, would argue for "fidelity, accuracy, and truth" as being essential components for evaluating adaptations (though Professor Kranz prefers the phrase *comparative criticism* to *fidelity criticism*). Others are more interested in evaluating the relationship between films and their sources in different terms, giving more consideration, for example, to cinematic form (Brian McFarlane), intertextuality (Thomas Leitch), or intellectual history (Donald Whaley) or positing that a film may surpass its source (in the case of Peter Lev's approach). Additionally, and finally, we have a few contributors such as Walter Metz and Sarah Cardwell—not coincidentally, they are among the younger authors in this volume—who work in adaptation studies but have little interest in the conventional relationship between films and their sources. Professor Cardwell advocates a "noncomparative" adaptation studies that analyzes British television adaptations of eighteenth- and nineteenth-century novels primarily as a genre and not as televisual versions of literary works.

Cinema studies did not begin to come of age academically until the 1970s, following the enthusiasm created by what *New Republic* critic Stanley Kauffmann called "the film generation" during the 1960s, picking up on the excitement created by the inventive filmmakers of the French New Wave and their "Second Wave" counterparts in Britain, Eastern Europe, and, finally, *Das neue Kino* in Germany. The Italian neorealists (Rossellini, Zavattini, De Sica, and, later, Antonioni and Fellini) had built a tradition immediately after World War II. Sweden was a world unto itself, ruled by the godlike dramaturg-filmmaker Ingmar Bergman. New ideas were found in France, thanks to André Bazin and his magazine, *Cahiers du Cinéma*, which provided an intellectual haven for such filmmakers as François Truffaut and Jean-Luc Godard, who began as budding film critics and who never quite lost their youthful enthusiasm for movie going, as well as filmmaking. Starting with the so-called auteur theory, simplified for Americans by *Village Voice* critic Andrew Sarris, French notions became ascendant.

Bazin was later eclipsed by Christian Metz, who borrowed semiotics from learned linguists and turned it into something called "semiology." Then in marched the structuralists, followed by the post-structuralists, the feminists, the queer theorists, and the postcolonists. Freud was rediscovered, along with Hitchcock; Derrida had his moment in the sun (as some began to probe his past), and Foucault and the wonderfully whimsical Roland Barthes listened attentively to "the rustle of silence." These critics gave all of us a lot to think about, but some of them also created a verbal fog of obtuse jargon that could only confuse and befuddle the common viewer (the cinematic equivalent of the common reader). Film, once called the "democratic art," was still for the masses, but criticism and theory began to levitate toward the ether, becoming ever more lofty and damnably abstract. This collection aspires to bridge that critical gap.

All of the authors represented here will be familiar to the readers of *LFQ*, an academic journal that has always taken pride in its readability as well as its academic substance. Most of the essays included in this anthology are original; a significant few have been culled from recent issues of *LFQ*. Many of our contributors have written multiple books. Brian McFarlane is Australia's foremost authority on adaptation and is the author of *Words and Images: Australian Novels into Film* (1983) and *Novel to Film: An Introduction to the Theory of Adaptation* (1996). Tom Leitch has specialized on crime films and has published two books dealing with the substance and style of Alfred Hitchcock, as well as writing an original work of adaptation criticism, forthcoming from Johns Hopkins University Press. Linda Cahir, who writes in the present volume on *The Manchurian Candidate*, has just published *Literature into Film: Theory and Practical Approaches* (2006). John C. Tibbetts has recently completed a book for Yale University Press that covers composer biopics; he is also the author of *Dvořák in America* (1994) and is as well informed about music as he is about cinema and theatre. J. P. Telotte, the author of *Science Fiction Film* (2001), is perhaps the foremost film genre critic in America. Odette Caufman-Blumenfeld, an expert on feminist drama, is the author of *Studies in Feminist Drama* (1998) and chair of the English Department at the Alexander Ion Cuza University in Iasi, Romania, where she has created a graduate program in cultural studies. The scholarly credentials of all of the writers invited to this anthology may be considered secure. We are pleased and proud to present their work on screen adaptation.

Note

1. Some of the material toward the end of this section—covering, for example, the dispute between Hitchcock and Selznick—has been reworked and rewritten from my foreword to Linda Cahir's *Literature into Film* (2006).

Works Consulted

Bazin, André. 1967. *What Is Cinema?* Trans. Hugh Gray. Berkeley: University of California Press.

———. 2002. "M. *Ripois*, with or without Nemesis." Trans. Bert Cardullo. *LFQ* 30 (1): 6–12.

Brownlow, Kevin. 1996. *David Lean: A Biography.* New York: St. Martin's Press.

Cahir, Linda Costanzo. 2006. *Literature into Film: Theory and Practical Approaches.* Jefferson, NC: McFarland & Co.

Caufman-Blumenfeld, Odette. 1998. *Studies in Feminist Drama.* Iaşi, Romania: Polirom Colecţia Ex Libris Mundi.

Crews, Chip. 2006. "'Bleak' in Name Only." *Washington Post,* 21 January, C1, C7.

Eberwein, Robert T. 1979. *A Viewer's Guide to Film Theory and Criticism.* Metuchen, NJ: Scarecrow Press.

Felperin, Leslie. 2005. "*Tristram Shandy: A Cock and Bull Story.*" *Variety,* 19–25 September, 63.

Lane, Anthony. 2005. "Hunting Dickens." *New Yorker,* 3 October, 106–7.

Leitch, Thomas. 2002. *The Encyclopedia of Alfred Hitchcock.* New York: Facts on File, 2002.

McCarthy, Todd. 2005. "*Oliver Twist.*" *Variety,* 19–25 September, 62.

McFarlane, Brian. 1983. *Words and Images: Australian Novels into Film.* Richmond, Victoria, Australia: Heinemann.

———. 1996. *Novel to Film: An Introduction to the Theory of Adaptation.* Oxford, UK: Clarendon Press.

McGrath, Charles. 2006. "Meta, Circa 1760: A Movie of a Movie of a Book about a Book," *New York Times*, 22 January, Sec. 2, 13, 28.

Morgenstern, Joe. 2005. "*Oliver Twist.*" *Wall Street Journal*, 23 September, W5.

Scott, A. O. 2005. "Dickensian Deprivations Delivered from the Gut." *New York Times*, 23 September, B6.

Smiley, Robin H. 2003. *Books into Film: The Stuff That Dreams Are Made Of*. Santa Barbara, CA: Capra Press.

Spencer, Liese. 2006. "The Postmodernist Always Wings It Twice." *Sight and Sound* *16* (2) [N.S.] (February): 14–17.

Telotte, J. P. 2001. *Science Fiction Film*. Cambridge, UK: Cambridge University Press.

Tibbetts, John C., ed. 1993. *Dvořák in America*. Portland, OR: Amadeus Press.

PART I

POLEMICS

CHAPTER ONE

∼

It Wasn't Like That in the Book . . .

Brian McFarlane

The idea for this piece grew out of a discussion with an English Department colleague on the 1993 film version of *The Age of Innocence*. This colleague had enjoyed the film and had found it attractive but added, "Of course it's not nearly as complex or subtle as the book." I'd thought the film was a masterpiece and had actually—and, I felt, daringly—said so in print; I'd also admired the novel for many years, though perhaps not so extravagantly. I'm not setting my judgment up as being more accurate (whatever that may mean) than my colleague's, but the exchange led me to reflect, not just on the matter of adaptation from literature to film, but also on the adequacy of a training in literature for dealing with film and, from the other corner, the adequacy of a training in film for dealing with literature. In Victoria where I come from, at least, it is now common for year 12 secondary school literature courses to offer one or more films as texts to be taught by trained English teachers. To the best of my knowledge, no comparable cinema studies course throws in a novel to be taught by trained teachers of film. I think "convergence among the arts" (in Keith Cohen's memorable and resonant 1979 phrase in *Film and Fiction*) is a desirable ideal but that it probably involves a kind of training different from what has been common hitherto.

On a related point, the other impetus for this paper came from Australian novelist Helen Garner's review of the latest film version of *Anna Karenina*, which she began by referring to "a class of literature that, by its very nature, is not adaptable to the screen" (1997, B27). What, I wondered, did she mean? That, in this case, it won't be Tolstoy's *Anna Karenina*? Or her idea of Tolstoy's Anna? Or that such a classic, by its very nature, is beyond the resources of film? Filmmakers, in such cases, are out of their league, she asserted. Her claim that a great novel's "central energy source" is its "narrative voice" may be unexceptional, but she goes on to insist that "nothing available to mainstream cinema . . . can translate the authority of that voice" (1997, B27), and here she is simply ignoring—or ignorant of—the nature of film narration, to which this paper will return, and its capacity for asserting its own authoritative voice. The review reminded me of a good deal of middle-class, middle-brow criticism, even from someone as distinguished as Dilys Powell, who wrote of David Lean's *Oliver Twist* that it is "careful in the preservation of the skeleton of Dickens's book (since skeleton is all a film has time for)" (1948, 334). There is at work here little sense that film may have at its command narrational strategies as potentially subtle and complex as those of any other narrative or dramatic mode, and such thinking has led to the perpetuation of such myths as "second-rate" fiction is easier to adapt to the screen.

Forty years ago, in his pioneering work *Novels into Film* (and the titles of such books, my own included, are depressingly similar), George Bluestone (1957) wrote of the overt compatibility but secret hostility between novel and film; in the intervening decades nothing has happened radically to challenge this perception. And when I talk to colleagues about film versions of novels or read the sort of criticism I've just been quoting, I am sometimes reminded of the late James Agee ,who wrote in 1946 that he had the idea that many serious-minded people wanted movies to offer more elevated themes or "a good faithful adaptation of *Adam Bede* in sepia, with the entire text read offscreen by Herbert Marshall" (he of the mellifluous tones) (216). It's as if they want film to be more like literature and are oblivious to what might make film cinematically exciting. In this way, I suspect that a training in literature doesn't simply fail to provide an understanding of how a film is working. I think it goes further, and more damagingly, to set up a sort of Leavisite evaluative judgment, a high culture/popular culture hierarchy, in which film inevitably comes below/behind the literary text. For such evaluations, the film is only really valuable as it approximates the precursor literary text.

I have to say that my experience is that those of us with a literary training are far more likely to hold forth about film, especially in relation to adaptation, than are the film-trained to lay down the law about literature. Most notorious, perhaps, among the former—the literary-trained—was F. R. Leavis, who described the idea of filming *Women in Love* as "an obscene undertaking" (quoted by Christie, 1969, 49). He was, of course, speaking sight unseen. It's partly, perhaps, a matter of the older discipline's being wary about according equal status to the newer one; it may also be something to do with the huge popularity of cinema, which perhaps makes it seem dubious as a basis for study comparable with literature. On that matter, incidentally, it has always seemed to me curious to hold the belief that it is easier to produce a work of art which pleases many than it is to produce one which will please only the few. At the risk of this chapter's containing something to offend everyone, I'd add that, as for the film-trained of today, they are often quite ignorant about literature, and indeed about the other arts in general, but, apart from, say, the reviewers whose favorite novel has been filmed in ways displeasing to them, they tend to limit themselves to the area in which their training has equipped them to recognize such qualities as complexity and subtlety. There are, though, younger film reviewers sometimes ready to court favor by expressing a hip impatience with, say, Shakespeare or Jane Austen, which leads them, almost as a reflex action, to prefer Baz Luhrmann's film *William Shakespeare's Romeo + Juliet* or Amy Heckerling's *Clueless* to more orthodox adaptations of classic literature.

Our training in literature equips us to read complexity and subtlety in novels (I'll stick to novels mainly for this chapter). We are trained to do more than to read for "mere" narrative, though, speaking as one who has recently read and taught *Lady Audley's Secret* and *The Woman in White* in a melodrama course, I have to say I don't think there is anything "mere" about narrative in the sense of referring to that skill that carries us breathless from one set of events to the next. We have been taught to be attentive to matters like how point of view is created: for example, to the different kinds of purchase on events which a first-person or omniscient author or a Jamesean "central reflector" allows us: how character is revealed by and precipitates action, how thematic concerns are articulated through character and action in collaboration, how to read—in more modern terminology—sometimes conflicting discourses of, say, gender and class. As a result of all this serious study of how literature works and means, we're unlikely to see *Pride and Prejudice* (the novel) as no more than a "merry manhunt" or "a picture of a charming and mannered little English world which has long since been tucked away in ancient haircloth trunks" as the *New York Times* reviewer described the MGM film of nearly sixty years ago (Crowther, 1940, 191).

The attitude of literary people to film adaptations of literary works is almost always to the detriment of the film, only grudgingly conceding what film may have achieved. My contention is that their training hasn't taught them to look in film for riches comparable to those they find in literature and that, in consequence, their filmgoing experience, especially when adaptation is in question, tends to seem thin by comparison. When viewing the film version of a novel or play they know, they want to find in the film what they valued in the literary work, without asking whether this is the sort of thing film can do. They are too often not interested in something new being made in the film but only in assessing how far their own conception of the novel has been transposed from one medium to the other. One hears such comments as "Of course, she [i.e., Gwyneth Paltrow] is not Emma," with little thought for what this might mean in the context of a move from the merely representational mode to what Barthes (1977) calls a "mode of the operable" (89). She is not whose Emma? I suspect there is a yearning for fidelity, not just among those with a literary training, but among quite wide sectors of the filmgoing public, without any real concern for how much fidelity is either possible or desirable—or what it might mean. And such thinking begs the question that there is such a thing as a "true" or fixed meaning for a literary text—for any sort of text for that matter. A certain kind of literary training seems also locked into a mimetic approach which sees divergence from realist expectations as some kind of failure. If you want the same experience (and believe you can have just that experience twice) that you had in reading the novel, why not simply reread the novel? It's much more likely to produce the desired effect. Fidelity is obviously very desirable in marriage; but with film adaptations I suspect playing around is more effective.

The discourse on adaptation is perhaps more enduring and pervasive than any other in relation to filmgoing. When we come out of a cinema, we rarely hear people saying, "What sophisticated control of the mise-en-scène" or "Did you notice the poetic use of lap dissolves?" It is, however, quite common to come out of a cinema after viewing an adaptation or to engage in casual conversation about it afterward and to hear such comments as "Why did they change the ending?" or "She was blonde in the book" or, almost inevitably, "I think I liked the book better." It is a subject on which everyone feels able to have an opinion, and most opinions, from the casually conversational to exegeses in learned journals, still tend to foreground the criterion of fidelity, whether in explicit terms or by tacit assumption. One such account in a scholarly journal is Nicola Bradbury's essay on the film version of *The Europeans* in *Essays in Criticism*. Speaking of one episode, she writes, "It is not, quite, a picture from James's novel, though it is thoroughly Jamesean in tone, and excellent cinema" (Bradbury, 1979, 299). By which she seems to mean, in her next sentence, that "every aspect of setting, action, dialogue, character, image, and theme is interrelated"—and she might just as well be talking about the book. The film, she makes clear, is sensitive and discreet insofar as it matches James. My dissatisfaction with this approach does not stem from the idea of enjoying a particular novel more than its film version; it would be surprising if one had no preference. My dissatisfaction grows from a failure to distinguish between what one might reasonably expect to find transferable from one medium of display to another and what requires the invoking of the processes of what I call "adaptation proper." Here, essentially, is where a lit-erary training proves most inadequate. It is easy enough to tell, even to quan-tify, what narrative kernels (in Seymour Chatman's term) or "cardinal func-tions" (in Roland Barthes's term—i.e., what he deems "hinge-points of narrative," opening up alternative narrative possibilities) have been trans-ferred from the wholly verbal sign system to the system of audiovisual mov-ing images. It is less easy, but a lot more interesting and rewarding, to con-sider how the processes of "adaptation proper" go about their business: This is where a knowledge of the strategies of film narration or enunciation be-comes crucial. I mean here essentially the ways in which the three large classes of film narration—mise-en-scène, editing, and soundtrack, in their various subcategories—put before us the narrative events which, in their bare bones, may have been transferred from page to celluloid. To be ignorant of these is to be ignorant of how film creates meaning in those large areas which pervade a text vertically, as distinct from the horizontal causally linked chain of events.

It's important for me to stress that merely being bold in the matter of adap-tation won't ensure a good/interesting/stimulating film, whether it outrages devotees of the precursor text or not. A recent example is Jane Campion's *A Portrait of a Lady*. A good deal of this seems to me intelligent in its rendering of a "young woman affronting her destiny," making a sad mess of her life, and maintaining her integrity the while. However, whenever the film's makers set out to be bold, their efforts look so self-conscious, so determinedly filmic, in the context of the naturalism of the classical Hollywood narrative style of the rest of the film, that these "touches" seem merely disruptive. I mean the opening with a lot of young Australian women talking on screen about kiss-ing, all done in black and white, and in no clear way related to what follows; or the home movie scenes of Isabel's travels; or the scene in which she imag-ines herself sexually fondled by three men. These constitute "bold" breaks with the expected in the sense, first, that they are departures from James, which one wouldn't on principle object to, and, second, that they challenge unproductively the validity of the dominant narrative mode of film story-telling in which they are cast. The black-and-white prologue and the washed-out old-photographs look of the home movies offers a disconcerting break from the prevailing Technicolor, and the scene of sexual fantasizing, while arguably an objectification of what is part of Isabel's confusion, sits strangely with the rest of the film in which sexuality is suppressed and its manifestations discreetly if powerfully encoded. I would argue that these apparently bold touches have the effect of being grafted onto, rather than imaginatively integrated into, Campion's incarnation of the novel's concerns, that they are jarring rather than enriching or provocative. She has not made the really bold leap that characterizes such transformations as Welles's *Chimes at Midnight* or Gus Van Sant's *My Own Private Idaho* or Amy Heckerling's *Clueless* or Alfonso Cuarón's 1997 version of *Great Expectations*. In each of these cases, what is offered is, in some sense, a radical reworking of the precursor text, a kind of commentary on its great antecedent, a new work.

But if *merely* being bold is no guarantee that the filmmaker will give satisfaction to audiences who may or may not have read the antecedent novel, neither is a slavish devotion to the original text: that is, to details of plot, character, and settings, for example. Not being bold can cripple the processes of adaptation, and one can end up with not so much an adaptation as an embalmment of a famous work. I place a good deal of BBC classic serial filmmaking in this category: I know enough people loved the serialization of *Pride and Prejudice* to warrant its being run twice in Australia within a few months (though I suspect the local chapter of the Colin Firth Fan Club of having a hand in that), but it seemed to me the work of an industrious bricklayer rather than an architect, with one event from the novel remorselessly following another, without any sense of shape or structuring, without any apparent point of view on its material. By this assertion, I mean a sort of dogged reproduction, incident by incident, of the novel's narrative. In fact, the old Hollywood film may have had a surer sense of what it was up to: that is, it was a light-hearted romantic comedy, fuelled by the sorts of star presences and narrative blockages and inevitable closure that characterized the genre. The BBC's version was eminently more respectable, as if it feared criticism from the academy; it took endless pains over the look of things in early nineteenth-century England; it filled out dialogue exchanges with no doubt well-researched episodes of country dancing and authentically got-up carriages travelling through picturesque countryside; but it seemed to have nothing to say dramatically about its material, except perhaps that sexual attraction was more potent than class or wealth—and we knew that if we'd read the novel, possibly even if we hadn't. Some of the Merchant-Ivory versions of James and Forster belong in this category in my view: the decorous, undaring, step-by-step, filmmaking-by-numbers approach to the adaptation of the classics, as if the aim was to placate an academy waiting with fangs bared to seize on any violation of the original. Violation, tampering: the sorts of terms used suggest deeply sinister processes of molestation.

It may be beginning to sound as if I can't be satisfied with adaptation of any kind, that I'm irritated by the merely bold and by the overreverent. I should say that this sort of captiousness is not the case and that, in relation to the latter (the close approximation in film terms of the functions of the original), fidelity to incident and character connections, to period and place, doesn't necessarily produce a poor film or a film that can't stand evaluative comparison with the novel. Peter Bogdanovich's *Daisy Miller* is a striking example of what I mean here: with one exception, admittedly an important one, it transfers all the major examples of what Roland Barthes would call "cardinal functions"; its characters are given to do what they do in the novel and almost always where they do it in the novel. Nevertheless, while observing this surprising degree of transfer, I'd say there is enough of Bogdanovich's own "commentary," making itself felt in the film's enunciatory procedures, on the action devised by James, to lead us to feel we are seeing something new. He seems to me, in adhering to the events of the novel, to provide a commentary on the nature and effects of repression, especially of sexual repression, rather than merely to reproduce the Jamesean complex fate. And one might also add that the Merchant-Ivory team achieve something similar in their adaptation of *Howard's End* when the brutalities of class oppressiveness are made so poignant.

The ideal seems to me to be, on the one hand, bold and intelligent and, on the other, determined to make something both connected to its precursor and new in itself. The film has the right to be judged as a film; then, one of the many things it also is an adaptation (it is also the product of a particular industrial system, a genre film, part of a tradition of national filmmaking, etc). That is, the precursor literary work is only an aspect of the film's intertextuality, of more or less importance according to the viewer's acquaintance with the antecedent work. In, for example, thinking about Olivier's *Hamlet*, it may be as important to have in mind the nature of British "quality" cinema, the works that accounted for its postwar prestige, its relation to the British theatrical tradition, the Freudian psychologizing of Dr. Ernest Jones, and the film noir stylistic and thematic preoccupations so common at the time, as it is to have Shakespeare's play. This is difficult for those of us trained in literature to accept: to approach a narrative mode which expends itself in, say, two hours and find in it complexity and subtlety in their own way as striking as those a novel may develop over several hundred pages and seven or eight hours of reading time. But I would claim that this does happen and that the great works of adaptation, particularly of the classics, of works that have been valued by many people over a long period, make us reconsider the original in the light of what a later period and another sign system have made of it, bearing in mind the sorts of other influences I have talked about.

I can imagine an approach to the recent film of The Wings of the Dove, which lamented the loss of the extended passages of interior analysis through which James gives us access to the machinations of Kate Croy and the reluctant acquiescence of Merton Densher in her scheme for him to marry the dying Millie Theale and then inherit her vast wealth. (Incidentally, I can also imagine an approach that welcomed such losses.) The film shears away many characters, reduces others to more or less shadowy figures in the wings and focuses the hard bright light of its intelligence and compassion on the central trio. Through decisions made about cutting between faces and the interception of glances, through the framing of faces either, say, in close-up or in sustained two-shot (e.g., Milly and Kate at oblique angles from each other as, from their balcony, they overlook Venice and talk of Merton), about costume and ways of looking, moving and sitting and gesturing, the interior nature of the drama at work among these three is conducted with a rigor that even the rigorous James might have approved. The film is updated to 1910, which may occasion purist objection, but it can also be argued that it enables convincingly just that much more freedom in the representation of sexual desire as to make Kate's conflict accessible to us now. That she is strongly sexually attracted to Densher intensifies the sense of what she is compelling herself to suppress in urging him to press his intentions on Millie.

On another aspect of the difficulties of her situation, that is the oppressiveness for a wellborn young woman in being without money, the film's mise-en-scène is persistently rigorous and complex in suggesting the different ways in which different settings can oppress. In London, the opening sequence on the Underground at once suggests the difficulty which impoverished lovers might experience in finding privacy: The silent journey in which their space is confined by jostling others builds up mutely a state of tension in which erotic release is finally given in the kiss in the lift. Elsewhere, Densher's rooms are located in a narrow street whose oppressive potential is created in the mise-en-scène: A low-angled shot stresses the daunting aspect of the slit of light between two high buildings of somber grey; color, light, and angle do the work of rendering not merely place but the quality of place, which, in a novel, might be done through the descriptive aspect of the discursive prose. At the country seat of Lord Mark, the aristocrat whom Kate's aunt wants her to marry, the sheer scale of the establishment, first indicated in an imposing exterior, then elaborated in shots of its overbearing interior grandeur, is again made palpable through the agency of the mise-en-scène, especially in the choices made about where to put the camera and where and when to move it. All these filming decisions are in the interests of making what Lord Mark has to offer the impoverished Kate seem as impressive as possible—and his motives as questionable. When the narrative moves to Venice, the mise-en-scène triumphantly furthers the whole drama of duplicity. Millie Theale's innocence is seen as threatened by an ambience in which nothing is solid, where the possibilities for deceit are unlimited. Especially in matters of color and lighting, in the juxtaposing of the superficial beauties of the place with the actualities of its decay and the masquerade in which the lovers make use of disguise to pursue their liaison, the complex web of corruption is rendered in terms of image and editing. The camera—what it chooses to attend to and from what angle and distance and according to what kind of focus, whether it is still or moving, how it frames what is presented to its lens, or what information it chooses to withhold—is, in collaboration with the editor who decides on the suturing of shots to act out the director's intention, as capable of complexity and subtlety, of ensuring emotional and intellectual engagement, as the writer is on the page in the exercise of a quite other sign system.

I began by talking about *The Age of Innocence*, so it is perhaps appropriate that I should try to demonstrate what I mean by a few direct references to it. About twenty minutes into the film is a wonderful long shot of a substantial New York apartment building (possibly Mrs. Manson Mingott's) standing at a snowy crossroads, while at the other three corners there is nothing to be seen but the earliest stages of foundation digging. This shot is preceded and followed by interiors, the former at Mrs. Mingott's house and on its steps, with Mrs. Welland saying it is a mistake for the Countess Olenska to be seen going about with the raffish Julius Beaufort, and the latter over Mrs. Welland's dinner table where the discussion is about Ellen's behavior.

The shot, intrinsically stunning in its composition, colors, lighting, and angle of vision, seems at first gratuitous. As I've said, it's placed between two interior scenes thick with elegant decoration and charged social talk, and it is apparently offered without comment. In itself, though, it does constitute a comment: it reminds us that this city, with its pretensions, dicta, and assiduously preserved rituals, behaving as if its decorums were sanctioned by generations of lawgivers, is actually still in the process of being built. The mere fact of its being an extreme long shot is itself significant: it implies that if you could stand back and view the city from some detached, sufficiently distant perspective, you might get a very different view on its life from that to be had in its socially acceptable purlieux. A single shot is, through the exercise of multiple cinematic strategies, including somberly dignified music on the soundtrack, imbued with a complexity and subtlety that cause it to stay in the mind long after the film is over. We can, of course, let it pass by without registering more than its aesthetic qualities, or not even that: I'm suggesting that, if we give it the kind of attention we expect to give the prose of a great novel, we shall be rewarded not only by its intrinsic beauty but by its commentative power as well.

The second example I want to draw attention to occurs even earlier in the film. The passage begins at the opera at the moment when Mrs. Julius Beaufort traditionally rises from her seat (in a box of course) to go home to receive her guests for the Beauforts' annual ball. A series of shots is joined by dissolves to remove Mrs. Beaufort at the usual moment from the opera to her waiting carriage to her home and to show the opulence of a home which can afford to have a large ballroom for use only once a year. Each successive dissolve signifies a lapse of time and a further stage in the preparation for the ball, over a period of days, perhaps weeks, before the night itself. The dissolves not merely link the shots but also comment on their interconnectedness: The first, for instance, gets Mrs. Beaufort from the opera house into her waiting carriage, as well as gives us a sense of the relative weight which these New Yorkers attach to high culture and high society—the latter wins hands down in any sort of competition for serious attention. This sequence of brief shots linked/separated by dissolves is accompanied by the narrator in ironic voice-over (and drawing on Edith Wharton's own words) drawing attention to the habits of the natives, then homing in on the Beauforts' pretensions in particular. The three shots of the ballroom itself represent the stages by which it is transformed from dust-sheeted emptiness to the gleam of readiness to the culminating moment of the orchestra's playing "Radetsky's March" as the dancers approach the camera with the exhilarating confidence of people absolutely assured of their place in society. The dissolves themselves act as signifiers of time passed, of time collapsed between three specific points, bringing us up to the moment of the dancing. And following the shots of the orderly dance, viewed in long shot from a high angle, to make the full formality of the occasion clear, the camera cuts to a close-up of the gentlemen's identical gloves awaiting later collection, a further point mutely made about the formality and conformity of this sample of New York society. I've deliberately chosen a moment of no particularly crucial importance to the narrative to show how the film's narrational resources can be marshalled in the interests of economical storytelling.

I'll finish by referring to a brief, much later extract, which is important to the film's main narrative line and in which, characteristically of this film, the visual and the aural work together in intricate ways, mediated by the subtlety of the editing. The scene dissolves from Ellen's stepping into the sunlit street to meet Newland, then dissolves again to the lakeside tea table, where in a series of alternating medium close-ups the situation between the two would-be lovers is revealed. This gives way to a tighter alternation of each seen over the shoulder of the other, a way of stressing the inextricable connection between the two and tightening the tension between them, and there is then a brief alternation between their hands touching on the table and the previous set of shots in which the camera looks over the shoulder of one at the other. In the two dissolves that follow, she first vanishes from the scene leaving him deserted, then he vanishes while the camera stays briefly and poignantly on the empty verandah and the voice of Enya on the soundtrack sings the famous song of a dream of love's tenacity, "I dreamt I dwelt in marble halls." That it is no *more* than a dream is reinforced by its being the aural link between this segment and the next, which returns us to thriving New York. The solitary building I showed of the earlier extract is now no longer isolated (the mise-en-scène effortlessly but unobtrusively making a point about material progress) and an army of uniformed businessmen, in top coats and bowlers held on against the wind, moving in slow motion, makes with visual eloquence Wharton's—and Scorsese's—point about the conformity which Newland will now find hard to escape. As the song on the soundtrack ends, he emerges from this anonymous crowd.

The three categories of narrational strategies—mise-en-scène, editing, and soundtrack—work together to imbue these two transitional sequences of shots with a complexity and subtlety which I think ought to have satisfied my colleague if her training had equipped her to look for these in film and to read the distinctive grammar of the medium. There is a good deal of overlap in areas of intellectual and affective response to a novel and to the film derived from it, but these responses are, of course, the result of two different processes of articulation. It may seem uphill work, but I think it is important for those of us involved in both film and literature to urge more strongly the dropping of a high culture/popular culture hierarchy or even dichotomy, the abandoning of the fidelity approach in favor of a more productive invoking of intertextuality, and the attention to what makes for such qualities as subtlety and complexity in film rather than complaining of the loss of what is peculiar to literature. Film is perhaps so easy to enjoy that it becomes even easier not to notice that a lot is going on.

Works Cited

Agee, James. 1946. *Agee on Film*. New York: McDowell Oblonsky. [Reprinted from *Nation*, 19 July 1947.]

Barthes, Roland. 1977. *Image-Music-Text*. Trans. Steven Heath. Glasgow: Fontana/ Collins.

Bluestone, George. 1957. *Novels into Film*. Baltimore: Johns Hopkins University Press.

Bradbury, Nicola. 1979. "Filming James." *Essays in Criticism* 29 (4), October, 293–301.

Christie, Ian Leslie. 1969. "Women in Love" (Review). *Sight and Sound* 39 (1): 49–50.

Cohen, Keith. 1979. *Film and Fiction*. New Haven, CT: Yale University Press.

Crowther, Bosley. 1940. "Pride and Prejudice" (Review). *New York Times*, 9 August, 19.

Garner, Helen. 1977. "Unhappy Families." *The Australian*, 9 July, B27.

Powell, Dilys. 1948. *The Dilys Powell Reader*. Oxford: Oxford University Press. [Reprinted in 1991.]

CHAPTER TWO

~

Literature vs. Literacy: Two Futures for Adaptation Studies

Thomas M. Leitch

These are great times to be writing about the cinematic adaptation of liter-ary texts, partly because there has been such a renascence of publications in the field, partly because a productive rupture has arisen between the theory and practice of adaptation studies. This rupture appears in ritual response to each new film adaptation of a canonical novel. On the release of Mira Nair's brisk, colorful adaptation of *Vanity Fair*, the director disputed an interviewer's remark that "Thackeray condemns Becky more than you do," arguing that the novel was serialized "in a tabloid and editors would respond to him con-stantly about his last episode. That's what I ascribe to the classic 'Hollywood interference mode': the inconsistencies of the character. . . . He was actually admonished: 'You're enjoying Becky too much. Make it clearer who's the vir-gin and who's the whore'" (Wilmington, 2004, 3).

Contributors to the Indiana University's VICTORIA listserv (n.d.) re-sponded with predictable outrage. Patrick Leary, disputing Nair's suggestion that "she has somehow rescued Thackeray's original, frustrated intention" as "pure fantasy," insisted that "the ever-compliant Bradbury & Evans never once in all their long association with Thackeray had anything in particular to say about the content of the fiction he published with them. Nor would Thackeray have paid them any attention if they had." Sheldon Goldfarb agreed that *Vanity Fair* was serialized not in a "tabloid" but in its monthly parts, adding, "The ending in the novel reflects the tension that builds up in its latter stages: a tension between the desire to get into high society (the social climbing impulse) and the fear of getting into it (the fear of then being set upon by all the high society ladies, etc.). This is a very interesting tension in the novel (I think reflecting a tension in Thackeray himself), and it is much better expressed by the novel's ending than the film's." Micael Clarke defended Nair's film as "follow[ing] the novel in important ways": its "surface sumptuousness," its critique of society, its sympathy for women. Sarah Brown added that "the Natasha Little version of a few years back [written by Andrew Davies and directed by Marc Munden, 1998] was conspicuously good—sophisticatedly alert to Thackeray's irony—and it had a real sense of narrative drive and momentum which I don't think is consistently true of the novel." Tamara S. Wagner added, "Talking about videos and dvds, I have just been given a catalogue by my university's AV department: a list of 'Highly Acclaimed Video Programs from Professor Elliot Engel (They're Light & Enlightening),' featuring such titles as 'The Brilliant and Bizarre Brontës' and 'A Dickens of a Christmas.' Has anyone ever seen (or used) any of those? (Otherwise, we'll rather go on and order movies like *Wild Wild West* or *Round the World in 80 Days* [sic] starring Jackie Chan—light and entertaining enough, I suppose, if one wanted to be entertained of course.)"

Despite their differences of opinion, all these statements, including Nair's, ignore fifty years of adaptation theory in uncritically adopting the author's intention as a criterion for the success of both the novel and any possible film adaptation. Only Brown suggests that the film could actually improve on the novel. Even she shares the habit, articulated most openly by Wagner, of ranking films based on canonical literary sources above merely "entertaining" films and, incidentally, in preferring evaluation to analysis when considering films in general and adaptations in particular. Although it is unlikely that these commentators or their colleagues would defend these positions as theoretical principles, they do not hesitate to adopt them in practice.

One reason that adaptation theory has had so little impact on studies of specific adaptations is that until quite recently, adaptation study has stood apart from the main currents in film theory. As the titles of most of the volumes listed above indicate, they trace their descent more directly from literary studies. Studies of Shakespeare on film, for example, use Shakespeare as a locus around which to organize their analysis of film adaptation. As the center around which individual adaptations orbit or the root from which the adaptations all grow, Shakespeare or Thackeray provides not only an organizing principle for the study of specific adaptations but an implicit standard of value for them all. Kamilla Elliott observes that "theories of the novel and of the film within their separate disciplines appear to have been significantly influenced by interdisciplinary rivalries" (2003, 13). More specifically, studies of adaptation tend to privilege literature over film in two ways. By organizing themselves around canonical authors, they establish a presumptive criterion for each new adaptation. And by arranging adaptations as spokes around the hub of such a strong authorial figure, they establish literature as a proximate cause of adaptation that makes fidelity to the source text central to the field.

Few empirical studies of adaptation accept these assumptions uncritically. In what is widely regarded as the founding text in adaptation study, George Bluestone notes that "changes are *inevitable* the moment one abandons the linguistic for the visual medium" (1957, 5) and concludes, "It is as fruitless to say that film A is better or worse than novel B as it is to pronounce Wright's Johnson's Wax Building better or worse than Tchaikowsky's *Swan Lake*" (5–6). Both Sarah Cardwell's study (2002) of television adaptations of four classic English novels and most of the essays collected in Deborah Cartmell and Imelda Whelehan's recent anthology (1999) question the primacy of literature as a touchstone for cinema. To the extent that adaptation study subordinates both specific adaptations to their canonical source texts and cinema as a medium to literature as a medium, it serves either faithfully or not, however, adaptations are studied under the sign of literature, which provides an evaluative touchstone for films in general.

This approach has dominated a half century of adaptation studies for several reasons. None of the first generation of scholars who led the charge to introduce film studies to the academy had received formal training in film studies themselves. Most of them came from English departments where they had been absorbed the pedagogical habits of close reading and the aesthetic values of literature—what James Naremore calls "the submerged common sense of the average English department . . . a mixture of Kantian aesthetics and Arnoldian ideas about society" (2000, 2).

Although Naremore traces these Arnoldian ideas to *Culture and Anarchy*, the program of comparative evaluation at the heart of Arnold's own aesthetics emerges more clearly in "The Study of Poetry." Having offered poetry, in which "the idea is everything," as a substitute for a religious tradition undermined by such heterodox facts as the discovery of ancient fossils and the theory of evolution, Arnold urges,

We should conceive of poetry worthily, and more highly than it has been the custom to conceive of it. We should conceive of it as capable of higher uses, and called to higher destinies, than those which in general men have assigned to it hitherto. More and more mankind will discover that we have to turn to poetry to interpret life for us, to console us, to sustain us. Without poetry, our science will appear incomplete; and most of what now passes with us for religion and philosophy will be replaced by poetry. (1903, vol. 4, 2)

If the burden Arnold places on poetry seems quaintly anachronistic, the passage may readily be freshened by replacing the term with *literature* or *novels* or indeed *cinema*—though not, clearly, with *popular culture*, from whose degrading influence Arnold assigns poetry, as successors like Tamara Wagner would presumably assign canonical cinema, the specific function of rescuing us.

The earliest films to come in for academic study under the Arnoldian dispensation that still ruled in American universities in 1960 fell into two categories: adaptations of canonical classics that served as adjuncts to the literary canon and classic works of cinema that could be studied as members of a supplementary quasi-literary cinematic canon. The first approach generated myriad courses in Shakespeare and film, the second courses in the masters of European art cinema from Dreyer to Bergman, Antonioni, and Godard, and, still later, in quasi-canonical American masters like Chaplin, Welles, and Hitchcock. Under this dispensation, many films were studied under the aegis of the literary works that gave them currency. Courses in Shakespeare and film were often courses in Shakespeare through film. Other courses were conducted under the sign of literature, analyzing and evaluating the films at hand as if they were literary works themselves, mining them for the ambiguity, complexity, penetration, and personal expressiveness traditionally associated with literature. In every case, specific literary works and literature in general were stipulated as touchstones.

Elliott has traced in trenchant detail the conflict between categorical approaches to adaptation, which follow Lessing's *Laocoön* in emphasizing the differences among such sister arts as literature, painting, and cinema that make them distinct modes with different expressive and representational possibilities, and analogical approaches, which follow Horace's "Ars Poetica" in emphasizing similarities among the arts that make it reasonable to imagine translations from one medium to another. What she does not emphasize in opposing these two approaches is their shared assumption that adaptation study is essentially aesthetic. Both categorical studies of adaptation and studies that emphasize analogies among the arts take as their central line of inquiry the question of what makes works of art successful—or what, in the more old-fashioned language adopted by both Horace and Lessing, makes them beautiful.

This inquiry is remote from the central inquiry of academic film studies, which from its beginnings had staked its insurgent disciplinary claims by rejecting the aesthetic appreciation of literature and developing a competing methodology of cultural critique rooted in the revolutionary intellectual ferment in France during the 1960s and 1970s. Films were valuable not because they formed a canon of fully achieved works of art according to traditional aesthetic criteria but because they raised illuminating questions, offered insight into overdetermined historical moments or the contemporary scene, exploded shibboleths that stifled critical discussion, or otherwise promoted a more thoughtful analysis of what Michel Foucault called the human sciences.

The rift between the aesthetic approach of literary studies and the analytical approach of cinema studies marked adaptation studies in two ways. It isolated adaptation studies from film studies, aligning it more closely with the programs in literary studies from which so many of its early practitioners had come. The further film studies drifted toward the left, unmasking film after film for political critique, the more firmly adaptation scholars dug in their heels on the right, championing the old-guard values of universalist humanism. At the same time, the rift widened between the theory and the practice of adaptation studies, which continued to take literary aesthetics as its touchstone and canonical works and authors as its organizing principle. It could hardly have been otherwise, since even potential methodological inversions of Shakespeare on film—Hitchcock's literary sources, for example—would have enshrined Hitchcock the auteur, film studies' version of the literary classic, in place of Shakespeare as the locus of meaning and value.

The persistence of humanist values in adaptation studies is not so much a triumph of Arnold as a triumph of evaluation that insists that originals are always touchstones of value for their adaptations, unless of course the adaptations are better. Even the staunchest partisans of textual fidelity, after all, urge their students to revise their papers. Fidelity makes sense as a criterion of value only when we can be certain that the model is more valuable than the copy. In the absence of this certainty, teachers license Hitchcock's free adaptations and urge students to revise, not because they make no assumptions about different versions' relative value, but because they make the reverse assumptions. Students may be starting with some promising material, but it stands to reason that they can make it better by reworking it because final drafts are more likely than first drafts to offer exemplary models. Hitchcock may be adapting literary originals, but he is making them into Hitchcock films, to which film scholars come to ascribe an even higher prestige value, though that value escaped Selznick. Hence Charles Barr's complaint that "a film criticism centred on directors . . . has not been concerned to follow up Hitchcock's statements . . . of indebtedness to English literary figures" (1999, 8). The only Hitchcock adaptation that has continued to attract anything like the harsh criticism Selznick leveled at *Rebecca* is *Sabotage* (1937) because its literary source, Joseph Conrad's novel *The Secret Agent*, has a still higher prestige value than Hitchcock. Michael A. Anderegg, for example, notes that "a Conrad enthusiast might be excused for feeling that *Sabotage* betrays its source on a rather fundamental level" (1975, 217).

In sum, the notion of fidelity as a criterion of value is based on a marketplace of competing models. Producers like Selznick insist on fidelity to literary models; filmmakers like Hitchcock get a special dispensation from following those models because they provide a brand name with even greater commercial and critical cachet; and production companies like Merchant Ivory or the BBC revive the Selznick legacy by providing what might be called a negative cachet, a guarantee that they will protect the audience from the shock of experiencing any new thoughts or feelings that would not have been provoked by their source texts. This surprising diversity of practice in the filmmaking industry and the corresponding diversity in beliefs about fidelity among different camps of film scholars raises an inescapable question. In the twenty years since Dudley Andrew complained that "the most frequent and most tiresome discussion of adaptation . . . concerns fidelity and transformation" (1984, 100), why has the field continued to organize itself so largely around a single one of these positions, the proposition that novels are texts, movies are intertexts, and in any competition between the two, the book is better?

One reason is that beneath the sharp disagreement between Hitchcock and Selznick is a deeper level of agreement most teachers of adaptation share as well. Although Selznick traces the success of a movie to its source text— "We bought *Rebecca*, and we intend to make *Rebecca*" (Selznick, 1972, 266)—and Hitchcock to its direction—"What I do is to read a story only once, and if I like the basic idea, I just forget all about the book and start to create cinema" (Truffaut, 1983, 71)—their shared view of a movie as the product of a single imagination is based on a classical view of art, grounded in both cases by a healthy respect for the marketplace. Though neither of them ever puts it this way, they share a view of art as a series of expressive works, whether literary or cinematic, whose value inheres in their finished, achieved qualities, their success in *being themselves*, which, for Selznick, forbids any tampering with a proven literary product and, for Hitchcock, justifies all possible uses of raw material in the service of a new work. This constellation of aesthetic appreciation assigns a doubly subordinate place to adaptation study. As the analysis of precisely those cinematic works that have failed to achieve the auteur status that would consecrate them as quasi-literature, it falls into the gap between the study of literature as literature and the study of cinema as literature. Standing outside the mainstream of both literary studies and film studies, its place is marginal and liable to shrink still further with the ebb of Arnold's idea of literature as a substitute for religion. This ebb is reflected by the passing of the belletristic ideal of appreciation in literary studies, in the waning influence of elitist cultural institutions like symphony orchestras and the Broadway theatre, and in the decline of au-teurism as the leading tendency in film studies.

An equally dim future for adaptation studies is implicit in the more pragmatic rationale for national literacy articulated in E. D. Hirsch's *Cultural Literacy* (1987). Unconsciously echoing the etymology of *literacy*, which did not appear in the language until 200 years after *illiteracy* as its antonym (*Compact Edition of the Oxford English Dictionary*, 1971, s.v. "literacy"), Hirsch traces a breakdown in "effective nationwide communications" to problems in the acquisition of the kinds of common ideas and referents that foster communication by stipulating the sorts of shared knowledge and assumptions that allow development and dis-criminations within that common area (1987, 2). The crux of Hirsch's argu-ment is that contemporary students communicate less effectively because their knowledge, though often considerable, is more parochial and ephemeral than that of their forbears; they are less conversant with the shared cultural markers that would allow them to grasp the meaning of what they read more precisely and effortlessly and to write with a surer sense of what their readers already know and believe. A knowledge of *Hamlet* is more useful than a knowledge of *I Love Lucy* because more past writers have used *Hamlet* as an analogy or point of departure in formulating their arguments and sharpening their examples, and referring to Hamlet provides contemporary readers access to a wider and more enduring audience than referring to Lucy and Ricky. Hence Hirsch proposes to reverse the modern pedagogical tendency from Rousseau to Dewey toward fos-tering critical thinking by subordinating rote learning to intensive study of a smaller number of texts and problems. Instead Hirsch reemphasizes an older ed-ucational ideal, the acquisition of specific information that will fit students to assume the unexpectedly onerous mantle of the common reader.

In "What Literate Americans Know," the appendix of 5,000 names, phrases, dates, and concepts Hirsch prescribes as essential to cultural literacy, Arnold's touchstones are pressed into a new function in this pre-Arnoldian ideal. Instead of serving as a suitably inspiring substitute for religious beliefs discredited by inconvenient facts, they are intended as a national lingua franca without which communication would be limited to the most obvious and primitive ideas. In principle, they help speakers and writers to develop, and readers to grasp, more complex ideas by allowing them to build on a sure foundation of common ground with their audiences—a program Hirsch, Kett, and Trefil develop in their *The Dictionary of Cultural Literacy* (1988), and Hirsch in a series of books titled *What Your Kindergartner Needs to Know: Preparing Your Child for a Lifetime of Learning* (1997).

The culture wars that have followed Hirsch's ambitious proposal to re-make American education have made the implications for film adaptations dismayingly clear. It is valuable to watch a screen adaptation of *Hamlet* be-cause it gives viewers access to something like Shakespeare's world and peo-ple and issues. And because, as Hirsch acknowledges, "the information es-sential to literacy is rarely detailed or precise" (1987, 14), something like that world is close enough to allow them to play along with other citizens more or less familiar with *Hamlet* as they all join in the national conversation.

Adaptation is at the heart of Hirsch's program for cultural literacy in a more general but equally limited sense as well. His emphasis on widely shared but superficially understood cultural touchstones presents every instance of a particular touchstone (e.g., Annie Oakley, NATO, "April showers bring May flowers") as in effect an adaptation of a single original that does not exist apart from its adaptations. Hirsch is not interested in ranking different ap-pearances of a single touchstone; evaluation enters his program only in the selection of touchstones. Just as a Google search ranks websites by their links to other websites, Hirsch's program ranks both literary or cinematic works and their consumers in terms of the number of touchstones they share.

Although the metaphor of adaptation might well be used to describe Hirsch's network of touchstones and their users, however, it relegates adaptation study itself to an even more marginal position than Arnold's aesthetic study of litera-ture. In Hirsch's post-Arnoldian program for literacy, adaptations have value only to the extent that they allow access to the world of the great originals that establish their credentials. Even when cultural literacy is defined in terms of ef-fective citizenship rather than aesthetic sustenance, adaptations are still to be consumed under the sign of literature. By valuing film adaptations to the extent that they make prescriptive cultural touchstones widely accessible, Hirsch's pro-gram is even more likely than Arnold's to treat Shakespearean adaptation as the spoonful of sugar that helps the Bard's medicine go down.

Under either Arnold or Hirsch, adaptation study seems condemned to a bleak and servile future. Yet a closer consideration of Hirsch's principles in-dicates an alternative future that is far more exciting, a future that subordi-nates the process of reading adaptations to the process of writing them.

A striking feature of Hirsch's program is the extent to which it neglects writing in favor of reading—not necessarily the reading of literature, but reading under the sign of literature, reading assuming the subordinate position of a receptive reader whose basic aim is to consume an informative text whose cultural authority is greater than the reader's own. Throughout his discussion, Hirsch assumes that if students learn to read, writing will take care of itself. Hirsch praises the conservative linguistic and orthographic and cultural presuppositions in the radical newspaper the *Black Panther*: "To be conservative in the *means* of communication is the road to effectiveness in modern life, in whatever direction one wishes to be effective" (1987, 23). Although he lauds their mastery of consensual norms of communication, Hirsch never explains how the Black Panthers acquired the ability to develop and advocate their revolutionary social and political principles, overlooking the fact that a mastery of the touchstones of cultural literacy would have given them only a shared vocabulary, not the means to formulate an original viewpoint. In fact, although Hirsch insists that "cultural literacy is represented not by a *prescriptive* list of books but rather by a *descriptive* list of the information actually possessed by literate Americans" (xiv), his list of markers must be framed by one of two unappealing alternatives. Either it introduces a prescriptive bias in its choice between designating "literate Americans" as the standard-bearers for public discourse, or it abandons all bias in the manner of the television quiz show *Family Feud*, in which contestants can win prizes by identifying Germany and Japan as modern countries with large armies, not because these answers are correct but because they are among the most popular answers in a survey the show has conducted. Like *Family Feud*, Hirsch's cultural schemata neither reward original analytical thinking nor explain how it could ever come to pass within such a rising tide of mediocrity.

Although he often pauses to pay lip service to critical and analytical writing, Hirsch clearly regards them as a simple extension of literacy instead of its crucial instance. In treating writing and critical thinking as skills that inevitably follow the acquisition of cultural literacy, Hirsch promulgates a strikingly passive ideal of literacy. Like the documentation for computer software, Hirsch's program acculturates its novitiates by reducing them to consumers of a prepackaged culture they are taught specifically to absorb but not to analyze, question, or change.

Hirsch offers the example of the *Black Panther* specifically to counter the objection that his program for cultural literacy is intrinsically conservative. But I suspect that American citizens are less passive than he assumes even when they are reading less obviously charged material. Do readers perusing the letters to the editor of a daily newspaper really ask what the writers mean, decide that they understand the meaning, and then either debate the meaning or turn the page in satisfaction? Such a hermeneutical model of understanding is at the heart of Hirsch's program. But readers left asking questions like "Is there compelling evidence for life on Mars?" or "Should poker become an Olympic sport?" or "Has the Electoral College outgrown its usefulness?" are having a reading experience other, and more, than hermeneutical, an experience that involved an active, critical analysis of what they read. Literary scholars have long accepted this view of professional discourse, but it seems even more true of such nonprofessional statements as "For tomorrow, a 30 percent chance of afternoon showers."

According to Hirsch, this analytical process is discrete from reading, as he had argued twenty years earlier in *Validity in Interpretation* by distinguishing between *meaning*, "that which is represented by a text," and *significance*, "a relationship between that meaning and a person, or a conception, or a situation, or indeed anything imaginable" (1967, 8). But although Hirsch's assertion that "significance always implies a relationship, and one constant, unchanging pole of that relationship is what the text means" has often come under attack, Hirsch maintains it under the sign of Herbert Spencer in his analysis of writing in *The Philosophy of Composition*, which advocates a normative, maximally "readable" prose based on Spencer's analogous distinction between "the decipherment of meaning" and "framing the thought expressed" (Hirsch, 1977, 78). The best writing, Hirsch implies, is that which is most easily consumed on the terms the author stipulates. Hirsch never considers the possibility that literacy might be in decline precisely because of the triumph of passive acculturation through repeated exposure—through television, through advertising, through political discourse—to utterances whose goal, like that of Hirsch's normative prose, is "readability" (74)—that is, discourse aimed at minimizing the likelihood of active analysis by indoctrinating readers rather than engaging them.

Consider the analogy between Hirsch's program for cultural literacy and what might be called music literacy or literacy in the visual arts but what is more commonly and revealingly called music and art appreciation. This sort of literacy involves the recognition of certain pivotal formal conventions, historical trends, and particular masterpieces in order to foster one's enjoyment at opera houses or concert halls or museums but not in order to be able to create new works by painting or sculpting or composing or to be able to reinterpret preexisting works in performance by mastering the steps of ballet or the fingerings of the violin. As the guardians of culture at the Book-of-the-Month Club used to remind us, this sort of literacy is useful mainly as a way of protecting one's reputation for cultural attainments. It is nothing more than an education in enlightened consumerism.

Such passive acculturation is the hallmark of the current orthodoxy of literacy that takes reading rather than writing as the central activity of the literate citizen. Hirsch anticipates the objection that "the very existence of such a list [as his 5,000 touchstones of cultural literacy] will cause students merely to memorize the bare items which it contains and learn nothing significant at all. Students will trivialize cultural information without really possessing it" by acknowledging that such misuse of the list is not only a danger but a near certainty" when "whole sections of our bookstores are already devoted to paring down complex information into short, easily digested summaries—crib sheets for every school subject" (Hirsch, 1987, 142). The years since the publication of *Cultural Literacy* have seen this dangerous tendency broaden to an extent that would be comical if it were not so perilous. Hirsch's own guides to what grade-schoolers must know have joined the proud ranks of primers on nonacademic subjects from *The Complete Idiot's Guide to Personal Finance in Your 20s and 30s* to *Sex for Dummies*. In the meantime, the No Child Left Behind Act, educational reform legislation whose formula for pedagogical accountability is based on students' performance in standardized tests, has spurred a national frenzy as teachers rush to teach to the tests in order to prevent their schools from being cited and themselves from being dismissed. The result has been an ever-widening gap between literature and literacy—that is, between reading under the sign of literature, whose goal is the consumption of information from authoritative sources, and the more active literacy Hirsch optimistically assumed would follow, a literacy whose goal is engagement, analysis, and reasoned debate. What the nation needs is a program for fostering active literacy as provocative and useful as Hirsch's program for consumerist literacy and a powerful and persuasive model for connecting the two.

In principle, we have long had a theoretical program for a more active literacy. Over twenty years before Hirsch wrote, Roland Barthes, in "From Work to Text," had distinguished the "work" on whose behalf defenders of established cultural norms from Arnold to Hirsch had fought from the "text" Barthes wished to liberate from the work. Unlike the work, "an object that can be computed" (Barthes, 1977, 156), Barthes's text is irreducibly "plural" (159), *"experienced only in an activity of production"* (157); instead of being designed for passive consumption, it "asks of the reader a practical collaboration" (163). Works are designed to be read, texts to be written—a distinction Barthes makes in somewhat different terms at the outset of *S/Z* when he distinguishes "the readerly"—"a classic text" designed to be consumed by readers limited to "the poor freedom either to accept or reject the text" (Barthes, 1974, 4)—from "the writerly"—"a perpetual present" which amounts simply to "*ourselves writing*," producing the texts we read (5). Barthes's analysis is echoed and amplified by Mikhail Bakhtin's distinction between the *authoritative discourse* of fathers, law, and scripture, which "binds us, quite independent of any power it might have to persuade us internally" (1981, 342), and *internally persuasive discourse*, "a contemporary word" or "a word that has been reclaimed for contemporaneity," whose "semantic structure . . . is *not finite*, it is *open*; in each of the new contexts that dialogize it, this discourse is able to reveal ever newer *ways to mean*" (346). Bakhtin finds internally persuasive discourse, "half ours and half someone else's," to be "of decisive significance in the evolution of an individual consciousness" (345).

For half a century and more, adaptation study has drastically limited its horizons by its insistence on treating source texts as canonical authoritative discourse or readerly works rather than internally persuasive discourse or writerly texts, refusing in consequence to learn what one might have expected to be the primary lesson of film adaptation: that texts remain alive only to the extent that they can be rewritten and that to experience a text in all its power requires each reader to rewrite it. The whole process of film adaptation offers an obvious practical demonstration of the necessity of rewriting that many commentators have ignored because of their devotion to literature. Any Thackeray novel must be better than the additions, subtractions, or transformations of any film version simply because it is literature. When theorists reverse this procedure and allow Hitchcock to adapt Daphne du Maurier more freely than she or Selznick might approve, they are actually confirming the same principle—except that this time, they assume that Hitchcock, a more canonical filmmaker than du Maurier is an author, has a greater claim to be producing the kinds of works typically associated with literature and so deserves all the rights and privileges pertaining thereto. And the first of all those rights and privileges is the demand to be read instead of rewritten.

Although Barthes's distinctions amount to an uncanny prophecy of the composition theory that would spring up twenty years later, they have had lamentably little impact on teaching on the larger terrain English departments generally. Most teachers continue to think of writing as the gradable symptom of critical thinking. As Barthes's distinction implies, however, it is more than that; it *is* critical thinking, even when the writer is not actually sitting at the word processor but preparing to do so by sifting, scrutinizing, actively engaging each given text. Writers are like the old lady in E. M. Forster's anecdote who asks, "How can I tell what I think till I see what I say?" (1927, 101). The distinction may seem like a quibble—is writing postreading, the visible sign of reading, or is reading prewriting, a necessary preliminary to writing?—but the overwhelming support for the first model over the second has produced a pedagogical orthodoxy of literacy which persists throughout the educational establishment, defining a literature of the readerly in a way that guarantees that adaptation study will remain as trivial as the adaptations it prescribes.

The real cost of our institutional attachment to literature, however, runs much deeper. Barthes complains that "what the (secondary) School prides itself on is teaching to *read* (well) and no longer to write" (1977, 162). The situation has changed remarkably little over the past forty years. Except for required courses in composition and electives in creative writing or preprofessional courses in journalism, college English courses are overwhelmingly devoted to reading rather than writing. They are named after what gets read in them and arranged according to these readings, and it is discussions of the reading that occupies most of class time. Even though students are typically graded almost exclusively on their writing, most of us spend little time teaching it, preferring instead to assume it is an adjunct to the reading we do teach. We end up teaching our students *books* instead of teaching them *how to do things with books* because our college English curriculum is organized around literature at the expense of the active, writerly engagement, the sense of performance and play, the unquenchable sense of agency even in the presence of canonical works, that we call literacy.

The privilege the educational establishment accords reading over writing continues to promote the evaluative tendency that shapes both Arnold's aestheticism and Hirsch's pragmatism in a widely deplored institutional snobbery about writing. As Charles Moran (1990), Christie Friend (1992), Peter Elbow (1993), David Barton (1994), Robert Scholes (1998), and James E. Seitz (1999) have all observed, the problematic opposition between reading and writing is a founding trope of the fields of literacy studies, composition theory, and institutional histories of English, and professors of English have long decreed that intensive work in writing ought to come before college and that if students cannot write, it is the fault of their high school teachers. Although college students are routinely asked to do writing assignments on which their grades depend, directed instruction in writing is commonly limited to elementary composition courses and preprofessional courses in business and technical writing.

Hence the college English curriculum is free to promote reading as a pedagogical goal to the virtual exclusion of writing. Courses are labeled and organized according to the reading students will do, not the writing required of them. Course descriptions typically go on for a paragraph about reading assignments before adverting in their closing sentence, if at all, to writing. The

few courses specifically designated as courses in writing are introductory, re-
medial, or preprofessional—as if only slow learners, freshman, journalists,
and authors of computer documentation needed instruction in writing—and
teachers mark their professional advancement by their growing success in
avoiding these courses. Except for the writing specialists hired specifically to
teach them, new colleagues are hired by a process that specifies areas of ex-
pertise in reading, not achievement in teaching writing. And despite all continuing debate about the wisdom of common texts and authors for core
courses for the major (should it be possible for students to graduate without
reading Shakespeare?), there is rarely any central oversight for the kinds of
writing colleges assign and the ways they assess it.

Although these priorities are not always shared by English departments in
nongraduate or emerging or two-year colleges, the sense of academic class
consciousness is. English departments that emphasize writing are schooled to
look up at those that emphasize reading as a universally desirable norm for
English studies. The profession does everything possible to underscore the
message to students, junior and part-time colleagues, and fellow colleges that
the teaching of writing is at worst something beneath the notice and abilities of higher education, at best something that does not deserve its top professional priority. Peter Elbow has summarized the resulting inequity: "When
writing programs are housed in English departments, as they so often are,
teachers of writing are usually paid less to teach more under poorer working
conditions—in order to help support literature professors to be paid more to
teach less under better working conditions" (2002, 533).

The educational establishment could do greater justice to both its texts
and its students if it paid greater attention to a vital countercurrent in English studies that goes back at least as far as Arnold. In "The Function of
Criticism at the Present Time," Arnold presses the aesthetic study of poetry
into the service of "*a disinterested endeavour to learn and propagate the best that
is known and thought in the world*" (1903, vol. 3, 42) in order "to create a
current of true and fresh ideas" (vol. 3, 20). The paradoxical goal Arnold
sets criticism is to change the world by renouncing any direct practical interest in it—not, in other words, to read one's culture more accurately, but to
rewrite it more compellingly. Hirsch himself acknowledges this countercurrent when he moderates his dissent from generations of skills-centered edu-
cators by concluding that "the polarization of educationists into facts people
versus skills people has no basis in reason. Facts and skills are inseparable"
(1987, 133). Although the foundation of Hirsch's argument about language
acquisition and the corresponding acquisition of cultural literacy is that active inferences greatly increase the ability to recall the particulars of a given

abstract schema, surely students ought to be trained to be more active readers than Hirsch acknowledges, reading not only to understand but to consider, to compare, to criticize, to debate. These skills are not superadded to training in rhetoric or literacy; they are the very essence of that training.

This is particularly true, of course, in college English courses, which are precisely forums for helping students get beyond a passive receptivity to texts toward an active engagement with them as literary studies' distinctive contribution to liberal education's goal of getting students to think better for themselves. In effect, college English teachers are not teaching their students how to read but rather how to read against simple understanding, to see further into a poem or play or novel than a literal reader, armed only with a general knowledge of cultural touchstones, could see. College courses commonly test the cogency and depth and power of those counterreadings by asking students to talk, and especially to write, about them, and that kind of testing seems uniquely appropriate, not only because English courses teach writing along with reading, but because the kind of active reading they teach is already tantamount to a rewriting of the text. Hirsch might well prefer to describe this project of reading against as *counterliteracy* because it aims at active interpretation and creation rather than neutrally receptive understanding. If we called Hirsch's cultural literacy a program for *preliteracy*, however, and reserved *literacy* as a label for the kind of active textual engagement that focuses more directly on writing than reading, we could hardly find a more effective focus for programs in literacy than cinematic adaptation.

The kind of adaptation study central to this discipline contrasts sharply with adaptation study under the sign of literature. Taking off from Frank Zingrone's anti-Hirschian remark that the "one-medium user is the new illiterate" (2001, 237), this alternative approach to adaptation study does not approach adaptations as either transcriptions of canonical classics or attempts to create new classics but rather as illustrations of the incessant process of rewriting as critical reading. It is informed by the conflict Bakhtin discerns between heteroglossia, whose protean, internally persuasive meanings are irreproducibly dependent on the contexts generated by particular readers and reading situations, and canonization, which seeks to standardize authoritative meanings for all readers (1981, 418). Just as Bakhtin celebrates, however prematurely, the novel's resistance to canonization, this approach to adaptation study treats both adaptations and their originals as heteroglot texts rather than canonical works, emphasizing the fact that *every text offers itself as an invitation to be rewritten*.

Emphasizing literacy over literature does not assume that all adaptations are equally valuable or that they are just as good as their originals. It simply waives the whole question of evaluation as peripheral to the discipline. After all, no matter how clever or audacious an adaptation is, the book will always be better than any adaptation because it is always *better at being the book*.

But this reductio ad absurdum, which is true by definition, indicates just
how trivial a claim we make when we argue that the book is better. Of course
it's better at being itself; so is the movie better at being itself; so is everything
in the universe. Fidelity as a touchstone of adaptations will always give their
source texts, which are always faithful to themselves, an advantage so enormous and unfair that it renders the comparison meaningless. In order to evaluate adaptations fairly, we would need to evaluate their source texts as well—
something that traditional adaptation study, which takes the literary text as
an unquestioned touchstone of value for any adaptation, has traditionally declined to do. In order to revitalize adaptation study, we need to reframe the
assumption that even the most cursory consideration of the problem forces
on us—source texts cannot be rewritten—as a new assumption: Source texts
must be rewritten; we cannot help rewriting them.

Whenever we teach a film adaptation—whenever we watch an adaptation as an adaptation—we treat it as an intertext designed to be looked
through, like a window on the source text. Although it is certainly true that
adaptations are intertexts that depend in a special way on their source texts,
thinking of them exclusively in these terms inevitably impoverishes them because it reduces them to the single function of replicating (or, worse, failing
to replicate) the details of that single source text. In practice, to extend
Bakhtin's argument, every text, from *Ulysses* to *Jay and Silent Bob Strike Back*,
is an intertext that incorporates, refracts, refutes, and alludes to many other
texts, whether literary, cinematic, or more broadly cultural. Taking fidelity as
the decisive criterion of an adaptation's value is tantamount to insisting that
it do the same job as its source text without going outside the lines that text
has established, even though adaptations normally carry heavier burdens and
labor under tighter restrictions than we would ever impose on an aspiring
novelist.

Sadly as such rules and regulations impoverish adaptations, they do even
greater damage to their source texts. By elevating Thackeray's *Vanity Fair*
above its film adaptations as a literary classic, they ignore its own status as an
intertext designed, just as surely as any of its adaptations, to be looked *into*
and *through* as well as *at*. To the extent that they praise a TV miniseries for
its fidelity to a Thackeray novel because it does not omit telling passages or
import irrelevant biases, they ignore the fact that every novel comes with
programmatic omissions and biases of its own, telltale traces of other novels
it could have been. When they focus on fidelity as the central problem of

film adaptation, they overlook the problematic nature of source texts that makes them worth studying in the first place by choosing to emphasize their privileged status as literature over their capacity to engage and extend our literacy.

It is ironic that literature and literacy, intimately related notions stemming from the Latin *littera* ("letter"), should have become so blankly opposed as centers for contemporary English studies. Elbow has noted that "the word *literacy* really means power over letters, i.e., reading and writing. But as *literacy* is used casually and even in government policy and legislation, it tends to mean *reading*, not writing" (1993, 13). As commentators from Arnold to Hirsch have acknowledged, however, reading and writing depend on each other, even if literature for over a century has claimed such precedence over literacy that it has often sought to repress or marginalize it as merely enlightened consumerism. The need to incorporate them both into what might be called the discipline of textual studies—the study of how texts are produced, consumed, canonized, transformed, resisted, and denied—offers a unique opportunity to adaptation studies, which can serve not as an avatar of literacy over literature but as a sorely needed bridge between the two.

Marilyn Hoder-Salmon offers a practical illustration of what new directions in adaptation study can combine the study of literature with the development of a more active literacy in her monograph on *The Awakening*, which uses the form of Hoder-Salmon's annotated screenplay of Kate Chopin's novel to consider "the omission from the Hollywood cinema of classics of women's literature and the counterpart phenomenon of reductive treatment when such classics are adapted" (Hoder-Salmon, 1992, 7). Hoder-Salmon's use of screenwriting as a medium of criticism is readily adapted to the classroom by getting students to write their own adaptations of specific scenes in the novel, turning them from readers looking up to Chopin into writers meeting her on their own ground and her own level. This approach does not neglect the traditional activity of interpretation; it simply changes the medium through which the novel must be interpreted from the critical essay into the screenplay, which selects what the screenwriter takes to be most important about the novel and rewrites it. Such courses are balanced between their loyalties to literature (its choice of a canonical text like Chopin's and its insistence on paying that text, or whatever text is chosen in its place, the compliment of intense and extended scrutiny) and literacy (its encouragement to students to become active producers of the text they might otherwise be content to read).

Teachers unwilling to reconfigure their literature courses as screenwriting courses could profit by encouraging their students to think of adaptation itself in different terms. Over the years adaptations have been studied as translations and transformations, as selections and specifications, as reimaginings and imitations, of literature. It would help redress the balance between literature and literacy to think of each adaptation not in terms of what it faithfully reproduces—what it selects, emphasizes, and transforms—but of what it leaves out. Instead of acting as if the power of a story lay in what it explicitly portrayed, we might explore further the "gaps" Wolfgang Iser calls "a kind of pivot on which the whole text–reader relationship revolves" because "whenever the reader bridges the gaps, communication begins" (1974, 169). The very process of supplying omitted material draws each reader closer to the story, its world, and the process of world making.

No story, of course, is the whole story, and no film adaptation of *Vanity Fair* can include every detail Thackeray does. But thinking about the elements a given adaptation strategically omits in order to engage their audiences' literacy—the details of family background, the thoughts we are allowed to infer, the authorial commentary so essential to our sense of Thackeray—can lead us back to the equally strategic omissions that make Thackeray's novel a performance text itself. Emphasizing the ways in which readers and viewers always complete the stories they think they are merely consuming can replace the pedagogical goal of inculcating a dutiful love and respect for literature with the goal of empowering students to think more critically about the ways they read, the ways writers write, and the surprisingly intimate connections between the two.

Whatever strategy theorists and teachers of adaptation pursue, it is unlikely to resolve a series of knotty questions about the relation between literature and literacy. Why should we study literature? If the goal of literary study is enlightened appreciation, how material is that goal to the more general goals of liberal education—effective national and global citizenship—and how is it connected to those other goals? If knowledge is power, is it more important to have a knowledge of what is in the canonical works of literature and cinema or a knowledge of how they can be used? Who ought to be empowered by literature and literacy and empowered to do what? Adaptation study has unique potential as the keystone of a new discipline of textual studies less ideologically driven, and therefore more powerful, than either contemporary literary or cultural studies, not because it resolves these questions but because it keeps them front and center—beginning with whether we want to organize textual studies around the question "What should we be reading?" or the question "What should we be reading for?"

Works Cited

Anderegg, Michael A. 1975. "Conrad and Hitchcock: *The Secret Agent* Inspires *Sabotage*." *LFQ* 3 (Summer): 215–25.

Andrew, Dudley. 1984. *Concepts in Film Theory*. New York: Oxford University Press.

Arnold, Matthew. 1903. *The Works of Matthew Arnold*. 15 vols. London: Macmillan.

Bakhtin, Mikhail. 1981. *The Dialogic Imagination: Four Essays*. Trans. Caryl Emerson and Michael Holquist. Austin: University of Texas Press.

Barr, Charles. 1999. *English Hitchcock*. London: Cameron & Hollis.

Barthes, Roland. 1974. *S/Z*. Trans. Richard Miller. New York: Hill and Wang.

———. 1977. "From Work to Text." In *Image-Music-Text*, trans. Stephen Heath, 155–64. New York: Hill and Wang.

Barton, David. 1994. *Literacy: An Introduction to the Ecology of Written Language*. Oxford: Blackwell.

Bluestone, George. 1957. *Novels into Film*. Baltimore: Johns Hopkins University Press.

Cardwell, Sarah. 2002. *Adaptation Revisited: Television and the Classic Novel*. Manchester, UK: Manchester University Press.

Cartmell, Deborah, and Imelda Whelehan, eds. 1999. *Adaptation: From Text to Screen, Screen to Text*. London: Routledge.

The Compact Edition of the Oxford English Dictionary. 1971. 2 vols. New York: Oxford University Press.

Elbow, Peter. 1993. "The War between Reading and Writing—and How to End It." *Rhetoric Review* 12 (Fall): 5–24.

———. 2002. "The Cultures of Literature and Composition: What Could Each Learn from the Other?" *College English* 64 (May): 533–46.

Elliott, Kamilla. 2003. *Rethinking the Novel/Film Debate*. Cambridge: Cambridge University Press.

Forster, E. M. 1927. *Aspects of the Novel*. New York: Harcourt.

Friend, Christie. 1992. "The Excluded Conflict: The Marginalization of Composition and Rhetoric Studies in Graff's *Professing Literature*." *College English* 54: 276–86.

Hirsch, E. D., Jr. 1967. *Validity in Interpretation*. New Haven: Yale University Press.

———. 1977. *The Philosophy of Composition*. Chicago: University of Chicago Press.

———. 1987. *Cultural Literacy: What Every American Needs to Know*. Boston: Houghton Mifflin.

———, ed. 1997. *What Your Kindergartner Needs to Know: Preparing Your Child for a Lifetime of Learning*. New York: Dell Publishing.

Hirsch, E. D., Jr., Joseph F. Kett, and James Trefil. *The Dictionary of Cultural Literacy*. Boston: Houghton Mifflin.

Hoder-Salmon, Marilyn. 1992. *Kate Chopin's The Awakening: Screenplay as Interpretation*. Gainesville: University Press of Florida.

Iser, Wolfgang. 1974. *The Act of Reading*. Baltimore: Johns Hopkins University Press.

Moran, Charles. 1990. "Reading Like a Writer." In *Vital Signs*, ed. James L. Collins, 60–71. Portsmouth, NH: Boynton/Cook.

Naremore, James. 2000. "Introduction." In *Film Adaptation*, ed. James Naremore, 1–16. New Brunswick, NJ: Rutgers University Press.

Scholes, Robert. 1998. *The Rise and Fall of English: Reconstructing English as a Discipline*. New Haven, CT: Yale University Press.

Seitz, James E. 1999. *Motives for Metaphor: Literacy, Curriculum Reform, and the Teaching of English*. Pittsburgh, PA: University of Pittsburgh Press.

Selznick, David O. 1972. *Memo from David O. Selznick*. Ed. Rudy Behlmer. New York: Viking.

Truffaut, François. 1983. *Hitchcock*. Rev. ed. New York: Simon and Schuster.

VICTORIA listserv. n.d. http://listserv.indiana.edu/cgi-bin/wa-iub.exe?A1=indo409b&L =victoria&D=o&H=o&I=-3&O=T&T=1#56 (accessed 24 October 2006).

Wilmington, Michael. 2004. "For Mira Nair, 'Vanity Fair' Was a World of Its Own." *Chicago Tribune*. Tempo section. 10 September.

Zingrone, Frank. 2001. *The Media Symplex: At the Edge of Meaning in the Age of Chaos*. Toronto: Stoddart.

CHAPTER THREE

~

Adaptation Studies and the History of Ideas: The Case of *Apocalypse Now*

Donald M. Whaley

Peter Lev, Thomas Leitch, and David Kranz have called for adaptation studies to move beyond the traditional problem of how a novel or play is made into a film and how faithfully the film reproduces the original. Lev believes that adaptation studies should investigate all sources for films, not just novels or plays. "Films," he argues, "are often based on multiple works, visual as well as textual. Paintings, photographs, news articles, historical events, films, television shows, and so on can be sources for films; one loses some of the richness of this impure art by limiting sources to novels and plays" (Lev, 2003, 7). Leitch (2003) has argued that we live "in a culture marked by the traces of thousands of texts" and that any "original" novel or play from which a film is adapted itself has an infinite number of sources, which he labels "intertexts." He calls for adaptation studies to be transformed into "intertextual studies, in which every text is a rereading of earlier texts and every text, whether it poses as an original or an adaptation, has the same claim to aesthetic or ontological privilege as any other" (6, 8). The key question of intertextual studies for Leitch would be to ask how and why any given text has rewritten the sourcetexts on which it was based. Kranz has contended that scholars of adaptation studies should move beyond the study of literary texts as sources for film and demonstrate an "openness to contextual approaches to adaptation," an "appreciation for the economic, historical, cultural, and ideological pressures which impinge on the production . . . of film adaptations" (Kranz, 2003, 3). If adaptation studies were to go in any of these proposed directions, scholars in that field would be doing something very close to what historians of ideas do.

The history of ideas is concerned with a simple question: Where do ideas come from and where do they go? Historians of ideas trace the movement of ideas through time as, in the words of Peter Gay, the ideas are "taken up, used, abused, dissected, by later generations" (1967, 111). (Gay would understand Leitch's argument that all texts are rewritings of earlier texts.) In tracing the movement of ideas through time, historians do not assume that an earlier text influenced a later one simply because of a resemblance between the two. Historians look for evidence of actual influence. One strategy for doing that is to research the biography and writings or other public pronouncements of the creator of a text for clues to the text's sources. Once the sources have been identified, the historian can, as James West Davidson and Mark Hamilton Lytle point out in *After the Fact: The Art of Historical Detection*, use the ideas in those sources to "reconstruct the intellectual worlds" behind the text in order to shed light on its meaning (2005, 60).

To illustrate the point, Davidson and Lytle use the analysis of the Declaration of Independence by Garry Wills in his *Inventing America* (Davidson and Lytle, 2005). Historians had known that the ideas of John Locke—the social contract, the government's duty to protect life and liberty—influenced the Declaration, but Wills argues that the ideas of the Scottish Enlightenment, especially those of Francis Hutcheson, were as influential in shaping the document. In the absence of direct evidence from the writings of Thomas Jefferson that he was inspired by Hutcheson and other philosophers of the Scottish Enlightenment when writing the Declaration, Wills drew on the next best thing, circumstantial evidence. He used the content of the lectures Jefferson's professor, Dr. William Small, a disciple of Hutcheson, gave when Jefferson was a student at William and Mary and the presence of Hutcheson's books in Jefferson's library to prove Jefferson's familiarity with Hutcheson's ideas. Hutcheson and other Enlightenment philosophers believed government should produce the greatest happiness for the greatest number of people and that happiness was measurable. "Happiness" for them meant the predominance of pleasure over pain, for example, and meant the absence of war and religious superstition, which they regarded as causes of pain and misery. According to Wills, when Jefferson wrote in the Declaration of "the pursuit of happiness" he had in mind precisely the definition of "happiness" put forward by Hutcheson and the other thinkers of the Scottish Enlightenment (Wills, 1978, 149–64, 201).

Historians of ideas define *text* broadly. The historian Ernst Cassirer, for example, listed among the "texts" amenable to study by the techniques of the history of ideas books, paintings, sculpture, architecture, coins, laws, public ceremonies, religious rites, and political constitutions (Gay, 1967, 115). Those techniques can also be applied to films.

Take, for instance, *Apocalypse Now*. The principal creators of that film were John Milius, who wrote the original screenplay, and Francis Ford Coppola, who directed the film and cowrote with Milius the final version of the script. Research into the sources these filmmakers used can help clarify the meaning of the film. *Apocalypse Now* was adapted from Joseph Conrad's novel *Heart of Darkness* (1990). Milius began his script while in film school at the University of Southern California after his professor told him about the many failed efforts to adapt the novel into a film, most notably the attempt by Orson Welles (Milius, 1998). Coppola kept a paperback copy of the novel in his pocket while directing the film, referred to the novel more often than to the script, and tightened the parallels between the novel and the film beyond those in the original screenplay (Coppola, 2000). The film borrows the novel's plot, a journey upriver toward Kurtz, a man who has given in to primitivism and savagery. In addition to Kurtz, other characters in the film are based on those in the novel. The accountant in *Heart of Darkness* is Colonel Kilgore in the film, the novel's black helmsman is the film's Chief Phillips, and the Russian harlequin in the novel is the photographer played by Dennis Hopper in the film (Cahir, 1992; Coppola, 2000).

Thomas Leitch has argued that even novels that serve as "original" sources for film are themselves rewritings of earlier texts. *Heart of Darkness* was a rewriting of the traditional adventure story, a kind of story told in every culture, the story that comparative mythologist Joseph Campbell (1949) has called "the monomyth." The plot of the monomyth always begins in the world of common, ordinary, everyday life. The hero is pulled out of this world on to the adventure, goes through a series of episodes in which he overcomes difficulties, and wins a climactic final victory, which spiritually transforms him. He returns from the adventure with the "boon," the power to regenerate society. Versions of the monomyth include, says Campbell, the story of a journey to unknown lands, as in *The Odyssey*; various tales of a journey to the underworld, as in the story of Dante in *The Inferno* or of Aeneas, who visits the underworld, the land of the dead, to consult his dead father and learn the future; and the story of Jesus, who leaves this world, ascends to heaven and returns with the boon, the good news of life after death. The victory won may be the gaining of wisdom or enlightenment (the story of the Buddha is a version of the monomyth, Campbell argues) or the killing of a tyrannical father figure (which Campbell says is a version of the Oedipus story in which the son kills his father and takes his place). Literary critic Paul Zweig (1974) contends that a group of nineteenth-century writers, including Conrad, Melville, and Nietzsche, rewrote the traditional adventure story to create a "new adventure myth." This new adventure myth portrayed nineteenth-century Western culture, with its emphasis on "domestic values"—the primacy of work, family, and obedience to law, conscience, and morality—as a prison from which adventure offered escape. The hero of this new adventure myth was a rebel against the established order who escaped the realm of domestic values into a realm beyond conventional morality, "beyond good and evil." For Zweig, Melville's *Moby-Dick* and Conrad's *Heart of Darkness* exemplify this new adventure myth (Campbell, 1949, 30–34, 58, 73, 245–46, 353–54; Zweig, 1974, vii–viii, 15, 17, 187, 209).

As an adaptation of *Heart of Darkness*, *Apocalypse Now* is a version of both the monomyth and the new adventure myth. Willard, a CIA assassin in America's Vietnam War, is assigned to travel up the Nung River by Navy patrol boat, locate the stronghold of Walter Kurtz, a Green Beret colonel who, with a private army of Montagnard tribesmen, is fighting a savage war without regard for the rules of conventional warfare. The officers in Nha Trang who assign this job to Willard argue that Kurtz has gone insane and is "out there operating without decent restraint, totally beyond the pale of any acceptable human conduct." Willard is to "terminate" Kurtz "with extreme prejudice." The officers in Nha Trang represent domestic values. The trailer in which Willard meets them is "furnished like a home" the screenplay tells us (Milius and Coppola, 2000, 7). Late in the film Kurtz calls them "grocery clerks" who have sent Willard as an "errand boy . . . to collect a bill." Chef, a sailor on the boat who just wants to go home and be a cook, also represents domestic values, with which his name and choice of occupation associate him. As Chef says about his woman, "Eva can't picture me in Vietnam. She pictures me at home, having a beer, watching TV." Chef, as a representative of domestic values, delivers the conventional moral judgment on Kurtz. The man is "worse than crazy," Chef says, "he's evil." Willard is caught between domestic values and the realm beyond good and evil represented by Kurtz ("I am beyond their timid, lying morality," Kurtz writes in a letter to his son); at the beginning of the film, we learn that Willard's wife is divorcing him because every time Willard is in Vietnam he wants to be home, but every time he is home he wants to be back in the jungle. As he studies Kurtz's file on the journey upriver, he finds much to admire, and it seems unclear whether he will assassinate Kurtz or join him.

The plot of *Apocalypse Now* is the plot of the monomyth. Willard embarks on a journey that consists of a series of episodes: a helicopter assault, led by Colonel Kilgore, on a village; an encounter with a tiger in the jungle; a Playboy bunny USO show; the killing of civilians in a sampan; a battle at the isolated Do Lung bridge; an attack by natives with arrows and spears. Willard achieves his climactic victory by assassinating Kurtz, the tyrannical father figure, and taking his place (at the end of the film Willard is the "new Kurtz," Coppola says in material included on the DVD version of *Apocalypse Now*).

John Milius, in writing his screenplay, had different versions of the monomyth in mind. One, he said in Eleanor Coppola's documentary film *Hearts of Darkness*, was *The Odyssey*. Colonel Kilgore, Milius said, was the Cyclops, an obstacle to be tricked and overcome, and the Playboy bunnies were the Sirens. The journey to the underworld also served as a basis for the plot of *Apocalypse Now*. Milius has said that he based Willard on Aeneas and Dante (Tomasulo, 1990). The film begins as does Dante's *Inferno*, with the protagonist alone, in midlife, having lost his moral and spiritual compass and undergoing a tortured, agonizing dark night of the soul. The descent into the underworld is symbolized in the film by the descending image of Willard's helicopter landing in Nha Trang to meet with the officers who will give him his mission. The Nung River in the film corresponds to the rivers of the underworld, and, as Frank Tomasulo has pointed out, the scene at the Do Lung Bridge in which soldiers stand in the water and beg for the patrol boat to pick them up calls to mind Canto XII of *The Inferno* in which the makers of war are submerged in a river of blood (Tomasulo, 1990). Milius also based Willard on Jesus and Oedipus (Tomasulo, 1990). The identification of Willard with these two figures is established in the opening scene of the film. As two soldiers drag a drunken Willard to the shower in his Saigon hotel room, Willard is in a crucifixion posture and the shower into which they put him becomes a symbolic baptism. The Oedipal theme is announced in the opening scene of the film by the use of the Doors's song, *The End*, about a son who kills his father and sleeps with his mother.

In addition to *Heart of Darkness*, Milius also drew on another version of the new adventure myth, *Moby-Dick*. Willard is Ahab, Milius has said (Tomasulo, 1990). The ethnically diverse crew of the patrol boat in the film is like the crew of the *Pequod* in that novel. The "Extracts" at the beginning of *Moby-Dick* and such chapters as "Cetology" and "Moby-Dick" interspersed between episodes in the novel gradually acquaint the reader with whales in general and Moby-Dick in particular. These chapters have their counterpart

in the film in Kurtz's file, excerpts from which are read in voiceover narration by Willard interspersed between action episodes in the film.

Willard returns with two things from his journey. One is a manuscript
written by Kurtz. The other is Lance, one of the sailors from the boat. Depending on which you take to be the boon, the film can be understood in different ways. That ambiguity reflects different positions taken regarding the
Vietnam War by Milius and Coppola. Milius believed the decision to go to
war in Vietnam was a mistake but that once in the war, the United States
should have done whatever was necessary to win, quickly and decisively
(Milius, 1998). Conrad's narrator in *Heart of Darkness*, Milius has argued,
failed to recognize Kurtz's wisdom. For Milius, Kurtz is crazy, but he is also
telling the truth (Milius, 2003). The wisdom that Willard is bringing back
with him, the wisdom that will regenerate society, is the message of Kurtz's
manuscript: "Drop the bomb. Exterminate them all." In Milius's favorite version of the film, the one first released in theaters, the closing credits are
shown over an air strike that destroys Kurtz's stronghold. Willard, the new
Kurtz, has acted on the manuscript's advice (Milius, 1998).

Coppola opposed the war (Milius, 1998). In a 1975 *Playboy* interview,
Coppola gave his thoughts about the state of America in the Vietnam era.
The career of Michael Corleone in *The Godfather*, Coppola said, was a
metaphor for America:

> Like America, Michael began as a clean, brilliant young man endowed with in-
> credible resources and believing in a humanistic idealism. Like America,
> Michael was the child of an older system, a child of Europe. Like America,
> Michael was an innocent who had tried to correct the ills and injustices of his
> progenitors. But then he got blood on his hands. He lied to himself and to oth-
> ers about what he was doing and why. And so he became not only the mirror
> image of what he'd come from, but worse. (Coppola, 2004, 27)

For Coppola, *Apocalypse Now* was an "antilie" film (Weschler, 2005, 71).
Kurtz was speaking truth, Coppola said (Chiu, 2004). The Vietnam War had
descended into primitivism and savagery, and America had become the mirror image of what it was supposed to be against. But, Coppola said, "unlike
America, Michael Corleone is doomed. There's no way that man is ever going to change. . . . But I don't feel at all that America is doomed." He added
that "as a nation, we don't have to go down that same road, and I don't think
we will" (Coppola, 2004, 27). As Coppola says in material available on the
DVD version of *Apocalypse Now*, Willard in becoming the new Kurtz becomes the leader of Kurtz's Montagnard army. Willard lays down his weapon

at the end, and the Montagnards do the same. Willard is leading them, Coppola says, into a future without war. In this version, the boon is Lance. Lance has given in to the primitivism and savagery represented by Kurtz, but Willard pulls Lance away from this savagery and brings him home, symbolically ending the war. In keeping with that interpretation, Coppola modified the film's ending. He realized that the air strike at the end clashed with his interpretation of the film, so he issued a new version with no air strike. The closing credits appear over a black background. Clearly the kind of analysis Leitch is arguing for works with *Apocalypse Now*. It is plain to see the intertextual relationship among *Heart of Darkness*, the new adventure myth, and different versions of the monomyth, and it is clear that *Apocalypse Now* can be understood as a rewriting of these earlier texts. But *Apocalypse Now* is also one of those films to which Peter Lev alludes, a film that has multiple sources, and the historian of ideas would try to identify them in order to better understand the film.

In the documentary *Hearts of Darkness*, Coppola says that on one level *Apocalypse Now* is an action-adventure story made in the tradition of Irwin Allen, a movie meant to be filled with thrills. That fact may account for what Peter Lev has seen as Coppola's "unresolved" feelings toward the war as expressed in *Apocalypse Now*. Coppola, Lev argues, is "critical of the war . . . but also caught up in the excitement of war," as illustrated by the scene in which Kilgore leads the helicopter attack on the Viet Cong village, one of the most exciting battle scenes ever filmed (Lev, 2000, 125). For his part, Coppola has said that he cannot "really accept that AN is prowar, though I can see that if you depict such violent acts in a stirring cinematic way, it's hard to avoid glorifying war" (Weschler, 2005, 71). As he was making the film, Coppola has said, he moved away from the idea of an action-adventure film and "the film became more surreal and reminiscent of the great Conrad novella" (Coppola, 2000, vii). Numbers of commentators on the film have remarked upon the film's surreal nature, especially the "bizarre" Playboy bunny USO show (Hillstrom and Hillstrom, 1998, 121); the scene at the Do Lung Bridge with its "phantasmagoric strings of lights" (Milius and Coppola, 2000, 124), a scene that features "bizarre, atonal music" and "disembodied voices" (Auster and Quart, 1988, 67); and "Kurtz's eerie stronghold" (Hillstrom and Hillstrom, 1998, 14). Walter Murch, who designed the sound for the film and edited it, has said in the scene that takes place on the French plantation (a scene cut from the 1979 release but included in *Apocalypse Now Redux*), Coppola had in mind the work of surrealist filmmaker Luis Buñuel. We are meant to ask, Murch says, as we do with scenes in Buñuel films, did this scene really happen or was it a dream (Murch, 2001)? Coppola's use of surrealism, in fact, appears to be his attempt to reproduce the dreamlike qualities of Conrad's book. Marlow, the narrator of *Heart of Darkness* says,

> It seems to me I am trying to tell you a dream—making a vain attempt, because no relation of a dream can convey the dream sensation, that commingling of absurdity, surprise, and bewilderment in a tremor of struggling revolt, the notion of being captured by the incredible which is of the very essence of dreams. (Conrad, 1990, 24)

Coppola also modified the original script's ending, which featured the action-adventure film's obligatory climactic battle. In thinking about the ending, Coppola said, "One of the books Kurtz quotes is *The Wasteland*. Something from T. S. Eliot kept teasing at me, almost advising me about the ending . . . 'Not with a bang, but with a whimper.'" As a result, he said, the new ending "is not another helicopter battle, but it's a guy, a face alone in a dark room, telling the truth" (Chiu, 2004, 49, 51).

The articles about Vietnam that journalist Michael Herr wrote for *Esquire* and later collected in his book *Dispatches* (1977) became a source for *Apocalypse Now*. Murch has claimed that Herr was hired to write the voice-over narration for the film because Milius borrowed so much from Herr's articles (Murch, 2001). Specific scenes in the movie are taken from Herr's essays, including the opening sequence in a Saigon hotel room in which Willard looks out the window on to the city and lies on the bed watching the ceiling fan and including the scene at the Do Lung bridge in which an American soldier locates by sound an enemy caught in the wire at the base's perimeter and kills him with an M-79 grenade launcher (Herr, 1977). Coppola says in *Heart of Darkness* that the photographer played by Dennis Hopper in *Apocalypse Now* is based in part on combat photographer Sean Flynn (son of actor Errol Flynn), who figures prominently in Herr's book. More importantly, Herr's work inspired the way the war is portrayed in the film, as a drug-soaked, rock-and-roll war, a "psychedelic war" as it is called in *Heart of Darkness*.

In one of his essays, Herr refers to Vietnam as "a California corridor cut and bought and burned deep into Asia" (1977, 43). That line probably inspired Milius's conception of the Vietnam War as "a California war," a "sort of East-meets-West thing, an ancient Asian culture being assaulted by this teenage California culture" (Milius, 1998, 273), and accounts for all of the references in the film to southern California and its culture—Charles Manson, Disneyland, Beverly Hills (the name of the command bunker at the Do Lung bridge), the music of the Doors, and, especially, surfing (Milius himself was a surfer). The beach party scene in which Kilgore and his men sit around a bonfire on the beach while Kilgore plays his guitar evokes similar scenes from such 1960s surfing films as *How to Stuff a Wild Bikini*. The movie *The Endless Summer* (1964) helped create what Joan Ormrod has called "one of the defining myths of surf culture," the myth of "the quest for the perfect wave" (2005, 39). The scene in *Apocalypse Now* in which Kilgore and his men attack a Viet Cong village in order to surf "Charlie's Point" both embodies and parodies that myth.

Other elements of *Dispatches* were incorporated into *Apocalypse Now*. Herr's (1977) reference to the tigers in the hills of Vietnam most probably inspired the film's scene of the encounter with the tiger in the jungle. More importantly, Herr tells stories of "irregulars" in the Vietnam War who were "lost to headquarters," on their own, without supervision, who exercised absolute authority over hamlets in which they operated; of people driven insane by the war, including "mad colonels" who were "nonchalant about the horror"; and of those Americans who wanted to drop the bomb on Vietnam, who "wanted a Vietnam they could fit into their car ashtrays" (52–53, 60–63). These references in *Dispatches* suggest the Vietnam story in *Apocalypse Now* that was grafted onto the plot of *Heart of Darkness*. The plot of *Apocalypse Now* had two other sources.

One was *Dr. Strangelove*. Milius has said that he wrote Kilgore as "a wildly drawn character—straight out of *Dr. Strangelove*" (1998, 273), a movie that was also one of Coppola's favorites (Ross, 2004). In fact, *Apocalypse Now* draws a parallel between Kilgore and General Jack D. Ripper in *Dr. Strangelove*. There is the similarity in their over-the-top names. In the scene at the beach party, Kilgore talks while chomping on a cigarette holder in the same way that General Ripper talks while chomping on a cigar. At Charlie's Point, Kilgore ignores incoming fire, responding to it deliberately and calmly without crouching, hiding, or taking cover in a way that echoes a scene in *Dr. Strangelove* when General Ripper's office is having its windows shot out by machine-gun fire as he calmly walks around. Frances FitzGerald has described the Kilgore episode as "black comedy" (1995, 290), and Peter Lev sees it as a "satire of the Vietnam War" (2000, 122). The origins of the episode in the black comedy *Dr. Strangelove* make it clear that FitzGerald and Lev are correct in their characterizations. For Lev, the Kilgore episode raises a question of Milius's attitude toward the war. Milius, Lev says, "is pro-war but also a satirist of war" (2000, 124). Milius has explained that seeming contradiction. He is a self-proclaimed "militarist," but he has also said, "In order to be great a movie has to be true. It must stay loyal to certain ideals and challenge them at the same time. *Apocalypse Now* challenged the inanity, the total unreasonableness of war" (1998, 277). (That idea of holding ideals while simultaneously challenging them also explains how Milius the surfer could parody in the Kilgore sequence the great myth of surfing, the quest for the perfect wave.) It seems clear that Milius took more than just Kilgore's character from *Dr. Strangelove*. The plot of *Dr. Strangelove* involves an air force general who goes insane and starts his own private war, ordering the B-52 bombers under his command to attack the Soviet Union with nuclear weapons. American troops are sent to assail the general's base in order to stop him. That plot is essentially the plot of *Apocalypse Now*: An American colonel goes insane, starts his own private war, and the American army sends an assassin to stop him. Milius did associate the title of his film with B-52 bombers: "The title came from the button hippies wore that said NIRVANA NOW with a peace symbol. I made one with a tail and engine nasals, so that the symbol became a B-52, and read APOCALYPSE NOW" (1998, 273). Milius's favorite ending of the film, in which Kurtz's compound is destroyed by an air strike, resembles the end of *Dr. Strangelove*.

The other source for the plot of *Apocalypse Now* was the "Green Beret murder case." In 1969, Colonel Robert B. Rheault, head of the Green Berets in Vietnam, was arrested for the murder of a suspected Viet Cong double agent, a charge similar to the one made against Kurtz in the film. The case exposed a rift between the regular army and the Green Berets in Vietnam. In effect America was fighting two wars in Vietnam: the war fought by conventional ground forces and a "dirty war" directed by the CIA, fought with the help of the Green Berets. That dirty war involved assassination of suspected Viet Cong. The assassinations took place under the Phoenix program, controlled by the CIA and headed by William Colby, which began as a program to identify and arrest suspected Viet Cong but ended in such excesses as beheadings of suspects. These decapitations became a signature of the program (Stein, 1992; Dubberly, 1998). (Significantly, in the film the name of the assassin first sent to kill Kurtz but who ends up joining him is "Colby," and Kurtz's compound is littered with severed heads.) The Green Berets operated with a great deal of autonomy in Vietnam and were not under the official chain of command. Rheault controlled a 40,000-man Montagnard army (similar to Kurtz's in the film) funded by the CIA. Green Berets ignored army discipline, growing their hair long, dressing like Montagnards, tattooing themselves, and adopting other native customs. Rheault himself had contempt for the regular army and was one of the critics within the military who believed committing conventional ground forces in Vietnam had been an error, that the war in Vietnam could be won through the "dirty war" tactics that were, in fact, modeled on the tactics of their Marxist adversaries.

Rheault had been expected to be in line for promotion to general but had been warned that he jeopardized his chances for advancement if he remained in the Green Berets. He rejected that advice and stayed in the kind of unit he loved. "To hell with my career," he said (Stein, 1992, 42–43, 58, 60–61, 64–65, 320). (Kurtz does the same in the film. "He could have gone for general," Willard says of Kurtz. "He went for himself instead.") Both General Creighton Abrams, commander of all American forces in Vietnam, and General George Mabry, head of the American army in Vietnam, resented the independence and lack of discipline of the Green Berets, and Mabry, a strong supporter of the Geneva Convention with regard to the treatment of prisoners, was appalled at the murder of a suspected Viet Cong agent in American custody. Both Abrams and Mabry saw the arrest of Rheault as a way to rein in the Green Berets (Stein, 1992). Peter Lev has demonstrated that Milius had this case in mind in writing *Apocalypse Now*. Rheault is mentioned by name in early versions of the script, and Lev argues that Milius probably got a good deal of the story, including details of Rheault's life that served as an inspiration for Kurtz, from the news coverage that was widespread at the time Milius was working on his screenplay in 1969. That news coverage, in fact, contained the term *terminate with extreme prejudice* as a euphemism for assassination (Lev, 2000). Milius had other knowledge of the Green Berets' role in the Vietnam dirty war. He claims that the story in the film about the Viet Cong hacking off arms of children inoculated by Americans was a true story, told to him by a friend who served three tours as a Green Beret in Vietnam. In retaliation the Green Berets rounded up "known" Viet Cong and murdered them. Milius says his friend was one of the models for Willard (1998, 273). As Peter Lev (2000) has argued, then, as symbolic and mythic as *Apocalypse Now* is on some levels, the use of the Green Beret murder case as a source for the film ensures that the film deals with real and significant issues in the way Americans fought the war in Vietnam.

Milius's use of the Green Beret murder case as a source ties in with his use of another source, the John Wayne western *The Searchers*. Milius has said that he puts something from *The Searchers* in every film he makes (Auster and Quart, 1988). Richard Slotkin (1992) has characterized *The Searchers* as a retelling of the American frontier myth, which first took shape in narratives about King Philip's War in New England in the 1670s and continued to be told in varying forms into the twentieth century. In the myth European Americans as they moved West were confronted with resistance by American Indians. European Americans were used to fighting a "civilized war" with rules that forbade making war on civilians or torturing prisoners. But American Indians fought a "savage war," an all-out war of attrition in which they tortured prisoners and killed women and children. The Europeans, the myth says, found themselves at a disadvantage in staying within the rules of civilized warfare and to win had to learn to fight a savage war. It was in part, Slotkin argues, the ideas in this myth that led in the Cold War to the creation of the Green Berets as American guerillas whose tactics would mirror those of the Marxist guerillas they were fighting. A key figure in this myth is "the man who knows Indians," the European American who understands how Indians fight and can teach other European Americans to fight a savage war. Ethan Edwards, the protagonist of *The Searchers*, is an example of the man who knows Indians (Slotkin, 1992). In *Apocalypse Now*, Kurtz is a variation of the man who knows Indians, the man who knows the Viet Cong. He has studied how they fight and advocates that to win the war, Americans must fight the kind of savage war the Viet Cong are fighting.

Finally, the Japanese code of bushido, the code of the samurai, in which Milius steeped himself, provides a source for *Apocalypse Now* (Milius, 1976). That code advocates that the samurai empty himself of ego, fear, and moral judgment and draw on instincts to kill without hesitation, thought, or remorse. Kurtz articulates that code in the film when he says that to win the war, you have to have men "who are able to utilize their primordial instincts to kill without feeling, without passion, without judgment. Without judgment. Because it's judgment that defeats us" (20).

Recreating the intellectual world behind a film by locating the film's sources in earlier texts, then, can help us to better understand the film's meaning. Historians of ideas, however, would go beyond looking for sources of texts in earlier texts. They would also look for the social sources of texts (Gay, 1967).

To identify the social sources of a text, historians of ideas ask specific questions about the social position of the creator of the text. What gender, ethnic group, or social class does the creator of the text belong to? Is he or she rising or falling in the class ladder? What social role or function does he or she have? What social, political, and economic pressures were operating on the creator of the text? How do all of these things affect what appears in the text? Ann Douglas, for example, in *The Feminization of American Culture* (1977), examines how the social position of ministers in the nineteenth century affected their ideas. She points out that Northern liberal, nonevangelical ministers in the early nineteenth century tended to be uncritical toward slavery. In the seventeenth and eighteenth centuries, when the colonies had official, established state churches and ministers had lifetime tenure, ministers could, and did, speak out fearlessly on the political issues of their day, but with the disestablishment of these churches and the end, in the early nineteenth century, of lifetime tenure, ministers became dependent on the good will of their congregations to retain their jobs. As Douglas argues, the Northern businessmen and merchants who were influential members of these congregations had a vital interest in protecting slavery, and the ministers could not afford to offend them by speaking out against the institution. These same ministers helped create the nineteenth-century stereotype of women as morally superior to men, more pious and more pure. A large proportion of these ministers' congregations were women, and by flattering these members of his congregation, a minister gained greater security in retaining his pulpit.

The method of the history of ideas applied to film can answer David Kranz's call for adaptation studies scholars to look at the cultural, economic, ideological, and historical pressures that affect a film's production. Let us return to *Apocalypse Now*. Francis Coppola and John Milius belonged to that first generation of film-school-trained directors who were imbued with the film-school ethos of revitalizing the film industry so that directors would be able to realize their distinctive artistic visions. Coppola, especially, tried to work within the Hollywood establishment with an eye toward changing it but found himself frustrated by studio executives more interested in deal making and the bottom line than art (Coppola, 2004; Gelmis, 2004; Phillips and Hill, 2004; Sragow, 2004). Coppola has said that "the film industry is entirely in the hands of a management mentality that would rather just keep repeating the same movies and sequels than use the tremendous resources of this country to invent and be creative" (Keough, 2004, 131). Milius has concurred: "Today in moviemaking, there's a pervasive fear of not being hip enough, not making the right corporate move, not having enough money. Corporate nazis have replaced individualism, dignity, and ethics" (1998, 277). Robert Lindsey (2004) has pointed out the parallel between Coppola's movie *Tucker* (1988) and Coppola's own social situation within the movie industry. The film is about Preston Tucker, an inspired inventor who creates a revolutionary, safer automobile but who is destroyed by American automobile companies who convince the public he is a fraud. In discussing *Tucker*, Coppola made an analogy between the automotive industry and Hollywood. The automotive industry, like Hollywood, he said, was "being run by huge, entrenched institutions completely hostile to . . . inventiveness" (Coppola, 2004, 39). "The time has come for industry—the entertainment industry, certainly the automotive industry—to let creative people be creative," he has said (Keough, 2004, 131). Coppola, Lindsey has argued, is "like Preston Tucker, convinced he knows a better way of doing things, but frustrated by his inability to convince others to accept it" (2004, 141).

Lindsey has characterized the plot of *Tucker*: "A creative, if perhaps impractical dreamer comes forth with a better idea that is quashed by a powerful establishment in order to maintain the status quo" (2004, 139). That description could equally fit the plot of *Apocalypse Now*. Willard tells us in the film's voice-over narration that Kurtz "was being groomed for one of the top slots in the corporation." The use of the term *corporation* evokes the image of the army as a powerful bureaucracy—like Hollywood studios. Kurtz, like Coppola, has worked within the system to try to change it. Kurtz had a vision of how the war could be won, and after his first tour in Vietnam, he had written a report to the Joint Chiefs of Staff pushing his ideas. His report was restricted and his recommendations ignored. Frustrated at his inability to change the system, Kurtz took action on his own. The regular army establishment sent out an assassin to kill him. Milius saw the parallel between Coppola and Kurtz. In making *Apocalypse Now*, Milius said, Coppola "became Kurtz." "In a way," Milius went on, "*Apocalypse Now* is about a guy who decides to make his own decisions. The further he gets in his career the more he is convinced he is not going to listen to the crap" (1998, 276, 277).

For the historian of ideas, fully illuminating the meaning of a text requires exploring all of the sources of the text, not only earlier texts but social sources as well. Scholars of adaptation studies seeking to expand their field beyond its traditional concerns, then, might find the method of the history of ideas to be useful.

Works Cited

Auster, Albert, and Leonard Quart. 1988. *How the War Was Remembered: Hollywood and Vietnam*. New York: Praeger.

Cahir, Linda Costanzo. 1992. "Narratological Parallels in Joseph Conrad's *Heart of Darkness* and Francis Ford Coppola's *Apocalypse Now*." *LFQ* 20 (3): 181–87.

Campbell, Joseph. 1949. *The Hero with a Thousand Faces*. Princeton, NJ: Princeton University Press.

Chiu, Tony. 2004. "Coppola's Cinematic *Apocalypse* Is Finally at Hand." In *Francis Ford Coppola: Interviews*, ed. Gene D. Phillips and Rodney Hill, 44–52. Jackson: University Press of Mississippi.

Conrad, Joseph. 1990. *Heart of Darkness*. New York: Dover.

Coppola, Francis Ford. 2000. "Introduction." In *Apocalypse Now Redux: The Screenplay*, by John Milius and Francis Ford Coppola, v–vii. New York: Hyperion.

———. 2004. "*Playboy* Interview: Francis Ford Coppola." Interview with William Murray. In *Francis Ford Coppola: Interviews*, ed. Gene D. Phillips and Rodney Hill, 17–43. Jackson: University Press of Mississippi.

Davidson, James West, and Mark Hamilton Lytle. 2005. *After the Fact: The Art of Historical Detection*, 5th ed., vol. 1. New York: McGraw-Hill.

Douglas, Ann. 1977. *The Feminization of American Culture*. New York: Knopf.

Dubberly, Benjamin C. 1998. "Atrocities during the Vietnam War." In *The Encyclopedia of the Vietnam War: A Political, Social, and Military History*, ed. Spencer C. Tucker, 29–31. Oxford, UK: Oxford University Press.

FitzGerald, Frances. 1995. "*Apocalypse Now*." In *Past Imperfect: History According to the Movies*, ed. Mark C. Carnes, 288–91. New York: Henry Holt.

Gay, Peter. 1967. "The Social History of Ideas: Ernst Cassirrer and After." In *The Critical Spirit: Essays in Honor of Herbert Marcuse*, ed. Kurt H. Wolff and Barrington Moore Jr., 106–20. Boston: Beacon.

Gelmis, Joseph. 2004. "Francis Ford Coppola: Free Agent within the System." In *Francis Ford Coppola: Interviews*, ed. Gene D. Phillips and Rodney Hill, 3–16. Jackson: University Press of Mississippi.

Herr, Michael. 1977. *Dispatches*. New York: Knopf.

Hillstrom, Kevin, and Laurie Collier Hillstrom. 1998. *The Vietnam Experience: A Concise Encyclopedia of American Literature, Songs, and Films*. Westport, CT: Greenwood.

Keough, Peter. 2004. "Coppola Carves a Cinematic Elegy: *Gardens of Stone*." In *Francis Ford Coppola: Interviews*, ed. Gene D. Phillips and Rodney Hill, 125–31. Jackson: University Press of Mississippi.

Kranz, David. 2003. "LFA/LFQ: Fidelity and Novelty." *LFA News* 1 (1): 3, 8.

Leitch, Thomas. 2003. "Where Are We Going, Where Have We Been?" *LFA News* 1 (1): 2, 6, 8. [This essay has been reprinted in chapter 23 of the current volume.]

Lev, Peter. 2000. *American Films of the 70s: Conflicting Visions*. Austin: University of Texas Press.

———. 2003. "The Future of Adaptation Studies." *LFA News* 1 (1): 7. [An expanded version of this essay appears in chapter 24 of the current volume.]

Lindsey, Robert. 2004. "Promises to Keep." In *Francis Ford Coppola: Interviews*, ed. Gene D. Phillips and Rodney Hill, 167–83. Jackson: University Press of Mississippi.

Milius, John. 1976. "Stoked: John Milius Interviewed by Richard Thompson." Interview with Richard Thompson. *Film Comment* 12 (4): 10–21.

———. 1998. "A Soldier's Tale." In *Rolling Stone: The Seventies*, ed. Ashley Kahn, Holly George-Warren, and Shawn Dahl, 272–77. Boston: Little, Brown.

———. 2003. "An Interview with John Milius." Interview with Ken P. http://movies.ign.com/articles/401/401150p1.html. Accessed April 19, 2007.

Milius, John, and Francis Ford Coppola. 2000. *Apocalypse Now Redux: The Screenplay*. New York: Hyperion.

Murch, Walter. 2001. "Apocalypse Then and Now." *Film Comment* 37 (3): 44–47.

Ormrod, Joan. 2005. "*Endless Summer* (1964): Consuming Waves and Surfing the Frontier." *Film and History* 35 (1): 39–51.

Phillips, Gene D. and Rodney Hill, eds. 2004. *Francis Ford Coppola: Interviews*. Jackson: University Press of Mississippi.

Ross, Lillian. 2004. "Some Figures on a Fantasy." In *Francis Ford Coppola: Interviews*, ed. Gene D. Phillips and Rodney Hill, 63–105. Jackson: University Press of Mississippi.

Slotkin, Richard. 1992. *Gunfighter Nation: The Myth of the Frontier in Twentieth-Century America*. New York: Harper.

Sragow, Michael. 2004. "Godfatherhood." In *Francis Ford Coppola: Interviews*, ed. Gene D. Phillips and Rodney Hill, 167–83. Jackson: University Press of Mississippi.

Stein, Jeff. 1992. *A Murder in Wartime*. New York: St. Martin's.

Tomasulo, Frank P. 1990. "The Politics of Ambivalence: *Apocalypse Now* as Prowar and Antiwar Film." In *From Hanoi to Hollywood: The Vietnam War in American Film*, ed. Linda Dittmar and Gene Michaud, 145–58. New Brunswick, NJ: Rutgers University Press.

Weschler, Lawrence. 2005. "Valkyries over Iraq." *Harper's Magazine*, November, 65–77.

Wills, Garry. 1978. *Inventing America: Jefferson's Declaration of Independence*. Garden City, NY: Doubleday.

Zweig, Paul. 1974. *The Adventurer*. New York: Basic Books.

CHAPTER FOUR

~

Adaptation Studies Revisited: Purposes, Perspectives, and Inspiration

Sarah Cardwell

Introduction: The Future of Adaptation Studies[1]

What does the future hold for adaptation studies? In addressing this question here, I have found it helpful to reflect upon my own experience of researching adaptation and in particular to consider the reasons the subject retains perpetual interest for me (I constantly return to it) and how I hope the field will develop. I shall examine and clarify my motivations for studying adaptation in order to ascertain whether the methodologies and perspectives I work with are indeed the most appropriate, given those motives.[2] My title touches upon the key concerns that have arisen from my reflections: purposes, perspectives, and inspiration.

I hope that the future of adaptation studies lies in exploring a vital and fertile area of aesthetics, contributing new questions, research, perspectives, and ideas to the study of literary, filmic, and televisual arts. Therefore, I propose in this chapter a future "aesthetics of adaptation" and elucidate two key areas that would constitute such an aesthetics.

Underlying my paper is an interest in what might be considered the core conundrum of the field: comparative versus noncomparative approaches. The term *adaptation studies* has historically implied a perspective of *comparison*, which admits a fundamental and determining relationship between "this book" and "this film" and leads frequently to "fidelity criticism." Such an understanding is intuitive and supports the longstanding comparative approach to adaptations. But there is another way of regarding adaptations. They can be considered as films (or programs) in their own right—that is, not in relation to a source book.[3]

In my book *Adaptation Revisited* (2002), I argue for a noncomparative approach to adaptations, rejecting comparison with source books. There is insufficient space here to rehearse the logical and conceptual foundations of that argument, and I refer interested readers to that earlier text.[4] Instead, I shall illustrate this position with an example from a recent literary adaptation. However, it is intriguing to realize that in recent articles, since the book was written, I have found myself being drawn back to a comparative approach in order to explore some aspect of film in contrast with literature, for example, temporality and tense, mood, or point of view. I find myself still torn between the two perspectives. This chapter is an attempt to establish more rationally which approach is suitable in which circumstances and to evaluate what the future potential of each approach is.[5] Both perspectives contribute in different ways to the development of an aesthetics of adaptation.

Against Comparison: Interpretation of an Example (*The Way We Live Now*)

Let us begin with the case against the traditional comparative analysis of adaptations. I have argued elsewhere that we should reject comparison with source novels for the purposes of interpretation and evaluation of adaptations (films and programs). At worst, comparison leads us to false expectations about the film's intentions and form, blinding us to what it itself is trying to achieve and allowing us to be biased against the adaptation from the outset, judging it by the standards of the book. At best, our close attention to the novel is restrictive: It shapes our reception of the adaptation, leading us to focus too narrowly on some aspects over others and to ignore other relevant contextual factors. Both interpretation and evaluation are therefore affected, and our attentive responsiveness to the film as an artwork is reduced. I would contend that in criticism we should be aiming for what Noël Carroll (2000) calls "sympathetic disinterest."[6] Comparison undermines this.

The most effective way of conveying this is through an example. Consider the opening sequence from *The Way We Live Now*, a British television adaptation of Anthony Trollope's book (1875), broadcast on the BBC in 2001. The serial opens differently from the book, which begins with an introduction of the characters; a new scene depicting Melmotte's arrival at his new home in Grosvenor Square is added. This sequence relates most closely to the introduction of Melmotte in the book.

The sequence opens with what appears to be an abstract shot composed of a number of vertical lines, some of which seem to be moving across the screen; as the shot progresses, the actual content becomes clearer: a polished door that reflects streams of light from an unknown source is being opened, and creates a mirror image (thus the curious kaleidoscope effect as the door moves). Two views of a man's head appear, his head being duplicated in the image as it is mirrored in the door (he thus appears to be looking in two different directions). It is unclear which of the images is real and which is the reflection.

The next shot is a long shot, symmetrically framed, showing a grand room empty of furniture yet warm, in honey-colored tones. The man (a servant) crosses the room from left to right to the heavy, closed curtains that shroud the tall windows. In medium shot, he briskly pulls the curtains open, and a cloud of dust whooshes toward him; bright light pours into the room as he gazes outside.

A sharp disjunction is made as the next cut takes us outside to an apparently unrelated location (this is not implied to be a point-of-view shot): A low-angle shot looks up at horses and then a carriage as they cross the screen from right to left. Another cut takes us to a big close-up of the very top of a globe so that we see the curve of its surface and part of its frame and axle. The colors are minimal—hues of brown and yellow—so that the image is a rather abstract one, focusing on tiny details. Movement in the background and the sound of rolling wheels alerts us to the fact that the globe is moving across the floor. The next shot is of the underside of the globe as it passes an ornately carved piece of furniture; this is followed by a low-angle close-up of the globe, making it seem enormous—and of the two men who are moving it and who, because of extremely bright back lighting, appear only as black shapes on either side of the globe. They leave the globe at the center of the screen.

A low-angle shot shows a servant's feet moving toward the back of a covered wagon, and then he pulls a dustsheet from a huge black chair being transported within it. An aerial shot shows the chair being unloaded by two men.

A medium long shot of the entrance of a country house reveals servants assembling at the doorway; they line up on either side of the front door in an orderly fashion and anxiously and hurriedly adjust their clothing. In long shot, a carriage arrives at the house. In mid shot, a servant approaches the carriage's door and unfolds the steps to allow the travellers to disembark.

Raised women's voices can be heard from inside the carriage as we look again at the waiting servants; a young woman stumbles ungracefully from the carriage, almost as if shoved rudely from inside; a woman (her mother) follows her. The two stand framed by the lines of servants and looking uncertain and embarrassed. They part and seem to join the two lines, one on each side, and everyone turns to look at the carriage (i.e., to look at the camera).

A long take follows: The camera moves rather unsteadily down from the carriage, up the front steps, and into the hallway of the house (this is implied to be a person's point of view—actually Melmotte's); just as he enters the hallway, an aerial shot catches his figure crossing the floor and swoops down to a rather odd angle, just missing Melmotte's face and instead capturing a young servant pushing another globe across the floor, followed by Melmotte's wife and daughter.

As the camera follows closely behind Melmotte, the screen is almost filled with the dark outline of his broad, hunched shoulders as he marches onward; then a reverse shot shows the front of him, but again he is only a black shape, with only the faint glow of his cigar visible, and with glimpses of the second globe behind him. A close up of Melmotte's black-gloved hands pulls back into a mid shot, showing him sliding a concertina door open: this is shown first from one side of the door and then the other, creating a jump-cut sensation as the sliding movement changes direction. There is a close-up of the hand in which Melmotte holds his glowing cigar, surrounded by a cloud of smoke; then, there is a full-length shot of him as he turns to us, and we finally see a clear shot of his face. He stands off-center in an empty room, and the camera moves in to a low-angle medium close-up of his face. He declaims, "Well, let us see what we can do here." Immediately the screen cuts to black, and then the title of the program is shown: *The Way We Live Now*, carved out on a block of grey-black stone in raised capital letters. The music which has accompanied the entire sequence, and which I refer to below, ends at this point with a dramatic chord.

One might choose to regard this program as an adaptation and compare it with the source novel, and to do so highlights some differences and similarities between the two. The program foregrounds Melmotte more than the book does, establishing him as the central character. Like the book, though, the program reveals Melmotte's effect upon those around him and his "reputation" before it shows the man himself and his appearance (his reputation precedes him, as it were). The sense that he is a go-getter, an entrepreneur who rushes at things, is implied through the fact that the household is not yet ready to receive him—he is there before they know it. This can be correlated with the sentence "All this had been done within twelve months."

The description of Melmotte's appearance corresponds closely with David Suchet's appearance, but in the novel this is an opportunity to introduce Melmotte in relation to his wife and daughter—in the adaptation he is a more solitary figure. The importance of travel and building up his global empire is implied by the presence of two globes—one is at the house, and one is with him, as if he cannot rest in marking out potential new territories upon it.

Looking briefly at the source novel in comparison then (and I shall come back to a couple of other points later), our attention is drawn to the presentation of Melmotte and his characterization, and this appears not incompatible with the adaptation's concerns in this scene.

However, I would argue in keeping with my previous contention here: that to take this approach is to ignore the program's own agenda, its artistic choices, its emphases and "voice." To comprehend the sequence as part of an artwork necessitates appreciating more fully its references to its artistic and cultural contexts and its medium. In this case, that means considering its locus within three contexts: its generic context, its authorial context, and its televisual context. Finally one needs to establish the sequence's aesthetic particularities—what defines it, how it is composed, shaped, inflected. And actually, once one has done this, as we shall see, it becomes clear that this sequence's most important aesthetic concerns can be reduced to the presentation of Melmotte or can be related to the novel. They are quite separate.

Generic Context

This program stands within the popular genre of (British) classic-novel adaptations. Its generic identity is marked by broad indicators, some of which are extratextual (for example, it was advertised as such, and the writer, Andrew Davies, is foregrounded and is renowned for classic-novel adaptations) and some of which are intratextual (for example, the costumes and the locations, which indicate a sense of the "past"; the presence of well-known British character actors; the overt use of symmetry as a compositional device; and the high production values). However, this program also declares itself as belonging to a new breed of costume dramas, following in the footsteps of other Davies adaptations, such as *Vanity Fair* and *Moll Flanders*, with its camerawork (handheld, wobbly, with partial views); its music, which is not sedate but lively, almost lurching, and which is employed more in the manner of a commentary rather than as a mood-inducing background; and its focus on small details rather than large landscapes. Thus *The Way We Live Now* clearly makes reference to recent examples of the genre of British television classic-novel adaptations.

Why is this important? Because the program refers to its membership of this genre more than to its relationship with the source book. This genre provides its framework, its ground rules, and a set of expectations for the audience. Most viewers will know this genre better than they will know the source book. They will have preconceptions about representations of the past, of gender and class in this genre; they will expect certain narrative and formal conventions. The opening of the serial conforms with some expectations and not others: it is like using the sonnet form but then experimenting within it. One cannot fully interpret a sonnet without being aware of the form/genre it uses; the same applies here. The adaptation's compliances with, differences from, and contrasts with generic norms give us clues for interpretation here. For example, we notice Melmotte's wife and daughter's undignified descent from the carriage and their trepidation in meeting the servants. This conveys the sense of their being outsiders, a sense which is emphasised by associating wobbly views to Melmotte's point of view, highlighting his unstable, disruptive influence in this ordered, formal world. Similarly, Melmotte's musical theme is one that is defiantly slower than the dominant theme, disrupting its timing, persistently forcing the music to slow down. This echoes Melmotte's forceful insistence on doing things his own way, on forging onward against the tide. It is details of the program's use of generic conventions, rather than any references to the source novel, that create significance here.

Authorial Context (Andrew Davies)

Furthermore, specific expectations are raised regarding the program's authorial context. Its place alongside examples of Andrew Davies's recent work implies something more particular for the knowing viewer: a certain tone or point of view that can be broadly understood as detached, sympathetic irony. Davies's recent adaptations tend to have great sympathy for often unsympathetic or wicked protagonists; they tend to use these protagonists to reflect upon the iniquities and double standards of the world that judges them (e.g., in his Moll Flanders [1996] and Vanity Fair [1998]); they tend to be amusing and amused; and they tend to exhibit a sense of ironic humour, which often arises from details of the program and from characters' performances.[7] So the program's place within, first, the genre and, second, Davies's oeuvre says more about its tone, intentions, and our engagement than the source book can tell us about the adaptation.

Televisual Context (and Performance)

The third pertinent context is that of television, and here it is useful to distinguish this television adaptation from film adaptations. First, one's attention is drawn in this adaptation to the use of framing and the emphasis on singular details. Historically, television has painted with broad brushstrokes, not overfilling the frame but focusing attention on a few salient details in each shot. (This no doubt arises from its historically poorer and smaller image.) The same is true here, leading us to observe details for their significance, as I have implied above. Further, the pace of television is said to be faster than that of film, as it must grab and hold the viewers' attention. Although the shot lengths here are generically fairly slow, the pace appears faster because of the spatial disconnection between cuts—the striking movement from one place to another.

Finally, *performance*, which one might understand to be a defining characteristic of television,[8] seems to be vitally important to the tone and structure of this sequence. The preparations for Melmotte's arrival take place in a very empty house, clearing the floor as if preparing a space for action—the servants are like stage hands awaiting the starring actor. Melmotte's face is hidden from us at first, as he walks purposefully to the large room, pushes back the doors, opens up the space, takes center stage, and dramatically announces, "Well, let us see what we can do here"—we then cut to the program title. This sequence thus forms a prologue before the action and enhances the theatrical mood. There is an emphasis on our awaiting the presence of both Melmotte and David Suchet as the star, so that Suchet's line becomes something with extradiegetic significance. As if calling upon a troupe of actors to begin, he opens the performance. This emphasis on performance is again important in establishing the program's links with other recent Davies adaptations, reasserting its connections with those. It does not refer to Melmotte's presentation in the novel. Indeed, in the novel Melmotte is presented by the author—he is not permitted to present himself in this way. The particular style of presentation employed here marks out the importance of the televisual context to the aesthetic choices of the adaptation.

Aesthetic Concerns

Finally, and briefly, for a full and responsive interpretation of this adaptation, one needs to consider those features that define its formal shape and aesthetic tone. The overriding air here is one of anticipation. This is created and sustained by partial views: The first shot is unclear—what are we seeing? Then we hear the wheels of the globe as it moves across the floor—what are we hearing? Then we sense the preparations—for whom are we preparing? And finally we are denied Melmotte's face—who is he (the question refers to both star and character)? Some formal details are notable: the way in which the music shapes the sequence, creating momentum, pace, and tension and governing when the sequence begins and ends; the creation of rhythm and intrigue through the use of spatial disorientation, jump cuts, and sudden changes in the direction of movements; and the manner in which details are valued not just for their narrative significance but also for the visual pleasure that they provide—their texture, sensuality, and form.

It is vital to recognize that, in terms of where one might wish to develop one's study of this adaptation, the program raises its *own* questions—ones that are unrelated to the source novel because they arise from its own aesthetic specificities. For example, I feel that one of the most striking features here is that familiar sense of sympathetic but ironic detachment from Melmotte that I expected from a Davies adaptation. But I found it difficult to dissect how this had been achieved. As I have shown above, it is fairly easy to pinpoint details in the sequence that confirm Melmotte as an outsider and a rather unpleasant man. Yet one is drawn to him somehow, and there is a feeling that the adaptation is presenting him sympathetically; it is this latter aspect that is hard to analyze. Reference to the source book is of no help to us in understanding this. Looking back to the novel, it presents a much blander relationship with the character. An explicit point of view on Melmotte is offered: Referring to the "wonderful look of power about his mouth and chin," the author notes, "This was so strong as to redeem his face from vulgarity; but the countenance and appearance of the man were on the whole unpleasant, and, I may say, untrustworthy" (Trollope, 1875, 31). The redemption from vulgarity implies, of course, the risk of it, and "unpleasant and untrustworthy" are damning adjectives. Also, note the "I may say"—an embedded narrator offering an explicit point of view.

But this does not help us, when we come to the adaptation, to look beyond details of physiognomy and performance. To answer any question about the attitude of this sequence to Melmotte, the viewer must discard the book and focus on what is there in front of him on the screen. Close attention to the details of the sequence reveals a sense of *collusion* between camera and Melmotte. Melmotte is the kind of character, as we see from his chair in this sequence, who is egotistical and showy. He would have chosen to make a grand entrance, take center stage. The sequence lets him do so. Indeed, the camerawork facilitates this, just "missing" his face when it could show it—allowing him to remain absent until he declares the action open. So the music (which is playful and bombastic and creates a jaunty pace and rhythm) and the focus on ironic details (the globes and chair) foreground the presence of a point of view that is sarcastic and ironic, commenting on the man. But the camera is also sympathetic to him, allowing him his pleasures, colluding with his performance. The novel's explicit view—"I may say"—

becomes much more diffuse and complex, being presented through so many facets, such as camerawork, editing, music, framing, and so on.

Here, then, comparison with the novel did not get us very far. Rather, attention to the details of the program was far more profitable and inspiring.

Purposes: A Case for Comparative Studies

The important feature of all this is to recognize what my *purpose* was here: to explicitly interpret and implicitly evaluate this program. Within that remit of interpretation and evaluation, there is no need for comparison. Everything I need to see I can see in the program, and it is not relevant to my aims to undertake a comparison with the book. However, for *different purposes*, comparison proves very useful, and that is what I shall address now.

The question that my film students ask, when we undertake a comparison of a book with a film adaptation, is "What's the point?" They want to know why looking at literature, even if a film is based on a book, tells us anything about film. It is a justifiable question. As a film studies scholar, it is important for me to consider the matter. What can the study of adaptation bring to my understanding of film? Why do I persistently return to it?

I see a uniquely valuable use for comparative studies of adaptation, and this is to offer a significant and singular contribution to film and television aesthetics and our understanding of literature. Through comparison of texts in different media, we can move to comparison of the media themselves, which can lead us to a fuller and more complex understanding of the specificity of the media involved. That is, the study of adaptation is uniquely able to advance the study of medium specificity. This is a vital and underdeveloped area of aesthetics: the study of the unique features of different art forms, those features that distinguish them from one another and constitute their artistic potential.

An example of such a practice can be found in an article of mine that was published recently in *Literature/Film Quarterly* (LFQ). In it, I considered the notion of tense as a starting point for exploring the temporality of film as compared with that of literature. This was with the aim of discovering aspects of the medium of film that were unique, specific, and possibly even determining. "Tense" was the obvious place to start, as it seemed to be something peculiar to literature and untranslatable to film. That is, tense poses a problem for filmmakers adapting literature. This problem, posed by the process of adaptation, precipitated my exploration of filmic temporality, exploring it first in comparison with literature but then stepping beyond that when that framework became constraining rather than enabling.

In short, I had a different *purpose* in mind from the one I had earlier when looking at *The Way We Live Now*. Although the article made references to the recent adaptation of *Lolita*, the fact is that I was not interested primarily in exploring this film's representation of temporal features or evaluating it. I was using the existence of this adaptation as a tool to explore an abstract feature of the literary and filmic media—their temporality. My purpose was to undertake an analytical, philosophical investigation into a key aspect of aesthetics (the medium specificity of film) by looking at one key feature (its temporal characteristics). Comparison with literature helped me enormously. It helped me to focus on the smaller details, as my focus on the words in Nabokov's novel encouraged me to focus on small constituents of the related sequence—single shots, frames. Also, it helped me to focus on the fundamental questions of ontology that have been glossed over: the inherently tensed nature of verbs in comparison with the tenseless nature of the image. It helped me later, when I returned to what had been said previously about time and film and tense and adaptation, to see the omissions, flaws, and circularity in what had been said. And it helped me to consider why those errors might have been made because of the different ways in which we experience and engage with film and literature. Literature highlighted the distinctive and different ways that film engages us. It inspired me.

Perspectives

Before concluding, there is something to be said about perspectives—not in the formal terms of methodology, such as with comparative or other approaches, but something broader—where we come from. It is my experience that the field of adaptation studies encourages the input of scholars from a wider range of perspectives than can be found in other areas of film and television studies. I have felt able, in my work on adaptation, to utilize approaches that are contentious or unpopular. In recent work I have drawn upon cognitive theories, philosophical approaches (including the philosophy of language, mind, and aesthetics), close analysis, and evaluation. Each time I have found an openness to my approach, to my style of thinking and expression, that I have not always found in film or television studies. Perhaps this is partly because adaptation theorists are knowledgeable about at least two fields and aware of a whole range of perspectives and methodologies; they are willing to give new methods and ideas a chance to prove themselves. It is surely also because the subject of adaptation studies has such fascinating and unaddressed questions at its core, which endows the field with a refreshing richness. When many ideas are becoming overused and redundant in literary and film studies, the existence of adaptations is vital. They cross the boundaries; challenge or reassert our notions of medium specificity and art, interpretation, and evaluation; and refresh our intellectual appetites—and we are intrigued all over again.

It is imperative, therefore, that we value the perspectives brought from both literary and film scholars to the question of adaptation. James Naremore (2000) expresses doubts about the "literary approach to film," such as that found in *LFQ*; he argues that such an approach leads to comparison and evaluation favoring the book. While Naremore is broadly right about the negative consequences, historically he fails to ask what positive qualities the approach can bring to our appreciation, not just of adaptation, but also of film and literature as distinct but related art forms. What can specialists in the "literary approach to film" contribute to an understanding of film aesthetics? What might they offer that someone trained only in film studies might not?

Many traditions in film studies do not pay great attention to detail, to argumentation, to seeking out questions and answers rather than offering theories. In comparison, some older traditions of literary criticism can encourage film scholars to enhance their close analysis of style and move beyond ideological and theoretical concerns. Similarly, in my experience, I have found that reading more widely in literary criticism and Anglo-American analytical philosophy has helped me to explore and express my ideas in a way that feels more natural, clearer, more logical, and convincing. If I am honest, these influences have aided me more than reading such film journals as *Screen*.

Vitally, I should emphasize that to draw upon older literary traditions is not to hark back to the past but is actually in keeping with moves afoot in film studies. The kind of traditional interests that come from literary studies— close analysis, aesthetics, careful argumentation, lucid expression, and so forth—advance film studies and indeed are gathering pace and force within that field at the moment. It is intriguing to see that some branches of film studies are beginning to see the value in approaches that literary studies deemed unfashionable a long time ago. Scholars are beginning to recognise that a very loose, uncritical, sloppy, or unengaged pluralism does not advance us in either theorizing abstractly about adaptation or appreciating particular instances of adaptation.

Furthermore, it is important to recognize that this process of learning from other fields works both ways. Adaptation studies has something to learn from the work that has been undertaken in film and television studies; in particular, the best film and television scholars have developed a respect for those media and a responsive attitude toward them, engendering the kind of "sympathetic disinterest" that should constitute our stance toward an artwork.

Inspiration

In conclusion, I would hope that in the future we might broadly understand adaptation studies as part of "aesthetics," enhancing the study of the art forms of film, literature, and TV, with adaptations providing a unique possibility for intermedia, interdisciplinary study, and that we might recognize that we adaptation scholars are among the people best placed to undertake this work. I have argued that the study of adaptation can be a valuable tool, but finally I would like to reiterate the *inspiration* that adaptation studies provides.

When researching *Adaptation Revisited*, I sensed that adaptation inspires passion in those who write about it. From the earliest writers who wished to defend either literature or film, the fact is that adaptations lead one instinctively to be on one's guard. As someone based in a film studies department, I might be expected to be a proponent of film, defending it and television as art, and indeed most of the time I am, celebrating their vividness. However, as someone who loves written language and literature and to whom the concreteness and exactness of the written text appeals, I am also drawn to literature's richness and precision. Perhaps this is one of the reasons I am constantly drawn back to adaptation. But my most direct and honest answer to the question "Why do I return to adaptation studies?" is that the subject offers me inspiration. One of my next projects is a book about film and time. It came about through researching adaptation. Another is a monograph on the work of Andrew Davies; most of his works are adaptations. Three other projects—on filmic mood, music in film, and point of view in film and literature—came about because of adaptations of Hardy's rural novels and the book *American Psycho*. I can see already how my brief comments on *The Way We Live Now* could spark off various investigations into, for example, performance, genre, tone, or attitude.

Much of that work may therefore move outside adaptation studies into film or literary or TV studies, but adaptation remains the source of inspiration. Many of those projects would not have happened had the films and programs in question not been adaptations, highlighting for me the specificity of film or TV through a comparison with literature. Adaptations illuminate points of contention, raise questions and problems, and allow multiple perspectives to suggest answers. What I hope to see in the future is an aesthetics of adaptation, entailing both the responsive appreciation of individual artworks (film and television adaptations) and thus the art of adaptation, and also a careful, conceptual, comparative exploration of key issues, including medium specificity, authorship, style, and evaluation, and a consequently greater understanding of the specificity and potential of the arts of literature, film, and television.

Notes

1. Readers should note that this chapter focuses on adaptations from literature to film and to television. That is not to suggest that other kinds of adaptation are not equally interesting. Further, when I refer to film, I usually mean to include television; I use the term *film* only for brevity.

2. In this spirit of openness and frankness, I shall admit from the outset that the spirit of this chapter is a proselytizing one: I hope to bring readers around to my way of thinking, nudge them in the same direction, and inspire them to join me.

3. Indeed, in some cases, particular adaptations can be more usefully regarded as part of a genre, such as the genre of classic-novel adaptations. This is a genre I postulate and explore in *Adaptation Revisited* (Cardwell, 2002).

4. In particular, interested readers should refer to chapters 1 through 3 of that book.

5. This is a question of methodology that I believe can only be answered by considering what the *purpose* of our study of adaptations is—we need to be honest about what we're really interested in and choose our methodology accordingly, depending on what we're trying to achieve. (I believe this is true more generally in film and literary studies.)

6. In his article "Art and the Domain of the Aesthetic," Carroll describes the necessary attitude of the critic to the artwork as "disinterested and sympathetic attention."

7. Chapter 7 in *Adaptation Revisited* (Cardwell, 2002) explores the serial *Moll Flanders*.

8. I propose "performance" as a fundamental feature of television in *Adaptation Revisited*; see in particular the section on television and performance (Carwell, 2002, 87–92) and chapter 7 (on *Moll Flanders*).

Works Cited

Cardwell, Sarah. 2002. *Adaptation Revisited: Television and the Classic Novel*. Manchester, UK: Manchester University Press.

Carroll, Noël. 2000. "Art and the Domain of the Aesthetic." *British Journal of Aesthetics* 40 (2): 191–208.

Naremore, James. 2000. "Introduction: Film and the Reign of Adaptation." In *Film Adaptation*, ed. James Naremore, 1–18. New Brunswick, NJ: Rutgers University Press.

Trollope, Anthony. 1875. *The Way We Live Now*. New York: Harper.

~

CHAPTER FIVE

The Cold War's "Undigested Apple-Dumpling": Imaging *Moby-Dick* in 1956 and 2001

Walter C. Metz

Editors' Note: This chapter about one novel and its various adaptations is "polemical" because of its insistence on not discussing Melville's novel as an essentialist text. Instead, the author proposes that "to seek out the contemporary significance of a classical novel, we must entertain the idea that the novel is extremely malleable."

On 10 September 2001, I was writing the following as a chapter in my book project about canonical novels adapted into Cold War American films: In *Approaches to Teaching Moby-Dick*, one of a series of pedagogically oriented Modern Language Association books on classic literature, Martin Bickman makes the following claim about the 1956 Hollywood film version of Melville's mid-nineteenth-century novel, directed by John Huston:

> There is widespread agreement . . . that the 1956 Warner Brothers film of *Moby-Dick*, casting Gregory Peck as Ahab and something like the Goodyear Blimp as the whale, is unsatisfying. Milton R. Stern, however, ingeniously shows in "The Whale and the Minnow: *Moby-Dick* and the Movies" how a comparison of the film with the book can highlight the nature and strengths of the latter. (Bickman, 1985, 15)

As much of my previous work on film adaptation has shown—for example, my defense of Martin Ritt's 1959 melodramatic film version of William Faulkner's *The Sound and the Fury*—the elitist assumptions imbedded in such a knee-jerk critical assault on Hollywood films need to be challenged.[1] This chapter proposes to question the "widespread agreement" that the only things to be said about Huston's film version of *Moby-Dick* are that it is obviously inferior to Melville's original and that it sports a rubbery special-effects whale.

To pursue such a project, I will explore a set of critical approaches to Melville's novel that center on the 1950s as a crisis point in *Moby-Dick* criticism. In particular, this critical strand centers on the New Historicism's assault on accepted notions of the meanings of the key texts of the American Renaissance. Led by "New Americanist" Donald Pease, this criticism has suggested that the increased attention to *Moby-Dick* in post–World War II America was driven by Cold War ideology. By reading F. O. Matthiessen's *American Renaissance* as expressive of these ideological concerns, Pease argues in his essay "*Moby-Dick* and the Cold War" (1985) that Melville's novel was appropriated during the Cold War as a direct expression of a simplistic battle of good and evil, between an Ishmael who allegorically codes for freedom and a totalitarian Ahab. Of course, more generalized studies of the Cold War critical establishment's ideologically driven readings of canonical literature have situated the *Moby-Dick* case within a larger paradigm. Geraldine Murphy's "Romancing the Center: Cold War Politics and Classic American Literature" (1988) is one such case in point.

This chapter will use such criticism as a methodology for interrogating John Huston's film as a critical act, engaging with the Cold War assumptions as to the meaning and scope of Melville's *Moby-Dick* as it would have been understood circa 1956. First and foremost, such criticism pushes the apocalyptic components of Melville's novel to the foreground. A novel that uses the Pequod as a microcosm of American diversity—in terms of class and race—ends with the destruction of that symbol. Furthermore, as Lakshmi Mani proposes in *The Apocalyptic Vision in Nineteenth-Century Fiction* (1981), Melville's apocalyptic ending relies on the vast ocean as the site of imperialist conquest and its failure, an ocean that clearly resonates with Pacific atomic bomb testing prevalent in the American consciousness of the 1950s. Thus, when Pease suggests, "That final cataclysmic image of total destruction motivated Matthiessen and forty years of Cold War critics to turn to Ishmael, who in surviving must, the logic would have it, have survived as the principle of America's freedom and who hands over to us our surviving heritage" (1985, 144), it can be made resonant with Huston's film's Cold War activation of Richard Basehart-as-Ishmael's ideological survival of the United States in its conflict with the Soviet Union.

Continuing with such top-down political readings of the film, one would observe that Melville's engagement with theories of leadership—contained in his examination of Ahab's ruination of the "ship of state" and its resonance with Thomas Hobbes's *Leviathan* (1950), for example—would be pertinent for a film made at the moment of Dwight Eisenhower's 1956 defeat of Adlai Stevenson. Or even more intriguingly, Charles Olsen's 1947 study, *Call Me Ishmael*—in which *Moby-Dick* is read as an examination of the birth of the modern petroleum industry—establishes the film's political context in reference to the quest for energy resources that drove the Cold War nations' partitioning of the Third World.

But my focus will be on issues of identity politics, a bottom-up political analysis of race, class, and gender. Melville's (1988) liberal engagement of the friendship between Ishmael and Queequeg—"Better sleep with a sober cannibal than a drunken Christian" (24) or better yet "the truth is, these savages have an innate sense of delicacy, say what you will; it is marvelous how essentially polite they are" (27)—becomes the meat of Huston's liberal film version, in which Queequeg "politely" drowns in his coffin so as to allow the white protagonist Ishmael to thrive under the American freedom Pease referenced earlier. Like the other great triumvirate of searchers in 1956 Hollywood cinema—Ethan Edwards, Martin Pawley, and Scar—the motley crew of Ahab, Ishmael, and Queequeg form a "primer" for American race politics (to borrow Brian Henderson's term for his analysis of Ford's film as an allegory for the *Brown v. Board of Education* Supreme Court case [1985, 429]). Ishmael benefits from the liberal consensus on race, bought with the blood of Queequeg, the person of color, to defeat Ahab's rabid resistance to Cold War centrist politics.

Interestingly enough, political readings of the novel in this vein, when they do mention film intertexts, avoid the Huston film and instead reach toward other prominent 1950s films. For example, David Leverenz's "Class Conflicts in Teaching *Moby-Dick*" makes an intriguing connection between *Moby-Dick's* politics of assimilation and those in Stanley Kramer's *The Defiant Ones* (1958): "When Queequeg is overworked, he simply makes his coffin and lies in it. The coffin ultimately saves his white friend, not himself, like Sidney Poitier's self-sacrifice for Tony Curtis in *The Defiant Ones*" (Leverenz, 1985, 93). While deeply appreciative of such intertextual criticism, I propose to return directly to the John Huston version of *Moby-Dick*, attempting to circumvent fidelity studies approaches to adaptation that a priori assume that because Huston's film has a different project than Melville's novel in its original nineteenth-century context, it is therefore incompetent and unworthy of serious academic analysis.

Such was my project on 10 September 2001. The next morning, as I faced teaching my courses to a very different world, I had to decide whether to discuss the geopolitical mechanisms of American imperialism or William Shakespeare's *Hamlet* (2002) and Plato's *Apology* (1976) and *Crito* (1956), the scheduled material for the day. I ended up doing both, using Hamlet and Socrates as characters who serve as testaments to humanity's ability to not succumb to thoughtless, barbaric violence in response to thoughtless, barbaric violence. Hamlet's thinking-induced delays and Socrates's decision not to escape his own execution, rationalized via the mantra, "never repay an injustice with an injustice," got me through that day feeling as if my rhetorical intervention to my students fulfilled the university's mission of containing emotion within the force field of reason.

I was confronted with how out of phase I am with my diabolically conservative culture, when on television that night, the former director of the CIA, one of a series of warmongering images (not the least of whom was George Bush) CNN foisted upon me, declared that it was important in dealing with terrorism not to get caught in "a Hamlet syndrome," which I interpreted to mean, "drop bombs now, ask questions later," a horrifying containment of reason within the force field of emotional hyperbole. Thus, the professor and the (Cold) warrior had in fact gathered the same data—that Hamlet is a pertinent intertext to 11 September—but we had processed that data in completely antithetical terms.

I consider this evidence for a claim that Jacques Derrida made at the inauguration of nuclear criticism as a discipline at Johns Hopkins University in 1984: that literary analysts, not politicians or physicists, are the most qualified to theorize the nuclear apocalypse because of the threat it poses to the literary archive. In a similar way, the events of 11 September—both the inhumanity of terrorism and the inhumanity of American imperialist response to it—produce a vacuum of the human that our field is uniquely positioned to rectify. The fact that we still care about what happened to Socrates is a testament to our ability to endure, not just as the animals that the terrorists showed us to be, but also as the humans that we have suspected we might be able to evolve into.

One astonishing thing about 11 September is how surprised people seemed to be that terrorists would target the United States. This should not have been the case. In 1994, James Cameron's *True Lies*, a film starring Arnold Schwarzenegger as Harry Tasker, an American family man who happens to work for the CIA's "Omega Sector" antiterrorism unit, viciously defined Americans' hatred of Arabs, at least in their filmed entertainment. *True Lies* forwards an arrogant belief in white males' superiority over people of color. The film encourages its audience to cheer Harry's facile dispatching of scores of Arab terrorists. No matter where Harry shoots, Arabs die. In the film's most absurd moment, Harry reconciles with his estranged wife, Helen (played by Jamie Lee Curtis), kissing her in front of an atomic blast set off by the terrorists. Whereas in real life, such a blast would have caused many people living on the east coast of the United States to die of radiation poisoning, here Arab incompetence becomes a ripe moment for inconsequential romance.

The Arab terrorists' incompetent deployment of an atomic bomb off the coast of Florida is part of *True Lies*'s systemic representational strategy that privileges the white American male as the master of high technology in contrast with Arab people of color and their sheer incompetence with such gadgets. In a moment played for comedy, the Arabs attempt to record their terrorist mantra into a video camera but fail when it runs out of batteries. On a totem pole of technological competence, Helen, a white woman, finds the middle ground, killing Arabs but only accidentally as she drops her machine gun down a flight of stairs.

This representational practice is horrifying because it replicates racist discourses of nineteenth-century eugenics, proposing that white men were superior to white women, who, in turn, were superior to men and women of color. After 11 September, I am horrified to say that Americans now understand the legacy of this sort of racist arrogance, a position that supported the decimation of the Arab world in the age of imperialism and which supported *True Lies*'s rise to blockbuster status. Arab terrorists may be horrifying, but they are anything but incompetent.

I thought about 1994's *True Lies* as I tried to tearfully explain to my three-year-old son, Alex, that the televisual images of planes crashing into the World Trade Center were not scenes from a movie. He did not believe me and still doesn't. I am not sure I can blame him: The alien destruction of the Empire State Building in *Independence Day* (Roland Emmerich, 1995) looks awfully similar to what was aired on CNN in the weeks after 11 September.

As George Bush delivered his warmongering address the night of the tragedy, a far more profound horror struck me. As I envisioned the retaliatory strikes killing thousands more innocent civilians, this time in the Arab world; the subsequent acts of terrorism in response to my tax dollars at work; and the never-ending cycle of violence, it dawned on me that I had completely undervalued the cultural significance of the contemporary Hollywood action-adventure film. *True Lies* and *Independence Day* were not merely films about identity politics; they in fact were serving a very specific function: to prepare Americans for the events of 11 September and their aftermath via a nefarious sort of brainwashing.

In these films, the terrorist or alien attacks happen relatively early. The anger generated by seeing our national landmarks obliterated then demands a formulaic response, centering on American pluckiness and its eventual triumph, to which the bulk of the movies are then dedicated. In *True Lies*, in a creepy form of before-the-fact catharsis for 11 September, Harry commandeers a jet and blows the Arab terrorists out of the skyscraper in which they are hiding. In *Independence Day*, black (Will Smith) and Jewish (Jeff Goldblum) men use American technological know-how to give the aliens a fatal computer virus.

For the sake of my children's future, I desperately believe we need to see how these films have programmed this nation's response to Bush's call for "Gulf of Tonkin" force against the Arab world. As 11 September indicated, *True Lies*'s basic premise about Arab terrorist incompetence was completely false. What makes us think that action cinema's facile solution—Americans get angry and kick ass—will be any more accurate?

Socrates argued for reason over emotion, even as he was about to be put to death. Let's pause and consider the most rational course of action. Let's consider what America's role has been in the perpetuation of poverty and injustice in the Arab world. After such difficult soul-searching, let our actions leave a world to Alex that has broken the chain of violence that was continued—but not begun—on 11 September 2001.

Herman Melville's *Moby-Dick* offers another such testament to the power of ideas to guide us in our response to 11 September. After all, what is *True Lies*'s Harry if not a modern-day Ahab who defeats his whale, the vilified Arab terrorists who "task" him? Melville's bitter warning about Ahab as a Romantic hero who does not win is a textual template that we would do well to consider when constructing arguments about the United States' potential course of action over the coming years. For in truth, George Bush is also Captain Ahab, hell bent on avenging the loss of his buildings, New York City's legs, if you will.

If ever there was good evidence for a political unconscious in the novel, it would be the imagined headlines about Ishmael's life presented in the first chapter, "Loomings": "Grand Contested Election for the Presidency of the United States," "Whaling Voyage by One Ishmael," and "Bloody Battle in Afghanistan" (Melville, 1988, 7), indicating if nothing else, the long-standing historical trauma that the Afghanis have had to endure. For the Afghanis suffering Bush's bombs, the distinctions between 1850 and 2001 that motivate my historical study do not pertain in the least.

The pertinence of this intertextual analysis of the Cold War's *Moby-Dick* as articulated in John Huston's film version can be seen most directly, perhaps, in the recent 1998 USA Network television production. This version, starring Patrick Stewart as Ahab, does not topple Huston's film's Cold War interpretation as we might hope a post–Cold War production would but instead perpetuates it by replacing Orson Welles as Rev. Mapple with Gregory Peck, he who played 1956's Ahab. In *The Errant Art of Moby Dick*, William Spanos argues for what is at stake here: "Pease's enabling contribution to the struggle to free Melville—indeed, American literature at large—from the bondage of American Cold War discourse is precisely his decisive displacement of the question of its contemporary intelligibility from the domain of the sovereign subject to that of hegemony" (1995, 274).

For precisely this reason, I believe that to effectively discuss *Moby-Dick* in light of 11 September, we must image the novel in ways that do not perpetuate, but instead transcend, its Cold War canonical reading. To do so, I want to focus on the identity political position from my earlier, now abandoned, project that I have not as yet breeched, namely questions of gender. I have chosen an extremely unlikely starting place, Chris Carter's sci-fi television show, *The X-Files*. There is a terrific moment in season 3, in the episode "Quagmire," first aired on 3 May 1996, when agents Mulder and Scully, having been on a case to catch a Loch Ness–style watery monster, have endured the sinking of their boat.

Stranded on a rock in the middle of a lake, Scully compares Mulder to Ahab, arguing that they both maniacally pursue some abstract and ultimately destructive paranoia that they label "Truth." If Mulder is Ahab, then who is Scully? There is a psychoanalytic possibility: Scully tells Mulder that her father used to call her Starbuck and she called him Ahab. Thus, Scully's dead father, much a source of trauma in the first season of the show, as he never approved of her becoming an FBI agent instead of a doctor, has been replaced by Mulder, her will-they-or-won't-they romantic foil, a position sealed by a season-ending episode in which Mulder and Scully kiss, having formed a "normal" family complete with newborn infant.

This line of reasoning would position Scully as Ahab's lover, a possibility that would seem all but ludicrous if not for the astonishing pre–Cold War film version of Melville's novel, made in 1930 by Warner Bros. as a star vehicle for John Barrymore. In this film, perhaps the most interesting adaptation I have ever seen, there is no Ishmael. Yes, that's right, the central character of the novel, Melville's grand solution to his crisis of how to justify the after-the-fact narration of an apocalyptic narrative, is left on the cutting room floor. Lloyd Bacon's film does not give a whit for the canonical reading of Melville's novel, largely because such a reading, an artifact of the Cold War, had not yet been articulated. Instead, Bacon's film produces a conventional Hollywood love story between Ahab and Faith, the invented daughter of Rev. Mapple, whose moral purity reforms Ahab from a bawdy sailor into a marriageable man. Being a pre–Production Code affair, the film is fairly aggressive about representing this transformation from sexual scoundrel to family man.

Once she has reformed him, Faith agrees to wait to marry Ahab when he returns from his next three-year whaling voyage. However, when Ahab's leg is bitten off by Moby-Dick (in a very funny scene thanks to an equally rubbery special effects whale), Ahab's brother tricks him into thinking Faith no longer desires him because of his handicap. Bitter at Moby-Dick for ruining his sex life, Ahab relentlessly pursues the whale, seeking vengeance. However, this time, Ahab wins. The men carve up Moby-Dick and return to New Haven, and Ahab marries Faith.

My point here is to entertain the possibility that to seek out the contemporary significance of a classical novel, we must entertain the idea that the novel is extremely malleable. Given the confines of a canonical reading, there is no question that the 1930 version of *Moby-Dick* is horrendous. However, once we highlight the complex ideological terrain of the canonical reading that contains the text, in this case, that the novel's misogyny is to be found in its marginalization of female characters, we have a path to begin appreciating extremely, shall we say, aberrant film adaptations.

The 1930 version—not being beholden to the idea that *Moby-Dick* is a masterpiece that should not be tampered with—produces a series of radical transformations of the novel. Sometimes these transformations seem absurd —the film focuses on the back story of Ahab, thus adding to what is already a 569-page novel. Thus, under no circumstances could a seventy-five-minute film hope to capture any significant thematic content of the novel. However, the introduction of Faith allows for an examination of gender that the Cold War reading pushes to the sidelines.

In her article, "Melville at the Movies: New Images of *Moby-Dick*," Susan Weiner (1993) pursues a similar gender studies agenda when she analyzes the references to *Moby-Dick* in Michael Lehmann's teen pic, *Heathers* (1988). *Heathers* focuses on J. D., an aptly initialed juvenile delinquent who murders off the popular girls in the school, all of whom are named Heather. Weiner argues of J. D., "This young rebel with a cause is the dark side of Veronica, just as Ahab was a buried part of Ishmael" (1993, 87). In this way, the radical approach of the 1930 film, by combining Ishmael, Melville's narrator and central character, and Ahab into the one character of John Barrymore's

Ahab, while not palatable to the canonical Cold War reading of Ishmael as freedom and Ahab as totalitarian, dovetails with the post–Cold War *Moby-Dick* as it is begun to be formulated by *Heathers*.

The 1930 film and *Heathers*, unified not by their historical contexts but instead by their insistence on not being Cold War texts, in fact make many of the same adaptational moves, including imposing a happy ending, about which Weiner argues,

> It is then that J. D. designs a plan for the annihilation of his society, an idea he finds in *Moby-Dick*. But *Heathers* rewrites the novel by offering a positive solution to the problem it poses. The good leader triumphs as Veronica kills J. D. and saves the school. Unlike Melville, this director changed his ending to stress optimism rather than nihilism. (1993, 87–88)

Victor Salva's *Powder* (1995), about an impossibly white albino boy with Christlike empathic powers, also extracts a happy ending out of *Moby-Dick*. As in Melville's novel, but not the 1930 film version, Powder, the sought-after white whale of Salva's film, defeats his pursuers and ascends to heaven (as Melville's whale descends triumphantly into his oceanic depths). Like *Heathers*, Salva's film directly invokes *Moby-Dick* as its primary literary intertext. When Jesse the social worker first goes down to the basement where Powder has been kept by his grandfather, she discovers that he has memorized Herman Melville's novel. Powder quotes a passage from near the end of the novel, from chapter 114, titled "The Gilder":

> Where lies the final harbor, whence we unmoor no more? In what rapt ether sails the world, of which the weariest will never weary? Where is the foundling's father hidden? Our souls are like those orphans whose unwedded mothers die in bearing them: the secret of our paternity lies in their grave, and we must there to learn it. (Melville, 1988, 492)

Obsessed with what he believes to be his impending death at the hands of the mad Romantic Ahab, Ishmael reflects upon all people's orphaned nature, curable only in death. Powder, Salva's film's white whale, reflects upon his own alienated position, as the representatives of "civilization" like the cruel neoconservative deputy, Harley Duncan, his Ahab, penetrates his basement abode, his oceanic depths.

To conclude, and to return to the larger political implications of my intertextual argument, I would like to throw one more *Moby-Dick* film intertext into the tank, 1975's *Jaws*. In an interview with Steven Spielberg, the director relates that he and the producers had to fire one of the early screenwriters because he insisted on calling the shark from Peter Benchley's novel a whale. The irony of course is that the screenwriter was right; Benchley's novel is a sort of popular culture version of Melville's novel.

The political significance of this observation is best appreciated by turning our attention back to William Spanos. To conclude his book, Spanos (1995) compares Melville's novel to Michael Herr's Vietnam novel, *Dispatches*, suggesting that Melville's "errant art" lies in its ability to indict the American imperialist project in its infancy. Unfortunately, no one listened to Melville and, when they did, reconstructed his critique of imperialism into a Cold War defense of freedom. The legacy of this, Spanos argues, is the disastrous American experience in Vietnam.

I believe *Jaws* is a *Moby-Dick* film in this Cold War sense. It is a film that features a crazed sea captain, Quint, who relentlessly pursues his object to the point of apocalypse. Both his boat, the Orca, and he himself, like Ahab, are destroyed by the shark. Like Melville's novel as read by the Cold War critics, the representatives of normative American whiteness survive in the guise of Chief Brody and Hooper, Ishmaels in their own way.

In terms of gender, the marginalization of women in *Jaws* is deliberate and diabolical in a way never approached by *Moby-Dick*. For *Jaws* is a backlash film against the women's liberation movement. A sexually active woman is the shark's first victim, predicting the narrative tradition of the slasher film for which *Jaws* is the prototype: one victim after the other dismembered by the monster. Chrissie's jog into the water is then answered at the end of the first act of the film, as Quint's sexist banter frightens Mrs. Brodie, the only other major female character in the film, away from the dock. Mrs. Brodie is literally banished from the film, forced to answer Chrissie's sexual advance into the water with a maternal retreat back to her children on shore. From this point onward, *Jaws* becomes a war film in which the grizzled sergeant, Quint, must train his recruits, the technologically inclined but green "lieutenant" Hooper and the equally green grunt "private," Chief Brodie.

A reading of Jaws as a war film is illuminated by Spanos's reading (1995) of *Moby-Dick* as a text that resonates with the Vietnam War. For *Jaws*, released the same year as the fall of Saigon, is a film that proposes how America should have won the Vietnam War. While drinking one night on the boat, Quint tells the story of why he will never put on a life jacket ever again: he was on the USS *Indianapolis*, the boat that delivered the atomic bomb at the end of World War II, but was then sunk by a Japanese submarine. Forced to fight off shark attacks day and night, Quint was one of the lucky survivors, as most of his buddies were eaten.

Like *Moby-Dick* before it, *Jaws* sets up a complex allegorical structure. When Chief Brody stuffs an oxygen tank down the shark's throat and uses his rifle to blow him up, *Jaws* is producing a multifaceted image. After Brodie blows up the shark, it sinks to the bottom of the ocean, looking distinctly like a sinking submarine. Thus, Brodie is able to avenge the shark's murder of his friend Quint, which is polysemically also revenge against the Japanese who traumatized him via his experience on the USS *Indianapolis*.

This collapse has frightening allegorical consequences on the 1975 context of *Jaws*. For if the use of the nuclear bomb at Hiroshima is celebrated by Quint ("We delivered the bomb . . . August 1945"), then the film's positioning of Brodie's lesson as doing the same to the shark means allegorically that the way to win Vietnam would be the reuse of similar atomic weaponry. Throughout the film, the shark is positioned as a Viet Cong–like entity: skulking around an underwater jungle, unseen, ready to spring out at any unexpected moment. And after all, the beach is the safe place for Americans, both in Vietnam and in *Jaws*.

On the last page of Spanos's book, he reflects on the significance of his study. He claims, "It is not, to extend a resonant motif in Michel Foucault, simply a genealogy, a 'history of Melville's present': it is also a history of the American future, of the present historical occasion that we precariously inhabit" (1995, 278). Unfortunately, this chapter concludes that George Bush as Ahab, the son of the George Bush who really did re-win Vietnam in the guise of the Gulf War, affirms the bleak prediction that Spanos made in 1995.

Note

1. My publications on film adaptation taking this critical approach include "Signifying Nothing?: Martin Ritt's *The Sound and the Fury* (1959) as Deconstructive Adaptation," *LFQ* 27, no. 1 (1999): 21–31; "'Another Being We Have Created Called Us': Point-of-View, Melancholia, and the Joking Unconscious in *The Bridges of Madison County*," *The Velvet Light Trap* 39 (Spring 1997): 66–83; and "Pomp(ous) Sirk-umstance: Intertextuality, Adaptation, and *All That Heaven Allows*," *Journal of Film and Video* 45, no. 4 (Winter 1993): 3–21.

Works Cited

Bickman, Martin. 1985. "Materials." In *Approaches to Teaching Melville's* Moby-Dick, ed. Martin Bickman, 3–15. New York: MLA.

Derrida, Jacques. 1984. "No Apocalypse, Not Now." *Diacritics* 14 (1): 20–31.

Henderson, Brian. 1985. "The Searchers: An American Dilemma." In *Movies and Methods: An Anthology*, vol. 2, ed. Bill Nichols, 429–49. Berkeley: University of California Press.

Hobbes, Thomas. 1950. *Leviathan*. New York: Dutton.

Leverenz, David. 1985. "Class Conflicts in Teaching *Moby-Dick*." In *Approaches to Teaching Melville's* Moby-Dick, ed. Martin Bickman, 85–95. New York: MLA.

Mani, Lakshmi. 1981. *The Apocalyptic Vision in Nineteenth-Century Fiction: A Study of Cooper, Hawthorne, and Melville*. Washington, DC: University Press of America.

Melville, Herman. 1988. "*Moby-Dick*, or The Whale." In *The Writings of Herman Melville. The Northwestern-Newberry Edition*, vol. 6, ed. Harrison Hayford, Hershel Parker, and G. Thomas Tanselle. Evanston, IL: Northwestern University Press.

Murphy, Geraldine. 1988. "Romancing the Center: Cold War Politics and Classic American Literature." *Poetics Today* 9 (4): 737–47.

Olsen, Charles. 1947. *Call Me Ishmael*. New York: Reynal and Hitchcock.

Pease, Donald E. 1985. "*Moby-Dick* and the Cold War." In *The American Renaissance Reconsidered*, ed. Walter Benn Michaels and Donald E. Pease, 113–55. Baltimore: Johns Hopkins University Press.

Plato. 1956. *Crito*. New York: New American Library.

———. 1976. *Plato's Apology of Socrates*. Accra: Waterville.

Shakespeare, William. 2002. *Hamlet*. Hauppauge, NY: Barron's.

Spanos, William V. 1995. *The Errant Art of* Moby-Dick: *The Canon, the Cold War, and the Struggle for American Studies*. Durham, NC: Duke University Press.

Weiner, Susan. 1993. "Melville at the Movies: New Images of *Moby-Dick*." *Journal of American Culture* 16 (Summer): 85–90.

~

CHAPTER SIX

Trying Harder:
Probability, Objectivity, and
Rationality in Adaptation Studies

David L. Kranz

Theoretical writings about the relationships of literature to film appeared sporadically throughout the twentieth century. They increased dramatically in number and focus in the last decades of the century, probably because the study of film adaptations of literature or theatre was becoming an established part of the humanities curriculum at this time. Much twentieth-century theorizing about film adaptation involved the ways in which literature and film or theatre and film were alike or different as arts, media, and cultural products. Meanwhile, starting about forty years ago, there was an explosion of new ideas about and approaches to literature. Literary scholars became embroiled in ever-increasing theoretical contestation, as traditional formalism, humanism, and historicism were challenged by post-structuralist developments, such as deconstruction, feminism, cultural/ideological studies, and postmodernism. During the same period, film studies was legitimized as an academic discipline within and alongside the established field of literary studies, and its core theoretical beliefs came under the spell of similar nascent post-structuralist theories, especially Freudian and Lacanian modes.

However, as interest in theory ebbed in departments of literature at the turn of the century, and as the primary theoretical paradigm in film programs based on neopsychoanalytic ideas about "the apparatus" faded in the face of cognitive reception theory, adaptation studies has, somewhat anachronistically, become the target of reform by several adherents of post-structuralist approaches within the now expanded field of film and media studies. Thus, just as literary theorists in the seventies and eighties transformed the traditional assumptions and practices of midcentury literary studies and gave film studies its first taste of sophisticated (and ponderous) theory, now film theorists armed with similar ideas seek to transform the study of literature and film at and after the turn of the twenty-first century.[1]

The Post-Structuralist Challenge

The precursor of recent calls for change was Dudley Andrew, whose highly anthologized chapter on adaptation from *Film Adaptation* in 2000 urged that adaptation studies become more sociological and historical (also in Braudy and Cohen, 1999; Corrigan, 1999). While reflecting that all film is in some sense adaptational and after defining three kinds of adaptation, Andrew laments that the third type, the "tiresome" discussion of fidelity with its premise that "the task of adaptation is the reproduction in cinema of something essential about an original text," breeds only "strident and futile arguments" about absolute differences in media and thus whether films can ever capture the spirit of novels or plays (31–33). To avoid these problems, Andrew emphasizes treating adaptation as a "complex interchange between eras, styles, nations, and subjects":

> Filmmaking . . . is an event in which a system is used and altered in discourse. Adaptation is a peculiar form of discourse but not an unthinkable one. Let us use it not to fight battles over the essence of the media or the inviolability of individual art works. Let us use it as we use all cultural practices, to understand the world from which it comes and the one toward which it points. (37)

This call for change has been seconded most recently by Walter Metz, who hopes that Andrew's "sociology of adaptation" will revitalize the field: "Given the exhaustion of current general theoretical studies [of adaptation], and the unproductive nature of individual studies of adaptation, this sort of culturalist middle ground represents, I believe, a fertile and open terrain for revitalizing our discipline" (Metz, 2003, 10).

But the interdisciplinary approach of cultural studies is not the only proposed panacea for future academic explorations of adaptation. A more expansive view comes at the millennium from Robert Stam (2000), who seeks a dialogical approach to the intersection of film and literature. Stam begins with the obligatory attack on fidelity criticism, this time as an inherently moralistic enterprise whose purported essentialism, he proposes, is utterly debilitating. Why? First, he finds that the differences between the media involved—"the shift from a single-track, uniquely verbal medium such as the novel . . . to a multitrack medium such as film"—make fidelity virtually impossible (Stam, 2000, 56). Second, so do the contingencies of each medium's operations, in particular the film's "complex material infrastructure" in contrast to the relative simplicity surrounding the individual writer (56). Third, Stam also contends, following post-structuralist literary theory, that the formalist assumption in fidelity criticism of "an extractable 'essence' . . . hidden 'underneath' the surface details of style" in the literary source is hopelessly naïve:

> In fact there is no such transferable core: a single novelistic text comprises a series of verbal signals that can generate a plethora of possible readings. . . . The literary text is not a closed, but an open structure (or, better, structuration, as the later Barthes would have it) to be reworked by a boundless context. The text feeds on and is fed into an infinitely permutating intertext, which is seen through ever-shifting grids of interpretation. (57)

Taking as gospel Derrida's (1970) concept of textual meaning as a fluid and infinite play of signifiers within a "boundless context" and an ever-changing and reciprocal set of related texts, themselves interpreted in ever-shifting ways, Stam (2000) seeks to shatter the simplistic paradigm he finds at the center of fidelity criticism. (Given the infinite and dynamic hermeneutic properties in his post-structuralist vision, however, one wonders if the possibility of useful interpretation hasn't also been shattered.)

Fourth, after raising but not answering the sensible "wider question: Fidelity to what?" (plot, character, authorial intention, style, point of view, etc.), Stam attacks the fidelity approach because it "quietly reinscribes the axiomatic superiority of literary art to film" by its prejudices in favor of seniority, iconophobia, and logophilia (2000, 57–58). But rather than arguing why this must be so or offering evidence that it is so, Stam concludes by reference to structuralist "and poststructuralist theoretical developments," which undercut the supposed literary biases of fidelity criticism:

> The Bakhtinian "translinguistic" conception of the author as the orchestrator of preexisting discourses, meanwhile, along with Foucault's downgrading of the author in favor of a pervasive anonymity of discourse, opened the way to a "discursive" and nonoriginary approach to all arts. . . . Derridean deconstruction,

meanwhile, by dismantling the hierarchy of "original" and "copy," suggests that both are caught up in the infinite play of dissemination. (58)

Using these theoretical (and jargon-filled) pronouncements as a self-approved trump card, Stam goes on to assert that a film can neither be faithful to a text or its author, nor subordinate to either.

More discourse on medium specificity in favor of the intertextual complexity of cinema follows:

As a rich, sensorially composite language characterized by what Metz calls "codic heterogeneity," the cinema becomes a receptacle open to all kinds of literary and pictorial symbolism, to all types of collective representation, to all ideologies, to all aesthetics, and to the infinite play of influences within cinema, within the other arts, and within culture generally. (Stam, 2000, 61)

Having made this post-structuralist claim for cinema in general, Stam concludes in a fifth point that translation, reading (especially misreading), critique, "dialogization, cannibalization, transmutation, transfiguration, and signifying" are better tropes than fidelity because "just as any text can generate an infinity of readings, so any novel can generate any number of adaptations" (62–63). In fact, for Stam, adaptation is really a small part of a vast "ongoing intertextual process" (64). To distinguish it from others, however, Stam dubs adaptation "intertextual dialogism" after Bakhtin and Kristeva, placing it alongside Gérard Genette's five types of "transtextuality": intertextuality, paratextuality, metatextuality, architextuality, and hypertextuality.

Interestingly, the latter category, which Stam finds "most suggestive" for his view of adaptation, posits the existence of "hypertexts" that relate to anterior "hypotexts which the former transforms, modifies, elaborates, or extends" (2000, 66). But while this type of transtextuality sounds suspiciously and ironically like the comparative relations underlying fidelity criticism, Stam comes to a different, euphoric conclusion: "Film adaptations, then, are caught up in the ongoing whirl of intertextual reference and transformation, of texts generating other texts in an endless process of recycling, transformation, and transmutation, with no clear point of origin" (66). And later, after a look at the intertextual roots and posttexts of the Robinson Crusoe story followed by a "long pageant" of cinematic adaptations, Stam suggests that this litany "can be seen as a kind of multileveled negotiation of intertexts" (67). He then offers quite a few examples of such intertextual negotiation, ending with Madame Bovary. (Ironically, however, his discussions of these manifestations of various intertextual relations, particularly the last, are very much like the detailed comparative analyses and evaluations which are the staple of fidelity criticism.)

Thomas Leitch has recently echoed Stam's call for a shift to intertextuality in adaptation studies (2003). In an essay on the past and future of *Literature/Film Quarterly* (*LFQ*) and the Literature/Film Association (LFA), the journal and organization primarily focused on cinematic adaptation, Leitch notes that both have taken a literary approach to film, using methods the field of film studies at large abandoned years ago in its worship of Lacanian high theory. Leitch bemoans the continued presence of this literary approach and its handmaiden, fidelity criticism, suggesting that, because the recent eclipse of neopsychoanalytic theory has opened up the discipline of film studies to new questions, now is the perfect time for change in adaptation studies. Echoing Stam, Leitch asks a number of provocative questions, including the following: "Since every text, including allegedly original sourcetexts, depends on numberless intertexts, why does it suit observers to elevate some intertexts to the status of sources and ignore others?" (8). Ultimately, Leitch surges past Stam to suggest a new discipline: an intertextual approach which "seeks to dethrone the English Department's traditional emphasis on *literature*, the existing canon that deserves close study and faithful adaptation, and replace it with *literacy*, the study of the ways [all] texts have been, might be, and should be read and rewritten" (8).

But Leitch's manifesto for change in the field of literature and film is not the first in our new century. Robert B. Ray opined five years ago that adaptation study has needed radical surgery for a long time: "Throughout much of the 1980s and 1990s, 'Film and Literature' fell into thorough disrepute, as if the sensed inadequacies of the field's principal books, journals, and textbooks had somehow discredited the subject itself" (2000, 38). Ray faults the field for not understanding, as did literary scholars well attuned to poststructuralism and active in the culture wars, that popular narratives, including cinematic versions, are radically intertextual and that "semiotic, reader-response, and structuralist accounts of the reading process (our negotiation with signs) converged in ideological criticism, a theoretical practice that the movies, a thoroughly commercial practice utterly exposed to the whims of the marketplace, have always demanded" (40–41). Blaming this blindness on a simplistic acceptance of the undertheorized assumptions of the New Criticism despite its critique by Derrida, Ray claims that adaptation case studies replay a broken record: "Without benefit of a presiding poetics, film and literature scholars could only persist in asking about individual movies the same unproductive layman's question (How does the film compare to the book?), getting the same unproductive answer (The book is better)" (44).

Based only on a list of ten titles from a lengthy bibliography of literature and film citations ranging from 1909–1977, Ray contends that literature has always been privileged in this simple equation, a result which helped "shore up literature's crumbling [academic] walls" in the face of the popularity of the movies as narrative vehicles (2000, 46). Likewise, in a Marxist mode, Ray suggests that the appropriation of film study by literature departments in these years was intended to stem falling enrollments in the humanities and that the plethora of fidelity studies at the time was the result of both bad market conditions for literature Ph.D.s and demands by the academic hiring and reward system for increased publications. Indeed, Ray thinks that LFQ was born of this bad job market and still serves a clientele of job-seeking graduate students and faculty from the least prestigious institutions, both greatly in need of publication opportunities. Finally, like Stam and Leitch, Ray proposes that film and literature embrace postmodernism and transform itself into the study of "transactions between word and image" by "imagining new ways in which words and images can be adapted or combined, as well as new purposes for those combinations" (48–49).

The latest book-length foray into adaptation theory comes from Sarah Cardwell, who revisits adaptation theory en route to analyses of famous novels adapted for television in the United Kingdom. She believes that traditional comparative studies fail to attend to the virtues of the filmic or the televisual product, to previous adaptations of the same source, and to the historical differences which separate source and adaptation (Cardwell, 2002). Not unlike Stam, Leitch, and Ray, for example, she is troubled that movies of historical figures like Kapur's *Elizabeth* (1998) are not identified as adaptations and that scholars haven't called Shakespeare's plays adaptations even though most are developed from earlier texts. Obviously, for Cardwell, the assumptions behind the source-to-adaptation model of the comparative method are flawed. Unsurprisingly then, following Roland Barthes and others, Cardwell argues for alternative approaches whose strength lies "in their very decentredness, comprehensiveness and flexibility, in their placing of adaptations within a far wider cultural context than that of an original-version relationship" (25). Like all the other recent theorists, she also finds biases in both culture and academe that favor source literature and resist the claims of media studies. After explaining additional problems with the concept of medium specificity and the comparative method in adaptation studies, Cardwell makes clear once again her support for approaches which enhance contextuality and intertextuality, eventually proposing that it "makes sense to reject a centre-based, comparative understanding and accept a more flexible conceptualization" (68).

However, unlike others influenced by post-structuralist theory, Cardwell offers a cautious view of its alleged theoretical advances. For example, she acknowledges that ideological readings are often reductive and biased and that the "impact of a plethora of theories from cultural studies, continental philosophy, traditional film theory and English literature is that sometimes the analysis of the films and programs themselves loses its proper place at the centre of discussion" (2002, 71). Moreover, she seems to balance her approval of the presentist and performative aspects of televisual adaptations with appreciation for the virtues of verisimilar recreations of the past, and she argues that both postmodern intertextuality (the playful, depthless pastiche of images and references) and traditional referentiality (which discovers deeper meanings and refers to concrete realities) are important in televisual artifacts if viewers can and will engage with them. Cardwell's ideal adaptation criticism, then, is to be as expansive and inclusive as possible without resorting to post-structuralist infinitude.

Overall, this review of recent theory makes clear that the primary post-structuralist arguments to transform adaptation studies in a radical fashion are as follows: (1) almost all past and much present writing on cinematic adaptation has been limited to the practice of "fidelity criticism," in which, it is asserted, more valuable analyses of both the film medium and film contexts and intertexts are effaced in favor of reductive narrative comparisons; (2) concurrently, evaluative judgments in this mode of criticism, it is supposed, invariably privilege literature over film and sources over adaptations; and (3) therefore, fidelity criticism should be terminated and replaced by an adaptation criticism based on post-structuralist theory which, it is alleged, better suits the complexities of the film medium because it opens up interpretation to infinite analytical possibilities via ever-changing intertextuality and contextuality; such a substitution, it is predicted, will resurrect adaptation studies from its apparent dead end, insuring its long life either as a subdiscipline within media studies or as part of a larger academic field of study involving infinite discourses, ideologies, and cultural constructions.

The seeds of these arguments to transform adaptation studies appear to have taken root in the journal most devoted to the relationship of film and literature. LFQ, now edited by Elsie M. Walker and David T. Johnson (2005), young scholars at Salisbury University, announces in a "Letter from the Editors" a paradigmatic shift from a time at the journal's inception in the 1970s "when 'faithfulness' to original literary sources was the primary concern in adaptation studies" to a new era:

> Now, over thirty years later, notions of fidelity, faithfulness, and authenticity have been interrogated and, to a large extent, replaced by much more permissive

approaches to adaptation: explorations of wide-ranging intertextuality are favored as much as finding direct correlations between pairs of texts; locating specific texts and adaptations of them within their own cultural moment takes precedence over arguments for the 'timelessness' of texts (whether verbal or visual); positivist arguments concerned with the essential qualities of any text have been challenged by a greater emphasis on why, how, and to what precise effect particular texts are adapted, made new, or remade; and essentialist arguments about the nature of literary versus cinematic storytelling or taxonomical approaches have been mostly displaced by more expansive understandings of different media as they intersect, inter-illuminate each other, and, sometimes, collide. Furthermore, the long-standing primacy of original literary texts over cinematic (re)creations has been consistently called into question. Anxiety about preservation is undone by the spirit of exploration. (2–3)

Indeed, articles in the new volume invoke neither "the stability of an original source" nor fidelity to it. Rather, they expand "notions of intertextuality" and place "texts in particular cultural and aesthetic contexts of production and understanding" (81).

Rational Reform, Not Radical Replacement

There is much to praise in this argument for transformation, especially its attempt to explode the theoretical paradigm which has purportedly limited critical exploration of adaptations in the past. Cinematic adaptations can do more than just be faithful or unfaithful to literary sources. Film adaptations can criticize aspects of those sources, debate their themes, and translate them into different cultures and times in ways which alter their meanings and effects, among other relational possibilities. What's important in comparing a source and an adaptation is not just its fidelity but the ways in which it interprets the source and uses it to create a new work of art. Thus, if fidelity criticism, as has been argued, harbors an automatic and unconsidered privilege, that criticism needs rethinking. Moreover, if there is even a tendency (perhaps suggested by the word *fidelity*) to assume that a film adaptation can never live up to or surpass its source, that evaluative straitjacket must be shed.

But how true are the characterizations of automatic bias in fidelity criticism aired above? Is it possible that post-structuralists have caricatured what is really more diverse than it appears, just as Derrida caricatured with his own binaries the rational ideals and practices of Western philosophy? While I'm willing to accept on faith that a preference for the literary has been largely the case in very early adaptation criticism, my reading of criticism in the latter decades of the last century leads me to believe that more recent fidelity criticism is more diverse and less biased than it used to be.[2] Perhaps the decline of reading in the face of an explosion of visual or mixed media along with the influence of auteurism have finally given the cinema evaluative parity with literature. In fact, were I pressed as a practitioner to take evaluative positions on cinematic adaptations I've analyzed, I'd say that often films are better than their sources (e.g., Julie Taymor's *Titus* is better than Shakespeare's *Titus Andronicus*, and Anthony Minghella's *The English Patient* is a tad better than Michael Ondaatje's novel of the same name). If we must evaluate, I'd also argue that both literary source and cinematic adaptation should be measured not in terms of each other but in comparison to similar works in the medium of each. But most of the formalist adaptation studies that I've read are more interested in how, why, or whether a film has altered its literary source than in whether the adaptation is better or worse than its original version. (Ironically, as shown below, complaints of infidelity come largely from post-structuralist critics!) Moreover, there's no necessary or inherent reason why fidelity criticism must include an evaluation of the relative quality of an adaptation with respect to its source. Why evaluate at all? We're not reviewers.

Secondly, if the comparative methodology at the heart of fidelity criticism skews or effaces the realities and complexities of filmmaking—its collective authorship, its sometimes numerous citations of past films and referents to the cultural and political givens at its creation, its economic infrastructure, its complicated reception, and the nature of its particular visual and aural medium—these shortcomings should be remedied in the interest of accuracy, fairness, and the quest for comprehensive truth. Clearly, a filmic adaptation is both a film per se and the legacy of a literary source, among other influences. Therefore, while literary and dramatic elements are usually the most important parts of feature films, *significant* cinematic elements—for example, mise-en-scène, cinematography, editing—*consequential* intertextual connections—for example, famous past films, screenplays, histories, media accounts—and *relevant* contextual data—for example, studio contracts; advances in cinematic technology; interviews with directors and actors; distribution statistics; and political, economic, or cultural events—count too.

However, there is no necessary reason why comparative or fidelity criticism must be exclusionary. Even if post-structural theorists are right about the cinematic evasions of fidelity criticism in the second half of the last century (and this is debatable, especially in the last twenty years), the cause is hardly inherent in the comparative method. My suspicion is that in the past an understandable priority for comparisons involving narrative and dramatic elements has caused the supposed absence of the filmic in adaptation criticism. After all, most traditional (*pace* the old New Critical heresy of paraphrase) and post-structuralist criticism of either literature or film to date attend to content before style and text over context. Moreover, extranarrative data is often irrelevant or only tangential to interpretations of cinematic adaptations. Depending on the movie in question, some directorial choices in cinematography, mise-en-scène, and sound will not be important in making interpretive claims. Furthermore, the very length of the usually detailed accounting of changes, additions, and omissions involving the story and the characters in past comparisons of literary source and film adaptation probably reduced time and space for treatment of cinematic, intertextual, and contextual elements. But nothing prevents the inclusion of the latter. Thus, overall, the post-structuralist challenge to adaptation studies is on solid ground in its effort to expunge the reductive practices of fidelity criticism. Comparative criticism of adaptations should include analysis of cinematic, intertextual, and contextual elements relevant to interpretive arguments emerging from analyses of narrative and other traditionally favored data. Not all such elements, however, are relevant or consequential.

Finally, if other potentially foundational theories can serve adaptation studies better than the formalism and humanism at the base of comparative adaptation analysis, they should be embraced. Why stick to comparative or fidelity criticism if competing theories present sound and exciting alternatives? The post-structuralists seem to offer such an alternative—the radical replacement that has been proposed. However, I wonder if adaptation studies will be well served by approaches based on relativistic post-structuralist theories which are currently being abandoned elsewhere. For the popular press now reports with some regularity that "some academics say postmodern theory is on the way out altogether. . . . In Chicago last spring at a discussion sponsored by the journal 'Critical Inquiry' cutting-edge thinkers such as Stanley Fish, Frederic Jameson, Homi Bhabha, and Henry Louis Gates Jr. spent two hours saying that postmodern theory was ineffective and no longer mattered in the world outside academe, if it ever did" (Kirby, 2004, 2).

Though Gates is about to publish a new book extending theory into multicultural areas (Kirby, 2004), Terry Eagleton, one of the early popularizers of theory in the 1980s, says in his latest book that formerly influential versions of theory are no longer worth attending to even in the academy. He groups these debased versions under the title of postmodernism, which for him includes deconstruction, cultural studies, and a few other schools of post-structural theory, defining the entire mix as "the contemporary movement of thought which rejects totalities, universal values, grand historical

narratives, solid foundations to human existence, and the possibility of objective knowledge" (Eagleton, 2004, 13). Eagleton does acknowledge
that literary theory has had a salutary effect in the penultimate decades of the
last century by challenging previous critical shibboleths which limited both
what and how we read, thereby making literary criticism more thoughtful
about its purposes and practices. He also acknowledges that post-
structuralists have made valuable contributions to literary studies by showing
that texts are full of gaps usually effaced by formalistic criticism, that cultural
paradigms can shape interpretation, and that all discourse has political implications, though these do not determine all understanding. And he still
finds value in both gender and postcolonial studies. However, Eagleton lam-
bastes current postmodern theory for its failure the engage the world:

> It has been shamefaced about morality and metaphysics, embarrassed about
> love, biology, religion, and revolution, largely silent about evil, reticent about
> death and suffering, dogmatic about essences, universals and foundations, and
> superficial about truth, objectivity, and disinterestedness. (101–2)

Among other points, Eagleton mocks the postmodern simplification of culture into the hegemonic binary of Self and Other and pillories its cult of "difference," its relativistic denial of truth and objectivity, its phobia against human nature and other "essentialisms," its inflation of the role of language,
and, most of all, its political impotence.

Other former adherents have preceded or followed Eagleton into reevalu-
ation. According to James Wood, as postmodernist criticism became system-
ically "insensitive,"

> many theorists themselves switched horses or turned tail. The genre of "con-
> fessions of a former theorist" is burgeoning at about the same pace as confes-
> sions of former supporters of the Iraq war. Some of the pioneers, such as
> Stephen Heath and Colin McCabe [just] dropped a few pounds of jargon. . . .
> Others, such as Christopher Norris, attacked what they saw as the new deca-
> dence of postmodernism. Harold Bloom . . . became a sort of Book-of-the-
> Month-Club armchair-alec. Frank Lentricchia recanted everything he had es-
> poused. (2004, 30)

Moreover, while only an occasional scholar took on post-structuralist theory
during its heyday (e.g., Vickers [1993] and Ellis [1997]), many more reform-
ers are criticizing postmodernist orthodoxy today. For example, I recently received a flyer from Columbia University Press announcing the publication of
Theory's Empire: An Anthology of Dissent (2005), edited by Daphne Patai and

Will H. Corral, in which forty-seven articles over 736 pages are said to question the ideas, delusory excesses, and jargon of now orthodox literary theory. Meanwhile, the Association of Literary Scholars and Critics, founded eleven years ago in reaction to the perceived dominance of theory in the Modern Language Association, has grown considerably and now sports a high-quality journal, an annual conference, regular newsletters, and the funding to underwrite a spirited defense of literature unencumbered by high theory.

Of course, adaptation scholars shouldn't wholly reject post-structuralism and postmodernism just because there is a growing chorus of apostates and critics in an adjoining field. Nor do I think we should reject them entirely; even turncoats like Eagleton have found much to value in the literary theory of the last forty years. Instead, I recommend that we filter out the relativistic excesses of postmodernist theory, such as its attack on rationality, its denial of any objectivity (that is, its ironic totalization of subjectivity), and its assumption of the virtue or necessity of infinite ambiguity (with simultaneous demonization of the essential, hierarchical, and probable), before using it to guide needed changes in adaptation theory. The filtering devices I suggest are (1) the application of probability to the infinite play of signifiers so championed by deconstruction and (2) the rational attempt to be objective by trying harder to reduce subjectivity, however impossible that empirical ideal is to achieve. It is only through filters like probability and the attempt at objectivity that a rational discourse community can maintain itself, avoiding both marginalization by the mass public and balkanization into numerous partisan niches.

With respect to probability, take the example of the recent attack on fidelity criticism. The post-structuralist critique suggests that the fidelity critic privileges the literary and especially the canonical because of the fundamental and unconscious linguistic preference for the primary term in an original versus copy dichotomy among other forms of unconscious bias. To remedy this prejudice, the post-structuralist recommends adoption of the claim that there are an infinitude of intertextual and contextual possibilities in any work of literature, film, or the "dialogic intertextuality" (Stam's substitute for adaptation) between them, none of which should be privileged. That is, we should trade in the simplistic essentialism of fidelity studies for the richness and complexity of numberless and ever-changing inter- and contextualities. However, what is the probability that most intertextual or contextual connections matter in determining what an adaptation is about? Is it crucial that a key grip fell ill on a given day in a shoot? Is a brief reference to an obscure silent film really going to change one's interpretation of an adaptation of Shakespeare? How many viewers catch most of

Tarantino's intertextual references? Probability suggests that only intertextual connections which are sustained or foregrounded will be recognized and possibly have a significant effect on the understanding of any given film. The post-structuralist vision of infinite connections to other texts and contexts is, from a practical standpoint, the height of academic silliness. The vision suggests that adaptation scholars should be compulsive consumers of novelty with an infantile wish to control every phenomenon in their reach, regardless of interpretive relevance.

Furthermore, there are good reasons to privilege a literary source over these "infinite" possibilities. First, probability suggests that producers, directors, and audiences share an understanding of the value of, say, a canonical or famous source, and that value—economic and artistic—is usually greater than the value of most other intertexts in the minds of those making and viewing films. That's why such a high percentage of films are adaptations and remakes of well-known novels and previous films. Directors and other creative participants also know that presentations to an audience by virtue of its even partial knowledge of a well-known or otherwise valued source (e.g., prize-winning, creation of famous author, epitome of generic distinction) can affect response to a greater degree than texts and events with lesser public prestige or visibility. Second, the critic and his or her readership understand that a pattern of changes made by the film adaptation to what is presented in the mutually valued source (or sources) is usually more persuasive evidence of the meaning of an adaptation than a plethora of textual, intertextual, and contextual elements with little or no relationship to that source. Even Dudley Andrew acknowledges that "the explicit, foregrounded relation of a cinematic text to a well-constructed original text from which it derives" has a heuristic value for interpretation (2000, 29). Of course, if the source text is neither canonical nor otherwise famous, the use of the comparative method embedded in fidelity criticism is less urgent, although its heuristic value is no less strong. Finally, the application of probability does not prevent consideration of other intertextual or contextual influences. When a literary source, however celebrated, is less than formative or only tangential to a cinematic adaptation, more relevant and influential intertextual or contextual connections can be given greater status. All of the above is common sense, of course, but that sense is apparently uncommon in many theoretical discussions.

Equally troublesome is the penchant in some post-structuralist circles to claim that objectivity is just an unacknowledged subjective position and thus not worth attempting. Following Freudian precedents, many post-structuralists, especially those of an ideological bent, often argue that we are subjected to a myriad of social constructions, ideologies, collective myths, and so forth, which determines our decisions and shapes our desires while simultaneously offering us only the illusion of choice, will, and agency. That is, we are unconsciously subjected by and/or consciously disguise oppressive assumptions and conclusions under the guise of "fair and balanced" discourse, using the concept of dispassionate and disinterested analysis to blind ourselves and others to thoughts which invisibly promote our self-interest, usually synonymous with those of a hegemonic political and economic system which victimizes others (and often, ironically, ourselves). Clearly, there is some truth to this charge. However, must all attempts at objectivity be so construed? Are we incapable of escaping the famous prison house of language and ideology? Is all rationality a blinding logocentrism? When thinking and arguing rationally, are we all victims of false binaries forced on us by language and Western culture? The answer, I believe, is no. Instead, post-structuralists themselves have been victimized by a limited linguistic understanding and a narrow, totalized view of rationality. Western culture accepts and debates competing paradigms all the time. Survey and experimental data is almost always presented as a range of probabilities, not absolute truths. Sophisticated arguments are usually highly qualified and only more or less persuasive, not utterly convincing or totally vapid.

Criticism Made Too Easy

More to the point of this discussion, however, is another question: if one adopts the post-structuralist or postmodernist take on objectivity and subjectivity, what are its consequences, especially for criticism? One possible result, I think, is that post-structuralists, lacking the option of even a partial objectivity and certain that the best they can offer is to acknowledge their ideological biases (their subject position), are less obliged to consider opposing arguments and contrary or qualifying evidence in hermeneutical endeavors. Another is that the evidence some scholars use in interpretation may be selected, even invented, and shaped to fit predetermined ideological positions with impunity. Subject position justifies limits on argumentation and evidence—the Alice-in-Wonderland of niche academe in the humanities.

Let me offer a few examples of these problems which suggest the intellectual costs of post-structuralist approaches to adaptation. First, in a previous article, I surveyed seven critical essays published between 1998 and 2000 on the relationship between Michael Ondaatje's novel *The English Patient* (1992) and Anthony Minghella's film of it (1996). The essays included two that praised Minghella for the ways he adapted the novel, largely on the basis of a formalist comparison of style and theme across the media; three that attacked the movie for unfaithfully turning a postmodern and postcolonial novel into an orientalist Hollywood romance; and two that stood somewhere in the middle, though in different ways (Kranz, 2003). Unsurprisingly, given the dates of publication, none of the authors referenced each other, but disturbingly all but two of the essays (especially the most theory driven), whether formalist (unconsciously so) or postmodernist and postcolonial (overtly so), failed to deal with obvious evidence, either within the works in question or without, which might have qualified their claims. To the contrary, my own analysis of The English Patient from novel to film included references to critical articles on Ondaatje's novel (which most of the adaptation critics could have cited but didn't) and a brief comparison of the film and its literary source (including contextual data and evidence of cinematic style unanalyzed by the others). This attempt to be objective ultimately showed that the extreme claims of adaptive fidelity or infidelity in the previous criticism were clearly overstated. There's no way of knowing once and for all, of course, whether well-defined or inchoate theory rather than weak scholarly methods led to these extreme views and to the apparent narrowness of critical focus and research that led to such findings. However, it is clear that these otherwise strong essays didn't try very hard to be objective or comprehensive, settling instead for conceptual and methodological limitations (whether or not authorized by untheorized formalist assumptions or by post-structuralist premises regarding the supposed subjective illusion of objectivity).

Second, I think a case can be made that critical reaction to Kenneth Branagh's Much Ado about Nothing (1993a, 1993b) also suggests the warping effect of post-structuralist assumptions and postmodernist ideology in adaptation criticism. As previously noted, the worst offenses, perhaps driven by overt ideological biases, involve the failure to consider contrary evidence and critical opinion. In one case, however, a post-structuralist critic of Branagh's film even invents evidence to support a very debatable interpretive claim about the adaptation. The story begins on the sceptered isle. According to Kenneth Rothwell, while American reviewers praised Branagh, British reviews were overwhelmingly negative. For example, he notes that Leslie Felperin Sharman of Sight and Sound deplores the film's "cinematic bardology" and echoes "the mantra of British cultural materialists that Kenneth Branagh is somehow darkly complicit with agents of capitalist imperialism" (Rothwell, 1999, 251). Calling Branagh "Mr. Ordinary" (Light, 1993, 16) in the same magazine, Allison Light attacks what she sees as the director's phony "cultural hybridity" (19). In her view, what Branagh presents is a conservative and sunny fairy-tale romance about an almost familial community, an adaptation which makes a mockery of the authoritarian patriarchy whose virginity fetish, she believes, gives the play its name. Light's essay is the first, if not the foundation, of several similar critiques in England and America.

Michael Hattaway (1998) continues the British academic attack on Branagh. Among other problems, he faults the director for not understanding the gendered gaze (presumably after Laura Mulvey's famous articles) and for not providing a cultural critique of Shakespeare. Since film mediates between audience and text, Hattaway opines that "the success of a screen version is going to be in proportion to its *difference* from the "original," to its *infidelity*, the degree it displaces, rearranges, and transforms, finds visual means to create a Derridean supplement to what an inevitably cut text provides" (1998, 195). Deborah Cartmell (2000) continues this trashing but on more explicitly feminist grounds. She alludes to the early modern misogyny of scolding, witchcraft, and whoring in order to argue that Branagh has evaded the play's recognition that Beatrice will, by eventual marriage, be placed in a state of "total submission," her "linguistic independence" silenced, as it is symbolically stopped by Benedick's kiss (51–52). Moreover, the film is "blatantly heterosexual," and "Branagh's ending evacuates the play of its ironies and historical context, reconstructing Shakespeare's comedy into a Hollywood romantic comedy" (53–55).

On this side of the Atlantic, Courtney Lehman (1998), citing Light several times and synthesizing Gramsci's theory of the "national-popular" with theoretical dicta from Foucault, Jameson, Žižek, Bhaba, and Sinfield, contends that Branagh's *Much Ado* is a politically regressive representation: "Despite its democratizing special effects, *Much Ado* remains sedimented in that post-modern no place where (life-enhancing) 'populism' is conflated with the 'popular,' generating conversation among the heterogeneous forces of the Renaissance and postmodernity only to the extent that multinational *capital* is the by-product of this merger" (Lehman, 1998, 2). From her cultural-materialist perspective, the film of *Much Ado* becomes a kind of ideological quilt which attempts to hide several real differences of race, class, and gender in a transcultural, transhistorical fantasy of universal harmony. Through setting, costume, and cinematic style, Branagh is partly successful in this manipulative covering, but, as Lehman argues in the final third of her essay, his casting of Denzel Washington as Don Pedro presents the inassimilable difference which gives the lie to the quilt and shows that Branagh's "multinational popular" has more in common with capitalism than multiculturalism (11–16).

Stephen Buhler's (2002) comprehensive taxonomy of the strategies of Shakespearean film adaptations from the silents to today echoes this nega-

tive chorus by including *Much Ado* in a chapter titled "Transgressive, in Theory." Buhler thinks Branagh's *Much Ado* cuts and undercuts the dark side of
Shakespeare's play in a number of ways in order to make the happy ending
more acceptable (2002). From one perspective, Buhler's take on Branagh
appears to oppose those above who think Shakespeare's text needs ideological deconstruction. But actually, the handful of critics from Sharman to
Buhler favor, more or less, an adaptation that clearly foregrounds the transgressive elements in the text (here fidelity is good) while simultaneously sub-
verting or critiquing the play's other elements, especially those which underscore conservative views or values which appear "natural" and apolitical
(here fidelity is bad). To be judged positively by any of these critics, then, a
film adaptation must toe an overtly materialist or feminist ideological line.
Though some may squirm at the directness of his statement, Herbert Coursen
makes clear that cinematic adaptations of Shakespeare, to be successful, re-
quire this interpretation in performance: "In other words, the critique coming from the left side of the political spectrum is the one that keeps the plays
'alive'" (1996, 116). Thus, with the exception of occasional qualifications,
ideological critics of Branagh find little or nothing in *Much Ado* to praise.

By contrast, academic critics who write approvingly about Branagh's
movie find plenty to praise while also bringing up at least some of the coun-
tervailing evidence repeated often by the naysayers. Buttressed in their views
by the overwhelmingly positive reception Branagh's *Much Ado* experienced
from audiences and most journalistic reviewers, Samuel Crowl (1993, 2000),
Ellen Edgerton (1994), Carol Moses (1996), Michael J. Collins (1997), and
Tanja Weiss (1999), as a group, find Branagh's film to be quite vital even
though it lacks the overtly subversive interpretive focus which, for Coursen,
is lifesaving. They approve of Branagh's "green world" setting in Tuscany as
appropriate for a romantic comedy which is looking sideways toward its festive and pastoral Shakespearean sisters and forward to Shakespearean ro-
mances and Hollywood's romantic and screwball genres. Most find the movie
as funny as it is romantic. They also think the film's emphasis on music appropriate, given the title's play on "nothing" as musical notation. Likewise,
the energetic nudity at the film's beginning fits both the genre of festive comedy and the title's punning play on female (and thereby also male) organs of
increase. Branagh's cinematic style, they believe, is appropriate both to his
popularizing goals and to his attempt to maintain in film both theatrical intimacy and repertorial collectivity, allowing him to bring out the inwardness
of a few characters and still assure the audience's reception of the social
harmony with which almost all versions of this genre end. Finally and most
importantly, while these critics acknowledge that Branagh reduces some

elements in Shakespeare's *Much Ado* which subvert either patriarchal practices or conventional class hierarchies, they show that he does not excise all
of them. Instead, these critics suggest that, among many other signs in the
film of the Bard's liberating unconventionality, Branagh's focus on Beatrice
(Emma Thompson), whose wit and emotive depth dominate the largely female space of the film's Tuscan setting, counteracts a blind acceptance of patriarchal proclivities among characters and audience alike.

But these and other discoveries of vital presentational and interpretive
virtues are largely ignored in leftist commentary. Of course, one could excuse
unacknowledged qualifications by noting that a few of the ideological reviewers and critics might have written before these virtues were manifested
by others, while the rest, knowing these virtues were already well publicized,
are justified in ignoring them. But the issue is not simply that the bulk of ideological analysis overlooks or appropriates what the majority has found positive and significant. Rather, though difficult to prove, I suggest the possibility that their arguments may also have been influenced by self-imposed
theoretical limitations which embrace subjectivity, thereby excusing the failure to acknowledge opposition, complexity, and ambiguity in sifting the evidence offered by Branagh's *Much Ado*.

For example, the attack on Branagh for "evacuat[ing] the play of its ironies
and its historical context" (Cartmell, 2000, 54–55), for presenting such a
sunny fairy-tale romance that patriarchal concerns are eviscerated from
the film (Light, 1993), for failing to subvert the male gaze (Hattaway, 1998),
and for other alleged absences of feminist interrogation in the film are, it
turns out, misleading at best. While Branagh has cut a few lines which foreground ironic comments on patriarchal practices, he has left many subversive
ones in the screenplay and film (e.g., Shakespeare, 1981, 1.1.274–75 and
most of 2.1.46–75). Furthermore, though feminist critics are right that
Branagh's casting of Robert Sean Leonard as Claudio creates more a youthful innocent than a dowry-hunting chauvinist, the character's verbal attack
on Hero in Shakespeare's first wedding scene is expanded in the film to include overt physical abuse. Don Pedro (Denzel Washington), moreover, the
highest-ranking male in the film, implicitly approves of this violence because
he accompanies Claudio throughout and does nothing to stop it. Indeed,
Branagh has the patriarch himself, the governor and father Leonato, resume
the physical attack on Hero after Claudio's departure. There is nothing in the
text that requires this violent abuse against the daughter. I suppose this
misogynistic treatment is not quite the equivalent of early modern tortures
like the cucking of a scold, but it comes close. Furthermore, lines alluding to
Hero's change in status from "maid" and "Dian" to "Venus" and "wanton"

(and thus the patriarchal paradigm of considering women either virgins or whores) are, *pace* Cartmell, oft repeated.

Additionally, in a play whose title suggests mistakes in observation, errors in noting, male errors are made even more palpable in the film than in the text by visualization of the Borachio–Margaret tryst followed by a cut to Hero sleeping soundly elsewhere. In this scene, cutting and camerawork make clear that the audience is seeing the point of view of Claudio, but the low-angle full and medium shots make questionable Claudio's acceptance of Don John's reading because Margaret, even with her back turned, doesn't look much like Hero. Also, as in the play, we know in Branagh's film that Don John is a schemer and that Claudio knows it too, not only from early exposition, but because Don John has fooled him at the masque and, as noted, because Hero is safely tucked in elsewhere. Thus, when Claudio accepts Don John's interpretation of events and then humiliates Hero at the wedding, he seems to us even more the fool and cad than in the play. At the very least, these visual enhancements qualify charges that the film has lost all the play's darker ironies. True, the setting is very ripe and sunny, but this Tuscan mansion can harbor a patriarchy as blind and violent as any in a Sicilian city. (Shakespeare, of course, never specifies that "Messina" be an urban setting.)

As for the alleged conventional gendering of the gaze, the film provides evidence that questions whether this old chestnut of feminist film theory is relevant. True, some of the first shots of the opening picnic feature women in passive poses exposing cleavages, but many of the men, themselves inactive, are utterly shirtless as well. Then, while the women's costumes do reveal some titillating jiggle en route the governor's mansion, the men arrive on phallic horseflesh, their tight, mostly leather trousers bouncing in slow motion. Later, during the exuberant bathing sequences, we also see bare backs and bums, but the quick editorial pace and the speed of the panning greatly sanitize this voyeurism, and the cross-cutting makes the objects of our collective gaze both male and female. Of course, Shakespeare's play does set up Hero as a largely silent object often fixed by the gaze of male suitors (and Branagh does not subvert her taciturn passivity), but the courtship of Benedick and Beatrice does not privilege either one as active pursuer, nor does Branagh's selection of shots favor either as object of the audience's or each other's gaze. If anything, the audience is moved to identify with Beatrice and see from her point of view when the director makes telling asides out of some of her lines, enabling us to hear her private thoughts in ways that Benedick's self-conscious soliloquies never allow. Branagh's *Much Ado* is no feminist film, but neither does it bear the marks of sexist Hollywood comedy.

Finally, let's turn to the problem of outright misinterpretation, or imagined evidence, this time with regard to race, not gender. Courtney Lehman finds that Branagh "fails to consider the implications" of his choice of an African American, Denzel Washington, for the part of Don Pedro (1998, 11). She thinks this tokenism fails when it becomes clear that Washington can't be part of the family at Messina unless his racial difference is minimized. Thus, he is "frequently left out of many of the film's depictions of mass reveling, where blackness might interrupt the homogenizing effects of the production values" (13), especially at the beginning and end of the film. Scenes where marriage is discussed become especially problematic because Washington's race raises the "spectre of just how costly the 'stain' of mixed marriage and miscegenation would be to an otherwise uniform social order" (13). Quoting Branagh's claim that his choice of Washington was colorblind, that race is not relevant to the role, Lehman concludes that Branagh tried to "'quilt' over the 'racial' with the 'filial,'" but this fantasy contrasted too much with his stated intention to bring difference to the Englishness of Shakespearean performance, and the result is "'hey nonny nonsense'" (15).

Lehman's analysis of *Much Ado* is the most sophisticated of all the poststructuralist critiques, but like the others it skews the evidence and eventually reports things that don't happen in the film. First, she fails to give direct credit to Branagh for putting his token black on top of the hierarchy; Don Pedro may be "unassimilable," but he is also the chief power figure in the play. Moreover, Branagh puts Washington's Don Pedro at the center and forward position in almost all of depictions of him with the ensemble in the first half of the film. Next, while Lehman complains that we don't see Washington's naked black skin in the "fleshy egalitarianism of the alfresco frolicking scene" (1998, 13), one of those depictions of mass reveling, she fails to note that we don't see Don John (Keanu Reeves) either, that we only see waist-up views of Benedick and Claudio, and that our view of the elder patriarchs is limited to an almost fully dressed comic moment. Finally, after the bathing, Don Pedro (in close-up) and Don John lead the men to the rendezvous with the household. Rather than subtle racism, then, it strikes me that throughout the credits montage, the relative nudity of both men and women is inversely proportional to rank (of course, Branagh may have let the male higher-ups off for reasons of dignity and perhaps the two American stars weren't paid enough to expose their backsides). But the point is that Lehman's implicit criticism of Branagh for Washington's absences in festive scenes is simply not born out by an unbiased, dare I say objective, examination of the film.

Lehman's reading of Branagh's handling of Don Pedro in the final scene continues to overstate some and even invent other cinematic evidence. For example, while she points out accurately that Washington is largely left out of the ending's "hey nonny, nonny" song of reassurance, she also risks incredulity by concluding that "we see Washington's Don Pedro blanch inwardly at the celebration that literally ghettoizes him" (Lehman, 1998, 14). While she rightly claims that "the contagious revelling *gradually* forces Washington's character out of the frame" (italics mine), Lehman also suggests, incredibly, that Branagh's stage directions offer a reminder of his leftover status by calling for a "DISSOLVE INTO BLACK" (14). In fact, in the film itself as opposed to the script, even an attentive audience could barely read these stage directions in the brief seconds that it sees Washington alone behind the revelers. This final isolation, furthermore, is a surprise because we have seen Don Pedro tightly framed with Benedick in a close-up as Don John is led away, after which Benedick, calling for the pipers, grabs Washington's hand to start the dance in a medium-to-full shot. Then, as the camera pans and starts to pull back quickly, Don Pedro is passed in the opening of the dance from Benedick to Claudio before standing aside, and he is smiling all the while. As in Shakespeare's text, Don Pedro will not marry here, but, though he exits the dance, he is hardly unhappy. Finally, at his long to extreme-long distance from the camera when the panning picks him up for the last time, viewers would never be able to detect any "inward blanching," Lehman's cutesy phrase for Denzel's supposed embarrassment and disappointment. For, though the speed of the tracking shot makes notice difficult, Washington actually waves a kiss to the dancers before he is seen no more. Lehman's attempt to make Washington's Don Pedro into a scapegoat and Branagh into a racist is ingenious but contrary to a fair-minded assessment of the cinematic evidence.

Let me suggest why ideological critics of Branagh's *Much Ado* fail to attempt fair-minded readings of the film, beyond obvious restrictions on article length imposed by their publishers. First, some are preaching to the choirs of editors who share their ideology (this is true of other critical schools as well, of course). Second, post-structuralist theories like feminism and cultural studies are reductive (as is also true of many other schools of criticism), demanding in art the subversion or transgression of the dominant patriarchal and bourgeois ideology of Western culture, with its mythic promotion of individualism and transcultural, transhistorical humanistic discourse. This latter, supposedly conservative ideology, so it is claimed, prevents us from seeing significant differences among races, classes, and genders while evading recognition of material realities which unjustly oppress the marginalized in each category. Given this predetermination, standards of evidence are easily compromised. Third, as noted earlier, post-structuralist theory suggests that no criticism can be objective; thus, criticism which is overtly ideological, which announces its subjectivity, is viewed as superior to criticism which pursues objectivity but, because of unacknowledged subjectivities, cannot achieve what is claimed. Given this theoretical position, even the attempt at objectivity is not worth making. Fourth, with respect to Branagh's *Much Ado*, my guess is that several left-leaning reviewers and critics, hoping his subversive moments in *Henry V* or his upbringing in Northern Ireland would lead to transgressive cultural productions, were deeply disappointed; as Sharman concludes, in *Much Ado*, "Branagh, financially independent yet toeing the [Tory] Party's aesthetic line, looks much less like the radical revisionist he first purported to be" (1993, 51).

Last Take

It should be clear that I believe there are dangers in making post-structuralist and postmodernist theory the basis for adaptation theory and criticism. Giving up on the ideal of objectivity and the attempt at rationality may lead to solipsistic practices which curtail mutual understanding and reduce or balkanize the audience for adaptation studies. Instead, we should try harder to achieve the ideal of objectivity even though we'll never attain it absolutely. At the same time, the post-structuralist challenge to the traditional fidelity mode of adaptation studies contains a number of valid points, as noted above. What scholars of the relationship of literature and film need to do, then, is reform traditional methods of adaptation study while avoiding the excesses of the theoretical movement which brought us the needed critique. That means we need to find a satisfactory mean or range between the essentialistic extreme of fidelity criticism as depicted by its detractors and the relativistic extremes of post-structuralist theory depicted above. Of all the approaches reviewed earlier, I think Sarah Cardwell's (2002) the most attractive. She advocates inclusiveness while not losing focus on adaptation itself. If, instead, we follow the theoretical recommendations of Stam (2000) and Ray (2000), for example, adaptation study loses its identity. With infinite and ever-changing intertexts and contexts to be sought and no distinctions made between them, all films become adaptations and adaptations become no different than any other films. It is akin to saying that because most feature films include music on the soundtrack that all films are musicals. Moreover, there is no reason to replace the comparative analysis at the heart of fidelity criticism; ultimately, one can't understand an adaptation without a comparison to the named or most likely literary source or sources; that's what we mean by adaptation. Thus, adaptations should maintain their distinctive status in the film medium. However, adaptation studies should both avoid the unconscious favoritism often granted the literary source and insist on the inclusive addition of information required to do interpretive justice to any film qua film. We need to cleanse adaptation studies of its errors but maintain its place as a subset of both literature and film studies. This reformulation probably means changing the name of fidelity criticism to comparative criticism, I suppose, making the issue of fidelity (still important for economic, audience-response, and hermeneutic reasons) only one of several related questions in the comparative equation. And we must ask the "fidelity to what?" question, breaking up the issue in various nonexclusionary ways. But let's keep the comparative heart of adaptation studies because it yields persuasive, probabilistic evidence that gives us confidence in at least a few tentative answers to our questions about the relationship of literature and film.

Why are such answers important? I think that scholars in this corner of the humanities need answers in which we can have some confidence. Asking numberless questions and proposing infinite complexities just isn't enough to satisfy most of us. Intelligent humans hope for and seek order as much as they seek difference, want some confident answers alongside infinite possibilities, desire security as we rage for variety and chaos. If we indulge ourselves only in the *jouissance* of an infinite play of signifiers and rule out the possibility of any signifieds, who will take our classes or support our studies? So far, like most academic groups in higher learning, we make our own rules and thus allow ourselves to suffer our own and our colleagues' foolish writings gladly, importing whatever we want into our inquiries, however tangential or obscure. All questioning and discovery is good, we say—knowledge for its own sake. But how long will that be enough for us and for others? To expand the issue, if only the sciences and the social sciences provide apparently useful answers to the infinity of questions and explorations we face in higher education, where will we in the humanities be in a few years? Already, student numbers and budgets in the humanities are shrinking. How long can scholars continue to speak only to their niche constituencies and ignore interests and financial realities beyond the ivory tower? To return to film and literature, how long will or should our society, especially the segments responsible for funding education, support the study of adaptation, particularly if it abandons probability for unfiltered theoretical inclusiveness or traditional standards of objective inquiry for overtly partisan subjectivity? Not long, I fear, and thus we need to make a case for an approach which continues to challenge unexamined and traditional understandings of adaptation, literature, film, and the humanities while also accommodating the fundamental principles and practices of academia writ large and the lasting economic, social, and cultural values and beliefs of American society as a whole.

Notes

1. See Corrigan (1999) for a brief history of the relationship of literature and film (15–78), for collected articles with varied relevance to that relationship (96–245), and for a few relevant end-of-century articles (262–304, 340–56). See Derrida (1970), Fish (1980), Althusser (1984), Lyotard (1984), and Showalter (1985) for famous examples of post-structuralist and postmodernist developments. Classic essays in film theory by Mulvey, Baudry, Heath, and Comolli can be found in Rosen (1986, 198–209, 299–318, and 379–443). See Bordwell and Carroll (1996) for a recent cognitive intervention.

2. For example, Charles W. Eckert's (1972) collection of essays on Shakespearean films stages the critical conflict between "those who feel that fidelity to Shakespeare's text is of prime importance and those who are willing to allow the director and adaptor creative authority both in cutting the original and in imposing simplistic or even eccentric interpretations upon it" (2). The volume is evenly split between both camps, suggesting that the principles of fidelity criticism were contested well before the end of the century. Furthermore, Kenneth Rothwell documents a century's attitudes to the Shakespeare film by pointing out that adaptation criticism has changed considerably over the last 100 years or so: "First, commentators rose to the bait of the impossible question: 'Is it Shakespeare?'; next, they avoided it or manipulated it; and, lastly, ignored it altogether. . . . That is to say, a text-focused preoccupation with literal translation of Shakespeare's language into film language has gradually and sometimes imperceptibly given way to a more open and adventurous foray by both auteurs and critics into discovering that which is special and unique about each movie" (2002, ix). Rothwell goes on to list numerous articles and books on the subject in the 1980s and 1990s which suggest that "the question 'Is it Shakespeare?' no longer concerns anyone" (xvi).

Works Cited

Althusser, Louis. 1984. *Essays on Ideology*. London: Verso.

Andrew, Dudley. 2000. "Adaptation." *Film Adaptation*, ed. James Naremore, 28–37. New Brunswick, NJ: Rutgers University Press.

Bordwell, David, and Noël Carroll, eds. 1996. *Post-Theory: Reconstructing Film Studies*. Madison: University of Wisconsin Press.

Branagh, Kenneth. 1993a. *Much Ado about Nothing, by William Shakespeare: Screenplay, Introduction, and Notes on the Making of the Movie*. New York: Norton.

———, dir. 1993b. *Much Ado about Nothing*. Perf. Emma Thompson, Kenneth Branagh, Michael Keaton, Denzel Washington. DVD. Columbia Tri-Star, 1997.

Braudy, Leo, and Marshall Cohen, eds. 1999. *Film Theory and Criticism: Introductory Readings*. 5th ed. New York: Oxford University Press.

Buhler, Stephen M. 2002. *Shakespeare in the Cinema: Ocular Proof*. Albany: State University of New York Press.

Cardwell, Sarah. 2002. *Adaptation Revisited: Television and the Classic Novel*. Manchester, UK: Manchester University Press.

Cartmell, Deborah. 2000. *Interpreting Shakespeare on Screen*. New York: St. Martin's Press.

Collins, Michael J. 1997. "Sleepless in Messina: Kenneth Branagh's *Much Ado about Nothing*." *Shakespeare Bulletin* 15 (Spring): 38–39.

Corrigan, Timothy. 1999. *Film and Literature: An Introduction and Reader*. Upper Saddle River, NJ: Prentice-Hall.

Coursen, H. R. 1996. *Shakespeare in Production: Whose History?* Athens: Ohio University Press.

Crowl, Samuel. 1993. "*Much Ado about Nothing*." *Shakespeare Bulletin* 11 (Summer): 39–40.

———. 2000. "Flamboyant Realist: Kenneth Branagh." In *The Cambridge Companion to Shakespeare on Film*, ed. Russell Jackson, 222–38. Cambridge: Cambridge University Press.

Derrida, Jacques. 1970. "Structure, Sign, and Play in the Discourse of the Human Sciences." In *The Languages of Criticism and the Sciences of Man: The Structuralist Controversy*, ed. Richard Macksey and Eugenio Donato, 247–72. Baltimore: Johns Hopkins University Press.

Eagleton, Terry. 2004. *After Theory*. New York: Basic Books.

Eckert, Charles W., ed. 1972. *Focus on Shakespearean Films*. Englewood Cliffs, NJ: Prentice-Hall.

Edgerton, Ellen. 1994. "'Your Answer, Sir, Is Cinematical': Kenneth Branagh's *Much Ado about Nothing*." *Shakespeare Bulletin* 12 (Winter): 42–44.

Ellis, John M. 1997. *Literature Lost: Social Agendas and the Corruption of the Humanities*. New Haven, CT: Yale University Press.

Fish, Stanley. 1980. *Is There a Text in This Class? The Authority of Interpretive Communities*. Cambridge, MA: Harvard University Press.

Hattaway, Michael. 1998. "'I've Processed My Guilt': Shakespeare, Branagh, and the Movies." In *Shakespeare and the Twentieth Century: The Selected Proceedings of the International Shakespeare Association World Congress Los Angeles, 1996*, ed. Jonathan Bate, Jill L. Levenson, and Dieter Mehl, 194–211. Newark: University of Delaware Press.

Kirby, David. 2004. "Theory in Chaos." *The Christian Science Monitor* 27 January. www.csmonitor.com/2004/0127/p11s01-legn.html (accessed 2 February 2007).

Kranz, David L. 2003. "*The English Patient*: Critics, Audiences, and the Quality of Fidelity." *LFQ* 31 (2): 99–110.

Lehmann, Courtney. 1998. "*Much Ado about Nothing*? Shakespeare, Branagh, and the 'National-Popular' in the Age of Multinational Capital." *Textual Practice* 12: 1–22.

Leitch, Thomas. "Where Are We Going, Where Have We Been?" *LFA News* 1 (1): 2, 6, 8. [This essay is reprinted in chapter 23 of the current volume.]

Light, Alison. 1993. "The Importance of Being Ordinary." *Sight and Sound* 3 (September): 16–19.

Lyotard, Jean-François. 1984. *The Postmodern Condition: A Report on Knowledge*. Trans. Geoff Bennington and Brian Massumi. Manchester, UK: Manchester University Press.

Metz, Walter. 2003. "The Future of Adaptation Studies." *LFA News* 1 (1): 3, 10.

Moses, Carol. 1996. "Kenneth Branagh's *Much Ado about Nothing*: Shakespearean Comedy as Shakespearean Romance." *Shakespeare Bulletin* 14 (Winter): 38–40.

Patai, Daphne, and Will H. Corral, eds. 2005. *Theory's Empire: An Anthology of Dissent*. New York: Columbia University Press.

Ray, Robert B. 2000. "The Field of 'Literature and Film.'" In *Film Adaptation*, ed. James Naremore, 38–53. New Brunswick, NJ: Rutgers University Press, 2000.

Rosen, Philip, ed. 1986. *Narrative, Apparatus, Ideology: A Film Theory Reader*. New York: Columbia University Press.

Rothwell, Kenneth S. 1999. *A History of Shakespeare on Screen*. Cambridge, UK: Cambridge University Press.

———. 2002. "Preface: How the 20th Century Saw the Shakespeare Film: 'Is It Shakespeare?'" In *Shakespeare into Film*, ed. James M. Welsh, Richard Vela, and John C. Tibbetts, ix–xxi. New York: Checkmark Books.

Shakespeare, William. 1981. *Much Ado about Nothing*. Ed. A. R. Humphreys. London: Methuen.

Sharman, Leslie Felperin. 1993. "*Much Ado about Nothing*." *Sight and Sound* 3 (September): 50–51.

Showalter, Elaine, ed. 1985. *The New Feminist Criticism: Essays on Women, Literature, and Theory*. New York: Pantheon.

Stam, Robert. 2000. "Beyond Fidelity: The Dialogics of Adaptation." In *Film Adaptation*, ed. James Naremore, 54–76. New Brunswick, NJ: Rutgers University Press.

Vickers, Brian. 1993. *Appropriating Shakespeare: Contemporary Critical Quarrels*. New Haven, CT: Yale University Press.

Walker, Elsie M., and David T. Johnson. 2005. "Letter from the Editors." *LFQ* 33 (1): 2–3, 81.

Weiss, Tanja. 1999. *Shakespeare on the Screen: Kenneth Branagh's Adaptations of Henry V, Much Ado about Nothing, and Hamlet*. Frankfurt: Peter Lang.

Wood, James. 2004. "Textual Harassment." *The New Republic*, 7 and 14 June: 28–35.

PART II

CLASSIC AND POPULAR LITERATURE

CHAPTER SEVEN

~

What *Is* a
"Shakespeare Film," Anyway?

James M. Welsh

The title of this chapter should be self-explanatory, intending to answer a very basic question made difficult only by the fussiness and peculiarity of theory. It reflects, perhaps, a certain irritation over the way theory came to dominate cinema studies and literary concerns as well at the end of the last, miserable century. The approach here is historic, filmographic, and bibliographic because the chapter surveys early films (some of them clearly adaptations, some of them merely "derivatives") and reviews the earlier scholarship before going on to discuss later scholarship trends that have proliferated over the past fifty years, in particular those approaches that have expressed special interest in Shakespeare "derivatives" and films that might be considered "almost" Shakespeare. But, as any serious Shakespearean might ask, is "almost" good enough? This chapter values Shakespeare for the distinctive poetry that has made the plays "timeless," demanding that Shakespeare's poetry and diction be valued and maintained. Derivative adaptations that ignore Shakespeare's language while exploiting his plots and characters should be considered misguided and corrupt.

Surely, everybody knows a Shakespeare film ought to be one intelligently adapted from a Shakespeare play, right? But the process has become pretty loose, lately, and would-be popular culture "scholars" have become pretty

adept at finding likely candidates far from Renaissance England. Director
Ken Hughes, for example, made a movie called *Joe Macbeth* updating Shakespeare's Scottish play to a twentieth-century gangster setting; so is that close
enough? Or how about the movie *A Thousand Acres*, based upon the novel
by Jane Smiley, set in Iowa, but conceived in a fit of feminist frenzy and spun
from a ghastly and simplistic distortion of the plot of *King Lear*? So is either
the original novel or the film, adapted by Laura Jones and directed by Jocelyn Moorhouse in 1997, anything more than Shakespeare with a Smiley face?
Director Delmer Daves made a Western called *Jubal* in 1956, marketed as a
"western take" on *Othello*. Does the mere claim make it ripe and ready for
classroom exploitation? Are we so desperate to make Shakespeare "relevant"?
Has the profession forgotten what it is or should be about? Or are we all sinking helplessly into the muck of a postmodern swamp?

What's Radically New on the Rialto? Othello Reformed

During the mid-1590s, Shakespeare wrote the perfect adolescent play. It was
called *Romeo and Juliet*. It's not set in Florida or California or Mexico City or
"Verona Beach," Baz Luhrmann to the contrary, though Luhrmann's *Romeo
+ Juliet* did manage, just barely, to hold on to some of the mangled music of
Shakespeare's poetry, or at least a token amount, delivered with varying degrees of competence by hoodlum youngsters including that darling, wild *Ti-
tanic* boy, Leonardo DiCaprio, a natural heartbreaker. On the other hand,
Othello was not an adolescent play, even though teenagers might no doubt
believe they can "relate to" the emotion of jealousy. (One imagines that "relating to" might be on the cusp of understanding.)

So how about wrenching *Othello* out of its Venetian and Mediterranean
context and plopping the plot and a few "updated" and barely recognizable
central but relatively incoherent characters down in a prep school in South
Carolina, updating it to the late twentieth century so that the contemporary
Moor would shoot hoops instead of Turks? Cool, eh? Director Tim Blake Nelson called it *O*, suggesting a metallic O, not a wooden O, a metallic O that
reflects the circularity of a basketball hoop, so that Cinthio's stolen fable
might be transformed into a preppie hoop dream. This foolish thing followed
the trend started by *10 Things I Hate about You* (1999), which also starred Ju-
lia Stiles and could have been tagged "*The Taming of the Shrew* Goes to High
School." But *Othello* is surely more problematic: Not only is it far more serious, but it is also far more difficult to update and dumb down. As the only
black male in an all-white high school, screenwriter Brad Kaaya presumably
might have experienced some of the anguish ascribed to his angry adolescent

version of Shakespeare's tragic protagonist, whose new name, Odin James, suggested the initials of yet another sports celebrity who, let's say, had trouble adjusting to a white-dominated world. Kaaya somehow thought it might be a good idea to turn *Othello* into a backcourt tragedy, without realizing that a basketball star might lack the authority, the *gravitas* and tragic dimension of the Moor, elevated to a position of military leadership. Shooting hoops instead of Turks is a less than subtle difference. So, is it *Othello*? (Not quite.) Is it Shakespeare? (Not really.) Or is it merely an angry and abortive derivative? Will it help contemporary students somehow to understand *Othello*? Where has the poetry gone? How can this enterprise be justified?

The "Bard Boom" of the 1990s

Since the academy has discovered the movies, there has been a veritable land rush to stake out claims to any goofy movie resembling theatre, drama, or Shakespeare. We can either praise (or blame, or praise *then* blame) Kenneth Branagh for the current Shakespeare boom, which started with his film adaptation of *Henry V* in 1989, a worthy effort, to be followed by other adaptations, some good, some strange, some very long, and one even (arguably) monstrous. Branagh's *Hamlet*, for example, is lavish, anachronistic, spectacular, often majestic and magnificent, and (at times) unbearably long, humping the quarto text to the folio, making the play more timely and, good grief, even Churchillian (even though Blenheim Palace does make a fine backdrop for Derek Jacobi's sleazy regal Claudius). The phalanx of films led by Branagh's "mirror for all Christian Kings" has been followed by a battalion of books, the best of these probably being Kenneth Rothwell's A *History of Shakespeare on Screen* (1999).[1]

Rothwell's *History* was certainly ambitious in the way it combined the earlier research of Robert Hamilton Ball's *Shakespeare on Silent Film* (1968) and Jack Jorgens's *Shakespeare on Film* (1977), the first really scholarly books to consider the filmed Shakespeare, though British critic and historian Roger Manvell's *Shakespeare and the Film* (1971) also provided a readable and useful survey of the topic and added as well interview material with the incomparable Laurence Olivier; Rothwell then continued his survey on to the Bard boom of the 1990s, including Lurhmann's *Romeo + Juliet* and Branagh's overlong *Hamlet*, but not Julie Taymor's *Titus* (1999) or Ethan Hawke's *Hamlet* in modern dress or the strange wedding of Shakespeare with Cole Porter in Branagh's *Love's Labours Lost* (2000). Rothwell's *History* (1999) was the culmination of a career that had started with *Shakespeare on Film Newsletter*, a periodical Rothwell founded with Bernice W. Kliman in 1976. By 1986 the advisory board included Robert H. Ball, Jack Jorgens, Roger Manvell, May-nard Mack, Sam Wanamaker of the Shakespeare Globe Center, and Louis Marder, the founding editor of *The Shakespeare Newsletter*, which incorporated the function of Rothwell's *Shakespeare on Film Newsletter* after Ken Rothwell retired from the University of Vermont in the 1990s.

Robert F. Willson Jr. took a far more tidy approach in his book *Shakespeare in Hollywood, 1929–1956* (2000), a little book equally interested in Hollywood as well as Shakespeare. By starting with the Douglas Fairbanks/Mary Pickford *Taming of the Shrew* (1929), Willson avoided the "Strange, Eventful History" covered by Ball in 1968. Chapters are devoted to the usual suspects, the Warner Bros. *Midsummer Night's Dream* (1935), the MGM *Romeo and Juliet* (1936), the Orson Welles *Macbeth* (1948), and the Houseman-Mankiewicz *Julius Caesar* (1953). The kicker comes in chapter 4, entitled "Selected Off-Shoots," where, with amusing logic, Willson (2000) makes cases for not only *Forbidden Planet* (1956) as an adaptation of *The Tempest* and *Joe Macbeth* but also several Western derivatives: Delmer Daves's *Jubal* (1956), the Western *Othello* and *Broken Lance* (1954) as a "*King Lear* on Horseback." Another (off)shoot-em-up is John Ford's classic *My Darling Clementine* (1946). Well, Victor Mature's Doc Holliday *does* recite the "To Be or Not to Be" soliloquy in this "classic," but John Ford is no William Shakespeare (Peter Bogdanovich to the contrary) and, besides, Jack Benny did it better in his wartime satire *To Be or Not to Be* (1942), Shakespeare truly "touched" by Ernst Lubitsch, who used tragedy for comic purposes in this stunning film and comedy for tragic purposes, when he has a Jewish actor in Nazi-occupied Poland recite Shylock's "Hath not a Jew eyes?" defense.

Just as *Hamlet* is embedded in the Lubitsch film, so *Othello* is embedded in George Cukor's *A Double Life* (1947), another "Shakespeare-influenced" film. Of course, "influence" is not adaptation per se, but despite a certain loopiness, this chapter poses an interesting question: What exactly is a Shakespeare "adaptation," anyway? Is *Last Action Hero* (1993) a "Shakespeare-influenced" movie because of its three-minute spoof of Olivier's *Hamlet* in a classroom presided over by Lord Olivier's widow? In *A Thousand Acres* (1997), Jane Smiley exploits *King Lear*, taking Shakespeare's concept for high drama but reducing it into a cornfed soap opera; a woman's film about a drunken and cantankerous father is the result. Can a film that utterly ignores the language of *Lear* be considered a worthy adaptation by any stretch? Robert Willson does not pose this question, but he should have.

No one should object to yet another book dealing with the filmed Shakespeare, so long as it is well informed and readable. Sarah Hatchuel's *Shake-*

speare, from Stage to Screen (2004) passes that test, even though it leans rather too heavily on French theory (but maybe since she teaches in Paris, she can't help it?). Hatchuel begins with a useful discussion of Shakespeare on stage, from the Globe to the Restoration to Drury Lane and nineteenth-century realism and then, inevitably, to cinema. When she poses the question, "What is a 'Shakespeare Film'?" (obviously not for the first time)—well, that is a definition devoutly to be wished for and one deserving a thoughtful answer. Hatchuel cautiously defines the genre so as to avoid the supposed Shakespeare derivatives that so titillated Richard Burt (1998) and so fascinated Robert F. Willson Jr. in his book *Shakespeare in Hollywood* (2000). So, how much caution is required here? How seriously should one explore the paths and thickets of intertextuality? Is Kurosawa's *Ran* really *King Lear*? Is Jane Smiley's *A Thousand Acres* close enough to *Lear*? How close is "close enough"? What, exactly, is one to make of a film adapted from a novel that is a feminist transformation of a male-centered Renaissance play? Does Jason Robards have enough dignity and gravitas to play a mean-spirited, cornfed Lear who runs like a deer? Sod that!

The problem of adapting Shakespeare falls under the larger umbrella of adaptation study or adaptation theory as defined most recently by Robert Stam and his New York University graduate student Alessandra Raengo in three books clearly intended to colonize and ultimately conquer the whole field, though the focus appears to be on novels rather than drama or Shakespeare. The first book suggests a method: Robert Stam's solo enterprise, *Literature through Film: Realism, Magic, and the Art of Adaptation* (2005), fortified by *Literature and Film: A Guide to the Theory and Practice of Film Adaptation* (Stam and Raengo, 2005b) and then a 460-page *Companion to Literature and Film* (Stam and Raengo, 2005a), incorporating the work of Dudley Andrew and Charles Musser (both from Yale), Richard Allen (from NYU), Tom Gunning (University of Chicago), the darlings of the Ivy League, and the cognoscenti of the Society for Cinema and Media Studies, determined to show that cinema is just as valid as literature or drama ever claimed to be. By and large the superstars are saved for volume 3. So here was a publication date to remember, one that (who knows?) might prove as important over time as 1623, not merely a single folio but *three* theoretical books!

Looking over this project, the first book seems reasonable enough. It's commonplace that because any adaptation of a novel or play requires an interpretation, it might be useful to teach literature through film. What drives the cognoscenti crazy is the usual assumption that "the book was better" and that cinema somehow does a disservice to literature, as is sometimes the case and more and more frequently the case when it comes to

Shakespeare. They are offended, moreover, by the jargon of the usual discourse, which seems to imply a moral judgment unfavorable to cinema: infidelity, betrayal, violation, bastardization, desecration, and vulgarization. Such terms will ring familiar to those who have followed the reception of a film adaptation of Shakespeare, whose diction is, after all, elevated and poetic, even "sacred" to true devotees. Stam is horrified by the way, as he so cleverly puts it, "adaptation discourse subtly reinscribes the axiomatic superiority of literature to film" (Stam and Raengo, 2005b, 4). Notions of *anteriority and seniority* assume that "older arts are necessarily better" ones. Stam lists other sources of hostility: *dichotomous thinking* (4) presumes a bitter rivalry between film and literature; *iconophobia* (5) recalls the second commandment's injunction against graven images; *logophilia* (6), or "the valorization of the verbal" supposes that the "text" is somehow sacred, as to some Shakespeareans it may well seem; *anticorporeality* (6) presumes that the "seen" will somehow be regarded as "obscene" because cinema "offends through its inescapable materiality" (a relatively silly assumption, seems to me); *the myth of facility*, which wrongly assumes that films are "easy to make and suspectly pleasurable to watch"; more on-target, perhaps, is the *class-based dichotomy* that assumes that cinema vulgarizes and dumbs down literature (which is surely to belabor the obvious); and, finally, the *charge of parasitism* (7), that adaptations are parasites that suck out the vitality of their literary hosts, a truly goofy notion, but one that Stam claims is endemic. Small wonder, then, that cinema scholars might feel slighted and inferior, but it's too bad that they should see the problem as an either/or equation.

But perhaps I have strayed too far from Shakespeare. Which brings me to another new book, this one edited by James R. Keller and a colleague at the Mississippi University for Women, Leslie Stratyner, entitled *Almost Shakespeare: Reinventing His Works for Cinema and Television* (2004). My response to this title is that "Almost" is not good enough and that "reinvented" Shakespeare is generally little more than *pretend* Shakespeare. Why should anyone bother with something that is "almost" Shakespeare when one could just as easily have the genuine item?

When Hamlet announces to the court that "we'll *hear* a play tonight," after conjuring up a production of *The Murder of Gonzago* to bait his "mousetrap," one supposes that Shakespeare himself might favor Hamlet's priority. The point I am attempting to make here is that, if the language cannot be *heard* as Shakespeare wrote it, the play cannot be understood as Shakespeare might have intended. So what if the language is not English? The Russian dramaturg Grigori Kozintsev directed a magnificent *King Lear* derived from the Russian translation of Boris Pasternak.[2] The original poetry will have been lost, but the plot and characters are respectfully retained, and the translation was, after all, written by a highly respected national poet. Those who know Shakespeare and have internalized his lines will have no problems following the action of the Kozintsev adaptation, whether they understand the Russian language or not. Unfortunately, the same cannot be said of Akira Kurosawa's *Ran*, a film set in feudal Japan and loosely based on *King Lear*, because not only is the poetry lost but the plot has been essentially and substantially reinvented. It is said to be "almost" Shakespeare, but I'm not entirely convinced. On the other hand, lacking any evidence of Shakespeare's poetry, Kurosawa's *Throne of Blood*, though wildly divergent from its source in rather too many places, is much closer to Shakespeare's *Macbeth* than *Ran* is to *Lear*. *Throne of Blood* might be close enough to Shakespeare, but *Ran* is ultimately a fine samurai epic that resembles *Lear*, in a way.

Kozintsev's film is one step removed from Shakespeare. Kurosawa's film is two steps removed, but *is* it Shakespeare? What about the adaptation of *Othello* entitled *Souli*, released in 2004, written and directed by Alexander Abela, and described by *Variety* as "a shimmering, full-palette Madagascar-set update of *Othello*" but "transposed to a primitive, isolated fishing village" (Scheib, 2004, 34). Should one quibble over intertextuality or simply accept the gushing praise of *Variety* reviewer Ronnie Scheib, predicting that "stunning imagery, sweeping primal emotions, handsomely gifted thesps and a clever recasting of the Bard in postcolonial idiom should wow arthouse auds" (34)? The dialogue, by the way, is in Malagasy and French. But for *Othello* we don't have to seek out such an exotic example. A far more ordinary domestic corruption of *Othello* can be found in your neighborhood video store under the title *O*.

Such films, although no doubt *inspired* by Shakespeare, are certainly not interchangeable with the plays that "inspired" them. The language is changed and the poetry is simply gone, lost, sacrificed, ditched. That is not the case, however, with Peter Greenaway's profoundly odd, disrespectful spectacle of Renaissance iconography, *Prospero's Books*, which contains the text of Shakespeare's *Tempest*, though that text is not exactly dramatized. It is recited by the most gifted Shakespearean actor still working at the time Greenaway made his film. Visually it is a bizarre feast for the eyes, a triumph of art direction (if not, exactly, of taste), but verbally it *is* Shakespeare. Of course that doesn't make it any more appealing to student viewers, who might rather be in *Scotland, PA*.

Although I may disagree with the rationale behind the *Almost Shakespeare* collection, I appreciate José Ramón Díaz Fernández's bibliography of "Shakespeare Film and Television Derivatives" (2004) and Dan DeWeese's essay entitled "Prospero's Pharmacy: Peter Greenaway and the Critics Play Shakespear's Mimetic Game" (2004). From Jacques Derrida's essay "Plato's Pharmacy" (1983), DeWeese characterizes Prospero as a *pharmakos*, which identifies Shakespeare's character as a wizard, magician, and prisoner. Hence in Greenaway's elegantly overloaded film, John Gielgud represents Prospero as actor, writer, playwright, wizard, magician, prisoner, puppetmaster, and, ultimately, Shakespeare himself, at the end of his dramatic career, just as Gielgud approaches the end of his stage career. Greenaway himself has explained that he sees the play as "Shakespeare's farewell to the theatre—and this might well be Gielgud's last grand performance. So this may represent his farewell to magic, farewell to theatre, farewell to illusion. So using that as a central idea, there was my wish to find a way of unifying the figures of Prospero and Gielgud and Shakespeare" (DeWeese, 2004, 160). But to expect typical students to see beyond the superficial spectacle of eccentric nudity into this unifying and cohesive elegance is to invite disappointment. Is the film too clever for a popular mass audience?

Conclusion

So what, finally, are the ground rules? Could any responsible scholar settle for diluted Shakespeare, reduced Shakespeare, stunted Shakespeare, faux Shakespeare? A film that presumes to adapt poetic drama should at the very least be "poetic" in style and substance. Shakespeare's prime achievement was his poetry. He should not be valued for his borrowed plots. What a Shakespeare film looks like is of secondary importance; what it *sounds* like is of primary importance. If it doesn't sound right, then it probably was not worth doing. Let's *hear* it for Shakespeare! Surely there is a line to be drawn between criticism and pop cultural folly. Surely clever, imaginative young filmmakers ought to be poetically challenged? Don't we, as filmgoers, have a right to demand something better than glib chatter?

Notes

1. For the earliest academic books treating film adaptations of Shakespeare's plays, see also Robert Hamilton Ball's *Shakespeare on Silent Film: A Strange Eventful History* (1968) and Jack J. Jorgens's *Shakespeare on Film* (1977). For a more popular and readable early treatment of the field, see Roger Manvell's *Shakespeare and the Film* (1971). And for a wide-ranging discussion of derivative films, see Robert F. Willson Jr.'s *Shakespeare in Hollywood, 1929–1956* (2000).

2. Kozintsev brilliantly staged and filmed both of Shakespeare's most demanding tragedies. See Grigori Kozintsev's "*Hamlet* and *King Lear*: Stage and Film" (1972, 190–99). See also Grigori Kozintsev's *Shakespeare: Time and Conscience* (1966) and *King Lear—The Space of Tragedy* (1977). For an intelligent survey in English of the Russian film director and dramaturg's career, see Barbara Leaming's *Grigori Kozintsev* (1980).

Works Cited

Ball, Robert Hamilton. 1968. *Shakespeare on Silent Film: A Strange Eventful History.* New York: Theatre Arts Books.

Burt, Richard. 1998. *Unspeakable ShaKKKspeare: Queer Theory and American Kiddie Culture.* New York: St. Martin's Press.

Derrida, Jacques. 1983. "Plato's Pharmacy." In *Dissemination*, trans. by Barbara Johnson, 63–171. Chicago: University of Chicago Press.

DeWeese, Dan. 2004. "Prospero's Pharmacy: Peter Greenaway and the Critics Play Shakespeare's Mimetic Game." In *Almost Shakespeare: Reinventing His Works for Cinema and Television*, ed. James R. Keller and Leslie Stratyner, 155–68. Jefferson, NC: McFarland.

Fernández, José Ramón Díaz. 2004. "Shakespeare Film and Television Derivatives: A Bibliography." In *Almost Shakespeare: Reinventing His Works for Cinema and Television*, ed. James R. Keller and Leslie Stratyner, 169–89. Jefferson, NC: McFarland.

Hatchuel, Sarah. 2004. *Shakespeare, from Stage to Screen.* Cambridge, UK: Cambridge University Press.

Jorgens, Jack J. 1977. *Shakespeare on Film.* Bloomington: Indiana University Press.

Keller, James R., and Leslie Stratyner, eds. 2004. *Almost Shakespeare: Reinventing His Works for Cinema and Television.* Jefferson, NC: McFarland.

Kozintsev, Grigori. 1966. *Shakespeare: Time and Conscience.* Trans. by Joyce Vining. New York: Hill and Wang.

———. 1972. "*Hamlet* and *King Lear*: Stage and Film." In *Shakespeare 1971: Proceedings of the World Shakespeare Congress, Vancouver, August, 1971*, ed. Clifford Leech and J. M. R. Margeson, 190–99. Toronto, ON: University of Toronto Press.

———. 1977. *King Lear—The Space of Tragedy: The Diary of a Film Director.* Trans. Mary Mackintosh. Berkeley: University of California Press.

Leaming, Barbara. 1980. *Grigori Kozintsev.* Boston: Twayne.

Manvell, Roger. 1971. *Shakespeare and the Film.* New York: Praeger.

Rothwell, Kenneth S. 1999. *A History of Shakespeare on Screen: A Century of Film and Television.* Cambridge: Cambridge University Press.

Scheib, Ronnie. 2004. Review of *Souli* (France–UK–Madagascar), *Variety*, September 6–12, 34–35.

Stam, Robert. 2005. *Literature through Film: Realism, Magic, and the Art of Adaptation.* Malden, MA: Blackwell.

Stam, Robert, and Alessandra Raengo, eds. 2005a. *A Companion to Literature and Film.* Malden, MA: Blackwell.

———. 2005b. *Literature and Film: A Guide to the Theory and Practice of Film Adaptation.* Malden, MA: Blackwell.

Willson, Robert F., Jr. 2000. *Shakespeare in Hollywood, 1929–1956.* Cranbury, NJ: Fairleigh Dickinson University Press/Associated University Presses.

CHAPTER EIGHT

~

Returning to Naples:
Seeing the End in
Shakespeare Film Adaptation

Yong Li Lan

The singular difference between the ending of a Shakespeare play and that of a film adaptation of it is that in the text and on stage, the ending is spoken by the characters, whereas on film it is visualized by the camera. Instead of events coming to an end through the characters' words, the endings of recent screen adaptations take place in extensive reframings of the scene, camera movements, and shifts away from the characters and the scene of their end. These interventions of cinematic editing change the image and scene to supplant and supplement the characters' ends in death, marriage, reunion, and farewell with the spaces or places, rather than the moment, of ending. This foregrounding of sight over speech in the narration of the ending alters the event from a temporal to a more spatial one. In so doing, it draws attention to another seeing of the play, in a difference unique to the medium and its means of presenting it, and to a cinematic culture of reproduction and consumption that demands its own, additional ending in a visual equivalent of the last word. In this sense, the displacements produced by the closing images clearly show the excess and the slippage of holding the play in place. Comparable to Prospero's verbal crossing back from the island to Naples in his epilogue, the pressure of concluding and returning from the story to the real world in which it belongs is felt in a supplementarity of spaces, self-conscious and surprising, interjected at the end and after it. The closing visual sequences thus represent the extra narration, or question, of where we should place the reproduction of the text. Negotiating the point of exit from the story, then, involves seeing rather than speaking one's way out of it. This chapter examines the differences that cinematic reproduction makes to the endings of Shakespeare in several recent film versions of the plays, in terms of the more—or less—that we see of the other, alternative ending and of the medium of cinematic space and visuality as a medium of revising through revisioning.

An ending can be thought of as constituting the finitude of the plot, and it can fulfill, resist, and transform what Frank Kermode has described as the "need for ends consonant with the past" (1967, 88). All modern production of Shakespeare, however, is properly speaking reproduction and therefore has to conclude double pasts: that of the events represented in the play and that of the particular production's interaction with the audience's prior knowledge and expectations of the "original" play, or even of other productions of it. According to how intertextual exchange has directed or disposed the form of the production, what Patrice Pavis terms "the context of utterance" (1988, 90) has, by the time we reach the end, refigured the events of the play in specific intertextual and intercultural terms. Consequently, the sense of an ending works toward multiple and disparate ends: of plot, the cultural framing of Shakespeare, the competition with Shakespeare for authorship, or with other productions for uniqueness, to name only the most obvious of the ends of reperformance. Pavis proposes that the mise-en-scène of the staging orders the confrontation between the dramatic text and its performance: "The fictional universe of the performance encompasses and permeates the fictional universe of the text uttered on stage, furnishing it with a specific context of utterance; and the fictional universe of the performance is liable to be at any moment contradicted and broken up from within by the text uttered in performance" (1988, 94). In cinematic reproduction, not only is the mise-en-scène much more dense than on stage and more equal in status to the actors as part of the total image, but mobile framing and editing between simultaneous spaces combine to retell and resell Shakespeare in terms of the performance of the image. The tensions of reproducing Shakespeare through the visual alterity of the cinematic medium can be seen in the strikingly divisive endings of recent film adaptations that reframe the ending and produce multiple spaces in which it takes place. In the recent box-office hit adaptation of *Romeo and Juliet, Shakespeare in Love*, the filmically realistic world of Elizabethan London is set dialectically against, yet often merges with, the theatrical space where the play is rehearsed and performed, thereby providing for a parallel story line, and a reopening of the question, after the first successful performance of Romeo and Juliet is over and the title characters are dead, "How is this to end?" (Norman and Stoppard, 1998, 149).

A play's ending is central and defining to how it is remembered (and the reproduction of that ending to how a production or adaptation will be remembered). To audiences participating in the reenactment of the play, it is the anticipated point of arrival, but while current film adaptations often reproduce the known ending as a highly ritualized event, the ritual is threatened with disruption or displaced by the counteraction of alternative, surprise endings. Prolonged, intense stillness surrounds the famous and familiar last moments of Gielgud speaking Prospero's epilogue in Peter Greenaway's *Prospero's Books* (1991), Hamlet's dying speech in Kenneth Branagh's version of the play (1996), and Romeo and Juliet's separate approaches to death in Baz Luhrmann's *Romeo + Juliet* (1996). This stillness solemnizes, not only the deaths and farewells of the characters, but the closure of the ritual of rewatching these plays. Marking the space, or more precisely the setting, of the ending, the long runways that frame the spectator's view of the characters in all three films function as a symbol for the ritual progression to the end. Above all, there is the repeated use of an unusually long take, with a very slow track-and-crane out from the scene to a long shot. This kind of shot deliberately protracts the moment of the spectator's final gaze, creating and indulging in a scene of visual farewell, for instance, in Luhrmann's crane shot of the dead lovers. The extravagant flooding of the image with candle flames in this scene, the clapping of the actors in *Prospero's Books*, and the soundtracks of all these films self-consciously produce, and invoke the spectator's conscious consumption of, the ending *as* a ritual of memory, nostalgia, and farewell.[1]

Stephen Heath points out that the long shot is a "master shot" derived directly from quattrocento codes of perspective, which center the spectator as the subject of an ideal vision: "The long shot . . . in classical narrative cinema . . . subsequently develops as the constant figure of this embracing and authoritative vision, providing the conventional close to a film, the final word of its reality" (1986, 384). While Luhrmann's shot does produce an idealized image of the lovers' death, this idealization is placed at an unrealistically high angle above the lovers (as it is throughout this scene), creating a sensational effect that increases as the camera rises. The shot destabilizes the authoritative, unified vision of *Romeo and Juliet* by drawing attention to the spectator's access to, and indeed constituting the excess of, spectacle from that particular viewing position in the scene. Heath cites Edward Branigan on the disturbance created by this kind of camera position: "To the extent that the camera is located in an 'impossible' place, the narration questions its own origin, that is, suggests a shift in narration" (Heath, 1986, 401). In this instance, "the impossible place" represents the pleasure of reenvisioning the scene: The only movements to continue the event are the camera's ever-so-slow withdrawal and the flickering of the recapitulatory images, and these together change that event of the lovers' deaths to the scene of our desire for and in it.

Explicit ritualization in these adaptations, however, neither seals the ending as inviolable nor performs our attachment to it as such but has the reverse effect of confronting the audience with what it expects and desires from watching Shakespeare. These strategies promote a self-consciousness about the desire for ritual reenacting and rewatching, such that desire becomes the field of play to which the tension and excitement of a challenge, a possible rupture to the ritual, is equally vital. In this sense, the scene of ritual closure and the scene of the alternative ending(s) stage a conflict which is not actually a conflict but a metadrama of completing, of our own knowingness. Hence the story line of John Madden's *Shakespeare in Love* (1998) depends quite openly upon the complicities of both our interest that *Romeo and Juliet* be written and successfully staged and our pleasure in the obstacles to its success. In Branagh's *Hamlet*, the repeated cross-cutting from Elsinore to brief, silent images of Fortinbras and his army generates a mounting anxiety, at first undefined but later crystallizing in a real threat to the ending as a vast battalion runs down the avenue toward Elsinore and assaults it, while so much remains yet uncompleted in the last scene taking place inside it. The continuous disruption of and return to the scene of the play's ending here constitute the rhythm of a confrontation between not only the text and its performance but the mediums of theatre and cinema. What is interesting in Branagh's reproduction of another ending to *Hamlet* is his expansion of another space, outside Elsinore, one that ostensibly provides the plot with a historical "context of utterance" closer to home but which makes itself felt as the cinematic and cultural space of the scale and spectacle of Hollywood historical epics. The cut from Horatio's farewell to Hamlet to the second story gallery as Fortinbras's soldiers crash through the windows in mass synchrony, SS style, clearly presents a spatially divided scene and the invasion of Hollywood spectacle into the play's ending. Thus the climax as it is reproduced is that of the competition between these two scenes of very different fulfilment, Hamlet's and Fortinbras's, and the split-second timing of their explosions in a single place. Hamlet's killing of Claudius and his last speech are made partner to, altered by, and ultimately subsumed in the context of Fortinbras's military coup, and this accounts for the strange sense of meta- or intertextual defeat as Fortinbras is crowned and takes over Denmark, a defeat objectified in the smashing of King Hamlet's statue.

To stress that another ending is produced as another space, and an alternative sightline, is to stress the editing of narrative space by which the story is redefined for cinematic cultures of watching. In both Branagh's *Hamlet* and Luhrmann's *Romeo + Juliet*, cross-cutting produces the double vision of "how it might otherwise end" by editing an "unseen" into the original endings. Luhrmann creates the contestational space of a possible alternative ending that would avert the expected tragedy, not by doubling locations as Branagh does, but by breaking up a unified scene into parts in conflict. The editing generates a cliffhanger by alternating between extreme close-ups that split the lovers spatially: When the close-up shows us Juliet's face stirring, Romeo is out of the frame putting the ring on her hand, and when it shows her fingers moving, Romeo is again off-screen at her face.[2] Thus the mechanism of dramatic irony that turns on Romeo's misapprehension is superceded by one that turns on his missed sight. This supplanting of what he does not know for what he does not see in the kind of tragic mistake made performs cinema's ingenious extension or appropriation of the verbal in the terms of the visual. But it also abandons the *space of time* between the two events of Romeo's death and Juliet's awakening (and the significance of that timing, however close) for the virtuoso effect of splitting the embrace of the lovers' bodies, dislocating a single event spatially. Although stage productions have also merged the two moments,[3] Luhrmann's reproduction of the mistake in terms of the simultaneously artificial and hyper-real close-up parodies the irony of fate with a trick of sight *played by the camera*; it is the build-up of conflict in the stimulus to the spectator's sight, not knowledge, that creates the suspense and delivers the shock of the climax.

The climax to this sequence of alternating close-ups is in fact preemptive, arriving before time at the instant Juliet's eyes snap open to look straight at us, intensely and abnormally close. The physical shock of her sudden awakening at such close range, the possibility that she may be just in time to change the ending, and the unexpected citation of Zeffirelli's version (1968), which used the same extreme close-up of Juliet's eyes to capture her reaction when Romeo catches her hand, combine to rupture the membrane of the screen separating seer and spectacle by "returning the gaze" and so exposing the spectator's watching.[4] In the conflated look of different Juliets (Shakespeare's, Luhrmann's, Zeffirelli's, our own), the spectator's part of remembering the play, while desiring a difference, is confronted and thus performed into the scene of reproduction. This direct, close-up meeting of the character's eyes with the spectator's occurs at crucial points in almost all the endings of recent adaptations, as an inevitable fold in the visual renarration at which the spectator becomes object, is included in the field of the spectacle.

One of the chief difficulties of discussing the looking structures in (and of applying theories of the gaze to) situations of cinematic watching is that the camera's eye cannot be taken as the spectator's: Its point of view is always as *if* it were our own and is not seamlessly joinable or fully identifiable with the spectator's own sense of seeing. The camera's eye has the double function of both presenting to our eyes and pretending to be our eyes, and this break or hinge in the jointure between the camera's point of view and the spectator's seeing is particularly felt when we are made to see against the grain. In the cinematic reproduction of Shakespeare, the camera is almost obliged to discomfort the spectator's sight as part of the difference of reperformance that it asserts. But the specific difference which the eye of the camera stands to make to the always intertextualized watching of Shakespeare is that it positions, and indeed creates, subject–object relations of viewing for the spectator: Just as reproduction looks back at us through Juliet's eyes in Luhrmann's film, it can enforce an alienated subjectivity through point-of-view shots. The closing moments of Branagh's film circulate the exchange of looks through Fortinbras's point of view, where the spectator alternately adopts Rufus Sewell's cold gaze around Elsinore and is in turn stared straight back at (and quite menacingly, too). The looking structures perform against the grain of the viewer's subjective identification with Hamlet in the space of the ending and produce the outsider and contender—for the throne and the ending—as the focal point, the subject matter.[5] Fortinbras's gaze is another sightline, which acts to change the place where events have ended by looking at them differently, but that direct, confrontational difference in point of view is threateningly opaque in that it is narratively inaccessible, unsecured by, and more than, the plot entails—in fact, taking its place.

Branagh's film returns to and ends at the cinematic space outside Elsinore: Following a dissolve that subtly transforms the image of Hamlet's body into one dressed for his state burial, the camera slowly tracks back and up to reveal the unexpected, enormous spectacle of amassed mourners in black arrayed outside Elsinore, at the same time gradually losing sight of Hamlet. This movement away from the scene of the play's end is pronounced and self-conscious in the films of Luhrmann, Greenaway, and Madden as well. Whereas Shakespeare usually leaves the characters' return undramatized, as the expected closure deferred until after the play has ended, the movement of images forms a visual crossing back, a passage of exit out from the place of the story. Its changes of the scene or place of the ending appear to proffer a new framework for capturing the play, that is, to use space as context and to effect that crossing as a connecting with scenes of habitual contemporary viewing. So Branagh re-places *Hamlet* in the Hollywood epic depicting the fall of regimes, and Luhrmann relocates *Romeo and Juliet* in a news broadcast on TV. However, the successive and conspicuous reframing or revisualizing of the space where the film ends does not so much resituate the scene as displace it because the cinematic stylishness with which images of a changing narrative space are crossed and joined, especially through mobile framing and dissolves, puts the performance of transition itself on display. When the process of editing becomes the primary action in this way, the scenes become illusionistic, screen spaces rather than representations of a real context, defined by their dissolving into and disruption of each other and by the visual pleasure and surprise of their combination.

As one might expect, it is the figure (not the idea) of the author that provides Shakespearean film adaptations with both a subject and site for transforming the ending in the correlative of his creative imagination. Greenaway's *Prospero's Books* maps its close onto the author's, while Madden's *Shakespeare in Love* closes with Shakespeare's affirmation of his art; these two films offer a neat contrast between how the image of Shakespeare takes its place in the narration that ends at the ending, and at the beginning, of the author. In Greenaway's final long take, the camera tracks slowly out from a close-up on Gielgud-as-Prospero-as-Shakespeare's face speaking the epilogue in what appears to be the ending, but as the camera moves out, his face is surprisingly disclosed and reframed as a two-dimensional image on a screen. This movement recontains the actor-dramatist's art within the filmmaker's and *makes space* in front of that screen-within-a-screen for the "live" eruption of three-dimensional images that break up and obscure the long farewell shot on it. Greenaway thus returns the plenitude of seeing to the spectator, after it had apparently been shed in the stripped-bare image of Gielgud's face and invokes our pleasure in the renewal of "magical" sight when Ariel dives into sudden water. As counteraction to the relinquishment of art, Greenaway's visual magic here takes over from Prospero's and Shakespeare's. This sequence is a virtuoso display of cinematic showmanship that is unsecured by narrative motivation, unlike Prospero's or Shakespeare's arts; it is a metaperformative rejection of the return at the end of *The Tempest* through a reassertion of the action of the magic eye of what cannot any longer be called the camera because it does not mediate objects as images but generates them. So even as the running of the child Ariel into our gaze to leap out of the frame prompts our uncomplicated identification with his joy, the increasingly slowed motion defines that pleasure of anticipation in terms of the artifice by which it is prolonged, expanded, and arrested. The story is superceded by the art—or the technology.

In *Shakespeare in Love*, the tragic ending of the play is a success in the real life of the film, and the tragic ending in real life is deflected into the start of a comedy. This circle of tragedy and comedy that turns life back into art and endings into beginnings is accomplished by revolving between three scenes that dissolve continuously into each other: the writer Will Shakespeare at his desk, his words being written on the page, and the underwater vision of his imagination. The effect of these dissolves is not merely to merge different scenes but to treat the cinematic screen as literally a screen that absorbs and merges other mediums of representation and action: the picture-perfect Shakespeare, writing on the page, water. More precisely, the screen converts the different physical natures of these mediums into the common currency of the cinematic image by drawing attention to their framing and filming—only the camera can show action underwater. In the visual match of the parchment and blank beach, they become merging images of a ground onto which the tiny figure of Viola materializes in front of the huge colon being written after her name. While the sequence seems directed toward a narrative epilogue, the merging mediums in fact persuade the spectator out of the need to conclude and into an imaginary circle starting afresh: The voice-over of the author narrating the prelude to *Twelfth Night* as a "new beginning" for Viola uses Miranda's words at the opening of *The Tempest* to integrate the scenes of Shakespeare's last play with his first as a professional. Thus the rhythms of the music and editing track a passage out of this adaptation's story that is actually a recursive starting again. Indeed, *Shakespeare in Love* returns to Naples in a celebratory fashion by beginning all over again where Prospero and Shakespeare ended, at the new place that is also the old one of Illyria, Prospero's island, America.[6]

In these film adaptations of Shakespeare, the action of visual metamorphosis replaces plot conclusion and resolution as the end of cinematic reproduction. This transformative drive seems both inescapable and confounding: It satisfies the compound imperatives to metamorphosis exerted by the cinematic medium, the differences of culture, the reauthorizing and reengagement of the story. In short, it represents the desire to say—or rather to show and see—something more as the end of the story. At the same time, the dissolves, reframings, and visual matches resist or avoid conclusion by reflexively deferring the placing of the story onto the medium of representation: the virtual space of the cinematic, televisual, or electronic image.

In the metanarrative of our relation to Shakespeare, what might otherwise be perceived as a fictional space in which the story concludes transforms into a virtual one in which such conclusions change form or format, not shift ground. In an alternative ending to the film, packaged with the collector's series release of *Shakespeare in Love*, Viola is met on the beach by two men, one white, one black, to whom she speaks her first line in *Twelfth Night*, "What country is this, friends?" and they answer, "This is America"; her reply is "Well then, good." Yet another ending was scripted but not filmed in which she moves past the line of trees blocking our vision at the shore to discover behind them the gleaming towers of Manhattan.[7] These alternatives, like a shadow behind the ending released, manifest what we already know in retrospect, that the film arrives at America—the Academy Awards, to be precise. More significantly, the proliferation of endings and the choice to leave "another shore" unnamed indicates the reluctance to form and fix a framing image of our space for Shakespeare's play or the reproduction of it. The transformative movements, then, take the place of any concrete representation of our context for remaking Shakespeare. Yet they also represent the effort to break the limits of a defining position. Walter Benjamin notes that "with the close-up, space expands; with slow motion, movement is extended. . . . Evidently a different nature opens itself to the camera than opens to the naked eye—if only because an unconsciously penetrated space is substituted for a space consciously explored by man" (1992, 229–30). In an ambivalent relation to this "different nature" of virtual space, each of these four films rejects dimensionality in favor of a flat two-dimensional image for the closing shot: Branagh's blocks, Luhrmann's television screen, Madden's beach, Greenaway's map, all present the end point of adaptation as a surface which seals off the spectator's interaction *in* any space at the level of the gaze.

Notes

1. The violins of Patrick Doyle's soundtrack are particularly noticeable in Branagh's *Hamlet* during all the key speeches of the play, marking out their value and evoking a nostalgic response to them.

2. This tactic of alternating close-ups is repeated in the second cliffhanger scripted into the ending in the screenplay, which was not part of the film released, where Father Lawrence nearly succeeded in getting the gun from Juliet and forestalling her suicide (Pearce and Luhrmann, 1996, 159–60).

3. In the Royal Shakespeare Theatre's production in 1976, with Ian McKellen and Francesca Annis in the title roles, Juliet began to move her hand over Romeo's back, unnoticed by him, as he held her in his arms during his dying kiss.

4. The notion of the "returned gaze" has been extensively theorized, especially by Merleau-Ponty, Lacan and Sartre, in terms of the otherness it produces in the subjective act of seeing, and some discussions of the relations between spectacle and spectator have adapted theories of the gaze to the situations of performance. Elizabeth Klaver for instance discusses how "the exchange of an object for a subject in the

spectacle that looks back . . . unmasters the privilege of viewing the world (or visual art) as a representation, but also catches up the relations between viewer and viewed in a performative modality"(1995, 312).

5. Russell Jackson's "Film Diary" records Rufus Sewell's performative appearance in this scene—"looks as though he really wants it, but knows it's easily won. Intense eyes, darkly handsome, calmly self-assertive"—and Branagh's remark, "No glam spared on this film" (Jackson, 1996, 197).

6. The last long shot, held throughout the titles, is scripted in the screenplay as "DISSOLVE slowly to VIOLA walking away up the beach towards her brave new world" (Norman and Stoppard, 1998, 155).

7. I am indebted to Russell Jackson, the production's textual advisor, for this information.

Works Cited

Benjamin, Walter. 1992. "The Work of Art in the Age of Mechanical Reproduction." In *Illuminations*, ed. Hannah Arendt, 211–44. Trans. Harry Zohn. London: Fontana.

Branagh, Kenneth, dir. 1996. *Hamlet*. Castle Rock.

Greenaway, Peter, dir. 1991. *Prospero's Books*. Miramax Films.

Heath, Stephen. 1986. "Narrative Space." In *Narrative, Apparatus, Ideology*, ed. Philip Rosen, 379–420. New York: Columbia University Press.

Jackson, Russell. 1996. "Film Diary." In *Kenneth Branagh*, Hamlet *by William Shakespeare: Screenplay and Introduction*, 179–213. London: Chatto and Windus.

Kermode, Frank. 1967. *The Sense of an Ending*. Oxford: Oxford University Press.

Klaver, Elizabeth. 1995. "Spectatorial Theory in the Age of Media Culture." *NTQ* 11 (44): 309–21.

Luhrmann, Baz, dir. 1996. *William Shakespeare's Romeo + Juliet*. Twentieth Century Fox.

Madden, John, dir. 1998. *Shakespeare in Love*. Miramax Films.

Norman, Marc, and Tom Stoppard. 1998. *Shakespeare in Love*. New York: Hyperion.

Pavis, Patrice. 1988. "From Text to Performance." In *Performing Texts*, ed. Michael Issacharoff and Robin F. Jones, 86–100. Philadelphia: University of Pennsylvania Press.

Pearce, Craig, and Baz Luhrmann. 1996. *William Shakespeare's* Romeo + Juliet: *The Contemporary Film, the Classic Play*. New York: Bantam Doubleday Dell.

Zeffirelli, Franco, dir. 1968. *Romeo and Juliet*. Paramount Studios.

CHAPTER NINE

~

Pop Goes the Shakespeare: Baz Luhrmann's *William Shakespeare's Romeo + Juliet*

Elsie Walker

Baz Luhrmann's *William Shakespeare's Romeo + Juliet* was number 1 in its first weekend at the United States box office, making US$11.1 million on 1,277 screens. But many critics and reviewers initially dismissed the production, despite (perhaps even because of) its popularity. In the 1998 New Casebooks collection of Shakespeare film essays (edited by Robert Shaughnessy), the film is not mentioned at all whereas subsequently made Shakespeare films (such as Kenneth Branagh's *Hamlet*) are already mentioned in the same breath as the aesthetically significant films directed by Welles, Kozintsev, Olivier, and Kurosawa. The film is a showy, audacious, often irreverent and playful appropriation of its Shakespearean source, so perhaps it was bound to prompt scepticism. The film is often measured against "the book"—Richard Burt, for example, condemns the spectacular, "dumbed-down" style of the film made "so teenagers can easily follow the plot": Insofar as the film has a message, it's not at all clear what use Shakespeare is in getting it across (1998, 230–31).[1] Crystal Downing (2000) defends the inventiveness of the film because it brings out "subtleties of Shakespeare's script"—however, rather than exploring the film as a new iteration of the text, the film is measured by the degree to which it brings out the latent qualities of Shakespeare's play (126). While Downing points out that "simulations of Shakespeare are always already simulacrums," she argues that the film nevertheless "works in the spirit of Shakespeare" (2000, 126, 130). So even when the film is defended and praised, it is accorded little "authority" in its own right. Rather than attempting to establish the film's credentials as a "faithful" representation of Shakespeare's play, I will examine the immediacy and sense of urgency in the film as a kind of social document. I will explore how the explicit film intertextuality and the postmodern mise-en-scène of Romeo + Juliet prompts an active and complex response hovering between detachment and engagement.

Most of the criticism of Luhrmann's Romeo + Juliet to date dismisses the production as "MTV Shakespeare": the kind of mindless visual candy we associate with rock videos. In an article for the Guardian newspaper, "Wherefore Art Thou, Will?" Gary Taylor (1999) claims that Luhrmann's film was a straightforward marketing exercise and, along with CD-ROM and Internet Shakespeare sites, "does not really expand the Shakespearean domain" but provides another alternative, popular way to satisfy existing markets (appealing to teenagers who must, apparently against their will, read Shakespeare in school) (4). Taylor describes the film as a vehicle for "easy access" to Shakespeare's work and places the film in the context of an argument that Shakespeare's status and the scholarly level of attention given his work is falling dramatically (1999, 4). Taylor implicitly assumes that Luhrmann's film provokes nothing but a passive response. Like MTV videos, the film contains a bombardment of imagery and music; it is a postmodern assault of the senses. But, I argue, the film demands more than a passive response.

Although many commentators have, like Taylor, described Luhrmann's Romeo + Juliet as an MTV production in a pejorative, negative way, an examination of the complexity of MTV videos offers reasonable parallels for the film. Will Straw (1993), for example, analyzes the characteristic stylistic heterogeneity of MTV videos. Straw writes that because most MTV videos are shaped by intertextuality, collections of anachronistic quotes, there is a tendency to see the "appropriation of historical styles and codes as a process of decontextualisation, as part of the diminishing of a sense of historical time within an endless present" (1993, 18). The resonance of artifacts or styles of the past become less important than the gesture of mixing or recontextualizing them in a clever way. Straw outlines a common, Jamesonian approach to postmodern, MTV productions: "In the absence of a style which . . . fully can be said to express the present, the attractiveness of styles which seem to embody the historical fullness of the past increases. At the same time, it is the plenitude of this embodiment, rather than the specific qualities of the historical moment, which threaten to become the important criteria" (18). In other words, the display of "ingenuity and connoisseurship" becomes more important than the specific resonance of the allusions made; style becomes more important than substance. Instead, Straw advocates a consideration of MTV's play with plundering the past as a "renegotiation of a relationship with its own history" (17). Similarly, Luhrmann describes his *Romeo + Juliet* as a response to doublet-and-hose Shakespeare, as an aggressive attempt to "reclaim" Shakespeare for an MTV generation.

Andrew Goodwin points out that MTV videos and programs are often described, like Luhrmann's film, as quintessentially postmodern products, as manifestations of "fragmentation, segmentation . . . stylistic jumbling, the blurring of mediation and reality, the collapse of the past and the future into the moment of the present, the elevation of hedonism . . . the intertextual fusion of 'high' and pop art" (1993, 45).[2] Both Goodwin and Will Straw also argue that MTV videos combine the conservative as well as the subversively challenging. These critics challenge the common assumption that MTV videos and the institution of MTV is only about pointless playfulness. Goodwin cites some specific examples:

> During its broadcast of the "Make a Difference" rock concert in the Soviet Union in August 1989, [MTV] repeatedly used the slogan "COOL MUSIC, NOT COLD WAR." And in January 1992 MTV screened Public Enemy's video "By the time I get to Arizona" with the stated intention of foregrounding that group's concerns about Arizona's non-observance of Martin Luther King's birthday. The clip, which intercut reconstructions of episodes from King's life with fictional footage of Public Enemy and its entourage assassinating white officials from Arizona, was a trenchant statement of black militancy which offended and upset many liberals. (1993, 63)[3]

This analysis of MTV production is also useful when considering Luhrmann's film: MTV and *Romeo + Juliet* are both "*ultimate* example[s] of commodification . . . of textual and psychological schizophrenia . . . and of new forms of resistance" (Grossberg, 1993, 185, original italics). Luhrmann's film, made for a comparatively small budget in Hollywood (about $25 million), was a massive box-office success. It was aggressively marketed though the two soundtrack compact discs, clothing and paraphernalia, a screenplay/play text edition, an interactive CD-ROM, and a sophisticated official website with downloadable extracts (Twentieth Century Fox, 1996). The film is "Shakespeare" with fiercely glamorous, designer flair: from the fashionable costumes, to the sleekly designed guns. While the film cannot be connected with a particular social event like the aforementioned MTV videos, I argue that the aggressive marketing, the commercial success of Luhrmann's

Romeo + Juliet, does not preclude the film's possible sophistication, its complexity, and its possible subversive social significance and resonance. Like MTV, the film is an audaciously beautiful and aggressive bombardment, an ironic fusion of old and new, a strange combination of Romantic nostalgia and postmodern style.

I should point out that the film was given more serious attention in a series of nine papers at the Shakespeare on Screen: The Centenary Conference in Benalmàdena, Spain, in September 1999. However, in open panel discussions, most commentators were critical of the conflict between postmodernist form and romantic sentiment in Luhrmann's film, calling it, at worst, a "weakness" and, at best, an "unsatisfactory contradiction." Such arguments do, it seems to me, miss the point. The presentation of irreconcilable opposites shapes Luhrmann's film. The central, unresolvable, and poignant tension is between postmodern notions of destructive fragmentation represented in the mise-en-scène and a romantic yearning for the certainty of positive absolutes represented by Romeo and Juliet. I believe this tension partly explains the extraordinary popularity and resonance of the film text as part of a broad social vision.

Romeo + Juliet is highly energetic, rhythmically quick, arresting cinema. Scenes and speeches are broken down into digestible snippets and sequences; their impact is created/supported/offset by visual paraphrases, music, and camerawork. In their screenplay, Pearce and Luhrmann (1996) allow themselves the interpretive flexibility that Dennis Kennedy and Anthony Davies ascribe to foreign directors working on Shakespeare in translation (Davies, 1988; Kennedy, 1993). The preservation of Shakespeare's dialogue loses preeminence. As James N. Loehlin writes (though in reference to Richard Loncraine's *Richard III*), "The inventive insouciance with which the film treats individual characters, scenes, and images makes it a consistently engaging riff on Shakespeare's dialogue, which it plays off against a number of other signifying systems." In Loehlin's words, the film is "a pattern of interwoven and overlapping visual codes" derived from both "high" and "low" (popular) culture (1997b, 68).

As with Loncraine's *Richard III*, due to the considerable cutting of the dialogue, characters like Mercutio, Lady Capulet, Capulet, and Paris do not have much time to develop. Each character is "fleshed out" through the cinematic shorthand of intertextual, visual associations. The languid movements, thick theatrical makeup, and slight southern drawl of Lady Capulet (Diane Venora), for example, simultaneously evoke Madonna, Elizabeth Taylor, and Vivien Leigh as Blanche Dubois. The costumes designed by Kym Barrett are particularly suggestive. Mercutio (Harold Perrinneau), wearing the bright red, sequinned dress of a drag queen to the Capulet ball, is imaged as existing on the social fringe. This suggests the subversiveness of Mercutio's character: the costume emblematically reflects his position as a kind of out-cast, seen as outrageous and seldom taken seriously. Filmmaker Zeffirelli com-pares Mercutio to Hamlet in the way that he is set apart from his people, em-bodying the anguish of Verona (1990). In Luhrmann's *Romeo + Juliet*, we see Mercutio on the beach, evoking Hamlet by literally taking arms against a sea of troubles, firing his gun into the sea. The Capulet ball of the film is a costume party where each character's costume serves as an analogue for their aspirations: Paris, being establishment minded, wears the space gear of an en-thusiastic astronaut—his immaculate dress, pronounced jaw, and squeaky-clean smile suggest privilege and vacuousness; Lady Capulet wears the gaudy get-up of a Cleopatra, which suggests her histrionic desire for tragic grandeur; Capulet (Paul Sorvino) wears the Caesaric robes of an august patriarch, sug-gesting his desire for tyrannical control over wife, family, and company; Romeo (Leonardo DiCaprio) wears the romantic armour of a knight; and Juliet (Claire Danes) wears the feathered wings of an earth-bound angel. The lovers are imaged as icons of a bygone era—they represent the kind of ideal-ism that is unsustainable in the postmodern world of the film.

The references to other films within *Romeo + Juliet* (another form of cin-ematic shorthand) highlight the different paces, rhythms, genres that Luhrmann finds in the single play: from the action movie whips, pans, zooms of the first showdown to the lingering, tight close shots of the central couple. In this way Luhrmann challenges Seymour Chatman's claim that "the cam-era, poor thing, is powerless to invoke tone" (Chatman, 1992, 415). This postmodern film is set apart from many other Shakespeare films because it "quotes" various films of diverse genres in a highly self-conscious way.[4] But Luhrmann and his team "sold" the idea to Twentieth Century Fox (in 1994–1995) as a "straightforward" youth film, featuring (then-rising) teen idol Leonardo DiCaprio.[5] (DiCaprio was flown to Sydney to film some clips with Luhrmann as part of the process—the clips were then presented to Fox executives.) The studio was persuaded to invest about US$15 million (the film cost around $25 million in the end)—although this is a relatively small budget for a Hollywood production, Luhrmann says this is "an enormous amount for Shakespeare" as far as major studios are concerned. Selling the idea to the studio was a question of pinpointing the desired youth audience. So the studios sold the film "very precisely as a youth market picture." Luhrmann is, however, careful to distinguish between the methods employed by Twentieth Century Fox to sell the film and his own directorial attempt to bring disparate elements together in one energetic film, to appeal to a wide audience. Luhrmann wanted to reflect "Shakespeare's lyrical, romantic, sweet, sexy, musical, violent, rude, rough, rowdy, rambunctious storytelling" with eclectic storytelling and diverse generic references (Brook et al., 1998, 48).

The other films directed by Luhrmann, *Strictly Ballroom* (1992) and *Moulin Rouge* (2001), are similarly eclectic. *Strictly Ballroom* includes documentary-style footage, one-reel archives, and stylized flashbacks in a story (not unlike Romeo and Juliet) about a pair of dancers who decide to "dance their own steps": Rather than adhering "to the book," the couple (Fran and Scott) perform at national championships with a breathtaking, showy routine, a snub to the conservatives of the Australian ballroom dancing federation. Luhrmann's "showy" *Romeo + Juliet* may be read as a similar rejection of stale, "by-the-book," traditional, or reverential approaches to Shakespeare. *Moulin Rouge* is a musical about a fashionable, bohemian club in Paris at the turn of the twentieth-century: The "millennium spirit" of 1999–2000 is imposed on the belle epoque through the Moulin Rouge in the film, which also "raises the spectre of Studio 54." *Moulin Rouge* is not only inspired by "classic" Hollywood musicals but also "nineteenth-century opera and literature and everything from Georges Méliès's primitive fantasy films to rave culture" (Fuller, 2001, 7). Before making the film, Luhrmann and his team "did an archaeological dig through the history of the musical. What we found is that the stories don't change, but the way in which you tell them does" (Fuller, 2001, 7). In all three films, postmodernity (generic eclecticism and playful anachronisms) is "balanced" by an idealistic, mythical, unifying, "timeless" vision of love.

I interviewed Baz Luhrmann on 9 July 2000 to find out about the process of conceptualizing, making, and marketing *Romeo + Juliet*. I should emphasize that although I was speaking to Luhrmann alone, he almost always spoke of collaborative visions and processes rather than referring to his own personal vision and input. He also spoke of the many script revisions and the reshoots of scenes within the film. So, I interpret his statements as more than the reflection of a predetermined, singular "author's" or "auteur's" perspective—he presented his views self-consciously as a representative of many people who participated in the evolution of the film.[6] Luhrmann's team researched for the film for two years: They were inspired by the generic heterogeneity of Elizabethan plays in particular, the combination of low comedy "cut with high tragedy and popular song" on the Elizabethan stage. Luhrmann's description of Elizabethan stage and theatre practice, as a result of this research, is both playful and idealistic, both demystificatory and mystificatory:

Shakespeare didn't think, "Well I'm doing a tragedy, so it must all be in a certain color and a certain rhythm." . . . Shakespeare was writing for a large audience next to the bear-baiting and the prostitution, who are mainly drunk, incredibly violent, and unbelievably noisy. He had to shut them up with jokes and *then* hit them with an emotional twist. Our *cinema* audience is much closer to his audience than an audience in a theatre today. They're a rowdy, noisy bunch who aren't going to be easily won over. So, we had to use the same aggression of device to shut them up.

This refreshingly "irreverent" view of the Elizabethan theatre is behind the energy, noise, and vibrant colors of *Romeo + Juliet*. Luhrmann and his team also included explicit allusions to many other popular films to arrest the audience's attention:

When Romeo's out in the desert, we're specifically quoting *Giant*, the James Dean film. The way Leonardo looks is a combination of Kurt Cobain and James Dean. . . . We spent a good year researching social and economic realities of the Elizabethan world, then translated them into a tear sheet of twentieth-century images.

In my interview, Luhrmann was determined to "authorize" the film by identifying a series of parallels between Elizabethan theatre and modern film audiences, between the form of Elizabethan plays and postmodern films, between early modern and modern societies. Identifying such parallels is perhaps a mystificatory move. However, Luhrmann was also determined to undermine and demystify the "revered" image of "Shakespeare": "the 'great Shakespeare' of the nineteenth-century—big sets, pantaloons, Leslie Howard climbing up a big piece of scenery." Luhrmann was determined to present the play with a sense of political and social urgency, to make the play "speak" to a wide audience. The film is seldom subtle in its effects and it's often described pejoratively as "accessible," "simplistic," as an example of, to use David Bordwell's often-quoted phrase, the prevalent, "excessively obvious" Hollywood cinema (Bordwell, Staiger, and Thompson, 1985, 3). But if we take Luhrmann's word, the film was not designed to condescend to its audience. Instead, Luhrmann argues that the film was made for a demanding, savvy audience:

It's more than just "funky Shakespeare." Shakespeare wrote for everyone, from the street-sweeper to the Queen of England, they all had to get it. And it's why I revere him so much as a storyteller because he was dealing with a supremely alive, real audience, who *had* to be absolutely and totally arrested into the story. They didn't come quietly.

For Luhrmann, the key thing is to recapture the vitality of Shakespeare's own theatres and the democratic appeal of the plays.[7] Above all, Luhrmann aims to emulate "Shakespeare" as a democratic, self-conscious, and "rapacious" story-teller. Ironically, Luhrmann's approach to adapting Shakespeare automatically alienated many of those most familiar with Shakespeare. Barbara Hodgdon writes about the "expectational texts" we bring to films of Shakespeare's plays: "private notions about the play and about performed Shakespeare, notions that I might not even recognise until I find them denied" (1983, 143). I suggest that the very audacity, popularity, immediacy, and accessibility of Luhrmann's *Romeo + Juliet* (taking considerable "liberties" with the text in the cuts and emendations made, representing the "democratic," rapacious combination of "high" [Shakespeare] and "low" [pop] allusions), has alienated many critics because it defies certain "expectational texts." As Michael Hattaway puts it, "all styles are equal" in this film, popular film allusions and Wagner's "Liebestod" are brought together in an unconventional way, "hierarchies are destroyed" (2000, 225).[8]

The "democratic" storytelling of *Romeo + Juliet* is anchored by allusions to other, diverse, popular films incorporated to draw in a wide audience. When watching a stage production, the audience must, in Anthony Davies's words, "play the game of theatre," investing a specific and defined area with special significance: "Our entering into complicity with the stage director and the actors is a crucial element" (Davies, 1988, 6). The play with film intertextuality in *Romeo + Juliet* prompts a similar response. Each shift in "genre" requires an imaginative shift on the part of the audience in complicity with the film director. Often the self-conscious camp cheekiness of the film invites its viewers to be detached onlookers, sitting back and enjoying the way in which Luhrmann "makes sense" of Shakespeare's verse in a nineties popular culture context. But more often, especially after the scenes of Mercutio's death, we are encouraged to sit forward, to be caught up in the action.

Within the opening moments of the film, a television screen frames a newscaster who delivers the prologue in the same calm tone, the false friendly attitude in which we are accustomed to hearing the news of modern life tragedies. The use of the television frame within the cinematic frame immediately makes our role as screen audience very self-conscious.[9] We are then "introduced" to the characters: each main character is shown in medium close-up facing the camera and their names and relationships to each other simultaneously appear in bold beside their faces ("Lady Capulet: Juliet's mother," "Mercutio: Romeo's best friend," for example). This may be an allusion to the opening sequence of Cukor's *Romeo and Juliet* where the characters are presented in framed head-and-shoulder portraits alongside their names. But in Cukor's film there is an important difference: During the sequence of "introductions," a small image of Shakespeare can be seen at the bottom right of the screen, providing the "stamp of authority." By contrast, the beginning of Luhrmann's *Romeo + Juliet* is more playful, obviously parodic, marking (even flaunting!) its difference from the way Shakespeare's plays are "traditionally" presented. The characters of Luhrmann's film are introduced to us like the characters of a soap opera. Indeed the materialism and fierce glamour of this Verona reminds me of *Dallas*, *Beverly Hills 90210*, and countless other productions by Aaron Spelling's company. The evocation of soap operas effects a comic distancing from the action. This "tone" of comic distance is maintained in the next few scenes.

The brawl at the beginning of the play proper is filmed at hysterical pitch. The cinematographer, Donald McAlpine, and the editor, Jill Bilcock, assault the viewer with various cinematic tricks (as loosely outlined in the Luhrmann/Pearce screenplay): impossible point-of-view shots (an extreme close-up of Tybalt's silver-heeled boots), quick cutting of pans, zooms, wipes.[10] The gas station shoot-out is filmed like a Hong Kong spaghetti western combined with *Terminator II*. The scene culminates in a characteristic contemporary action genre device; something potentially destructive moving at great speed is shown in slow motion, to evoke the anticipation of the horror to come—here that moment is when Tybalt draws his weapon upon Benvolio (Arroyo, 1997). The film intertextuality, the self-conscious and amusing allusions to the spaghetti western and the action movie, distances the audience from the action somewhat. This evocation of the worlds of westerns and action movies is chiefly entertainment; we are at a "safe" distance in that what we see is familiar and hermetically sealed off from "reality." The film places us in a privileged position, seeing the characters (as they cannot) locked within recognizable genre frames. The overt, parodic allusions to various generic film templates foregrounds the appropriation of an early modern "classic" with postmodern playfulness. At this point in the film, the self-conscious aesthetic distancing makes us laugh at the action, at the exploits of the Montague and Capulet boys. It allows us, along with the Prince, to temporarily wink at their discords. This cheeky self-consciousness is also manifested in the billboards which dominate certain early scenes: One billboard advertises "Prospero's finest whiskey: the stuff dreams are made of," another advertises a make of gun with the slogan "I am thy Pistol and thy Friend" (from *2 Henry IV* 5.3.93), and another billboard (shown above the Montague boys as they discuss going to the Capulet ball) displays the white words "Wherefore l'amour?" against a red background—the colors and script imitate an advertisement for Coca-Cola. The comedy in these billboards is in the meeting of "high" culture (allusions to Shakespeare) and "low" (popular, commercial) culture. The film is similarly, self-consciously cheeky in the representation of weaponry: the rapiers, swords, and longsword of Shakespeare's text become guns with the words *rapier, sword, longsword* recast as trademarks. Romeo and his mates hang out in a dilapidated pool hall called "the Globe."

Several commentators at the Shakespeare on screen centenary conference assumed that Luhrmann's choice of title, *William Shakespeare's Romeo + Juliet* suggested a claim to authorial authenticity.[11] (Luhrmann revealed in a radio interview that he gave the film that title so that even when audiences saw the wordless images and music of the preview they would still know to expect Shakespearean dialogue in the film [Hill, 1997].) I argue that the film is a more self-consciousness appropriation of Shakespeare's play than this assumption suggests. Rothwell writes that the close-ups on guns with Shakespeare's words *sword* and *longsword* as trademarks are attempts "to slide around an awkward anachronism" (1999, 243). But the film does not merely provide a "neat conceit that gets rid of any historical bumps in the verse" (Anthony Lane cited in Worthen, 1998, 1104) but forces us to "mind the gap" even as it bridges one; the film marks its derivative relationship to an "original," to Shakespeare's *Romeo and Juliet* at the precise moment that it marks its distance from the original conditions under which that play was produced. Luhrmann's *Romeo + Juliet* calls into question the notion of citing *a* text, problematizing straightforward notions of reiterating *Romeo and Juliet* by "placing" the text within a late twentieth-century texture of verbal citation (the billboards which place Shakespeare's lines within the language of commercialism), visual citation (the explicitly intertextual camerawork and mise-en-scène), and musical citation (the eclectic soundtrack, including a parodic punk song called "Pretty Piece of Flesh," also "places" the Shakespearean text in a new way). As Worthen points out, the film invokes and displaces "a textual 'origin'" by performing the text in a specific situational environment that self-consciously draws attention to its own construction, a construction that emphasizes difference and otherness rather than a construction of "transcendent" cultural homogeneity (1998, 1103–4).

However, in the scenes focusing on the interaction between Romeo and Juliet; the barrage of noise, the cheeky billboards and accessories, the noise and bright colors, the explicit and amusing film intertextuality fade into the background. These scenes represent the fantasy of a simpler world of absolutes, of "transcendent," "timeless" love and the certainty of unmediated, "true" contact and intimacy. Close-ups are predominantly used whereas medium and long shots are prevalent in other crowd scenes (including the first brawl). Romeo and Juliet's scenes are suffused with white and blue, with gentleness, moments of silence, the purity of water. The water imagery in the lovers' scenes obviously emphasizes the idealism of their relationship existing within a chaotic, corrupt, and frightening context. Romeo and Juliet believe that they are hermetically sealed off from the rest of Verona, able to guide their own destinies. (The balcony scene where they swim secretly together in a pool while one of the Capulets' armed guards sits nearby epitomizes this.) We are, albeit temporarily, allowed to believe this too: The close-ups draw us into a highly personal, sealed-off world. As in *Strictly Ballroom* and *Moulin Rouge*, the high-spirited central couple wins our admiration by the resilience they show in asserting themselves despite their stifling surroundings.

It is also worth considering the portrayal of Mercutio's death in contrast with the opening brawl. The cheeky metacinematic nature of the first brawl is followed and displaced by a much more frightening duel. In contrast with the camerawork of precise zooms, wipes, and pans featured in the first brawl, the handheld camera circles and jumps unsteadily, chaotically with Romeo, Tybalt, and Mercutio as they fight. The duel takes place by the ruins of an outdoor stage. We were visually introduced to Romeo when he was sitting on this stage "as" rebel without a cause, smoking and writing poetry. We have seen Mercutio dance in drag with his friends (also in costume) on this stage before leaving for the Capulet party. In the second duel scene, after Tybalt stabs him, Mercutio staggers toward the stage, slowly rises, and with a flourish of one hand proclaims "a scratch." As in Zeffirelli's *Romeo and Juliet*, Mercutio's friends momentarily believe they are watching another "performance"; the use of the stage painfully underlines this. Mercutio stumbles from the stage and dies. The retreat into self-conscious pretense is no longer possible. Besides, the stage is literally crumbling. The "reality" of Mercutio's death is the opposite of the hyperreality, the fast cars and flash guns, of the opening brawl. Romeo cries and clutches his friend in his arms, then runs to his car in the distance; we see Benvolio running after Romeo and trying, in vain, to stop his friend leaping into the car. Throughout this sequence the camera maintains a deep focus shot with Mercutio's dead bloody body in the foreground.

Luhrmann's *Romeo + Juliet* emphasizes the tonal shifts which many critics find within Shakespeare's text—the play is, arguably, set apart from the other Shakespeare tragedies in that the action and characters begin in familiar comic patterns and are then transformed to compose the pattern of tragedy. In the final moments of the film, the camera cuts from the lovers' lifeless bodies to show a montage recapitulation of their happy moments together. The montage finishes with a slow-motion shot of them kissing underwater, from the balcony scene—the image suggests they are baptized by the purity of love, that they are "drowning" in the high of love, and it also points to the potential danger in any attempt to escape, to "block out" the outside world. Then the television newscaster delivers the epilogue and the lovers end as they began, the subjects of a rhyming epigram delivered in an emotionless monotone. Their bodies, wrapped in white sheets, are shown being hoisted into an ambulance: the picture is slightly fuzzy suggesting the footage of a documentary or a news broadcast. The kind of comic, self-conscious detachment invoked by the newscaster's delivery of the prologue becomes a poignant reflection on the media's ability to trivialize and, through glib sensationalism, to empty a tragic event of meaning. This performance of the epilogue ironically heightens our sense of the story's grandeur: The discrepancy between the newscaster's summary and the passion we have witnessed is marked.[12]

In a sense *Romeo + Juliet* is two films in one: the metacinematic elements, the profusion of popular culture signifiers set ripples of association in motion, speaking to an audience not necessarily familiar with Shakespeare while the parodic, "irreverent" sequences appear especially surprising and novel for the "initiated," for those with Shakespearean "expectational texts," and for those familiar with the performance history of *Romeo and Juliet*. Various elements of Luhrmann's film (the popular culture references, the symbolism, the setting, music, and camerawork) comprise a composite art of storytelling. The film claims and rewards the attention of viewers while ensuring that they will be alerted to everything they need to know. Zeffirelli's (1990) and Luhrmann's (Pearce and Luhrmann, 1996) treatment of Shakespeare (in their respective screenplays) parallels Shakespeare's treatment of his own sources. As Hapgood points out, Shakespeare was not only a popular artist but also a *popularizer*, transferring "from page to stage and from narrative to drama some of the central writings of his time" (1997, 84). Zeffirelli argues, "Cinema creates a different chemistry with the audience [than theatre] . . . and the attention of the audience moves so fast . . . fantasy gallops in the audience in the movies . . . your mind flashes-flashes-flashes" (Hapgood, 1997, 82). Zeffirelli's and Luhrmann's film versions are similarly bold appropriations of the Shakespearean playtext. Given the similarities between these popular, big-budget films, both of which successfully targeted contemporary young audiences, it is surprising that Zeffirelli rejects Luhrmann's film as emotionally hollow, shaped by compromise, pandering to the youth market: The Luhrmann film didn't update the play, it just made a big joke of it. But apparently the pseudo-culture of young people today wouldn't have digested the play unless you dressed it up that way, with all those fun and games

(Brook et al., 1998). But Luhrmann's *Romeo + Juliet* "places" the Shakespearean play in an aggressively postmodern, disturbing social and multicultural context. I argue that while the film is playful, it is much more than "fun and games."

Luhrmann's *Romeo + Juliet* conveys a *world* of attitudes and tendencies in the succinct accumulation of visual clues. Like the forest of Kurosawa's *Throne of Blood* (1957) or the Elsinore of Kozintsev's *Hamlet* (1964), the world of Luhrmann's *Romeo + Juliet* functions essentially as a concept rather than a particular, "realist" location. In Kurosawa's *Throne of Blood*, the threatening representation of "cobweb" forest—disorienting, jump-cut close-ups of tangled branches glimpsed through foggy filthy air—is a "multi-layered embodiment of the film's thematic substance" (Davies, 1988, 16). Kozintsev argues that it was impossible to "translate" his concept of Elsinore, a place of steel, high walls, state oppression "directly and completely into plastic form. . . . The screen must show separate parts; the general plan can only be imagined. Otherwise, everything seems small, reduced" (Kozintsev, 1967, 266). The high concrete walls of Elsinore are often only partially seen, extending beyond the limits of the frame—they are signs of insidious and oppressive state power pointing to what the spectator cannot see. In watching Kozintsev's film, the spectator is "responsible for assembling not merely a spatial whole, but a *metaphysical* whole which relates to the significance of the action" (Davies, 1988, 21). In a different way, Luhrmann's film demands a similar kind of imaginative positioning from its audience. Signifiers of the modern Western world (emblems of mafia gang-land hostility: guns, fast cars, tattoos; emblems of lurid wealth, of consumer culture, excess and decay: gaudy colors, huge billboards, cheap ostentatious jewelry, a massive cityscape dominated by the skyscrapers of Montague and Capulet) carry a string of associations which constitute a metaphysical whole. But it is not simply a matter of having placed the action in a recognizable, "realistic," nineties world. As José Arroyo (1997) puts it, the film is "set in a 'constructed' world, one that is different enough to allow for different ways of being and knowing, but with enough similarities to permit understanding" (6). Arroyo argues that the film world "which combines the real with the imagined, the past with the present, results in a depiction of time and space which is quasi-mythic." This "mythic" aspect "renders understandable a world where filial duty, religious devotion, family honour and the institution of marriage have an importance that they do not have in ours" (Arroyo, 1997, 6).[13] At the same time, Verona is imaged as a cultural mirror through which the film asks urgent questions about the Western world of the 1990s. This Verona is a place beset by urban

violence, obsessive consumerism, depersonalization, the suffocation of innocence, and faithlessness: patterns of oppression which may be seen in our
modern Western world. It is a world where a regular American girl of Juliet's
age can easily find a gun.

The setting for Luhrmann's *Romeo + Juliet* is especially interesting in comparison with the "safer," "museum-piece," fifteenth-century Italianate settings for Cukor's, Castellani's, and Zeffirelli's films of the same play (dated
1936, 1954, and 1967, respectively). The studio set for George Cukor's
Romeo and Juliet was an expensive attempt at historical "authenticity." The
Hollywood set was designed in detail from carefully selected photographs of
Italian Renaissance architecture. The massive, elaborate "period" sets do
tend to dwarf the characters (perhaps to evoke a world closing in on them).
Similarly, Castellani's film version received acclaim at the Venice Film Fes-
tival because it was "a splendidly colourful reincarnation of fifteenth-century
Italy in Technicolor" (Davies, 1996, 154). The film is filled with "authentic"
architectural and artistic detail without the irony of Loncraine's *Richard III*
(Roger Manvell in Davies, 1996, 156). And the glorious scenery of Zeffirelli's
Romeo and Juliet, designed to evoke "the history and atmosphere of familiar
paintings, . . . belongs firmly in the lineage of the Victorian interpretation
and production of the plays of Shakespeare" (Hamilton, 2000, 119). Despite
the sexiness and violence of Zeffirelli's film, it now appears overly pretty,
more straitjacketed by reverence toward the Shakespearean source than
Luhrmann's version. Of course, ironically, Zeffirelli's film initially prompted
as hostile a response as Luhrmann's film because it appeared too irreverent
and simplistic (Pilkington, 1994).[14] The mise-en-scène of Luhrmann's *Romeo
+ Juliet* is a more frightening, surreal, postmodern collage of decadent, violent, and chaotic images.

The love between Romeo and Juliet is the most "real" thing in a world
made of simulacra, quotations, irony, and parody. One of the most affecting
aspects of this film is that the idealism, purity, sweetness of Romeo and
Juliet's love is offset, defined by the world around them. Objects, the spatial
detail can have in film an anthropomorphic dimension, can have (for Balázs)
a "violent expressive power," an "intense physiognomy" against which the
"human characters pale into insignificance" (Davies, 1988, 9). Luhrmann's
Romeo + Juliet takes this notion to a polemic extension. Indeed, the characters of the film are dwarfed by the profusion of meaningful objects around
them. Every object in the film world is an important component of a "tear-
sheet" of twentieth-century images, which, in Luhrmann's words, "all serve
the story." This does not mean that the film features "fussy" attention to the
slightest period detail, frames cluttered with objects for their own aes-

thetic/historic appeal. The specific attention to details which constitute a believable, metaphysical whole, seems in keeping with Brook's approach to setting Shakespeare:

> "Authenticity" seems to invoke an enormous amount of detailed and painstaking research, devoted to making the film as exact as possible in regard to the surviving records of a period. Now this may be some delight to the historian but has nothing whatever to do with the convincing of an audience. One wants an audience to accept the world in which a story is happening as being . . . something with which they can feel familiar from the moment the film starts. The one place where this is unlikely is a museum. The other danger, "timelessness," is merely the danger of a cop-out; if you don't know enough about a period, or if you don't have clear enough ideas about the atmosphere you want to build up, then you find something so neutral that it amounts to no period and no atmosphere. (Brook cited in Manvell, 1971, 139–40)

The objects in *Romeo + Juliet* may have particular symbolic meaning: for example, the numerous religious icons which ironically foreground the faithlessness of this Verona or the guns which, sleekly designed and seductively photographed, seem almost omnipresent signalling a world driven by hostility. But they also indicate that this Verona is a world of gaudy, oppressive materialism. Paradoxically, the film appears to both revel in and condemn this kind of superficiality.

Some critics have claimed that the aggressive marketing and financial success of the film works against its effectiveness as a critique of late capitalist consumerism. Loehlin, for example, notes the various merchandising tie-ins and the bankable power of DiCaprio (DiCaprio was a rising star at the time the film was made; after the first screenings of *Romeo + Juliet*, he became a major teen idol). After the first chart-topping weekend at the box office, Tom Sherak (then in charge of distribution for Twentieth Century Fox) cried, "If you don't believe this is the greatest love story ever told, look at these numbers" (Loehlin, 1997a, 132). But do the commercial and materialist imperatives and responses to the film necessarily preclude its provocative, even subversive power? Just as the film self-consciously features signs of commercialism (most obviously, by using Shakespearean lines as advertising slogans), it also forms an ironic critique of the kind of corporate enterprise, power, and ingenuity behind its making and marketing. Even as the film represents gaudy materialism and was aggressively marketed, the film evokes a longing for a story beyond corporate imperatives. The impossibility of escaping social realities is played out in the final gorgeous but gaudy, devastating but aesthetically beautiful, final scene. The slim, lifeless figures of Romeo and

Juliet are small amid the elaborately decorated Capulet tomb: large blue and gold neon crosses, a multitude of candles and flowers, rose petals strewn thick across the floor. But Luhrmann told me that he wanted to avoid making the last scene appear too "artificial" and "theatrical." He wanted to make a scene of relative naturalism and simplicity. Originally, he imagined that Juliet would lie in state in a mausoleum. A mock mausoleum studio set was built, but, for Luhrmann, this set simply did not work:

> I kept looking at the set . . . and then I realized that the problem is that mausoleums are theatrical sets. By their very nature they're not naturalistic real rooms; they're like stylized theatrical sets. So . . . we found that very extraordinary church in Mexico with the Jesus on the top—it really exists. . . . The whole end scene was filmed in a church, a real church, and the only stipulation was that we didn't blow Juliet's head off on the altar. (Because we had to shoot on the altar.) So there's a tiny little trickle of CGI blood out of her, but basically, it was shot, all of that, in a real church in Mexico City and we dressed it.

Although Luhrmann hoped to avoid making an "artificial," "theatrical" final scene, the heavily, beautifully decorated church is, arguably, as "unnatural" and "stylized" as Luhrmann's description of a mausoleum. The perfectly placed drop of computer-generated-imagery (CGI) blood and the painterly shots of the lovers during the death scene suggest that Romeo and Juliet cannot escape the "excess," materialism, glamour, the overdecorated, stifling superficiality of the world around them; they cannot escape to a separate, more "pure" space.

In this film, Romeo and Juliet try to define a separate, personal space for themselves within Verona city. If, as Barthes insists, "the city is a discourse and this discourse is truly a language," we should pay close attention to what the city of this film "says" (1976, 92). The setting could be a prototype for imaging a postmodern city as described by the architecture specialist David Harvey.[15] The urban world of this film is a "collage" of highly differentiated spaces and mixtures. This startling, eclectic "collage city" is comprised of the decrepit fairground, the ruined stage, the corporate cityscape flanking an immense statue of Christ, the massive Capulet mansion, which is comprised of Edwardian (a parquet floor, ionic columns, gardens structured into squares) and modern (Juliet's pink bedroom décor, the massive pool and security guard booth) elements. The ruined stage, in particular, prompts a sense of spatial and metaphysical dislocation because it does not seem "real," does not appear as an integral part of the city but rather as an old fragment inserted into a new context. At times, the use of Shakespeare's verse invokes a similar sense of dislocation placed, as it is, in such a modern, eclectic context. In the collage mise-en-scène, in the quoting of various films of diverse genres and the portrayal of the characters themselves (of various nationalities and colors, from the camp black Mercutio, to the Blanche Dubois Lady Capulet), the film presents and alludes to many kinds of cultures, "realities" and "texts" which collide, which interpenetrate explosively.

The film plays upon various different cultural stereotypes to evoke a postmodern world of irreconcilable differences, differences that cannot be elided through a "transcendent" Shakespearean text. Luhrmann does not use the Shakespearean text to authorize a vision of cultural homogeneity as seen in, say, Kenneth Branagh's Shakespeare films. Arroyo (1997) alludes to the "colour-blind casting" in Branagh's *Much Ado about Nothing* (1993), for instance, noting Denzel Washington's "straight" delivery of the Shakespearean text in particular (like Captain Prince in Luhrmann's *Romeo + Juliet*, Washington speaks in the usual received pronunciation and declamatory style expected of Shakespearean actors) (8). Arroyo then notes, with surprise, Harold Perrineau's different, "recognisably black-American inflection" as Mercutio in Luhrmann's film (8). Paul Sorvino (Capulet) and John Leguiziamo (Tybalt) speak with Hispanic accents. As in *West Side Story*, Romeo's family is white and Juliet's family is Hispanic. For Arroyo, this eclecticism makes the film "more relevant to contemporary culture," more "realistic" (even if there is cultural stereotyping involved—Tybalt, for example, imaged in a Matador jacket with pencil-thin moustache and Cuban heels, his angry yet graceful bursts of movement like a flamenco dancer) (8). The "ancient grudge" between the families and the transgressiveness of Juliet's refusal to marry Paris (a Hispanic-looking man selected by her father) are potently and painfully emphasized through these ethnic differences.

Such a representation of different cultures might sound freeing, but in this film, the coexistence of many styles and the evocation of many cultures does not, overall, convey a sense of freedom of expression but overwhelming oppressiveness. What Harvey calls the postmodern "themes" of destructive fragmentation, ephemerality, collage, rapid flux, and chaotic change shape this film (1990, 44, 64). Harvey distinguishes between the "destructive fragmentation" of postmodernist works which may produce chaotic and/or violent effects and the "positive fragmentation" of modernism. T. S. Eliot's modernist poem *The Waste Land* would be, using Harvey's definitions, an example of "positive fragmentation": The "heap of fragments" may, for the reader, collide, interact, and eventually "cohere" in a harmonious whole greater than the sum of its parts. Conversely, the fragments of an eclectic, postmodernist work, like Luhrmann's *Romeo + Juliet*, interact, collide, and remain in conflict rather than present the possibility of some final unification.

The personalized close-up space of Romeo and Juliet is juxtaposed, and is incommensurable, with the space of Verona city. The city is an "antagonistic, voracious world of otherness," where different cultures, texts, architectures, and personalities clash and jostle for supremacy.[16] Metaphysical absolutes, like the love Romeo and Juliet seek to create and preserve, have no place in this world. The close-ups on Romeo and Juliet sometimes "block out" the setting, conveying the search for an illusory fantasy world that takes them and us beyond immediate physical "realities" into pure imagination.

Luhrmann likens DiCaprio as Romeo to a kind of *Rebel without a Cause* (1955) James Dean or a young Marlon Brando in that the character is fighting against many things without exactly knowing what it is he is fighting against.[17] Aspects of the story, as discussed by Luhrmann, are linked to *Rebel* in that Romeo and Juliet are alienated from their elders and, in American teen movie fashion, they are battling against "society." But there is a profound difference between the tone of *Rebel* and Luhrmann's *Romeo + Juliet* because the former does implicitly suggest the possibility of a positive, alternative reality, the resolution of conflicts. In this *Romeo + Juliet*, the possibility of an ultimate positive, in the portrayal of the lovers, is only fleetingly held out. Perhaps DiCaprio's Romeo "doesn't know what he's fighting against" because the forces opposing him and Juliet are too big and multifaceted to be "contained" by being named. There is seemingly no possibility of an absolute enduring "positive" to counteract all the "negatives" of this film world: gangs, drugs, violence, oppressive media, intergenerational conflict, warring corporate owners, faithlessness, destructive fragmentation, racial tensions, chaos, and despair.

Burt (1998) argues that the film represents a "debased" but "commodified" vision of love. He argues that the film *only* represents the commercialization of love and of Shakespeare (he cites the large Coca-Cola-like billboard which reads "Wherefore l'Amour," "as if love were a product like Coke," as well as the billboards featuring slogans from Shakespeare's plays) (230). But if the film subjects love to the logic of late capitalism, I also detect the film's (or at least the director's) desire to break from such postmodern, ironic distancing devices, to celebrate "true" love. This comes through most powerfully, and painfully, in the scenes featuring Romeo and Juliet. Love is finally "a value that remains beyond the market" (Belsey, 1994, 72). As Belsey (1994) writes, "The postmodern condition brings with it an incredulity towards true love" but when it seems that everything else can be bought, love "becomes more precious than before because it is beyond price, and in consequence its metaphysical character is intensified." In postmodern culture love is "infinitely uniquely desirable on the one hand, and conspicuously naïve on the other" (73).[18] After all, post-modernism "repudiates the modernist nostalgia for the unpresentable, in-effable truth of things" (77). In a postmodern Western culture, love is silent (or struggles to be heard) partly because, Belsey (1994) argues, we recognize its banality. How can we capture the extraordinary experience of love when, as Barthes points out, "every other night, on TV, someone says: *I Love you*" (74). The famous story of Romeo and Juliet is littered with overused familiar phrases ("Romeo, Romeo, wherefore art thou Romeo" being the most obvious) which are, through repetition and familiarity, in danger of being (un)heard as worn-out clichés. Repetition obliterates the distinctiveness and integrity of such phrases. Making Juliet deliver her famous balcony scene lines by the Capulet poolside (with Romeo hiding behind her) rather than from the height of a balcony (as in the long tradition of performances) reinvests the lines themselves with some degree of novelty and surprise (Belsey, 1994, 82).[19] Luhrmann's *Romeo + Juliet* repeatedly, self-consciously "places" the familiar Shake-spearean dialogue in new ways.

The Coca-Cola-style billboard which appropriates the most overquoted Shakespearean line as "Wherefore l'amour" playfully points to the way in which Shakespeare's text has been appropriated for the purposes of a finan-cially lucrative feature. The slogan simultaneously, playfully, points to the longing of the film—where can love be found in a world like this, how do we preserve the language of love when it becomes the language of marketing?

Luhrmann's *Romeo + Juliet* confronts the vivid realities of the present. The temporal disjunction between early modern verse and postmodern set-ting works to make strange the familiar, to make new the text(s) we know as *Romeo and Juliet*. The obvious, emphasized disjunction between verse and setting in the film throws the verse *and* its filmic context into a kind of de-familiarizing relief.

Each of the three Bazmark films, *Strictly Ballroom*, *Romeo + Juliet*, and *Moulin Rouge*, attempts to represent absolute love within the context of a postmodern milieu. The self-conscious way this desire is represented in all three films is what makes them disarmingly engaging. This is not the unproblematized, standard ("bottled") romanticism of other Hollywood productions—*Message in a Bottle* (1999) is a conveniently titled example. In-stead, the Bazmark films represent a painful awareness of the elusiveness and the unsustainability of absolutes while, at the same time, willfully celebrat-ing their desirability.

Notes

1. Ignoring the immense popularity of the film (especially among teenagers), Richard Burt (1998) even argues that the production reveals less about youth culture than the way the middle-aged director perceives it. Burt cites the "restatement" of the prologue as an example of the film pandering to a teen audience through repetition.

2. Here, Goodwin uses D. Tetzlaff's description of postmodern art.

3. More recently, at the MTV Europe 2001 awards, Joshua Jackson presented a Free Your Mind Award for T.A.C. (the Treatment Action Campaign). The Free Your Mind Award aims to raise awareness of key social issues and encourage freedom of all kinds from intolerance and injustice around the world. T.A.C. is a South African organization working against multinational drug companies to bring down the price of patented medicine for the many victims of HIV in South Africa. With support from the South African government, T.A.C. smuggled cheap HIV medicine from Thailand into South Africa, and the big drug companies voluntarily lowered their prices in response.

4. In claiming this, I disagree with James N. Loehlin who places Luhrmann's film in the company of other recently released Shakespeare films like Trevor Nunn's *Twelfth Night* or Olivier Parker's *Othello*, which employ "mainstream conventions in a straightforward, unself-conscious way" (Loehlin, 1997b, 67).

5. Unless otherwise stipulated, *all* quotations in this chapter are from my interview with the director on 9 July 2000 at the Bazmark Company House of Iona in Sydney, Australia.

6. Luhrmann worked in closest collaboration with other members of his company, Bazmark Productions: Catherine Martin (production designer), Craig Pearce (screenwriter), Martin Brown (producer-art director), Jill Bilcock (film editor), and John "Cha-Cha" O'Connell (choreographer). (The company is called Bazmark to incorporate the two Martins.)

7. The latest film directed by Baz Luhrmann, *Moulin Rouge*, grew from similarly democratic, infectiously romantic aims. For Luhrmann and his researchers, the Moulin Rouge nightclub represents "the democratization of leisure" during the belle epoque of Paris at the turn of the last century "that heralded the twentieth-century invention of mass culture." On the official film website, Luhrmann and his researchers describe the Moulin Rouge (which opened in Paris in 1889) as attracting "highbrow and lowbrow society alike," "making a radical break with the country's relentless class divisions," attracting Bohemian artists like Toulouse-Lautrec who "broke with the ultra conservative Academies and took art to the streets." The film is like *Romeo + Juliet* in that there is no attempt at period "authenticity" or "consistency"—instead of attempting to portray Paris 1889, the film is playfully anachronistic and eclectic, the official film website describes the Moulin Rouge nightclub presented in the film as "a can-can-besotted version of Steve Rabell's disco-crazed Studio 54 crossed with Bangkok's sex market meets Mardis Gras carnival" (Twentieth Century Fox, 2001).

8. Lesley Stern is similarly fascinated with the way Amy Heckerling's 1994 version of Jane Austen's *Emma* (entitled *Clueless*) "actually assumes, through the heterogeneity of its references and allusions, that quotidian knowledge is informed by and woven out of diversity of cultural practices—not distinguishable according to 'high' and 'low' markers." Los Angeles, the city of the film, is, like Verona in *Romeo + Juliet*, "an intertextual site spun by movies, television series, MTV, and a variety of remakes and adaptations" (Stern, 2000, 225).

9. The device echoes Brecht's notes for his *Hamlet* adaptation—a voice breaks in at the end of 3.4 (the "closet scene") to announce "we interrupt our broadcast to bring you the extraordinary news of Ophelia's death" (Whall, 1981–1982, 132).

10. The cinematographer, Donald McAlpine, says he "aimed to remove . . . every hint of highbrow 'classic'" by trying to "develop as much movement and change of perspective as possible, [using] every cinematic trick we [could] think of" (McAlpine cited in Hamilton, 2000, 122).

11. James N. Loehlin also assumes that the title is "a gesture to bardic authority" (1997a, 121).

12. Perhaps the ending of this *Romeo + Juliet* is influenced by the ending of Michael Bogdanov's 1986–1987 RSC production in which there was "little assurance of a brave new world in Verona." In the final scene of Shakespeare's play, Montague and Capulet each promise to build a gold statue as a ceremonial tribute to the other's child. In Bogdanov's production, the golden statues were presented as "an empty public relations event with the Prince speaking from cue cards and paparazzi photographing all the surviving principals in appropriate poses. The handshake of Capulet and Montague become a photo op" (Snyder, 1996, 162).

13. Arroyo goes on to point that, in a broad sense, every film presents a "constructed" world—even if we accept the city in which *Casablanca* is set as "stand-in" for the real city, we know that does not mean it is even remotely like that real city. However, Arroyo is more concerned with "constructed" worlds in a narrower sense, the way science fiction movies often place contemporary dilemmas in futuristic settings, for example, or the "constructed" worlds most commonly associated with particular genres, including sci-fi, fantasy, horror, and, to some extent, musical features (1997, 6).

14. Many reviewers now hold up Zeffirelli's film as an "ideal" in comparison with Luhrmann's "travesty" (Downing, 2000, 125).

15. As Fredric Jameson points out, the postmodern "modifications in aesthetic production" are "most dramatically visible" in architecture (1991, 2).

16. I use Harvey's description of postmodern cities (1990, 49).

17. As he explained in the interview with Kim Hill (1997).

18. Belsey (1994) contextualizes this argument in relation to Ferdinand De Saussure's arguments about the impossibility of making perfect translations. Saussure showed that "meanings are not held in place by objects in the world, or by concepts independent of language." Instead, meaning resides "in language, or, more broadly, in signifying systems." The world cannot be known outside of systems of differential

signification: Ideas "are an effect of difference, not its cause. They are, moreover, deferred by the signifier which produces them. Differed and deferred, supplanted, relegated by the signifier, the signified has no autonomy, no substance." Belsey goes on to argue that in a world where there is "no certainty that our linguistic, signifying, differential cognitive maps are accurate," where "we cannot guarantee the positive content of what we know by pointing to some extra-linguistic ground of truth," certainty itself only exists in the language used to evoke it. "The possession of any certainty, any truth" (including absolute love) is "not an option" (Belsey, 1994, 73).

19. Of course, as Belsey points out, there is a long history of representing love and desire as citational. In *Romeo and Juliet*, for example, the lovers' first conversation forms a conventional sonnet. But what is specific to postmodern texts is that they "foreground the citationality of desire" (1994, 82).

Works Cited

Arroyo, José. 1997. "Kiss Kiss Bang Bang." *Sight and Sound* 3: 6–9.

Barthes, Roland. 1976. *The Pleasure of the Text*. Trans. Richard W. Miller. London: Capo.

Belsey, Catherine. 1994. *Desire: Love Stories in Western Culture*. Oxford, UK: Blackwell.

Bordwell, David, Janet Staiger, and Kristen Thompson. 1985. *The Classical Hollywood Cinema: Film Style and Mode of Production to 1960*. London: Routledge and Kegan Paul.

Brook, Peter, Peter Hall, Richard Loncraine, Baz Luhrmann, Oliver Parker, Roman Polanski, and Franco Zeffirelli. 1998. "Shakespeare in the Cinema: A Film Director's Symposium." *Cineaste* 24 (1): 48–55.

Burt, Richard. 1998. *Unspeakable ShaXXXspeares: Queer Theory and American Kiddie Culture*. New York: St. Martin's Press.

Chatman, Seymour. 1992. "What Novels Can Do That Film Can't (and Vice Versa)." In *Film Theory and Criticism: Introductory Readings*, 4th ed., ed. Gerald Mast, Marshall Cohen, and Leo Braudy, 403–19. New York/Oxford, UK: Oxford University Press.

Davies, Anthony. 1988. *Filming Shakespeare's Plays: The Adaptations of Laurence Olivier, Orson Welles, Peter Brook, Akira Kurosawa*. Cambridge, UK: Cambridge University Press.

———. 1996. "The Film Versions of *Romeo and Juliet*." *Shakespeare Survey* 49: 153–62.

Downing, Crystal. 2000. "Misshapen Chaos of Well-Seeming Forms: Baz Luhrmann's *Romeo + Juliet*." *LFQ* 28 (2): 125–30.

Fuller, Graham. 2001. "Baz Knows the Score." *Observer*, 19 August, Review sec., 7.

Goodwin, Andrew. 1993. "Fatal Distractions: MTV Meets Postmodern Theory." In *Sound and Vision: The Music Video Reader*, ed. Simon Frith, Andrew Goodwin, and Lawrence Grossberg, 45–66. London/New York: Routledge.

Grossberg, Lawrence. 1993. "The Media Economy of Rock Culture: Cinema, Post-Modernity and Authenticity." In *Sound and Vision: The Music Video Reader*, ed. Simon Frith, Andrew Goodwin, and Lawrence Grossberg, 185–209. London/New York: Routledge.

Hamilton, Lucy. 2000. "Baz vs. the Bardolaters, Or Why *William Shakespeare's Romeo + Juliet* Deserves Another Look." *LFQ* 28 (2): 118–24.

Hapgood, Robert. 1997. "Popularising Shakespeare: The Artistry of Franco Zeffirelli." In *Shakespeare, the Movie: Popularizing the Plays on Film, TV, and Video*, ed. Lynda E. Boose and Richard Burt, 80–94. London/New York: Routledge.

Harvey, David. 1990. *The Condition of Postmodernity*. Oxford, UK: Blackwell.

Hattaway, Michael. 2000. "Classic Adaptations of Shakespearian Texts: Contradiction in Terms?" Paper presented at the July 2000 ANZSA Conference in Auckland, New Zealand.

Hill, Kim. 1997. Interview with Baz Luhrmann. "Nine to Noon" show, *National Radio*, Wellington, New Zealand, 4 February.

Hodgdon, Barbara. 1983. "Two *King Lears*: Uncovering the Filmtext." *LFQ* 11: 143–51.

Jameson, Fredric. 1991. *Postmodernism, or the Cultural Logic of Late Capitalism*. London/New York: Verso.

Kennedy, Dennis, ed. 1993. *Foreign Shakespeare: Contemporary Performance*. Cambridge, UK: Cambridge University Press.

Kozintsev, Grigory. 1967. *Shakespeare: Time and Conscience*. Trans. Joyce Vining. London: Dennis Dobson.

Loehlin, James N. 1997a. "'These Violent Delights Have Violent Ends': Baz Luhrmann's Millennial Shakespeare." In *Shakespeare, Film, fin de Siècle*, ed. Mark Thornton Burnett and Ramona Wray, 121–36. London/New York: Routledge.

———. 1997b. "'Top of the World, Ma': *Richard III* and Cinematic Convention." In *Shakespeare, the Movie: Popularizing the Plays on Film, TV, and Video*, ed. Lydia E. Boose and Richard Burt, 67–79. London/New York: Routledge.

Manvell, Roger. 1971. *Shakespeare and the Film*. New York/Washington, DC: Praeger.

Pearce, Craig, and Baz Luhrmann. 1996. *William Shakespeare's* Romeo and Juliet: *The Contemporary Film, the Classic Play*. New York: Bantam Doubleday Dell.

Pilkington, Ace G. 1994. "Zeffirelli's Shakespeare." In *Shakespeare and the Moving Image*, ed. Anthony Davies and Stanley Wells, 153–79. Cambridge, UK: Cambridge University Press.

Rothwell, Kenneth S. 1999. *A History of Shakespeare on Screen: A Century of Film and Television*. Cambridge, UK: Cambridge University Press.

Shaughnessy, Robert, ed. 1998. *Shakespeare on Film*. New Casebooks series. New York: St. Martin's Press.

Snyder, Susan. 1996. "Ideology and the Feud in *Romeo and Juliet*." *Shakespeare Survey* 49: 153–62.

Stern, Lesley. 2000. "*Emma* in Los Angeles: Remaking the Book and the City." In *Film Adaptation*, ed. James Naremore, 221–38. London: Athlone Press.

Straw, Will. 1993. "Popular Music and Post-Modernism in the 1980s." In *Sound and Vision: The Music Video Reader*, ed. Simon Frith, Andrew Goodwin, and Lawrence Grossberg, 3–21. London/New York: Routledge.

Taylor, Gary. 1999. "Wherefore Art Thou, Will?" *Guardian* (Saturday Review), 24 April.

Twentieth Century Fox. 1996. *William Shakespeare's Romeo + Juliet* (home page). www.romeoandjuliet.com.

———. 2001. *Moulin Rouge* (home page). www.clubmoulinrouge.com.

Whall, Helen M. 1981–1982. "The Case Is Altered: Brecht's Use of Shakespeare." *University of Toronto Quarterly* 51 (2): 127–48.

Worthen, W. B. 1998. "Drama, Performativity, and Performance." *PMLA* 113 (5): 1093–1107.

Zeffirelli, Franco. 1990. "Filming Shakespeare." In *Staging Shakespeare: Seminars on Production Problems*, ed. Glenn Loney, 240–70. London/New York: Garland.

~

CHAPTER TEN

Reframing Adaptation: Representing the Invisible (On *The House of Mirth*, Directed by Terence Davies, 2000)

Wendy Everett

"The text tells you everything and you try to keep in mind its tone, which is important, and the look and the feel of it. But it's got to be cinema as well." Typically, this comment, by the British director Terence Davies, goes immediately to the heart of the adaptation debate: "it's got to be cinema *as well*" (Davies, 2001). As well, that is, as all the rest; as well as all the various issues and concerns that inevitably surface in discussions dealing with theories and practices of adaptation: issues such as "fidelity," "truthfulness," and "authenticity" (highly problematic terms in whatever context), which may equally be applied to the language that the film employs, the (period) detail of its costumes, settings, and artifacts, or even the physical characteristics of its actors. All these elements may matter, to varying degrees, Davies admits, as does the basic *tone* of the text, its *look and feel*, but unless the film works on its own terms, unless it can stand on its own as a piece of cinema, then it has failed.

For too long, critics and spectators alike have been so concerned to establish whether or not a given film has succeeded in exactly replicating a particular text (or—to be more precise—their individual experiences of that text) that they have simply ignored the aspect of filmic identity that Davies posits as essential. Along with its outmoded privileging of literature over cinema and its tendency to reduce both to simple story line and character, such an approach may more worryingly reveal a fundamental lack of understanding of what filmic identity might be; of the nature and specificity of film itself. It is these issues that are explored in this chapter, with particular reference to the work of Terence Davies.

Already famous for his powerful and elliptical autobiographical portraits of life in postwar Liverpool (in iconic films such as *Distant Voices, Still Lives* [1988] and *The Long Day Closes* [1992]), in 2001 Terence Davies released his adaptation of Edith Wharton's *The House of Mirth* (1905). The film attracted considerable international attention and became the focus of widespread critical debate. Opinion was predictably divided, and whereas a good many critics found the film striking in its originality and vision, others were puzzled by an adaptation that seemed to undermine so many of their expectations. On the one hand, it was described as a "triumph" (Johnston, 2000, 5), an "unpredictable, unformulaic success" (Horne, 2000, 15), a "glorious . . . if sometimes harrowing" adaptation (Fuller, 2001, 54), and characterized by its "intelligent fidelity" (French, 2000, 7); on the other it was criticized for being deliberately self-conscious, for omitting certain aspects of the text (particularly its anti-Semitism) and altering others, for example, by combining two of the women in the novel, Grace Stepney and Gerty Farish, into a single character (Nochimson, 2001, 41–42). Such comments are revealing, for while the film could certainly not be faulted for the "authenticity" of its images or for its "fidelity" to Wharton's language, it stubbornly rejected both the easy formula of *Heritage* and the reverential approach to the novel as historical artifact so common in adaptations of classic literary texts. If it is in this independence of approach that we can begin to understand Davies's film, it is through its fundamental self-consciousness, its clear-sighted awareness of its status as film, that we may be able to explore what Davies would classify as the fundamental objectives of filmic adaptation.

In many ways, Davies's decision to adapt and direct Wharton's novel could be seen as particularly bold. He had previously made only one adaptation, his film of John Kennedy Toole's *The Neon Bible* (1995), and the result, while fascinating in all sorts of ways—not least because of the film's transitional status within his own oeuvre—nevertheless proved problematic. Interestingly, in this case, criticism centered on the perceived overlap between this film and Davies's earlier narratives rather than on any relationship between film and text (Everett, 2004, 110–35). One can only suppose this to be because *The Neon Bible* was not widely known, certainly in comparison with *The House of Mirth*—an acknowledged literary classic with all the cultural baggage that entails. It is certainly the case that critical treatment of

The House of Mirth almost invariably involves a comparison of the film with the original text, rather than an evaluation of the film as a film, in clear justification of McFarlane's often repeated complaint that discussion of adaptation continues to be "bedevilled by the fidelity issue" (McFarlane, 1996, 8). Moreover, as is so often the case when classics are adapted for the screen, the film's reception was further complicated by widespread familiarity with existing adaptations of novels by the same author, particularly, in this instance, Scorsese's version of *The Age of Innocence* (1993) (which, for a range of reasons, seems to have acquired a mythical status as adaptation). Thus, Davies's film could be found lacking on two counts: First, it was not the same as the book; second, it was not the same as Scorsese's adaptation of *The Age of Innocence*. In this way, its identity as a film remained largely unexplored.

While it is not possible, in a short article, to provide a detailed examination of the complex debates concerning, on the one hand, the nature of adaptation and, on the other, the specificities of film itself, by identifying and exploring a number of the techniques used by Davies in *The House of Mirth*, I shall analyze the transition from literary text to innovative, powerful, self-conscious film and, in so doing, shall pinpoint a number of issues that are central to any evaluation of the present and future status of adaptation studies.

Choice of Text

Davies has long been familiar with Edith Wharton's writing, declaring that *The House of Mirth* impressed him particularly not only because of its powerful visual images but also because of its overwhelming "modernity." In its obsession with money and appearance, he insists, the world the novel depicts clearly reflects our own. "It's about what do you look like and how much money have you got. And what is modern society about? Nothing's changed except for the frocks that are worn. . . . That's why the book is very modern, it's about surfaces. It's the perfect example of that line from *The Importance of Being Ernest*: We live in an age of surfaces. We did then and we do now" (Stone, 2001, 1). Tellingly, Davies relates this world to what he sees as its contemporary cinematic equivalent—Hollywood—and finds it to be equally sinister and cruel. Moreover, Lily Bart, the protagonist of the novel, is entirely trapped within her world in a way that recalls the situations of Davies's earlier characters, including his autobiographical persona (as indeed it recalls that of Edith Wharton herself). Within this constricted setting, Wharton explores, through Lily, ways in which individual identity may be shaped and strengthened by adversity, and the story is ultimately as much about Lily's journey to self-awareness as her social decline. Davies's adaptation therefore reflects the contemporary relevance of the novel as well as its key themes. He is not interested in using film as a means of replicating the novel as artifact, as stasis, but rather as a way of exploring its insights into contemporary life and identity.

Just as *The House of Mirth* explores themes that dominate Davies's autobiographical films—entrapment, exploitation, social exclusion, cruelty, and the desire for freedom—so, too, it reflects the male/female dialectic that is no less central to his personal experience and work: Lily Bart's vulnerability, her suffering, and her eventual downfall can all be understood as the direct outcome of the dictates of a patriarchal society. This is because Lily, like the other women in the book, is essentially a commodity to be purchased or rejected by men, and both her social status and her ultimate fate are thus dependent upon them. Wharton stresses these concerns right from the opening chapter of the book when, in her conversation with Lawrence Selden, Lily reflects on the difference between their respective situations and comments "What a miserable thing it is to be a woman" (1995, 22). Watching Lily as she measures the tea into the pot, Selden presciently notes that "she was so evidently the victim of the civilization which had produced her, that the links of her bracelet seemed like manacles chaining her to her fate" (23). From the first, therefore, Lily is presented as a victim in a society that prizes appearance and money above all else. However, like the women in Davies's autobiographical accounts, she is a fighter, and Davies is attracted to this aspect of her character. In his reading of the text, it is Lily's fierce and uncompromising morality which ultimately proves her downfall because it prevents her from agreeing to marry for money rather than love and from playing by the hypocritical rules of her society.

As a lover of literature, music, and art, and a published writer in his own right, Davies was as fascinated by the novel's linguistic and cultural resonances as by its moral dilemmas and powerful narrative. Lily, like the world she belongs to, is a linguistic creation; both her weaknesses and her strengths are a construct of Wharton's vivid prose. It is this formal aspect as much as the narrative itself that Davies addresses in his filmic interpretation: the nature of Lily and her world as fictional construct and the tones and rhythms of the text that create them.

Processes of Adaptation

Davies is keenly aware that the process of reading and understanding a text involves an imaginative and creative response that is shaped as much by the book's formal construct as by its narrative development, and his initial response to a text is to its language and its formal style, which will ultimately dictate his pace and rhythms. But what he also realizes is that fundamental to the process of reading is the ability to read *between* the lines of the text, to see beyond and between the words on the page, to engage creatively with the silences and intervals that lie at its heart. Recognition of this essential element, of the role in literature of silence as source of the reader's ultimate freedom, and of the importance for the director of ensuring its filmic equivalent is, I suggest, precisely the quality that sets Davies's adaptations apart, creating their particular and powerful resonance.

Davies' idea is interesting in a number of ways, not least in its contradiction of the widespread belief that whereas film is ideally suited for the reproduction of visual detail, unlike literature it is not able to deal with subtle ambiguities or hidden subtexts, so that the spectator inevitably has less creative freedom than the reader of a novel. He refutes such suggestions with passion: Indeed, in his opinion, cinema is a *uniquely privileged medium* for exploring what goes between lines, behind the images (Davies, 2001). It may well be that in studying the repercussions of this idea in his work, we will reach new insight into adaptation itself.

Let us consider, for example, the question of narrative voice-over, an essentially literary device frequently used in adaptations as a way of underlining their "fidelity" to the original text. Voice-over is one of a number of strategies successfully employed by Scorsese in his adaptation of *The Age of Innocence* as a way of retaining Wharton's authorial voice and foregrounding the film's close, even "fetishistic" relationship with the text (Taubin, 2001, 62). In striking contrast, there is no voice-over in Davies's *The House of Mirth*. It is not that he rejects this safe and "easy" solution (Dick, 1990, 21–22) merely out of perversity but rather that given his desire to ensure maximum freedom for the spectator, he rejects the control that voice-over would impose (since it constitutes an authoritative voice in film, encouraging the viewer to accept its [single] version of events). Moreover, given that film is not only, or indeed mainly, a linguistic medium, there are other ways of allowing Wharton's voice to emerge. These include the rhythms and nuances of the dialogue, of course, but also the film's visual images and cadences, the camera's angles and rhythms, and the internal dynamic between and within each shot. While Tibbetts and Welsh (1998), for example, argue that Scorsese uses voice-over, not merely to convey the novelist's voice, but also to reconstruct the social atmosphere of New York at that time, Davies would claim that film has other and more powerful tools at its disposal to achieve this "reconstruction." And, as we shall see, these have little to do with authentic costume and historical detail.

There is, however, a further reason for Davies's rejection of voice-over in *The House of Mirth*: The novel is about the gaze, the nature of appearance and sight (both physical and metaphorical), and the complex power struggle between *looker* and *looked-at*. Much of what we learn about Lily comes from other people's descriptions of and reactions to her; such observations are frequently partial and flawed, often revealing more about the speakers themselves than about Lily. Thus readers must gradually construct their understanding of Lily through an independent and creative response to the text. Davies believes it essential to retain the interplay of fluid and unstable gazes that lie at the novel's core, and he foregrounds the multiplicity of gazes (not least through the camera's close-up observations of faces and eyes and the repeated play with mirrors and windows). Without the guidance of an omniscient narrator, the spectator, like the reader, must deal independently with the unmarked, shifting viewpoints and, within this process, responding to what is not directly represented as supremely important. Moreover, within the film's status as construct, it is the camera that performs the role of narrator and, because it acknowledges this function openly, it involves the spectator directly within the creative process. The transition from literary text to self-conscious, self-reflexive film through the gaze of the camera is particularly fascinating, and in the following section, we shall consider some of the elements that lead to this ultimate transition.

Visual Detail and Authenticity

Adaptations of period novels frequently reveal an obsessive concern with authentic detail, with costumes, décor, and historical artifacts. Indeed, heritage cinema is characterized by this fundamental concern. Films such as *A Passage to India* (David Lean, 1984), *A Room with a View* (James Ivory, 1985), and *Howards End* (James Ivory, 1991), for example, characterized by large budgets and high production values, star-filled casts, and polished camerawork and lighting, were essentially concerned with, and often even judged by, their minutely researched décor and costume (Vincendeau, 2001). If we consider *The House of Mirth* in this context, we realize that, despite its striking visual coherence, it reveals a fundamentally different attitude to both location and detail.

Although locations are important for Davies, they are valued less for their "realism" than for their ability to conflate exterior and interior spaces within a psychological realism composed of interwoven times, places, and viewpoints. To him, therefore, it was relatively unimportant that his very limited budget made it impossible to film in New York; instead the civic buildings in and around Glasgow had to serve. While not "authentic" (a point that seemed to worry a number of American reviewers), the locations nevertheless appear entirely credible within the film: "If like me you believe that what you don't see is just as important as what you do see, then we're in New York in 1905," Davies comments (2001).

Successfully compensating for an inadequate budget requires originality and inventiveness grounded in a fundamental understanding of the nature of the medium and of its difference from the literary text that inspired it. One example in The House of Mirth was the filming of the Van Osburgh wedding for which, as Davies explains, the script required an Episcopal church. Unfortunately, such churches are not to be found in Scotland, and because there was no money to build the necessarily complex set, he was suddenly faced with the need to find a solution, which he did with typical imagination and flair. "So what is the easiest way to tell you about a wedding? What do all weddings have in common? They have photographs. Well in those days the image in the camera was upside down. So you see them upside down. . . . 'I now pronounce you man and wife,' and they're the right way up. It's witty, it's succinct. And it's cheap" (Davies, 2001). Thus by including a single frame showing an inverted image of a bride and groom, a device that could not have worked in another medium, Davies both creates an entire wedding in the spectator's imagination and enables his narrative to move coherently and smoothly to the reception.

Davies shows a similarly creative and irreverent attitude to period artifacts which are never included in his film merely because they are authentic but only if they contribute directly to its fundamental meanings. This approach gives his film an essential and unusual focus, a point recognized by critic, Romney, for example, for whom The House of Mirth feels altogether "un-British" in its rejection of what he calls the "comforts of heritage cinema" and the "touristic distractions of costume drama" (Romney, 2000). In Romney's opinion, Davies's directing is characterised by its "matter-of-fact austerity," and this judgment is justified if we compare Davies's film with the essentially filled-in camera work, surfeit of period detail, authoritative voice-over, and relentless romantic background music that characterizes so many other adaptations. In Davies's methodology, there is no justification for paying excessive attention to detail unless, in so doing, the camera replicates the gaze, thoughts, or feelings of (one of) the characters or unless it is in some other way contributing a new dimension to the film's deeper meanings. Whereas Scorsese claims that the visual detail in his film replicates

Wharton's descriptions, Davies would argue that in *The House of Mirth*, it is precisely Lily's indifference to such details that both frustrates her aunt (in her constant requests for graphic accounts of what was eaten, how it was served, and what was worn on specific social occasions) and renders them largely irrelevant within the film. Lily does *not* pay attention to such details because they form part of her everyday experience and are thus taken for granted. Accordingly, Davies sees no justification for allowing the camera to linger on such details unless germane to the meaning of the scene. For example, he does pay intense attention to the silence inside Aunt Peniston's drawing room, foregrounding the smallest sounds of a clock ticking or a floorboard creaking, because this is central to the intense claustrophobia that Lily is experiencing. Similarly, when Lily—and we—do notice objects or furniture, it is because she is suddenly reminded that she has no space of her own but must always exist according to the rules and habits of those whose space she inhabits.

Music

Another device that sets film apart from literature, of course, is its ability to include music within the experience it offers its viewers. Interestingly, this aspect of adaptation has received only scant attention perhaps because music is not seen as part of the original text, and it is therefore regarded as relatively unimportant. It is also true that scores used in adaptations are frequently derivative and may simply act as temporal signifiers, music being one of the most powerful of all pointers of period, place, and memory (Everett, 2000). Very often in adaptation music is accorded the most conventional of roles: silent, "unheard" shaper of emotional mood and response (Gorbman, 1997, 73; Brown, 1994, 1). Again, *The House of Mirth* breaks the rules, foregrounding music as one of its most powerful signifiers.

In Davies's score, which comprises six different works dating from the early eighteenth century to the 1970s, music never functions simply to support the narrative or manipulate the spectator. Indeed, at moments which express most fully the passions and desires of the characters, the soundtrack is often silent, either reflecting their tight emotional restraint or serving to focus attention on other modes of expression in the scene. For example, when he wants us to experience Lily's feelings of claustrophobia, he foregrounds silence and stasis in a way that recalls "the intense, hushed, charged sound world of Bresson, Rohmer, late Kieslowski or of Ingmar Bergman's harrowing *Cries and Whispers*" (1972) (Horne, 2000, 16). When music is included, it is used much as Davies uses light: to highlight detail, to create depths and texture, to suggest layers of meaning that cannot be represented directly. In this context, Davies's choice of Baroque music is important not only because its delicate control and balance so perfectly represent the period he is dealing with but also because its intricate structure reflects the character of Lily herself: complex, apparently delicate and fragile, yet possessing great inner strength. In the opening scene in which Lily and Selden meet, we hear a short extract from "Oboe Concerto in D Minor" by Alessandro Marcello, and that same piece is heard again when they first kiss. However, instead of the same recording, the version we hear now has been transposed to F-sharp minor and is performed not by an oboe but by a string quartet. While the change is subtle, its effect is to make the textures and tone more delicate than in the original version. This, along with the fact that the excerpt ends on an imperfect, unresolved cadence, warns us that Lily and Selden's relationship, too, is unresolved, open-ended. At the end of the film, as Lily takes her fatal dose of chloral and as Selden discovers her body, it is heard for a third and final time. While its function is not that of a traditional leitmotif, we do, however, come to associate the piece with Lily, and Davies extends and deepens this association through a key visual metaphor.

During the credits, as the Marcello is heard for the first time, we watch a series of increasingly intricate patterns developing on the screen. These patterns are immediately repeated in the lace of Lily's veil as she arrives at the station and appear again in the lace curtains in Selden's flat. At the end of the film, when Selden raises the blind in Lily's bedroom, he seizes the lace curtain and holds it tightly in his hand before looking at her body. Why? If the patterns in the lace, with their apparent fragility but underlying strength, are actually created by the gaps between the threads, then equally we might argue that musical structures, too, are a function of rhythmic patterns and intervals between the notes. By associating the two with Lily, Davies foregrounds the need for our creative response to the gaps and silences of her character.

The role of music is intimately related to that of all the other signifiers, and each new piece is used to create new references and meanings. Thus, for example, the "simple, delicate, fragile sounds" of Morton Feldman's *Rothko Chapel: Why Patterns?* heard during the milliners' sequence articulate Lily's particular vulnerability at that moment (Griffiths, 1990, 172), while the composition itself, a tribute to Mark Rothko and originally written for performance in the Rothko Chapel a year after its opening, is essentially conceived as a spatial construct shaped by chance and time, particularly relevant to Davies's film. Moreover, it contains references to Stravinsky's funeral, and to traditional Jewish music, and may have been included by Davies as part of his reaction against the anti-Semitic context of Wharton's novel.

In addition to these works, three different excerpts from Mozart's comic opera *Così fan tutte* are heard, foregrounding the work as a dominant theme. Davies's choice of this opera reflects both his determination to use "Soave sia il vento" for his transition sequence and his understanding of its narrative focus upon women as objects and potential victims of the male gaze.

The Wider Contexts of Adaptation: Film

Acknowledging the importance of music in Davies's film highlights one of the dangers of considering adaptations exclusively in relation to the original text: the obfuscation of the film's identity as film. If, however, this identity is recognized as primordial, not only does it becomes possible to situate the original text as merely one of many influences, but it also opens up critical awareness in important new ways. No film can be fully understood without an awareness of its broader filmic and cultural contexts, and as an essentially self-conscious director, Davies openly acknowledges the filmic context in which *The House of Mirth* should be situated. The following section identifies some of its filmic references and examines their overall significance.

Among the many influences Davies acknowledges is *Letter from an Unknown Woman* (Max Ophuls, 1948). This film, whose powerful narrative, lyrical camera work, and richly lit and textured mise-en-scène all fascinate him, acquires a particular resonance in relation to *The House of Mirth* through its atmospheric recreation of turn-of-the-century Vienna. The film recounts the story of a young woman's doomed love for a self-obsessed concert pianist who seduces and abandons her, leaving her pregnant, and later does not even remember her, so that like Lily Bart, its heroine Lisa Berndl is a victim of a patriarchal society. The film is structured as a series of flashbacks triggered by Lisa's voice reading the letter she writes as she is dying, and the hopeless circularity of its plot is emphasized by the letter's opening sentence: "By the time you read this I shall be dead." While not initially successful, *Letter from an Unknown Woman* subsequently acquired the status of classic, and it is significant that Scorsese also cites it as an important influence on *The Age of Innocence* (Christie, 2001). For Davies, *Letter from an Unknown Woman* served as a form of "template," and its atmospheric shots, for example, the opening sequence showing a horse-drawn carriage moving along wet cobbled streets gleaming in the gaslight or the sumptuous and intricate interiors of its houses and cafés, may have influenced the composition of a number of his New York shots. Interestingly, he describes the film as "a kind of opera," relating its structure and its emotional power to that of music while also acknowledging its essential theatricality. Certainly, the beautiful crane shot of the crowd climbing the opera steps in *The House of Mirth* makes visual references to the equivalent sequence in *Letter from an Unknown Woman*, and even the presentation of the characters in their opera house boxes suggests various parallels, while Davies's wish to include a panning shot of the whole opulent interior (thwarted by the lack of funds) reflected his love of just such a shot in *Letter from an Unknown Woman*.

Other important reference points include *All That Heaven Allows* (Douglas Sirk, 1955), *Magnificent Obsession* (Douglas Sirk, 1954), *The Little Foxes* (William Wyler, 1941), and *Love Is a Many Splendoured Thing* (Henry King, 1955). Like *Letter from an Unknown Woman*, all these films can be classified as melodrama, specifically as "weepies" or "women's movies": "Absolute crap, but there's a great gusto about them. There's something about the vulnerability of a woman in that era," muses Terence Davies (Horne, 2000, 17). While their narratives are frequently trite, these films have an underlying power, and Davies is receptive to many of their qualities. He admires, for example, Sirk's expressionist use of color in *All That Heaven Allows*, possibly reflecting this in *The House of Mirth* in the way the tonal range and color intensity diminish as the story develops until, in the final freeze frame of Lily's body, all color gradually leeches away until she appears entirely insubstantial. Many of the tight framings and complex settings with which Davies creates Lily's claustrophobic world may also reflect generic devices of melodrama, particularly its use of a highly stylized mise-en-scène as expression of inner emotions (Elsaesser, 1987).

Another, less predictable, reference point in Davies's film is *Some Like It Hot* (Billy Wilder, 1959), particularly the shot of Marilyn Monroe walking along the platform through the steam. This example is interesting in a number of ways. First, because Marilyn Monroe is being acknowledged as an icon of femininity. "Jello on springs" is how Jerry (Jack Lemmon) describes her, as he and Joe (Tony Curtis) watch in awe as she passes. And it is true that the silhouette we see of Lily emerging from the steam in the opening shots of *The House of Mirth*, for all the differences of costume and period, similarly articulates the essence of femininity. Moreover, the fact that Lily appears in silhouette, her face invisible, foregrounds her position as object of our (and Selden's) gaze and possibly reflects that of Marilyn Monroe, both as Sugar Kane (the object of our gaze and that of the two male protagonists) and as a star whose life was destroyed by the exploitative gaze of the public. Such references to film in *The House of Mirth* further our understanding of its meanings while also reminding us of its identity as film.

The Wider Contexts of Adaptation: Art

Paintings and photographs play a key part in Davies's films, particularly in relation to his fascination with light and texture, and they too should be recognized as key signifiers. In *The House of Mirth*, the turn-of-the-century interiors with their opulent fabrics and rich colors enabled Davies to experiment with chiaroscuro in ways largely inspired by Dutch interiors. In particular, Davies references Vermeer, whose small, detailed domestic scenes are notable for their innovative use of light and perspective. Many of Davies's interior shots, particularly those in Aunt Peniston's house, use daylight filtering through a curtained window to create perspectives and textures that strikingly merge the rich stillness of Vermeer's canvases and the claustrophobic silence of Lily's world.

The artist whose role in *The House of Mirth* has been most widely recognized is John Singer Sargent. Davies used Sargent's society portraits as a guide to the period, much as, in filmic terms, he used *Letter from an Unknown Woman*. It has been widely reported that in casting the film, he chose Gillian Anderson, not because of her fame and popularity (never having previously seen her or *The X-Files*), but because he was immediately struck by her beauty: "I was trying to find someone who looked like she might have stepped out from one of John Singer Sargent's portraits, and there she was" (Johnston, 2000, 5). John Singer Sargent was a fashionable turn-of-the-century portrait painter whose work was in great demand by upper-class society on both sides of the Atlantic, and his canvases, with their dramatic use of light and shadow and their detailed recreation of the sumptuous gowns and rich furnishings of the period, clearly influenced Davies's visualization of the novel.

If some of the above observations seem marginal to the assessment of the process of adaptation, my response is that, on the contrary, they are fundamental. Film is a different medium from literature and has at its disposal a whole range of different techniques, devices, and references. If these are ignored in analyzing an adaptation, the identity of the film itself will not be adequately understood. The final section of this chapter examines a single sequence from *The House of Mirth* to illustrate some of the diverse and complex ways in which Davies approaches his adaptation, referencing in particular his concern with reading between the lines of the text and offering the spectator an equivalent creative freedom.

The novel is divided into two books: The first opens with Lily's chance meeting with Selden at Grand Central Station and ends with the arrival of a telegram from Bertha Dorset inviting her on a Mediterranean cruise. Book

2 opens with Selden already in Monte Carlo, enjoying "the whole outspread effect of light and leisure" (Wharton, 1995, 261), and ends with him kneeling beside Lily's lifeless body. Davies's film retains this two-part structure, but whereas Wharton executes an abrupt cut from New York to Monte Carlo, he instead creates a three-minute-long transition sequence. At one level, the sequence provides a lyrical interlude; at another it articulates the hidden, innermost experiences of Lily.

The length of the sequence is dictated by the duration of the trio from Mozart's *Così fan tutte,* and the music both motivates and sustains the constantly mobile camera and lap dissolves that deconstruct space and time and merge inner and outer worlds. Apart from the Italian lyrics, there is no dialogue, and the sequence—an abstract composition of movement, light, texture, and sound—seems only loosely linked to the narrative. The journey Davies makes from the stasis and entrapment of the New York house to the freedom and color of Monte Carlo is created entirely through the combination of music with changing light on the surface of water.

It might be tempting to suggest that, beautiful though it is, this sequence has little to do with the original text and is entirely self-indulgent. Such criticism could be countered by a close narrative reading of the text. For example, the extraordinary desolation created by the shrouded furniture at the start of Davies's sequence may reflect Wharton's comment that "Mrs. Peniston had kept her imagination shrouded, like the drawing-room furniture" (1995, 181). Similarly, the movement from darkness to light, from entrapment to freedom, suggested by the move away from rigid architectural structures to the vastness of sea and sky, echoes Selden's emotions and desires upon leaving "surroundings made for the discipline of the senses" (261), where "the ugliness of things rasped the eye as the gritty wind ground into the skin" (262), for the light and exuberance of Monte Carlo, brimming with "sensuality and implied sex" (Cahir, 2001, 169).

However, more importantly, the sequence exemplifies the process of reading between the lines, and if it creates an abstract portrayal of journey and escape through it and without showing Lily or having recourse to dialogue or voice-over, Davies transports us deep inside her mind. In the bleak deserted house we experience her despair, and in the movement toward light and space, we discover her deepest longings. Ironically, while Selden successfully makes the transition to freedom, Lily remains trapped; as he stands gazing out to sea, she is confined to the yacht (itself the object of the gazes of those on shore, including his). And although the yacht functions as facilitator of movement and change, Lily's place in it is entirely prescribed. As the camera returns to the interior of the boat, we see her, seated in a corner, tightly framed by vertical and horizontal bars, trapped in a situation over which she has no control and from which she cannot escape.

Davies's transition sequence, therefore, serves to move the narrative on through its temporal and spatial shifts, but more importantly it explores the silences and spaces of the novel; and essentially, its lack of dialogue or closed narrative structure ensures that the spectator, too, is free to explore and create, and the means by which this is achieved are specifically, often uniquely, cinematic.

Conclusion

By choosing to focus on Terence Davies's *The House of Mirth*, it was never my intention to suggest that this film should serve as a model for adaptation in general nor that it is necessarily more successful than any other. Even the implication that there is any such thing as a "typical" adaptation or a single route would be grossly misleading. However, it is clear that by examining a number of the innovative and self-conscious techniques used by Davies within the context of an adaptation that is premised upon the specificities of film, and the importance of ensuring the creative freedom of the spectator, it is possible to highlight new areas that are fundamental to the study of adaptation. Those of us who are privileged to explore the relationship between literature and film should always recognize the creative potential of both and should, above all, value their fundamental differences and their equivalent power to excite, enlighten, and fascinate.

Works Cited

Brown, Royal S. 1994. *Overtones and Undertones: Reading Film Music*. Berkley and Los Angeles: University of California Press.

Cahir, Linda. 2001. "The House of Mirth: An Interview with Director Terence Davies and Producer Olivia Stewart." *LFQ* 29 (3): 166–71.

Christie, Ian. 2001. "'Passion and Restraint,' Ian Christie Talks with Martin Scorsese." In *Film/Literature/Heritage: A Sight and Sound Reader*, ed. Ginette Vincendeau, 66–76. London: BFI.

Davies, Terence. 2001. Commentary on the film by the director included as one of the special features on the DVD recording of *The House of Mirth*. London: Granada Film Limited and Film Four Limited.

Dick, Bernard. 1990. *Anatomy of Film*. London: St. Martin's Press.

Elsaesser, Thomas. 1987. "Tales of Sound and Fury: Observations on the Family Melodrama." In *Home Is Where the Heart Is: Studies in Melodrama and the Woman's*

Film, ed. Christine Gledhill, 43–69. London: BFI. First published in 1972 in *Monogram* 4.

Everett, Wendy. 2000. "Songlines: Alternative Journeys in Contemporary European Cinema." In *Music and Cinema*, ed. James Buhler, Caryl Flynn, and David Neumeyer, 99–117. Hanover, NH/London: Wesleyan University Press.

———. 2004. *Terence Davies*. Manchester, UK: Manchester University Press.

French, Philip. 2000. "Daylight Snobbery." *Observer Review*, 15 October, 7.

Fuller, Graham. 2001. "Summer's End." *Film Comment* 37 (January/February): 54–59.

Gorbman, Claudia 1997. *Unheard Melodies: Narrative Film Music*. Bloomington: Indiana University Press.

Griffiths, Paul. 1990. *Modern Music: A Concise History from Debussy to Boulez*. London: Thames and Hudson.

Horne, Philip. 2000. "Beauty's Slow Fade." *Sight and Sound* 10 (October): 14–18.

Johnston, Trevor. 2000. "Even My Therapist Hates My Father Now." *Independent*, 1 October, 5.

McFarlane, Brian. 1996. *Novel to Film: An Introduction to the Theory of Adaptation*. Oxford: Clarendon Press.

Nochimson, Martha. 2001. "*The House of Mirth*." *Cineaste* 19 (2): 41–43.

Romney, Jonathan. 2000. "British Filmmaker Terence Davies's Adaptation of Edith Wharton's *The House of Mirth*." *Film Comment* (May/June). Reproduced at http://gauk.net.

Stone, Judy. 2000. "Old Obsessions Remain." Interview with Terence Davies published on the *Official Gillian Anderson Website* at http://gaws.ao.net/hom/print/oaklandtribune.html (accessed 2 February 2007).

Taubin, Amy. 2001. "*The Age of Innocence*: Dread and Desire." In *Film/Literature/Heritage: A Sight and Sound Reader*, ed. Ginette Vincendeau, pp. 61–65. London: BFI.

Tibbetts, John C., and James M. Welsh. 1998. *The Encyclopedia of Novels into Film*. New York: Facts on File.

Vincendeau, Ginette, ed. 2001. *Film/Literature/Heritage: A Sight and Sound Reader*. London: BFI.

Wharton, Edith. 1995. *The House of Mirth*. New York: Simon and Schuster. First published in 1905.

~

CHAPTER ELEVEN

Sucking Dracula: Mythic Biography into Fiction into Film, or Why Francis Ford Coppola's *Dracula* Is Not Really *Bram Stoker's Dracula* or Wallachia's Dracula

James M. Welsh

There are many reasons Romania should be more famous than it is in the West: The admirable spirit of its long-suffering people, for example, who have endured centuries of hardships imposed by foreign powers, from the Huns to the Hapsburgs to the Ottoman Turks vying to control the gateway to Europe. The natural beauty of its landscape, the rugged beauty of the Carpathians and Transylvanian Alps. The accomplishments of its poets (such as Mihai Eminescu), playwrights (Eugene Ionescu), writers (Ion Creanga and Mircea Eliade), composers (George Enescu), and artists (Constantin Brancusi). Its folklore and Orthodox traditions, such as the remarkable "painted" monasteries of Bucovina in the northeast. Its vineyards that have produced such fine wines as Cotnari Grassa, as yet undiscovered in the West. Its spirituality, as nurtured by the monasteries of the Neamţ region, and the teachings of Father Cleopa from the mountain monastery, Mănăstrea Sihăstria, famous for his piety and wisdom.

But, unfortunately, the bad has driven out the good, and the image of Romania in the West has too often been dominated by those twin icons of evil: the dictator Nicolae Ceausescu, who was executed in December 1989 but whose legacy lived on and the fierce Wallachian Prince Vlad Ţepeş, Vlad III Dracula, whose cruelties inspired the Irish novelist Bram Stoker

(1847–1912) to write his demented Gothic fantasy, *Dracula* (1897), without ever once having set foot in Romania (a feat later replicated by the beautiful and beautifully self-assured Elizabeth Kostova in the twenty-first century); those who spin evil fables out of Romania should at the very least have to live there and work there and know some of the people, so as to understand the culture. Thus was a historical figure demonized in what was to become one of the most celebrated classics of Gothic fiction. Thomas Carlyle once described history as "a distillation of rumour," and there is no better demonstration of that than Stoker's utterly grotesque distortion of the historical *Dracula: The Vampire* (derived from the Magyar *vampir* or "blood-sucker"). How did this transformation come about?

The many transformations of the Wallachian Prince Vlad III Dracula is an example of what University of Cardiff research professor Stephen Knight was to call "mythic biography" in his book *Robin Hood: A Mythic Biography* (2003). Taking his lead from that "bible of English biographic pomposity, *The Dictionary of National Biography*," Knight notes that his outlaw hero lurks "among all the forgotten politicians and forgettable aristocrats," in an entry written by *The Dictionary of National Biography (DNB)* coeditor Sir Sidney Lee identifying Robin Hood as a "mythical forest elf." Like Robin Hood, Count Dracula is "neither solely a myth nor merely biographic," Knight explains in his introduction (2003, xiii), adding that his book "is a mythic biography in two ways: it deals with both the human and the superhuman manifestations and meanings of the figure; but it is also a biography of the myth." As is also the case with Dracula, one cannot separate the man from the legend from the myth, which keeps growing and morphing grotesquely.

According to Clive Leatherdale (1985), while Bram Stoker was on vacation at the Yorkshire port of Whitby in 1890, he came across a book in the Whitby library written by William Wilkerson in 1820, entitled *An Account of the Principalities of Wallachia and Moldavia*. Unlike Stoker (and others who have presumed to write about Romania and Vlad Ţepeş and Dracula), Wilkerson had actually been to Romania and served as British consul in Bucharest. In Wilkerson's "account" Stoker read about the exploits of the fifteenth-century Wallachian *Voivode*, Prince Dracula, born circa 1430 in Sighişoara. The Holy Roman Emperor Sigismund had given Vlad's father the throne of Wallachia and invested him with "The Order of the Dragon." (*Dracul* in Romanian means "Dragon"; *Dracula* simply means "Son of the Dragon.") Thus Vlad Dracul (Vlad the Dragon) was made Prince of Wallachia as a reward for fighting the Czech Hussites and the Turks. He seized the Wallachian throne in 1436 but was put to death in 1447, and in 1453 Constantinople fell to the Turks, bringing an end to the Eastern Roman Empire. The son, Vlad Dracula, better known as Vlad Ţepeş (which translates as "Vlad the Impaler"), ruled Wallachia with an iron hand from 1456 to 1462 and became a Romanian folk hero for fighting the Turks, but he also fought and impaled Saxons and Hungarians. He besieged but never captured Castelul Bran (Bran Castle, presented to suckers as "Dracula's Castle") outside the Saxon city of Braşov on the southeast frontier of Transylvania and was finally imprisoned by the Hungarian King Matthius Corvinus for twelve years, from 1462 to 1474, and not released until he converted from Orthodox Christianity to Roman Catholicism. Thereafter, he again became supreme ruler of Wallachia from 1474 to 1476, when he was killed fighting the Ottoman Turks. But Stoker was not especially interested in the exploits of the historical, that is, the "real" Dracula.

The working title for Stoker's novel was "The Un-Dead," derived from the word *Nosferat* (plural *Nosferatu*, literally "plague-carriers"). The Greek Orthodox Church "declared that excommunicants and other heretics would not decompose in their unhallowed graves" (Leatherdale, 1985, 27). The devil would claim their bodies, making them "undead" spirits who could never "rest in peace"—hence, *Nosferatu*.

Sighişoara, then, became famous as the birthplace of Vlad Ţepeş. A bronze plaque marks the spot, a few hundred paces from the bell tower entrance to the walled Old City. It should also be famous for being one of the most remarkable medieval cityscapes in Europe. Bran Castle has become known as "Dracula's Castle" (one of many), though Vlad never occupied it. It seems to be the setting for *Nosferatu—The Vampyr*, Werner Herzog's 1978 remake of the F. W. Murnau classic silent film. This remarkable Saxon fortification, 100 miles from Braşov (once ruled by the Teutonic Knights), commanded a view of the trade routes cutting through Romania to the north.

Stoker's *Dracula* has been adapted both to stage and screen many times over. The "unofficial" screen version of Stoker's novel was F. W. Murnau's silent classic *Nosferatu*, loosely adapted by Murnau in 1922, changing the European locale from England to the continent and even changing Dracula to Graf Orlak. Murnau changed the story substantially because he had not obtained the rights to the novel from Stoker's estate. Stoker himself had worked unsuccessfully on a stage adaptation that was simply too long and cumbersome, until it was later reshaped by Hamilton Deane's stage adaptation, set entirely in England. The Deane version toured England in 1926 before opening in London in 1927. The later American stage version was revised by the London-based American journalist John L. Balderston. This version opened on Broadway on 5 October 1927 and was the basis for the 1931 Tod Browning film, starring the forty-six-year-old Hungarian expatriate actor Bela

Lugosi (Bela Blasko), whose appearance epitomized the image fabricated by Deane. Other films, such as the one directed by John Badham in 1978, followed the Deane–Balderston stage adaptation.

Of course Bram Stoker and his followers have been joined by legions of blood-sucking exploiters, the most recent of which was Elizabeth Kostova, who constructed her novel *The Historian* (2005) on partially understood legendary folklore, though she had not bothered to visit Romania while "researching" her novel, which explains why so much of the action takes place elsewhere, in Spain, in Bulgaria (which is, at least, close to Romania), and in Istanbul (Turkey—Vlad indeed fought the Turks!), and Budapest (which is even closer to Transylvania). She managed to mangle and confuse all known elements of the Dracula myth and Central European geography and as a reward ended up on the *New York Times* bestseller list with a looming movie contract. The novel pretends to be "a quest for the truth about Vlad the Impaler," but almost certainly the novelist didn't know where to look, until ABC News took pity on her and had Elizabeth Vargas accompany her to Romania with a camera crew to document her enlightenment. Of course, Romania had been an open society for the preceding fifteen years.

Francis Coppola intended to go back to Stoker's novel, but his film was not to be shot on location. Presumably, like Stoker himself, he never set foot in Romania (though, according to *Variety*, he visited the country in 2005, scouting out possible locations for a later project). His notion of authenticity was to have the characters set in his mythical "Romania" and speak in Romanian. The project originated with screenwriter James V. Hart, who had worked with Steven Spielberg on the movie *Hook* (1991, freely adapted from James M. Barrie's *Peter Pan*), his first produced screenplay. This "success" enabled him to become coproducer on the *Dracula* project. Born in Shreveport, Louisiana, and educated in Texas at Southern Methodist University, Hart had studied finance and economics as an undergraduate before taking his master's degree in film and broadcasting. He started working on what he called "the real Dracula" project during the 1970s, greatly influenced by Leonard Wolf's *Annotated Dracula* (1975), and claims to have been "completely spellbound" by Stoker's writing. His first-draft screenplay, entitled "Dracula: The Untold Story," was about to become a cable television movie when actress Winona Ryder read for the role of Mina and was so impressed by the screenplay that she passed it along to Francis Coppola, who also became interested because, he believed, no one had ever really filmed the book. Let's say at the very least his intentions were good.

Coppola's film, which claims to be "*Bram Stoker's Dracula*," begins with a "back story" to explain to ignorant Americans how Dracula became Dracula in a grotesquely fashioned Gothic fabrication that shows Vlad the Impaler (Gary Oldman), suited-up in red-tinged reptilian armor, who leaves his castle to do battle with the Turks, leaving his beloved spouse, Elizabeta (Winona Ryder), behind. She is tricked by the Turks into believing that her husband was killed and in grief and desperation commits suicide by leaping from the castle wall. When Vlad returns home to find his beloved wife dead, he is then told by a tiresome Orthodox priest (Anthony Hopkins) that, as a suicide, she cannot be buried in consecrated ground. Devastated and outraged, he renounces God and the holy church and forms a bizarre pact with the devil that turns him into the mythic vampire.

None of this fanciful and spectacular back story is to be found in the novel. But the back story gives Dracula a context that seriously distorts Bram Stoker's original design, shifting the story from one of Gothic terror to one of Gothic romance. The novel begins with solicitor Jonathan Harker (the memorably anguished Keanu Reeves) being sent on a mission to Transylvania to visit Count Dracula, leaving his betrothed Mina (Winona Ryder) behind in England. In the film, but not in the novel, Mina seems to be Elizabeta reincarnated; not only is the Count attracted to her, therefore, but she seems to have medieval memories of her former marriage to Vlad before he became Dracula. Moreover, the priest, whose ruling concerning Elizabeta's burial drove Vlad to the devil, seems to be reincarnated as Dr. Abraham Van Helsing (also played by Anthony Hopkins, with little or no restraint in a high camp style), the peculiarly obsessed scientist and metaphysician.

As played by Gary Oldman, Coppola's Dracula has a sense of power and majesty. We next see him hundreds of years later, when Jonathan Harker arrives at his haunted castle in Transylvania, a passage filmed with eerie effectiveness. Made up to look 300 years old, Oldman's Count recalls Bela Lugosi most nearly when he hears wolves howling and speaks his familiar line "Listen to the children of the night!" Otherwise, however, the visual conception is strikingly original. Harker completes his real-estate transaction with the Count but is then imprisoned in Dracula's castle for a month as he makes arrangements to transport Dracula and his strange retinue to the ruined abbey the Count has purchased on the outskirts of London. (But why, one wonders, would this prince of darkness choose to settle upon consecrated ground?) Left behind, Harker has to resist carnal seductions by three randy female vampires but finally manages to escape via the river to a convent, where he is gradually nursed back to health.

Dracula has seen a photograph of Harker's fiancée, Mina, whom he immediately recognizes as the reincarnated Elizabeta. When he stalks and then seeks her out in London, he appears to her as a much younger man (his youthful appearance is consistent with Stoker's novel); but this shifty devil also appears as a red-eyed wolfman for the bestial rape of Mina's aristocratic best friend, Lucy. Oldman undergoes eight different changes of make-up in the film. We see him as an old man, as a younger man, and in various bestial incarnations, including that of a shriveled, upside-down man-sized bat.

Coppola's film constantly seeks to be inventive and moves toward multiple excesses, working a rather scrambled metaphor on extravagant sexual behavior and the exchange of contaminated blood. This would seem to be a glib and potentially repulsive allusion to the AIDS dilemma, evocative, perhaps in a way, but essentially cheap and sensational. At one point Van Helsing is seen giving a lecture on vampire bats, diseases of the blood, venereal diseases, and civilization, making the absurd comment that "in fact, civilization and syphlization have developed together," while his students thump their desks in delight and approval. In the film Van Helsing apparently works in Oxford, not in Amsterdam. Coppola works in other ways to move the narrative forward in time, as he attempts to show how much of an anachronism Dracula has become in the early twentieth century, dominated by science and technology rather than religion and superstition. Mina uses a typewriter (invented in 1859), for example, to keep her journal. The learned doctors in England use a recording device to keep their notes. Then there are the microscopes that magnify blood platelets and a device for blood transfusion. Some of this technology can be traced to the novel but by no means all of it. The modern, mechanized world revealed by the film has changed so much that an ancient demon from a more superstitious era seems not only awkward and out of place but a pathetic misfit.

The action is set in 1898 (though the novel was published in 1897), about the time the movies were born, and Coppola sets up a meeting between Vlad and Mina at a cinematograph because the age of mechanical reproduction has just begun. This gives Coppola an excuse to indulge in his own enthusiasm for early cinema. During the early 1980s Coppola had exploited the work of the French film pioneer Abel Gance by bringing a chopped-down version of Gance's 1927 silent epic Napoleon to Radio City Music Hall. Dracula gives Coppola an opportunity to imitate Gance's shock-cutting techniques and breathtaking camera movements. He replicates Gance's pendulum-swing camera work, for example, as the spirit of Dracula speeds up a staircase then withdraws just as rapidly. The mysterious passage of Dracula's coffin over the sea vaguely recalls the famous double-tempest sequence in Napoleon. Gance also seems to have inspired mattework and various iris effects Coppola uses throughout the film. Coppola's cinematographer Michael Ballhaus began his career in Germany with Rainer Werner Fassbinder and Volker Schlöndorff and would have been well aware of the techniques required for creating Coppola's visual spectacle, which takes precedence over the international cast.

The narrative framework of Stoker's novel is epistolary. The story is told through letters, journal entries by Mina Murray, Jonathan Harker recounting his journey to the Carpathians, and newspaper clippings. In the film the back story is narrated by Anthony Hopkins using one funny accent, which is later replaced by another, still in the Hopkins voice, which voices over the captain's log of *The Demeter*, the ship that carries Dracula to England. The Hopkins narrator intrudes at other times, giving vampire lore as when, for example, he says "Contrary to popular belief, the vampire can move by day, though it is not his natural time, and his powers are weak." The voice is consistently that of Anthony Hopkins but not consistently that of the same character. There is also a comic bluntness about the film's Van Helsing that is not really in keeping with the novel.

The film is governed by a different context than the novel and a whole different logic determines the behavior of the main characters, Dracula and Mina, who are locked into a beauty and the beast relationship that tends to leave Jonathan out of the loop. The film also gets the tone of the novel and of Victorian England all wrong by turning Mina's aristocratic friend Lucy into a randy tart. One of her suitors is a gentleman from Texas who packs a bowie knife the two women discuss in prurient terms: "It's so big," Lucy gushes with a telling double entendre that is not at all in keeping with the novel's decorum. Her dirty mind makes Lucy a willing victim for her later ravishment by Dracula, who comes on to her as a werewolf. Coppola's version is consistent with the mores of the late twentieth century rather than those of the late nineteenth century. The moral atmosphere is simply wrong. In this regard, the adaptation fails.

The compounded complications here are stunning, as history has been adapted to legend, a perverse exercise in mythic biography that has produced a film representation of a fifteenth-century Wallachian *Voivod* (prince) as a mythic vampire, the "son of the devil," notorious for his cruelty, as adapted from history to novelistic fiction to the theatre, then to cinema many times over, until Bram Stoker's *Dracula* morphs into Francis Ford Coppola's *Dracula*, telescoping F. W. Murnau's *Nosferatu* (originally plagiarized in 1922 from Stoker's popular novel) and Bela Lugosi's *Dracula*, shaped for the stage by John Balderson's dramatic adaptation. To even think about discussing the popular culture implications of the Dracula myth and its many permutations, one must attempt to do justice to these complications. And what of the persistence of fidelity here? All but a few traces have disappeared into this intertextual maze. Of course, that is only to be expected in a Hollywood treatment of popular myth and legend. Still, some will be offended, no doubt, no doubt with reason.

And, yet, the adaptation is not so offensive as, say, the latest adaptation of *The Scarlet Letter* (1995), starring Demi Moore as an utterly absurd Hester Prynne or Tim Burton's *Sleepy Hollow* (1999), which takes outrageous and absurd liberties with Washington Irving's "The Legend of Sleepy Hollow," turning it into a loathsome bloodbath and turning Ichabod Crane into a goofy forensic detective sent from New York City to investigate mysterious multiple decapitations occurring outside Tarrytown, New York. But whatever merits Coppola's film may offer (and, indeed, there is much to recommend the art design, the nineteenth-century reconstruction, and the visual pyrotechnics), it should not be called *Bram Stoker's Dracula*. That's a misnomer, and this glorious shipwreck of a film has even less to do with Romanian history. Do authenticity and fidelity to one's source matter when applied to historical or literary projects? Arguably, they do and should be of importance. If liberties must be taken with the novel (as was done when the novel was adapted to the stage) and if a faux "historical" subtext must be added, then the fabricators could at least get the "historic" material right, in terms of biography and character relationships, as well as geography, and also in terms of the late Victorian mores that would have governed polite society in England. Just as Dracula sucks (as is in his nature), so does this motion picture as an adaptation. Would it were better.

Works Cited

Kostova, Elizabeth. 2005. *The Historian: A Novel*. New York: Little, Brown.

Knight, Stephen. 2003. *Robin Hood: A Mythic Biography*. Ithaca, NY: Cornell University Press.

Leatherdale, Clive. 1985. *Dracula, the Novel and the Legend: A Study of Bram Stoker's Gothic Masterpiece*. Rev. ed. London: Desert Island Books.

Stoker, Bram. 1897. *Dracula*. Westminster, UK: Constable. Rptd. 1995. New York: Barnes and Noble.

Wolf, Leonard, ed. 1975. *The Annotated Dracula, by Bram Stoker*. New York: Clarkson Potter.

Works Consulted

Coppola, Frances Ford, and James V. Hart. 1992. Bram Stoker's Dracula: *The Film and the Legend*. New York: Newmarket Press.

Erskine, Thomas L., and James M. Welsh. 2000. *Video Versions: Film Adaptations of Plays on Video*. Greenwich, CT: Greenwood Press.

Florescu, Radu R. 1972. *In Search of Dracula.* Greenwich, CT: New York Graphic Society.

Florescu, Radu R., and Raymond T. McNally. 1989. *Dracula: Prince of Many Faces.* Boston: Little, Brown.

Joslin, Lyndon W. 2006. *Count Dracula Goes to the Movies: Stoker's Novel Adapted, 1922–2003.* Jefferson, NC: McFarland.

Lennig, Arthur. 2003. *The Immortal Count: The Life and Films of Bela Lugosi.* Lexington: The University Press of Kentucky.

Tibbetts, John C., and James M. Welsh, eds. 2005. *The Encyclopedia of Novels into Film.* 2nd rev. ed. New York: Facts on File.

Treptow, Kurt W. 2000. *Vlad III Dracula: The Life and Times of the Historical Dracula.* Iaşi, Romania: Center for Romanian Studies.

CHAPTER TWELVE

~

Vertigo, Novel and Film

Peter Lev

The study of film adaptations (of literature, drama, and biography) is a fast-growing subject area in the humanities, but certain limitations of this nascent field remain to be explored. For example, what are the boundaries of "literature"? Should literature be limited to the novels and plays canonized by high culture, or does it extend from Dostoevsky to comic books? Both positions are encountered in critical work on film adaptations, the first stemming from adaptation study's roots in literature departments and the second from the newer, more inclusive orientation of cultural studies. Instead of choosing between these positions, the current chapter explores a third alternative: Adaptation study can bring to light neglected works of literature that nevertheless have a sophistication worthy of serious study.

Consider, for example, the French mystery novel *D'entre les morts* (literal translation "From among the dead") by Pierre Boileau and Thomas Narcejac (1954). This novel is the literary source for Alfred Hitchcock's *Vertigo* (1958), often considered Hitchcock's finest work. Hundreds of thousands of words have been written about *Vertigo*, yet the relationships between novel and film have been almost undiscussed. Even book-length studies of *Vertigo* by Dan Auiler (1998) and Charles Barr (2002) provide only plot summaries of the novel. Robin Wood's *Hitchcock's Films* (1965) is the exception that proves the rule: He discusses *D'entre les morts* for three paragraphs but only to disparage it. I would posit three interrelated reasons for the lack of critical analysis: (1) Boileau and Narcejac have not received much attention from either high culture institutions or the reading public. (2) *D'entre les morts* has been out of print for most of the last fifty years. (The novel was republished by Bloomsbury Press, London, in English translation under the name *Vertigo* in 1997, but that welcome reissue is now itself out of print.) (3) Alfred Hitchcock has a towering reputation as an "auteur" that might be undercut by investigation of his source material. Nevertheless, *D'entre les morts* is a thoughtful and innovative work of mystery fiction that deserves study both in its own right and as the precursor to the film *Vertigo*.

Pierre Boileau was a professional writer specializing in crime fiction, and Thomas Narcejac (pen name for Pierre Ayraud) was a teacher with a philosophy degree and several published crime novels when they decided in 1948 to write as a team. Their joint works include a long list of novels and short stories published between 1951 and the 1980s, and they also wrote plays, screenplays, and teleplays. Boileau–Narcejac's best-known novels are clearly *Celle qui n'était plus*, 1952 (basis for the film *Diabolique*, 1954), and *D'entre les morts*, 1954 (basis for the film *Vertigo*). According to biographer Jean-Pierre Colin, both men were marked by the experience of World War II, which gave them a deep skepticism about the goodness of human beings. Another theme that pervades their work is the fragility of identity, which Colin describes via the following quote from Narcejac (1999):

> It seems that this consciousness of being a "me," a privileged point of the world, a new beginning of everything in the light of reflection, will always be precarious and assailed by doubts, as if the world were only an appearance and logic were only a tool of limited usefulness. (28; trans. P. Lev)[1]

Colin also describes as a repeated theme/technique of Boileau–Narcejac the use of a weak protagonist whose thoughts and behavior are swayed by emotion.

D'entre les morts takes place in Paris and Marseilles in the period just before and just after the occupation of France during World War II. The protagonist, a lawyer named Flavières, is asked in 1940 to follow a woman named Madeleine, who is behaving strangely. Gévigne, Madeleine's husband in the book, has some evidence that Madeleine is possessed by her great-grandmother Pauline Lagerlac, a woman who committed suicide. Flavières follows Madeleine, saves her when she jumps into the Seine, observes other strange behavior, and becomes convinced that the story is true. Flavières also falls in love with this beautiful and strange young woman. Madeleine even-tually commits suicide—or so it appears—by jumping off a church bell-tower. But in 1945, after the war, Flavières finds a young woman in Marseilles named Renée Sourange who looks amazingly like Madeleine, though she is of a lower social class. Renée becomes Flavières's mistress, but he remains obsessed with Madeleine. Flavières hounds Renée to admit that she *is* Madeleine, a reincarnated Madeleine a Madeleine risen from the dead. Fi-nally Renée does admit to being Madeleine but with an unexpected twist: She "acted" the role of Madeleine so that Gévigne could kill his rich wife (she was murdered and then thrown from the bell-tower). Enraged by this deception and by the end of his illusions, Flavières strangles Renée.

Those familiar with Hitchcock's film will recognize the substantial com-monality between the film's plot and the novel's. In both narratives, a woman's playacting suggests a return from the dead. And in both versions, this supernatural theme is ultimately debunked by the woman's confession. Within this schema, some of the variations between novel and film seem re-lated to *Vertigo*'s conditions of production. For example, the historical con-text of the novel, which allows a balancing of Flavières's individual trauma and France's national trauma, is abandoned by a film intended for American and international (but not primarily French) markets. Hitchcock and his screenwriters substitute a visually evocative San Francisco. Also, the theme of vertigo (dizziness or imbalance caused by heights), mentioned briefly in the novel as the reason Flavières cannot rescue Madeleine, becomes far more important in the film. In the opening scene the film's protagonist, a plain-clothes detective named Scottie (James Stewart), has a vertigo attack on a rooftop that leads to a policeman's death. In the novel, this scene is only re-ferred to in conversation—it is the reason Flavières has left the police and started a private law practice. Also, Hitchcock suggests vertigo via camera shots combining zoom in and track out and makes this unique technical de-vice a key symbol and embodiment of an unstable world. A third difference is that in *Vertigo* Scottie does not sleep with Madeleine or Judy, a modifica-tion probably necessitated by the censorship requirements of 1958 (Judy is the film's version of Renée; both Madeleine and Judy are played by Kim No-vak). The French version—Flavières has a sexual relationship with Renée—is interesting because it shows that one can be physically intimate with a woman without knowing her in any profound sense. The American version (Scottie and Madeleine/Judy do not get beyond kissing) is interesting be-cause it shows that Scottie's passion is not primarily physical. Though these differences are significant, the one crucial break between novel and film lies in the ending, which I address later in this chapter.

The key stylistic similarity between Boileau and Narcejac's novel and Hitchcock's film is that both are subjective, passionate narratives. However, the subjectivity and the passion are expressed in dramatically different ways. The novel is told in the third person but with a great deal of emphasis on what Flavières is thinking. It therefore merges, quite successfully, objective and subjective material using what linguists call "free indirect discourse." Though *D'entre les morts* takes place essentially within one consciousness, it is in some ways a talky book—full of thoughts and internal dialogue, as well as conversations occurring in the external world. Flavières is constantly thinking about analogy and significance—about turning reality into a story. The book thus illustrates Narcejac's concept of "the world" as an "appearance" created by the protagonist's not-entirely-trustworthy logic. Here are some examples of Flavières's analogic thinking:

p. 21 (on seeing Madeleine for the first time): "Perhaps he ought really to have been a novelist, with this host of images which so readily and of their own accord flooded his brain."

p. 52 (after Madeleine jumps into the Seine and Flavières saves her): "From that day on he playfully called her Eurydice. He would never have called her Madeleine. Besides, Madeleine was a married woman, another man's wife. Eurydice belonged to him and him alone."

p. 83: "He had to admit, as he got into the car and slammed the door, that he had almost from the first regarded himself as Madeleine's real husband."

p. 117 (Flavières' early impression of Renée): "He had the impression he was looking at a badly dubbed film, with some nonentity speaking the part of the star."

p. 143 (Flavières talking to Renée and comparing her reappearance to Christian doctrine): "I came near to believing in the Christian God because of the promise of the resurrection. . . . Now . . . now I believe my shout was answered. . . . I want so desperately to believe it. If it were true . . . if you could tell me."

Flavières is acting like an intelligent reader, or like the viewer of a film, trying on various hypotheses to see what matches his experience. The novelty of this approach is that the process of finding meaning is usually left to the viewer/reader. By making such "readerly" speculations part of the text, Boileau and Narcejac are suggesting a free play of signifiers with little connection to signifieds. Or, to put the authors' technique into a more suitable 1950s context, they are presenting a Surrealist emphasis on the imagination with a lessening of interest in everyday reality. Flavières is free to try out any number of hypotheses, to see himself as Madeleine's real husband, or to envision Renée as the proof of Christian resurrection. Because of this swirl of ideas, *D'entre les morts* retains reader interest although it takes place primarily within Flavières's head.

How innovative Boileau and Narcejac's technique is here may be open to debate. American crime novelists of the 1950s such as Jim Thompson and David Goodis (both well-known in France) combine objectivity and subjectivity in clever ways. Also, Boileau and Narcejac's *Celle qui n'était plus* uses free indirect discourse—the protagonist's wild thoughts as he tries to figure out what happened to his wife—in a limited way (1954b). However, the extent to which *D'entre les morts* is taken over by the protagonist's thoughts seems to me unusual, more reminiscent of literary modernism than of the crime novel tradition.[2]

Alfred Hitchcock and his scriptwriters take a far different approach to presenting a story with subjective and interpretive dimensions.[3] Hitchcock tells us a romantic and apparently supernatural story with fairly conventional cinematic means. Except for four brief excursions into dream, daydream, or flashback, the film appears to be a representation of objective reality. The character Scottie has no privileged interior monologues, so the flow of thoughts in the novel becomes a much more external experience in the film. However, colors, movement, setting, pacing, speech rhythm, music—indeed, the entire palette of cinematic creativity—turn this superficially objective view into a richly subjective experience.

To begin with, the film's San Francisco, beautifully photographed by Robert Burks, has a muted, crepuscular beauty well-suited to this story of the supernatural. Landscapes show hills and water in green, blue, and gray tones; cityscapes are picturesque and sometimes colorful but always slightly desaturated; interiors range from the brown, masculine tones associated with Gavin Elster (Madeleine's husband in the film, played by Tom Helmore) to the plush red of Ernie's restaurant to the feminine pastels of the upscale dress shop. Madeleine herself has an understated elegance and a wardrobe of muted colors that, combined with her gliding walk, make her seem almost unworldly. Judy is a brasher, more obvious presence, and the film's lighting becomes less diffused when she appears. However, as Scottie transforms Judy back into Madeleine, the muted lighting of the film's first part returns.

Movement in the film is graceful, romantic, perhaps even transcendental. Scottie and Madeleine, "wandering" (the characters' word) by car through the countryside, are seen in uncannily clear and stable medium shots in front of moving landscapes. The effect was produced by back projection, which often looks artificial but here matches the narrative mood. Back projection operates similarly in an earlier hyperromantic Hitchcock film, *Rebecca* (1940). Madeleine moves with a calm, elegant grace, especially when Scottie first sees her at Ernie's. Scottie walks hesitantly, as befits a man who is not quite sure about anything. The intense, desperate kisses of Scottie and Judy are shown with a panning, revolving camera. And the shots expressing Scottie's vertigo are strongly kinesthetic, expressing his disequilibrium as a physical sensation. Movement and image benefit from the widescreen technology of Vista-Vision (pioneered by Paramount, the film's producer, in the mid-1950s), which provides more depth and sharpness than conventional 35 mm film.

Bernard Herrmann's musical score revolves around two major motifs. The motif associated with Madeleine is romantic, wistful, and melancholy. A second, harsher motif occurs at moments of action and stress; it might be called the "vertigo motif." The film's musical high point comes when Judy, already dressed in Madeleine-like clothes, emerges from the bathroom with her hair up; she "becomes" Madeleine. This moment is marked visually by a soft, greenish, otherworldly light and musically by a swelling of the Madeleine theme, which here becomes strongly reminiscent of the "Love Death" from Wagner's opera *Tristan and Isolde*. The musical reference is not only appropriate but stunning.

The film's images and sounds certainly solve all problems of atmosphere and symbolism stemming from the novel, but they don't create the equivalent of the novel's swirl of ideas. It is part of *Vertigo's* originality to take a manic flow of words and thoughts and turn it into a serene flow of images. However, Hitchcock does need additional techniques to solve problems of exposition and to reproduce at least some of the book's intellectual richness. One means of accomplishing this is the introduction of a new character, Scottie's old friend Midge (Barbara Bel Geddes). Midge is the equivalent (in a functional sense) of Flavières's more rational and critical thoughts in the novel. Midge's pragmatism and sense of humor present an alternative to Scottie's extreme romanticism. She also helps with the film's backstory. For example, Midge introduces Scottie to a book dealer who knows the early history of San Francisco, and this allows us to hear the story of Madeleine's beautiful and tragic ancestor Carlotta Valdes (equivalent to Pauline Lagerlac in the book). In terms of visual imagery, Midge provides an image of woman as safe, comfortable, practical, unexciting. It is worth noting that Midge resembles Hitchcock's daughter Patricia (who plays a prominent but unromantic role in *Strangers on a Train*) and Madeleine resembles the cool, elegant, idealized blondes of many Hitchcock movies. Not surprisingly, Scottie prefers poetic Madeleine to prosaic Midge.

The four dream or flashback episodes in *Vertigo* add essential depth and mystery to what is otherwise a conventionally told tale. These are (1) Scottie's dream, dominated by the sensation of falling. This sequence suggests a repetition of Madeleine's death, a desire for his own death, and also perhaps a desire to penetrate illusion to arrive at the truth. (2) Judy's flashback describing her participation in Elster's plot to murder his wife and to use Scottie as an unwitting accomplice. This fascinating scene "solves" the mystery of Madeleine/Judy soon after the introduction of Judy (though the casting of Kim Novak in both roles is itself a strong tipoff). The visual excursion into Judy's consciousness is followed by a scene of Judy writing, then discarding, a confessional love letter (we hear the text in interior monologue). (3) When Scottie succeeds in remaking Judy as Madeleine, an intensely romantic kissing scene with swirling camera follows. In the midst of this romantic scene, the background changes from Judy's hotel room to the carriage house at Mission San Juan Bautista, where Scottie had kissed Madeleine. But the carriage house is a kind of museum, not a fully reconstituted past, and so this scene may signal the limits of Judy's makeover.[4] And (4) soon after the kissing scene, Judy changes her dress and primps in front of a mirror. She puts on *Carlotta's* pendant, which Madeleine supposedly inherited. At this moment the supernatural story breaks down, and we see—presumably from Scottie's point of view—an image flickering from Judy to the Carlotta portrait and back again. The moment illustrates a rational process (the realization that Judy and Madeleine are one person) and at the same time portends a mental breakdown.

Numerous critics have suggested that *Vertigo* is not only a story of romantic obsession but also an allegory of cinema. Scottie creates his "perfect woman" out of memories, fantasies, deceptions, clothes, beauty products, and a willing subject (Judy). Similarly, a film director creates a character or a story out of memories and fantasies plus materials available in the real world. Madeleine is intense, vivid, emotional, yet she never existed; similarly, film is an emotional yet unreal experience. This allegory of cinema reveals something about Hitchcock, who created any number of mysterious/romantic blonde beauties in his films and yet lived quietly with his wife Alma over a long marriage. It also reveals something about Kim Novak, who was never comfortable with the glamorous star image Hollywood figures including Harry Cohn and Hitchcock created for her.[5]

Vertigo as allegory of cinema is sometimes presented as the most personal and most original theme in Hitchcock's long and illustrious career. Nevertheless, this theme is prefigured by the novel *D'entre les morts*. Throughout the novel, Flavières's restless mind is trying to impose his fantasy on the world. The beautiful-woman-connected-with-death is more in Flavières's mind than in the real world, though the deceptions of Gévigne and Madeleine link the mental template with a real (but playacting) woman. In passages quoted above, Flavières specifically relates this connection between fantasy and reality to the work of the novelist or the filmmaker. The lonely middle-aged lawyer in the book thus becomes an image of the novelist/creator, of Boileau and Narcejac, just as the melancholy retired detective of the film becomes an image of the filmmaker/creator Hitchcock. And in both cases, the work of the creator can be seen as the obsessive behavior of the lovesick male. Both Flavières and Scottie are driven to create, and re-create, their ideal female, just as novelists and filmmakers re-create their obsessions in a fictional world. An additional theme of the novel would be that we are all writers, creators, and philosophers because we all attempt to impose meaning on the world. Sad, lonely Flavières thus becomes a version of Everyman, or perhaps even Everyhuman.

The one crucial difference between *D'entre les morts* and *Vertigo* lies in the two endings. The novel concludes, like most crime novels, with the solution to the various mysteries of the plot. Renée confesses to Flavières that she pretended to be Madeleine to help her lover Gévigne murder his wife. Flavières then strangles Renée in their hotel room. The story of transcendental love becomes a rather ordinary case of murder, and Flavières's wild speculations are diminished by the revelation of his at least temporary madness. Certainly the allegory of the lovesick male as literary creator remains part of the novel, but it is distanced by the final murder. In the last few paragraphs, we are removed from Flavières's subjectivity as, speaking aloud, he tries to make sense of his situation: "A love like a marvelous tapestry—on one side it told a wonderful legend, on the other . . . I don't know . . . I don't want to know." (158). He fails or refuses to perceive the true situation, continuing to address "Madeleine" rather than Renée. The murder in this context seems to be a refusal to accept reality; Flavières is insane.

The divergent ending of *Vertigo* actually starts with Judy's flashback showing her complicity in the murder of Madeleine. This confession to the spectator (not to Scottie) solves the primary mystery of the plot and allows Hitchcock and his writers to concentrate on character and theme. Here the contrast between novel and film reverses expectations—for one generally expects the popular medium of film to be plot driven, whereas literature can spend more time on character and ideas. However, the deviation from conventional structure may have affected the film's commercial career. Though Hitchcock was an exceptionally well-known and well-loved filmmaker in 1958, *Vertigo* was only a modest box-office success upon first release.

With Judy's confession out of the way, the emphasis shifts to how Scottie will discover the truth and what he will do next. Scottie understands some of Judy's duplicity when he sees Carlotta's pendant. But instead of confronting Judy in the hotel room (as in *D'entre les morts*), Scottie drives her to the church at San Juan Bautista. He thinks that by reenacting the crime of Mrs. Elster's death, he can be free of the trauma (including vertigo) that it caused him. The idea that understanding a previous trauma will be therapeutic stems from Freud; let us note in passing that Hitchcock's American films are strongly influenced by Freudian psychoanalysis. The return to the church also allows for a visually exciting climactic scene. But Scottie's attempt to cure himself is only partly successful. He does climb to the belltower, but instead of exorcising a moment of loss, he repeats it as Judy falls or jumps to her death. Scottie is left emotionally shattered and profoundly depressed. As to the spectators, we are left to ponder the repetition of emotional disaster.

An important difference between novel and film is that Scottie at the end of *Vertigo* is not a criminal. Thus we cannot disengage from him as we do from Flavières at the end of *D'entre les morts*. Instead, we feel for him, and we feel with him. But Hitchcock doesn't tell us or show us what Scottie is feeling at this point. Our last image of Scottie shows him on a ledge near the top of the bell tower, looking down at Judy's body (unseen by the film viewers). He is hunched over in a private agony but not likely to jump. We are free at this point to project our own fantasies, our own stories, upon Scottie's passive figure. Perhaps he will return to active life, though this seems unlikely, and then be hurt again by romantic love. Perhaps he will remain forever unresponsive, lost in his obsessions. Because Scottie's character is curiously unresolved, his emotion and his anguish continue to reverberate with the film's viewers. The "unfinished" aspect of the story is a considerable part of its brilliance.

This comparative study of *D'entre les morts* and *Vertigo* leads me to several conclusions. The first is that the novel *D'entre les morts* is a remarkable work in its own right. Its study of romantic love via an obsessive protagonist and free indirect discourse provides aesthetic and intellectual experiences far beyond what one would expect of a modest mystery novel. In this case the reputation of a major film has led us to an unknown gem of a novel. The second conclusion is that *D'entre les morts* and *Vertigo* are mutually illuminating. Both works make interesting choices based on a generally similar plot. Some of these choices are medium influenced; for example, Hitchcock chose to evoke Scottie's literal and emotional disequilibrium via kinesthetically powerful shots of vertigo. Some of the choices are context influenced (Boileau

and Narcejac wrote for French readers in the 1950s), and others are influenced by the creators' personal interests and obsessions (Hitchcock's
blondes). Looking at the two works comparatively highlights the choices
that are made. A third conclusion is that, despite the aesthetic richness of
both works, evaluative judgments are still possible. Though I contest Robin
Wood's characterization of *D'entre les morts* as a minor work of "drab, wilful
pessimism" (1965, 72), I do think that *Vertigo*'s ending is far superior to the
ending of the novel. Boileau and Narcejac diminish and criminalize their
character at the novel's end, so we don't need to think about him. On the
other hand, Hitchcock's Scottie is not guilty, except perhaps of not forgiving
Judy, and so we are left to think about his obsessive love, and romantic love
in general.

A fourth and final conclusion is that the most common paradigms for literature and film adaptation studies are not adequate to cover or explain
many interesting cases. Adaptation studies that begin from the literary canon
(e.g., "Shakespeare and film") are fine, except that they leave out so many
paths of investigation. What, for example, is the relationship of the Western
novel (the genre set in the American West, usually in the late nineteenth
century) to the Western film? Conservative literary scholarship would have
no incentive to ask this question. Similarly, the auteur theory, by now a conservative approach to film studies, opens up many subjects of investigation
but closes down others. For example, most studies of *Vertigo*, my own included, owe a debt to Hitchcock's stature as an auteur. But the auteur theory,
with its emphasis on directorial originality, has discouraged study of Hitchcock's source materials; at a certain level, auteurists "don't want to know."
We need to get beyond this prejudice in order to arrive at a far more open
and flexible version of adaptation studies.

Notes

1. The original source of this quote is a critical work on crime fiction by Narcejac: *La fin d'un bluff* (Paris: Portulan, 1949).

2. Thomas Leitch, who suggested the Thompson and Goodis examples to me,
points to Edgar Allan Poe as the originator of this whole tradition of mixing objectivity and subjectivity in crime fiction (personal communication with the author, 17
August 2004).

3. Another understudied area of Hitchcock criticism is the contributions of
screenwriters—in *Vertigo*, Alec Coppel, Samuel Taylor, and Maxwell Anderson (uncredited). Because Hitchcock frequently met with his writers, it is difficult to know

whether a particular idea originated with director or writer(s). However, Barr does credit Coppel and Taylor with specific contributions to *Vertigo's* shooting script.

4. The past as a frozen museum is central to Chris Marker's *La Jetée* (1962), a film greatly indebted to *Vertigo*.

5. See Byars (1997) for a feminist account of Kim Novak's career.

Works Cited

Auiler, Dan. 1998. *Vertigo: The Making of a Hitchcock Classic*. New York: St. Martin's Griffin.

Barr, Charles. 2002. *Vertigo*. London: BFI.

Boileau, Pierre, and Thomas Narcejac. 1954a. *D'entre les morts*. Paris: Denoel.

———. 1954b. *The Woman Who Was No More*. Trans. Geoffrey Sainsbury (English translation of *Celle qui n'était plus*). New York: Rinehart.

———. 1958. *Vertigo*. Trans. Geoffrey Sainsbury (English translation of *D'entre les morts*). New York: Dell. [Reprinted in 1997 by Bloomsbury Press, London.]

Byars, Jackie. 1997. "The Prime of Miss Kim Novak: Struggling over the Feminine in the Star Image." In *The Other Fifties*, ed. Joel Foreman, 197–223. Urbana: University of Illinois Press.

Colin, Jean-Pierre. 1999. *Boileau/Narcejac: Parcours d'un oeuvre*. Amiens, France: Ancrage.

Wood, Robin. 1965. *Hitchcock's Films*. London: A. Zwemmer.

CHAPTER THIRTEEN

~

Heinlein, Verhoeven, and the Problem of the Real: *Starship Troopers*

J. P. Telotte

The typical modern human is characterized by a life under the dictatorship of the screen.

—Paul Virilio (1991)

No wonder you're having nightmares: You're always watching the news.

—*Total Recall*

As the above comments suggest, the "typical modern human," as Paul Virilio offers, seems to live a rather precarious, even nightmarish existence, partly as a result of the audiovisual culture we inhabit. And as a character in Paul Verhoeven's *Total Recall* (1991) attests, within that culture even the "news," which we might think of as a means of linking us to the world, of tying us to events just beyond the small circle of personal experience, even of a kind of liberating potential, can produce an unsettling sense of reality. In his various efforts to explain this contemporary situation, Virilio suggests that we have become subject to a process of what he terms "cinematic derealization," thanks to the way media culture has "denatured direct observation" and even "common sense," providing us with a kind of "substitute" reality (1991, 111). Within this context, the world around us increasingly comes to seem little more than a kind of detached spectacle, and we find ourselves essentially re-constituted as its spectators. In his various science fiction films especially, Verhoeven has repeatedly explored this same problem, although it shows up most clearly in his *Starship Troopers* (1997), an adaptation of Robert Hein-lein's famous Cold War–era novel (1987). In fact, as we compare the novel source to the film, we find one of the major shifts is its focus on our position within an audiovisual culture, as the film foregrounds its own mechanisms and explores the ways in which that culture conditions our sense of reality.

Of course, the science fiction genre has always made great capital from vi-sualizing alien, futuristic, and apocalyptic environments, from catering to our wonder at what strange realities "could be"—usually elsewhere and in other times. All of Verhoeven's science fiction films clearly follow this pattern, as they evoke various sorts of strained and artificial contexts, environments hostile in diverse ways to the human, both on and off Earth. An obvious ex-ample is *Robocop*'s (1987) depiction of a crumbling Old Detroit and its in-tended replacement by a new, gleaming Delta City, a world that is essentially a corporate dream—and exploitation—of what modern life should be like (even to its "planned" and corporate-controlled crime and corruption) and one that is already being sold to people through the various commercials in-terspersed in the narrative. While *Total Recall* begins as a dream, that dream quickly turns into a nightmare about being trapped in a depressurized space suit in the airless atmosphere of Mars. And the film ends with more than a hint that its central characters may still just be living in this dream, despite their seemingly happy ending on a transformed Martian world. Although *Starship Troopers* doesn't interrogate its reality in quite this problematic way, it places its key figures constantly on alien worlds, in damaged spaceships, in nightmarish, seemingly hopeless situations, far removed from their home planet and out of contact with their fellow human beings. In fact, we might say that alienization is the order of the day here and in Verhoeven's other sci-ence fiction films, as they repeatedly suggest how we have come to inhabit a very unnatural and ultimately threatening place, how we have, in great part through our audiovisual media, come to fashion a very unreal world for our-selves.

Such a perspective might seem a strange one to be drawn out of the work of Heinlein, an author often praised for his efforts at realistically grounding his science fiction narratives. Yet while Heinlein has been described as "the most mature, forceful, and influential" of the early modern science fiction writers, particularly for his attention to convincingly detailing even his most fantastic environments, some of his work has also been criticized for the larger context of its detailing (James, 1994, 64). In the 1940s and 1950s, like other noted science fiction authors such as Andre Norton, he produced a body of what has been termed "juvenile" science fiction, most of it published in a Scribner's series aimed at an audience typically conceived of as pre- and early-adolescent males.[1] These dozen early novels, as Jack Williamson explains, follow a fairly consistent "story-of-education pattern" (1978, 30) and emphasize an "optimistic vision of space conquest" (31). And some of them, as Edward James judges, could well be ranked "among the best novels he wrote, introducing young readers to the excitement of frontier life on the planets and to the challenge of different social structures and difficult moral dilemmas" (1994, 84–85). In short, they contain many of the hallmarks of Heinlein's most effective work, including very clear reference to the social context in which he was then writing.

At the same time, all of these early works are clearly marked by exaggeration, often veering into what Heinlein himself termed the "romantic" (1989, 43), and—more significantly—frequently push in the direction of what he called "my own propaganda purposes" (41). On the one hand, Heinlein seems to have been under no illusions about his efforts for the juvenile market. He obviously saw them as a somewhat different sort of writing from his "adult novels," as constituting an attempt "to write wholesome stories which were able to compete with the lurid excitements of comic books" (72). Yet on the other hand, these juveniles betray a typical Heinlein signature, his own sense of the "wholesome." Like the adult novels, they consistently emphasize the hard details of science—such as the complexities of colonizing the planets and the difficulties of space flight (seen especially in his contributions to the script of the landmark film *Destination Moon* [1950])—portray the problems of everyday living (on Earth and elsewhere), and detail the psychological lives of their characters. The result of this dual pull, of a juvenile exaggeration and of Heinlein's trademark fascination with detail, would result in what we might term a rather problematic sense of reality.

We can partly measure out this tension between the requirements of the juvenile genre and an emphasis on what James describes as "not only some hard-headed extrapolation but also . . . a carefully realized social and cultural context, with a 'lived-in' feel" (1994, 66) in some of the strained responses to the novels. Well chronicled are Heinlein's frequent censorship battles with his Scribner's editor Alice Dalgliesh and the reactions of reviewers who objected to elements of sex, violence, and the Heinlein world view that inevitably surfaced even in the juveniles, particularly, as Philip E. Smith argues, the pattern of a cold and inescapable "social Darwinism" (1978, 137). Many of his stories finally seem to be about a kind of cosmic survival of the fittest and the difficulties his young protagonists face in learning this fundamental truth of life. Their emphasis is frequently on the sort of discipline that would be needed to endure in new and often harsh environments —and by extension, for his juvenile readers to survive in a potentially harsh and constantly challenging future, such as he saw facing the United States in the Cold War era. That emphasis has led many to see in all of his work a rather troubling ideology. Thus, Barton Levenson sums up one focus of recent Heinlein criticism when he argues that, "in the clearest sense of the word, his political and ethical beliefs were fascist" (1998, 10).[2]

That charge certainly resonates with the novel *Starship Troopers*, for its militaristic focus, emphasis on the unquestioning obedience to orders, and championing of the elitist group easily suggest such an authoritarian and nationalistic ideology. And partly as a result of that ideology, along with its emphasis on the violent details of war and, as Williamson says, its "glorification of the fighting man" (1978, 30), *Starship Troopers* was rejected for the Scribner's juvenile series. While the novel shares many characteristics with the other, more "innocent" works of the juvenile group, it also points toward a more troubling dimension of Heinlein's canon, one that might help us see how it appealed to Verhoeven as a possible vehicle for his own science fiction perspective.

Certainly, all of Verhoeven's work in this genre suggests a similar tension between the real and the exaggerated, even excessive effect. In assessing his own career, he notes that while working in his home country of the Netherlands, particularly in collaboration with screenwriter Gerard Soeteman, he "went much more to a realistic approach"; at this point his sense of "reality and realism" generally dominated his films (Shea and Jennings, 1993, 11).[3] However, upon coming to America to work on *Robocop*, he says he felt as if he "was going back to my childhood," to the sort of "special-effect movies" he liked as a kid (Shea and Jennings, 1993, 11). In fact, he cites a rather obvious ancestor of *Starship Troopers*, *The War of the Worlds* (1953), as one of the formative films of this juvenile period. While Verhoeven might have initially seen working on *Robocop* as his own kind of juvenile turn, he also found in it something more—an opportunity to deal with elements he "had repressed . . . for twelve or fifteen years" (Shea and Jennings, 1993, 11). The end result seems to have been a rather different approach to reality itself. By the time of *Total Recall*, that developing perception produced a narrative that resolutely refuses to situate its audience in a verifiable actuality; rather, it suggests, as Verhoeven says, "that there are different realities possible at the same moment. What I wanted to do in *Total Recall* is . . . a movie where both levels are true" (Shea and Jennings, 1993, 19). The very indeterminacy built into this approach not only let him draw on his own juvenile perceptions of his world—perceptions honed during the violent Nazi occupation of his homeland and ones that saw violence as "normal" and peace as "anormal" (Shea and Jennings, 1993, 5)—but also allowed him to reflect on how, as a culture, we have managed to construct such a strange and pervasive sense of reality.

The film *Starship Troopers* certainly seems to many like a comic-book exaggeration of reality, much in the vein of *Robocop*; thus Roger Ebert (1997) described it as "the most violent kiddie movie ever made." And in a tone that might recall much later Heinlein criticism, it has been scored for its political posture—or more precisely for lacking one. Richard Schickel (1997), for example, suggests that a key "unexplored premise" of the film is the way that it simply depicts without question "a happily fascist world." And in this same vein, Mike Clark (1997) describes the seductive lure of the film's "army of sweet-tempered, fresh-faced fascists." Perhaps these and other reviewers were drawing in part on Heinlein's own political reputation in this regard, yet what they seem to miss is the great extent to which the film diverges from its novelistic source, particularly as it deploys its exaggerations to explore the very reality from which such a politics would arise—in effect, the extent to which it very precisely examines that "premise." For while Heinlein, in *Starship Troopers* and elsewhere, carefully constructs his world and his characters in painstaking detail and with the sort of rigorous attention to scientific possibility that his pulp editor, Joseph W. Campbell Jr., early on demanded of him and also emphasizes the sort of dictatorial, authoritarian figures that he saw as necessary for survival in such a world, Verhoeven plays rather loosely with his science instead focusing his attention on how our culture does the constructing—of both our world and ourselves.

Of course, Verhoeven's adaptation of the novel undeniably shows many traces of the juvenile tale's influence. For all of its changes, the film still follows the Heinlein pattern of youthful education, in large part because, the movie implies, we have all become very much like juveniles in the process of being molded by today's media culture and its powerful methods of "derealization." *Starship Troopers* takes Johnny Rico and his friends from high school, Diz, Carmen, and Carl, through various forms of military training; it emphasizes the rigors and even deadly dangers of that training; and then it shows several of these figures in combat against the insect foe from the planet Klendathu. Yet its focus is never the same as Heinlein's, on what these characters learn, on Johnny's maturation in particular; rather, it consistently focuses on how people are educated in this future world, indoctrinated on every level, from the classroom, to the sports they play, to the training they undergo in the military, to the pervasive media, to the very structure of society, which rewards those who follow the paths it lays out. When early in the film Johnny rebels against one sort of indoctrination, his parents' efforts to send him on an expensive vacation and then to Harvard for college education, arguing that "it's my decision, not yours," is less the sort of triumphant assertion of individuality that we would expect to find in a Heinlein novel than an ironic note in the face of the many factors we have seen that are already shaping Johnny's future, determining his path to federal service more surely than any conscious decisions he makes.[4]

Especially telling in this case of reality construction are a number of things that disappear from the original story, as well as several others that have been grafted on. Foremost among the missing is the variety of dominant, authoritarian figures. Johnny's father, for example, is killed off early in the film, rather than, as in the novel, reappearing as one of Johnny's own troopers who has accepted and adopted his son's world view. That early death provides Johnny with a purely emotional stimulus for his desire to fight the bugs of Klendathu, in place of the novel's gradually developed and thoroughly rationalized devotion to duty and to behaving as a citizen should. The authoritarian yet, beneath a gruff exterior, fundamentally caring Sergeant Zim simply becomes the hard taskmaster, the stereotyped drill sergeant who teaches through violence, breaking one recruit's arm and throwing a knife through another's hand—both vivid teaching tactics and further steps in the mental conditioning of these would-be soldiers. Although he disappears from most of the film, Zim reappears at the narrative's end as the person who has succeeded in capturing a "brain" bug—in effect, one who has managed to bring an unruly and threatening rational impulse under his violent control, under the control of a race that apparently believes, as Mr. Rasczak asserts, that "violence [is] the supreme authority from which all other authority derives." A key scene added to the film is a live-fire training exercise in which Johnny allows a squad member to remove a protective helmet because he cannot see with it on. When the cadet is subsequently shot in the head and killed, Johnny is blamed and receives a public lashing for his negligence— essentially, for allowing one of his charges to remove the sort of blinders that this culture places on those it wishes to use and control.

Just as important is a significant shift in the narrative mechanism itself. For while Heinlein's novel is a first-person narrative told from Johnny Rico's vantage point, Verhoeven's film unfolds, not from the perspective of any individual, but rather from the point of view offered by the audiovisual culture itself. It is a most fitting shift, for with it, the film is able to establish a rather different authoritarian voice, and indeed a subtly tyrannical power, one that is the real heart of its satiric vision. Here, the book's multiple, powerful authoritarian figures are largely transformed into the media, which, through their substitute reality, become precisely the sort of dictatorial voice of which Paul Virilio speaks.

While the repeated use of commercials in both *Robocop* and *Total Recall* pointed out the extent to which our media have influenced the formation of contemporary consciousness, *Starship Troopers* from its very start establishes the media context of all that we see. In fact, the entire narrative is framed in "reports," news coverage of the struggle with the bug adversary of Klendathu. The film opens on a recruiting video for federal service, showing a young boy in the ranks with regular soldiers, suggesting just how early this culture begins constructing its violent regime. That introductory video is interrupted by images of what those recruits must realistically face in a newsfeed that is being beamed live to Earth, showing the mobile infantry invading Klendathu. The disastrous results of this first action, though, emphasize the problems of such "reality" reporting, as both the on-air reporter and cameraman are killed. Clearly, reality does not want to follow the "script" of heroic warfare and victory that the media has, as we see, already begun shaping for the public back home. The conclusion, too, is a combination of recruiting appeal and newsfeed, detailing a single victory over the bugs, the capture of a "brain bug," and the subsequent testing and experimentation on the creature. A carefully shaped presentation, this last video suggests how the calamitous situation of the war has been carefully reconfigured for public consumption, particularly with its closing affirmation that our forces will "keep on fighting" until they win. And that shaping reminds us how, as Virilio (1989) contends, "the concept of reality is always the first victim of war" (33).

Perhaps the most pointed reminder, though, is the form Verhoeven gives the various other interpolated newsreels/newsfeeds that, from time to time, intrude into and give shape to the narrative. They are a curious combination of the old and the new, of World War II propaganda films and present-day webcasts that together fashion an illusion of the democratic dissemination of information and freedom of choice. On the one hand, the titles of these media messages pointedly evoke Frank Capra's famous World War II *Why We Fight* series and his *Know Your Enemy* films. As Capra (1985) explains, while his films were certainly propaganda, they were a necessary part of the "struggle for men's minds" in that era (329). Couched in the form of rhetorical argument, they examined the causes leading up to the war, examined documents that clarified the ideologies of the combatants, and compared and contrasted the aims of the countries involved; in short, they gave the illusion of a thoughtful, reasoned debate. However, *Starship Troopers*'s videos offer no pretense at argument. Instead, they provide us with exaggerations, sloganeering, and cheerleading, as if the audience were much like the fans we see earlier rooting for Johnny Rico's football team. When one of these feeds does offer something akin to hard information, in a piece titled *Know Your Foe*, it is footage of a cow being slaughtered by a captured bug to demonstrate that species' capabilities and its ferocity; interestingly, much of the slaughter occurs behind a "censored" patch across the screen. In turn, another feed shows a bug, perhaps the same one, being blasted to bits by soldiers who are instructed how to hit its central nervous system in order to make a quicker kill—and here nothing is censored. It is a telling illustration of just what this culture sees as obscene, as a censorable reality, and a clear indication of how it has set about sanctioning a most horrific violent response to the bug foe. More importantly, it drives home the extent to which the sense of reality here seems driven by emotion, impulsive reactions, and spectacular effects.

The film couches this display of propagandistic technique, though, in a thoroughly contemporary context by letting us see these video feeds on screens that suggest the streaming news formats that have become familiar on websites like CNN Interactive and MSNBC. Along with each "news bite" we see a question, "Want to know more?" and a prompt to a hypertext link that is supposed to bring us that "more." However, the narrative's rapid movements from one brief clip to another never follow any of these links, never provide us any in-depth coverage, just the sort of superficial, headline-style information with which both the contemporary evening news and the Internet have made us so familiar. More than just logical, futuristic extensions of the *Mediabreak* news show that begins and frequently cuts into *Robocop*'s narrative—a show that promises, "You give us three minutes and we'll give you the world"—these brief video feeds mock the promise of today's electronic communications, the Internet, and the democratic diffusion of information supposedly available through the World Wide Web. For in one chief respect, these offerings differ little from those propaganda films produced by Capra for the U.S. government in World War II: The illusion of choice and access to "more" information offered here is no great gain in a world where no one seems to have even those three minutes *Robocop* mentions for thoughtful consideration.

Still, the film emphasizes how the people here are all linked together through the latest in communication devices, essential parts of the artificial technological environment that has been crafted for them. Even from deepest space, Johnny can talk to his parents on a video link—at least until that link completely fails when a bug-sent meteor hits Earth. Carmen seems to be talking to Johnny until a track back reveals that she is simply watching a disk he has sent her. In nearly similar fashion, we see Johnny view a communication from Carmen, a video "Dear John" letter—appropriately for this context, a communication that terminates a human relationship. Later, Carmen sends out a distress signal prior to crashing into a bug-occupied planet, but the signal breaks up and is lost before Johnny's squad can get a fix on it. What these and numerous other such failed, interrupted, or faulty communications suggest is the difficulty of living in a mediated world. For as those various technological links, the very ones that so condition our sense of reality, repeatedly fail, leaving humans stranded, alone, trapped by the bug enemy, trapped essentially by our own flight from our humanity, they also point out the fragility of that constructing network on which these people have come to rely.

And yet, as Verhoeven's film suggests with its final lines, we probably shall "keep on fighting" in this alien environment; we shall, for all of our efforts, probably remain a most violent and even self-destructive species, far removed from its home reality. It simply seems, as the title of another of his films suggests, one more "basic instinct" of postmodern humanity. But while for Heinlein this combative nature and predilection for artificial environments are keys to our destiny, a sign of our species' strength, even a mark of our ability to cope with the various challenges with which the conquest of the universe—which he sees as humanity's inescapable destiny—presents us, for Verhoeven it is only a terrible postmodern symptom, part of our retreat from reality itself, a sign of how much we have lost touch with, lost the signal from, or been Dear John-ed by the very real, human world into which we were born. Within this strange, artificial, and ultimately quite fragile environment we have fashioned for ourselves, within the bubble of audiovisual culture, we see—and understand—only what we have culturally decreed that we should see and understand. We almost blindly follow not some fascist leader but a fascist spirit of control incubated in a derealized environment.

Verhoeven's films, then, much like Virilio's work, suggest that today we face something far more disturbing than anything Heinlein might have conceived, more repressive than any political system, in fact, something that all ideologies seem intent on mobilizing for their benefit. That is the cinematic derealization of our world. In response to this pervasive effect, he has in his films tried to trace the shape and visualize the power of this strange audiovisual environment we inhabit. And it is in this respect that he does share a real kinship with an author like Heinlein. *Starship Troopers*, like Verhoeven's earlier science fiction forays, conveys a sense of purpose akin to that which propelled its novelistic origin. For while Heinlein set about trying to awaken his readers from what he saw as an ideological apathy—an apathy that, he feared, could help pave the way for a Communist subversion and takeover—

Verhoeven seems intent on exposing another kind of apathy: our passive acceptance of an increasingly cinematic or mediated reality. He does so by painting that world in broad, satiric strokes, by offering us images that foreground and, in the process, challenge the very ways in which we see our world—or are allowed to see it by the supposedly protective blinders we wear. By exposing our own sort of disconnected, ungrounded astronautic identity, as Jean Baudrillard (1988) has described this postmodern condition,[5] his films attack the much greater and subtler subversion we face in a post–Cold War, postmodern world, that of derealization itself.

Notes

1. For a discussion of the science fiction "juvenile" and its role in helping to create a dedicated adult readership for the genre, see James's *Science Fiction in the Twentieth Century* (1994), especially pp. 84–85.

2. Levenson (1998) bases this conclusion on Heinlein's consistent embrace of what he terms five fundamental tenets of fascism: his fondness for autocratic leaders, his support of militarism, his elitist attitudes, a consistent resorting to consequentialist ethics, and a general contempt for the mechanism of traditional democracy. These elements, he argues, surface repeatedly across the Heinlein canon and are all forthrightly supported in *Starship Troopers*. See his "The Ideology of Robert A. Heinlein."

3. As Verhoeven explains, all of his European work "was based on reality. I mean *Soldier of Orange* was an autobiographical book, *Keetje Tippel* was autobiographical, *Turkish Delight* was, *Spetters* was based on newspaper articles and all taken from magazines—all real things. Even *The Fourth Man*, even though it looks like a fantasy, was for eighty percent an autobiographical novel" (Shea and Jennings, 1993, 11).

4. In the novel Johnny's father rather easily dismisses his son's initial assertion that he will join the federal service, noting that "this family has stayed out of politics and cultivated its own garden for over a hundred years—I see no reason for you to break that fine record" (Heinlein, 1987, 23). And Johnny's actual enlistment suggests no well-devised rebellion against this traditional apolitical stance but rather a sudden surge of youthful enthusiasm; as he notes, "my mouth was leading its own life" (28). To Heinlein's credit, such initial stances and nearly knee-jerk reactions pave the way for his characters to gradually and credibly move toward their true commitments.

5. Baudrillard offers this astronautic metaphor in his *The Ecstasy of Communication* wherein he describes the postmodern human as one who "sees himself promoted to the controls of a hypothetical machine, isolated in a position of perfect sovereignty, at an infinite distance from his original universe; that is to say, in the same position as the astronaut in his bubble, existing in a state of weightlessness which compels the individual to remain in perpetual orbital flight" (1988, 15).

Works Cited

Baudrillard, Jean. 1988. *The Ecstasy of Communication*. Trans. Bernard and Caroline Schutze. New York: Semiotext(e).

Capra, Frank. 1985. *The Name above the Title*. New York: Random House.

Clark, Mike. 1997. "'Troopers' on Beeline to Blockbuster." *USA Today*. www.usatoday .com

Ebert, Roger. 1997. Review of *Starship Troopers*. http://rogerebert.suntimes.com/apps/ pbcs.dll/article?AID=/19971107/REVIEWS/711070305/1023

Heinlein, Robert A. 1987. *Starship Troopers*. New York: Ace Books.

———. 1989. *Grumbles from the Grave*. Ed. Virginia Heinlein. New York: Ballantine.

James, Edward. 1994. *Science Fiction in the Twentieth Century*. Oxford, UK: Oxford University Press.

Levenson, Barton Paul. 1998. "The Ideology of Robert A. Heinlein." *The New York Review of Science Fiction* 116: 1, 8–11.

Schickel, Richard. 1997. "All Bugged Out, Again." *Time*. www.time.com/time/magazine/ article/0,9171,987338,00.html

Shea, Chris, and Wade Jennings. 1993. "Paul Verhoeven: An Interview." *Post Script* 12 (3): 3–24.

Smith, Philip E., II. 1978. "The Evolution of Politics and the Politics of Evolution: Social Darwinism in Heinlein's Fiction." In *Robert A. Heinlein*, ed. Joseph D. Olander and Martin Harry Greenberg, 137–71. New York: Taplinger.

Virilio, Paul. 1989. *War and Cinema: The Logistics of Perception*. Trans. Patrick Camiller. London: Verso.

———. 1991. *The Lost Dimension*. Trans. Daniel Moshenberg. New York: Semiotext(e).

Williamson, Jack. 1978. "Youth against Space: Heinlein's Juveniles Revisited." In *Robert A. Heinlein*, ed. Joseph D. Olander and Martin Harry Greenberg, 15–31. New York: Taplinger.

PART III

POLITICS AND ADAPTATION

~

CHAPTER FOURTEEN

Literary Hardball:
The Novel-to-Screen Complexities
of *The Manchurian Candidate*

Linda Costanzo Cahir

A defining legacy of postmodernism is that the sharp lines that separated genres and that distinguished high art from low, lines which once appeared so very clear, have become blurred. In no single academic discipline is this characteristic more celebrated than in cultural studies, that discourse which explores the ways in which humans understand and articulate their world. Boundaries are not as definable as we once believed. In the wake of this realization, it is important to examine the relationship between culture as lived experience (popular culture) and culture as creative and philosophical expression (high culture). Current scholarship suggests that both canonical literature and popular works merit detailed analyses that draw on artistic, social, and historical contexts.

Popular films based on sources from the Bible to Shakespeare to modern novels are studied and understood as cultural artifacts and political polemics, subtly or overtly proselytizing the filmmakers' viewpoints on societal issues. *The Manchurian Candidate* provides a strong example of how the study of a novel translated into popular film can be explored within the contexts of political science, history, literature, film, and psychology.

Published in 1959, the novel *The Manchurian Candidate* is Richard Condon's unrelenting assault on Cold War tactics, on the use of pernicious means to secure ascension to American political power, and on the hypocrisy, chicanery, and simple indecency that are the hidden, but abiding, values behind American success stories. The story centers on Raymond Shaw, stepson to Senator John Yerkes Iselin, who, with the aid of his wife, Eleanor Iselin (Raymond's mother), is engineering a bid to be president of the United States.

Raymond Shaw is a recipient of the Medal of Honor for his outstanding and heroic conduct as the leader and savior of a squadron of American soldiers captured during the Korean War. However, we learn later that Shaw never really saved his platoon at all. The story of his heroism was manufactured by Communist operatives attempting to infiltrate American politics. These operatives brainwashed Shaw, psychologically programming him to be a political assassin. To test the success of their brainwashing efforts, the Communists have Shaw kill two of his own men, then have him demonstrate that he feels no remorse and retains no memory of the act. The entire platoon witnesses the murders, but, mentally reconditioned themselves, they have been brainwashed into believing that Shaw saved them.

As a result, Shaw returns to the United States as a highly decorated war hero, while he is actually a helpless tool of Communist chieftains attempting to destroy American democracy by placing a puppet of the Communists in the White House. Raymond Shaw is their perfect killer because he is devoid of any hesitancy, guilt, and memory of his crimes. As Condon (2004) writes, "Without the consciousness of guilt . . . he had been made unique" (104).[1] He had also been made utterly alone: "motherless (by choice), fatherless (by treachery), friendless (by circumstance), and joyless (by consequence)" (12). He is incapable of forming close ties with other people, and, while amply skilled (he is intelligent, handsome, and "the greatest natural marksman in the division"), Shaw has "no ability to make friends" (27, 104). He lives fully isolated and detached.

Condon's novel posits a Freudian explanation for Shaw's emotional isolation, adding psycho-biographic information which seeks to link the crucial influence Shaw's mother had on his abnormal emotional development. A psychoanalytic approach to the novel would certainly center on Shaw's mother, whom he hates; but such a reading would also include consideration of Shaw's Oedipal conflict and repression; of Eleanor Iselin's lust for power as attributed to a repressed Puritan conscience; of the network of male and female sexual symbolism present in the novel; and of the importance of dreams as they relate to Freud's theory of displacement (where an image is replaced by a psychologically more significant one) and Freud's theory of secondary revision (where disparate, seemingly illogical elements are shown to comprise an intelligible, coherent, revelatory whole).

Within Condon's ever-darkening world, the novel slowly reveals how Eleanor Iselin has manipulated every detail of her son's life. When he was a young man, she put an abrupt halt to Raymond's plans to marry Jocelyn Jordan. Unbeknownst to her son or to Jocelyn, Eleanor met with Jocelyn's father, Senator Thomas Jordan, and explained to him that "his daughter was far too fine a girl to be hurt or twisted by her son, that Raymond was a homosexual and in other ways degenerate, and that he would be far, far better forgotten by this sweet, fine child" (115). Eleanor's claims are a string of treacherous lies intended to yield the results she wants: Politically, she succeeds in severing a potentially damaging family alliance that would come of a link between her husband, the conservative John Iselin, and the liberal Tom Jordan; and, personally, she triumphs by obliterating from Raymond's life the one woman he loves, and, who, in turn, loves him, and whom Eleanor Iselin jealously loathes. The novel strongly hints at an incestuous mother/son relationship, which Eleanor commands as she commands all the men in her life: bringing their "dependence on her to a helpless maximum" (76). As she is described, Ellie Iselin is a woman who "calculated without hesitation," who "played all her key scenes with consummate art," and who "contrived all" with absolute "precision" (80, 81).

Raymond attributes his father's earlier suicide to his mother, whose very public affair with, and assertive political promotion of, Johnny Iselin—Mr. Shaw's own law partner—brought the senior Shaw shame, humiliation, loneliness, and despair. Raymond knows that his mother is vacuously depleted of all concern for anything outside of her drive for power. He even understands that she pragmatically viewed the premature death of her second son (Raymond is her first) as something that could be spun to political advantage: "greatly helping Johnny Iselin's bid for the governorship by interjecting that element of human sympathy into the campaign" (71). At her most horrific, Eleanor Iselin was instrumental in her son Raymond's being brainwashed and reconditioned into a murderer and a political pawn who could be used whenever and however the covert powers would choose.

Mrs. Iselin's self-made life, in all its wealth, power, social status, and personal triumphs (she raised a son who is believed to be a highly decorated war hero, and she is married to a man who could become president), ostensibly embodies the American dream. However, her realization of the dream has been attained through a highly calculated string of horrible acts in which people closest to her are nothing more than instruments in Ellie Iselin's campaign for worldly success. Eleanor "sought power the way a superstitious man might look for a four-leaf clover. She didn't care where she found it" (74). She thrives in an ethos of murder and betrayal, involving her own husbands or her own son in each as game pieces throughout her strategic maneuvers. Outwardly, she appears to be a poised and selfless advocate for numerous worthy organizations, but her son recognizes her as the consummate monster that she is.

Eleanor Shaw is not an isolated case of reprehensibility. Condon created a world populated with base and vile people. Eleanor's second husband Judge John Iselin secured the governorship when and because his wife (with his knowledge) procured the crucial support of Senator Banstoffsen through "one simple sprawl on an office desk" (90). Eleanor's first and second husbands were not only law partners but also best friends, however this did not stop Johnny Iselin from double-crossing and humiliating Raymond's father. The senior Mr. Shaw was no better. He had married Eleanor when she was just sixteen (he was twenty-nine), doing so "after two ecstatic frictions on an automobile seat" (73). As an attorney, he was the sole executor of two large estates; the fiduciary for "the substance of two maiden ladies and an institution-committed schizophrenic," and, over the period of sixteen years, he systematically looted them (77).

The novel's style is hard boiled, hard edged, and hard hitting. Its plot reveals the darkest sides of humanity and society and the darkest underpinnings of the American dream. *The Manchurian Candidate* takes place in a complicated, corrupt world of dark secrets and ambiguities. At its heart, it is a crime story set against a backdrop of uncertainty, with the only predictable outcome being that humankind's conduct will invariably be base: self-serving, ignoble, cowardly, unapologetic, and unregenerate.

In its style, its subject, its depiction of character, and its theme, *The Manchurian Candidate* is in keeping with the tradition of hard-boiled American crime fiction. A literary approach to the study of this novel might include an analysis of the ways in which *The Manchurian Candidate* continues and expands upon American crime fiction of the 1920s and 1930s. This literary tradition started with the short stories that appeared in the magazine *The Black Mask*, created in 1923 by editors George Jean Nathan and Henry L. Mencken. The tradition reached its golden age in the work of Horace McCoy,[2] Raymond Chandler,[3] Dashiell Hammett,[4] and James M. Cain,[5] whose fiction became central in the Hollywood film industry.

Central to this tradition are plots constructed around lies, double-dealings, betrayals, and misrepresentations. Often cruel and brutal, the world, as presented in these works, is always uncertain, an environment which compels the protagonists to find their way through mazes of duplicity. Unable to be certain of the authenticity of any facts that emerge and necessarily wary of all people, the protagonists are deeply cynical and hardened.

They live alienated from a society they know to be corrupt. Themes and recurring images of alienation and entrapment abound in an atmosphere where
one's lover is underhanded, where all judges are corrupt, and where political
machinations and governmental malady abound. The protagonists have no
faith in legal justice or in stable, predictable patterns of life; instead, they understand that life is morally deplete, chaotic, and subject to ethical and situational randomness. Two types of people populate the world of the hard-
boiled school of fiction: transgressors and victims. The writers in this
tradition share a distinctive view which Raymond Chandler famously describes in *The Simple Art of Murder*:

> Their characters lived in a world gone wrong, a world in which, long before the
> atom bomb, civilization had created the machinery for its own destruction and
> was learning to use it with all the moronic delight of a gangster trying out his
> first machine-gun. The law was something to be manipulated for profit and
> power. The streets were dark with something more than night. (1972, 121)

Richard Condon clearly shares this view. *The Manchurian Candidate* depicts a world gone wrong. Throughout the novel, the law is manipulated, to
ghastly extremes, by Eleanor and Johnny Iselin—as well as other governmental and military officials—motivated solely by personal profit and power.
The American public is a willing, if unwitting, accomplice to its own victimization; and the American political system is both the enabler and ultimately the dupe of their strategies. Johnny Iselin, the corrupt judge, ascends
to become Johnny Iselin, the corrupt senator. Modeled on Senator Joseph
McCarthy, Iselin fabricates accusations of Communists lurking throughout
America's Defense Department, which results in an annihilation of reputa-
tions and a ruination of lives.[6] Just as crucially, the red scare that he sets off
ultimately makes a mockery of senatorial proceedings, transforming the democratic and deliberative body into a tyrannical and despotic combination of
court, jury, and executioner focused on one, single issue. Throughout it all,
Johnny Iselin acts in accord with Eleanor Iselin's grand plan and with the
"moronic delight of a gangster trying out his first-machine gun" that Raymond Chandler describes as central to this literary tradition.

Central also to this tradition is the femme fatale, that woman who is as
beautiful, resourceful, and smooth talking as she lethally conniving, double-
crossing, and murderous, a role taken to a consummate extreme by *The
Manchurian Candidate*'s Eleanor Iselin. Strong minded, tough, and independent, Ellie Iselin is described as "an exceptionally handsome woman . . . straw
blond, in the Viking tradition" and as someone who held a "pre-eminence in

any group of women" (84–85). She is also lethally dangerous, operating with an instinctual, sophisticated, and complex understanding of the inculcating power of her sexuality. Void of any conscience, she manipulates, controls, and betrays the men in her life who once loved her most. Without qualm and in service of her appetence to power, she destroys her first and second husbands and her own son.

Raymond Shaw functions as the novel's protagonist. In keeping with the hard-boiled tradition, he is emotionally detached, abides in an ethical limbo, and becomes the dupe of a femme fatale. In Condon's Freudian expansion of and variation on this literary tradition, the femme fatale happens to be Raymond's own mother. The book's innuendos suggest that they share a complex sexual relationship. Underhanded and lethally duplicitous, she manipulates, traps, betrays, and ruins her son, making her the most pernicious of femme fatales.

Hard-boiled American fiction clearly developed its complexity and literary prowess under the direction of Joseph T. "Cap" Shaw. Made editor of *Black Mask* in 1924,[7] Shaw understood, better than anyone else at the time, the pith and substance of hard-boiled fiction. He articulated a clearer, more expansive concept of this genre and functioned as an effective editor and recruiter of writers for his publication. It was Cap Shaw, for example, who recognized the talent in Dashiell Hammett, an ex-Pinkerton agent who had written just a few stories. Cap Shaw convinced Hammett to write much more seriously and to appreciate and to explore the depth possible in the genre. *The Manchurian Candidate* brings to this literary genre the political, philosophical, and psychological depth that Cap Shaw envisioned; and Richard Condon's decision to name his protagonist "Shaw" very well may be a quiet homage to Cap Shaw and his legacy.

In keeping with hard-boiled fiction, *The Manchurian Candidate* functions as a sociopolitical critique of what Chandler describes as "the machinery humanity created for its own destruction" (1972, 11). More specifically, the book is a critique of the Cold War and the ethos that drove it. Thus, in addition to being fertile ground for psychology and literary study, *The Manchurian Candidate* lends itself to inclusion in twentieth-century political science and history discourse.

The novel has been made into a film twice: 1962 (United Artists) and 2004 (Paramount); however, the 1962 film, *The Manchurian Candidate*, was unavailable for screening (as discussed later) from the early 1970s through 1988. Its subsequent rerelease prompts new discussion in film adaptation studies, including the exploration of the complex reasons for and effects of the film's having been prohibited.

Much like the book, the 1962 film adaptation functions as a critique of the Cold War and, simultaneously, as a more general critical exploration of a world gone wrong and the reasons for it. Within the mazelike plot that the film adapts from the book, the movie causes us to contemplate the socio-political machinations that abound in world politics and leads us to conclude that the defects of society—whether a democracy, a Communist state, or otherwise—can consistently be traced back to the defects of human nature.

The film, *The Manchurian Candidate*, had its American theatrical release on 1 January 1962, a date that coincidentally became sandwiched between two defining Cold War events: the April 1961 Bay of Pigs invasion and the October 1962 Cuban missile crisis. The movie depicts an assassination attempt on an American presidential candidate; and, while the assassination plan was designed by Soviets and Chinese conspiring to seat a Communist-controlled candidate as president of the United States, the plan was orchestrated, in part, by a powerful American politician. At its heart, the film is pointedly critical of the American political process and the corrupt politicians who serve it and chilling in its suggestion that some political leaders, driven by personal ambition, may covertly be operating in collusion with the very leaders they openly oppose. This 1962 movie is unabashed in its assertion that political ascendancy frequently is achieved through duplicity and crime, and, as such, stands as example of art heralding life. At the time of its release the president was John Fitzgerald Kennedy, whose own father, Joseph Kennedy, had amassed the family's huge fortune largely through duplicitous and illegal means. Released at the time it was (merely nine months after America's involvement in the Bay of Pigs), the movie was bold in its political criticism; and United Artists exhibited a certain bravery–or temerity—in financing it. The movie certainly functions as a comment on its times, although it is largely remembered, in political terms, for its broad-stroke lampooning of Senator Joseph McCarthy and the House Committee on Un-American Activities and for its satire of the paranoia that reigned during the Cold War.

The Manchurian Candidate (1962) is a film which has been honored by the American Film Institute as one of America's 100 greatest movies. A traditional translation of Richard Condon's 1959 novel of the same title, the 1962 film maintains the overall traits of the book—its plot, settings, and stylistic conventions—but revamps particular details in the specific ways that the filmmakers saw as necessary and fitting. The film accelerates the novel's slower-paced unfolding of plot detail and dispenses with a few minor characters (Ed Mavole's father and Senator Banstoffsen, for example) doing so, however, without diminishing the novel's story, character development, theme, or tone.

The tone of Condon's novel presents an uncompromisingly cynical opinion of the workings of politics, as does the film. Condon's brutally critical stance is integral to the novel's meaning; and the film conveys, with force and ferocity, the weight of Condon's dark convictions. The screenplay (by George Axelrod) remains true to the literal details of the story, while integrating much of Condon's prose in with the characters' dialogue. While the 1962 film does soften the novel's references to drugs (in the novel Eleanor Iselin is a drug addict), sexuality, the incestuous history of Raymond Shaw, and the dirty dealings of his unconscionably ambitious mother, the film never backs off from the book's greater significance: showing the vastly iniquitous machinations carried out by politicians who look so respectable in their outward aspect.

These machinations are carried out in the political arena of the Cold War. The Cold War between the Soviet Union and the United States was defined by the great divide of political ideologies: Communism and democracy. The two ideologies carried propagandizing points of view. For the Soviets, the world was divided into two camps: the dehumanizing and degrading imperialist, capitalist regimes and the progressive Communist humanists. For the Americans, there were also two diametrically opposed ideologies: one free and dedicated to personal independence and liberty and one treacherously determined to divest the people of all nations of their inalienable human rights. However, the film, in keeping with Condon's views, sees the Cold War as less of an ideological struggle than a struggle for world dominance. In both the novel and the 1962 film, the political banner—Communism or democracy—that the power brokers carry seems to be of no more significance to them than a team color would be, even as they speak out passionately in the language of their convictions. The Chinese and the Soviet Communists, brothers in ideology, are competitive rather than cooperative; combatant rather than monolithic; and downright petty in their needs to assert national—and personal—supremacy. Senator Iselin's public outrage against Communist infiltration of America's Defense Department is a construction of lies solely created to propel the unknown senator into American prominence, with a view to the White House as the end. Against the backdrop of the Cold War, the film, like the novel, posits the notion that power, not political principle, drives the real workings of world politics.

The movie centers on Raymond Shaw (Laurence Harvey); his overbearing, dictatorial mother (Angela Lansbury); and his step-father, Johnny Iselin (James Gregory). Like the novel, the film is as much about the literal 1950s Cold War politics of Communism and democracy as it is about the corruption that Condon believes is inherent in all political practices. Like the novel, the film is constructed around mounting suspense, based on intricacies of plot. One of these intricacies involves concurrent action in which two men from Shaw's platoon, Captain/Major Bennett "Ben" Marco (Frank Sinatra) and Corporal Alvin "Al" Melvin (James Edwards), independent of one another, experience the same recurring nightmare. Early on in the film, their dream is conveyed in a memorable sequence which is created, in part, by an uninterrupted pan in which the camera tracks a full 360 degrees.

Director John Frankenheimer and cinematographer Lionel Lindon create striking images using high speed, monochrome film. Frankenheimer and Lindon integrate, with wonderful success, techniques that they learned from watching *Citizen Kane*: deep focus, wide angles, and chiaroscuro lighting. Like *Citizen Kane* (also shot in black and white), *The Manchurian Candidate* incorporates overlapping dialogue, montage, and shock editing, the last of which creates a wonderfully unsettling and unpredictable rhythm to the entire movie.

The Manchurian Candidate, now considered a classic of American film, would not have been made had Frank Sinatra not succeeded in having then-president John F. Kennedy intervene. Kennedy reassured Arthur Krim (president of United Artists and finance chairman for the Democratic party) that he was a fan of Condon's novel and was untroubled by its subject matter being brought to the screen. However, from the early 1970s through 1988, the movie was unavailable. Sinatra had bought the rights to the film and forbade its exhibition in any form. While Sinatra never explained why he prohibited screenings of *The Manchurian Candidate*, most film historians speculate that the presidential assassination that occurs in this 1962 film, which might never have been made had Kennedy not given his imprimatur to the project, is a painful reminder of John F. Kennedy's actual assassination, which occurred within a year after the film's release.

The novel is hard hitting and absent of any courageous, admirable, or welcoming characters. Departing from Condon's relentlessly dark vision, the 1962 film provides a star personality, Frank Sinatra, and the story invariably becomes more focused on his more competent and likeable Ben Marco. The audience could identify with and cheer for Sinatra's Marco, the regular guy who becomes the reluctant hero, trying, at great personal cost, to stop the insidious political machine run from the shadows.

The 1962 film *The Manchurian Candidate* demonstrates a successful collaboration of talents—direction, acting, production design, editing, and sound—resulting from the particular chemistry of the particular elements assembled for that particular movie. Condon's novel has been brought to the screen one more time. The 2004 movie, *The Manchurian Candidate*, directed by Jonathan Demme from a screenplay written by Daniel Pyne and Dean Georgaris, relocates Condon's setting to contemporary time.

Instead of the Korean War, Sergeant Raymond Shaw (Liev Schreiber), Captain/Major Ben Marco (Denzel Washington), and their platoon served in the first Persian Gulf War (1991). During a routine reconnaissance mission in Kuwait, they were ambushed by the enemy, brainwashed, and programmed to recall the experience as Raymond Shaw's heroic feat. (They claim that Shaw seized a machine gun and single-handedly annihilated the enemy.) Shaw returns home and is awarded the Congressional Medal of Honor; however, fully unknown to him, the enemy has implanted a subcutaneous microchip in Shaw which transforms him into an unthinking, unfeeling minion of the enemy. The majority of the film is set thirteen years later. Raymond Shaw, handsome and appearing (ironically) fully self-possessed, is an up-and-coming young congressman; and his mother, Senator Eleanor Prentiss Shaw (Meryl Streep), acting with Mephistophelean skill, is engineering a bid for Raymond to be vice president.

Rather than focusing on Raymond Shaw, as Condon's novel does, this film centers on Ben Marco, whose nightmares have been diagnosed as Gulf War Syndrome. Unable to find anyone in the military who will countenance his suspicions that *something* nefarious did happen to his platoon in Kuwait and afraid to sleep because the Iraqi nightmare will recur, Denzel Washington's Bennett Marco lives all alone, on cup-a-noodles and No-Doz. Very different from Frank Sinatra's more bravura-filled depiction of Marco, Washington's character is frightened, haunted, despondent, and unsure of his own sanity; and, as such, he stands closer to the character Condon created. When Marco learns that a fellow platoon member, Al Melvin (Jeffrey Wright), is experiencing the same recurring nightmares as he, Marco grows determined to get at the source of these recurring dreams. In the process of getting at the truth, he uncovers layers of political perfidy and discovers duplicitous connections among Raymond Shaw's election campaign, Senator Eleanor Shaw, and a vast, global corporation: Manchurian Global.

Meryl Streep plays the powerful Senator Eleanor Prentiss Shaw as a composite of contemporary, high-profile women politicians, most particularly Senator Hillary Rodham Clinton, Senator Kay Bailey Hutchison, and Governor Ann Richards. Often dressed in soft pastels and a modesty of pearls, Streep's Eleanor Shaw is a skilled political ambusher, whose soft cashmere and cultured pearls serve as camouflage for a menacingly entrapping force who is coldly calculating, made more of concrete and steel than human flesh.[8] Rather than being icy and pugilistic as Angela Lansbury's Eleanor Shaw was, this Eleanor Shaw has an easy, confident demeanor, complete with a charmingly intelligent giggle (we see why her constituency votes for her), but there is a perverse quality in the tingle of her laughter and a sinister edge to all she does.

One particularly sinister moment occurs in a political backroom during the presidential convention. The ethical Senator Thomas Jordan (Jon Voight), his party's top choice for vice president, is unexpectedly dropped from the ticket by means of Eleanor Shaw's power-play, which lands her son in the favored spot. Senator Jordan understands that Eleanor Shaw's vast political power comes from her relationship with the Manchurian Corporation, and he quips about her son's nomination, "Just think. He'll be the first vice president wholly owned and operated by a major corporation." The quip, an indirect lampooning of the current American vice president, Richard Cheney, and his ties to Halliburton, is a signature trait of this film. Barbed political comments on real, contemporary issues are made throughout the film but never directly. Instead, innuendo delivers the hits. Thus, the seemingly constant television feed that plays in the film's background is a satirical reference to Fox News and the role that Fox plays in attempting to shape political opinions rather than reporting political facts. The real motive behind America's Patriot Act, the film implies, has little to do with diminishing terrorism. Multinational corporations control the politicians who, in turn, control the government; and the Patriot Act allows the government—and the corporations—to work more efficiently without the inconvenient encumbrances created by responsibility for civil liberties, which interfere with the corporations' ability to make ever-larger profits in an expanded and well-controlled world market.

Bennett Marco stands alone against the perversely corrupt forces that he discovers; and though he wants to, he cannot restore order; he cannot set all to right. The basic narrative pattern of hard-boiled crime fiction pits the lone investigator, Marco, against brutal thugs, often in league with a corrupt power. In this case, the brutal thugs and corrupt power all emanate from a multinational corporation, Manchurian Global, comprised of greedy business people with so much power that they can place one of their minions in the White House.

The corporation in the film carries the name "Manchurian," to tie it to the book, and the name "Global," to modernize it. The malevolent force is no longer a power from a particular geographic area, then the mysterious, Communist Manchurian region of China. It is now a power more insidious because it's everywhere; it's global.

The 2004 The Manchurian Candidate is an adaptation that tells much about the time in which it was made, a period which witnessed an uneasy melding of politics, big business, and entertainment in America. Lines became blurred in an age when politics became a spectator sport, packaged and pushed by cable news networks, media conglomerates, and publishers taken over by megacorporations, all seeking to attract viewers and readers. Filmmakers have entered the fray, as well, making films to express political viewpoints and to sell tickets.

Some films in 2004 were decidedly and openly partisan. Such films, deliberate in mission and tone, include *Stolen Honor*, the anti–John Kerry film, produced by Red, White, and Blue Productions and narrated by its president, investigative reporter and Vietnam veteran Carlton Sherwood; the anti–Michael Moore films, Michael Wilson's *Michael Moore Hates America* and Larry Elder's *Michael and Me*; and the anti–Bill Clinton movie, *Mega Fix: The Dazzling Political Deceit That Led to 9/11*. Each of these films was screened at the American Renaissance Film Festival, the first-ever conservative film festival, staged in Dallas, Texas, on the third anniversary weekend of the 9/11 terrorist attack.

Control Room (2004), directed by the Harvard-educated Egyptian American Jehane Noujaim, is a documentary which offers an unadulterated look into the international perception of America's invasion of Iraq and into Al Jazeera, the Arab world's most popular news network, widely regarded as Osama bin Laden's mouthpiece. Ms. Noujaim's film depicts Al Jazeera as largely an instrument of anti-American propaganda and implies that American journalists (we see reporters from CNN, Fox News, and NBC) are under a similar pressure by the Bush administration, which exerts influence over how they report the news.

Michael Moore's Cannes Film Festival, *Palme d'Or*–winning film, *Fahrenheit 9/11*, takes aim at George W. Bush's abuses of power. Moore edits together documented film clips with some staged scenes and his own voice-over narration to piece together an exposé of the Bush family's business links to the Taliban, the bin Laden family, and the intricate, global maze of Halliburton. The issue the film raises is similar to that of *The Manchurian Candidate*: There is a crisis created by the secretive, duplicitous, and self-serving actions of those who would control government and the media-manipulated populace. Moore, himself, plays a Ben Marco character, the regular guy poking his nose behind the scenes in an attempt to discover the truth.

Much as these films provide comments on America's political climate in 2004, the two film versions of *The Manchurian Candidate* comment on their political era, the Cold War and post-9/11 America, respectively. John Frankenheimer's 1962 film shows how the anti-Communist paranoia that reigned during the Cold War was used by corrupt politicians who manipulated that fear in order to gain political power. Jonathan Demme's 2004 film, with its multiple references to America's war on terror, shows how adroit political marketing can be used to exploit the fears of an entire nation victimized by the terrorist threat. A. O. Scott (2004) wrote in his *New York Times* review of the film, "The shadowy desire for total political control that scared us in the cold war . . . seems impossibly quaint next to the mundane, insatiable drive to wring profit out of the world's instability."

The brainwashing that occurs in the novel and the 1962 film is replaced in the 2004 movie by implanted microchips. Ours is an age of computers and arcane, high technology, the film reminds us; and in an era when election results can be determined by the reprehensible, yet almost undetectable, manipulation of electronic voting machines, Demme's film hints that we all—not just Raymond Shaw, but all of us—can become the unknowing pawns of thugs in high places. If Manchurian Global is meant to function as analogy to Halliburton, then the duplicity that occurs in the film's political backroom during the national convention might very well be a comment on the corporate strategies that won George W. Bush and Dick Cheney the White House in 2000 and a prognostication of the invariable outcome of the 2004 presidential election.

The nationwide release of *The Manchurian Candidate* on 30 July 2004 was sandwiched between the American Democratic National Convention (26–29 July 2004) and the Republican National Convention (30 August–2 September 2004), a time of heightened political awareness in the United States. The crucial scene in *The Manchurian Candidate* takes place at one such national convention (it could be either or any major party). Thus, as the film's political party is selecting its vice presidential and presidential candidates, the same process was actually occurring in the United States. The American people are in the exact same position as the American public in the film, and the concurrence can give the film audience the sense that they are behind the scenes, peering in at what really happens in the back rooms of politics during an American convention. The timing of the film's release is meant to make people think about what really might be going on throughout the national convention; and the movie's use of a television feed that often plays in the background may cue the film audience to the great divide that exists between the slickly spun, highly edited broadcast news we receive and the actual political workings. Released when it was, the movie is bold in its political criticism; and Paramount, like United Artists before it, exhibited a certain bravery—or temerity—in financing its adaptation of *The Manchurian Candidate.*

The novel and the two films show how politicians seek to be the manufacturers rather than the upholders of reality. The Manchurian brainwashing carried out in the novel and the 1962 film, like the Manchurian Corporation's microchip implant of the 2004 film, results in the manufacturing of a war hero and the simultaneous manufacturing of a programmed political assassin. In 1962, brainwashing was a very real national fear, much as the arcane world of technology is in post-9/11 America. Thus, the implantation of a microchip in 2004, like brainwashing in 1962, is a fictional device born of reality. Technology has advanced so far beyond the understanding of the average person that instead of inspiring faith that it is bettering society as a whole, it drives a suspicion that it is being used by the few to control the many. People who feel overmastered by the ever-growing complexities of their VCRs and PCs suspect that self-serving corporations, so much the subject of modern scrutiny, wield computers the size of pinheads as nefarious wizards once wielded wands. In 2004 America, technology, like the earlier brainwashing, is a means of potent, invisible, and clandestine control; and in all three versions of *The Manchurian Candidate*, the enemy is insidiously unidentifiable but certainly among us.

In all three versions of *The Manchurian Candidate*, we witness the power brokers attempting to dominate the world as they manufacture heroic personalities out of people whom they utterly control. In American politics during the 2004 presidential election, both major parties sought to manufacture their candidates as heroes, even as each side tried to tear down the heroic status of the other's candidate to win the election of 2004.

Decorated Vietnam War hero John Kerry was touted as such by his Democratic Party and then denounced by the opposition for falsely creating his own heroic persona. Republican George W. Bush strutted on the deck of an aircraft carrier off Iraq after landing a jet in front of a banner proclaiming "Mission Accomplished." The opposition denounced him for staging a manufactured photo opportunity, blatant and self-promoting, in a moment when the country needed a strong leader who came by his heroism the old-fashioned way.

The 2004 *The Manchurian Candidate* came out to a polarized electorate and during a time when the distinction between news and entertainment media grew fiercely blurred. Media coverage of the 2004 election was a grand melange of politics, sociology, spun political commentary, hard news, and entertainment meant to persuade, inform, indoctrinate, and entertain viewers. One was left with the uneasy feeling that the reality behind the *news* that reached us was, perhaps, more horrifying than that occurring in *The Manchurian Candidate*.

All three versions of *The Manchurian Candidate* are revelatory about their times, as much about the politicians and the age in which they govern as about the writers and filmmakers who chronicle human behavior in the arena of politics. Each of the three versions warns that we should have real fears that the system is corrupt beyond repair. Even if the 2004 film version of *The Manchurian Candidate* loses some of the novel's hard-boiled edge in order to fit Hollywood's star-studded stock character of the likeable, noble underdog and the panacea of the neatly packaged ending, it should inspire students of politics and broadcasting to wonder if the American electorate is justified in its acute skepticism of politicians and broadcasters. The novel and the two film versions very well might be fictional renditions that better explain the reality of politics and people, media and ambition gone unchecked than any news network or political documentary film might.

New directions in film adaptation studies and cultural studies mean that popular movies have worth as texts to be closely studied through a multitude of approaches. *The Manchurian Candidate* serves as an example of a literature-to-film translation that addresses issues and raises complex questions in many areas, most notably in political discourse. It stands as a prime example of a fictional narrative being able to provide a more accurate and a more telling account of the state of American politics than real media coverage (so-called news) provides.

Notes

1. Unless otherwise indicated, parenthetical page citations are to this source.

2. Horace McCoy's best-known filmwork includes *Kiss Tomorrow Goodbye* (1950, novel); *The Lusty Men* (1952, screenplay); and *They Shoot Horses Don't They?* (1969, novel).

3. Raymond Chandler's best-known filmwork includes *Double Indemnity* (1944, screenplay); *The Big Sleep* (1946, novel by Chandler, screenplay by William Faulkner); *Lady in the Lake* (1947, novel); and *Strangers on a Train* (1951, screenplay).

4. Dashiell Hammett's best-known filmwork includes *The Maltese Falcon* (1931, 1941, novel); *The Thin Man* (1934, novel); *The Glass Key* (1935, 1942, novel); *Watch on the Rhine* (1943, screenplay); and *Miller's Crossing* (1990), based on Hammett's novels *Red Harvest* (1929) and *Glass Key* (1931). *The Thin Man* became a series of films (1936, 1939, 1941, 1945, 1947) on which Hammett worked to varying degrees.

5. James M. Cain's best-known filmwork includes *Algiers* (1938, additional dialogue); *Double Indemnity* (1944, 1973, novel); *Mildred Pierce* (1945, novel); *The Postman Always Rings Twice* (1946, 1981, novel); and *Interlude* (1957, story).

6. Senator Joseph McCarthy, like the fictional Johnny Iselin, had an unimpressive senatorial career until his incendiary speech (in Wheeling, West Virginia, 9 February 1950) in which he announced that he held a list of fifty-seven people in the State Department who were known members of the Communist Party. In a direct lampoon

of McCarthy, Johnny Iselin also accuses fifty-seven Defense Department members of being Communists, a number Eleanor Iselin fabricates because its association with a popular advertising slogan ("Heinz 57") will make the falsified number easier to remember.

7. One of his first functions as editor of *Black Mask* was to drop the "The" from the magazine's title.

8. Camouflage functions as a trope throughout the film in the disguised cameo appearances of political humorist Al Franken as a TV journalist; performance artist Bill Irwin as a scout master; actor Dean Stockwell as an executive in the Manchurian Corporation; singer-songwriter Tom Chapin as Governor Edward Nelson; actor/director Simon McBurney as a doctor specializing in the brain; singer-songwriter Robyn Hitchcock as a British guide in Kuwait; and, perhaps most humorous of all, iconoclastic filmmaker Roger Corman as a powerful politician.

Works Cited

Chandler, Raymond. 1972. *The Simple Art of Murder*. Boston, MA: Houghton Mifflin.

Condon, Richard. 2004. *The Manchurian Candidate*. New York: Pocket Star Books.

The Manchurian Candidate. 1962. Dir. John Frankenheimer. Perf. Laurence Harvey, Angela Lansbury, James Gregory, and Janet Leigh. United Artists.

———. 2004. Dir. Jonathan Demme. Perf. Denzel Washington, Liev Schreiber, Meryl Streep, and Kimberly Elise. Paramount.

Scott, A. O. 2004. "Remembrance of Things Planted Deep in the Mind." *New York Times*. 30 July. http://www.nytimes.com/2004/07/30/movies (accessed 2 February 2007).

Works Consulted

Asinof, Eliot. 1993. *1919: America's Loss of Innocence*. New York: Donald I. Fine.

Brands, H. W. 1993. *The Devil We Knew: Americans and the Cold War*. New York: Oxford University Press.

Whitfield, Stephen J. 1991. *The Culture of the Cold War*. Baltimore: Johns Hopkins University Press.

CHAPTER FIFTEEN

~

The Oak: A Balancing Act from Page to Screen

Odette Caufman-Blumenfeld

*Editors' Note: The novel and film described in this chapter were a part of the political tur-
moil surrounding the Romanian revolution of December 1989. They therefore were directly
involved in political change and the search for social equilibrium. By contrast, American and
Western European films rarely if ever participate so fully in the political life of a nation.*

The release in 1992 of Lucian Pintilie's *The Oak* marked the triumphant return of this gifted Romanian director to the cinema after an absence of almost twelve years. Although as a stage and opera director Pintilie earned a
worldwide reputation by working abroad, beginning in 1974, with well-
known companies in France, England, Canada, and the United States, he
chose to shoot all his films in Romania. All of these films deal with native
themes of which Pintilie had a firsthand knowledge. Conscious of the documentary value of the film medium, Pintilie made a name for himself in the
international motion picture industry by testifying and reflecting on what
he was best acquainted with—the Romanian reality of his time, with all the
absurdities of the Communist regime.

Eugenia Voda (1992) considers *The Oak* "the first truly world-wide smashing success of Romanian cinematography" (17). This statement has constantly been reinforced by those Western critics who have enthusiastically

217

related its significance for today's cinema to the strong influence of Wajda's *The Marble Man* on its own time. For them, Pintilie's film is a thrilling social and political fresco, a stunning picture of the commotions shaking up Eastern Europe nowadays. Vincent Ostria, the reviewer of *Cahiers du Cinéma*, went as far as to correlate the penultimate episode of the film—a bus full of children first taken hostage and then mercilessly shot by soldiers because the authorities preferred to sacrifice them rather than negotiate with "the terrorists"—to a similar "real" event that took place in Yugoslavia those very days (Ostria, 1992, 28). Camille Nevers, another critic for *Cahiers du Cinéma*, made a pertinent remark that can function as an explanation for the differences between the novel on which the film is based—Ion Baiesu's *The Balance* (1985)—and the script itself: Although the action is placed at the end of Ceausescu's era, what the film shows and says, in a climate of more freedom of expression, undoubtedly makes it a post-Ceausescu film (Pintilie, 1992b).

The Romanian critics unanimously acclaimed *The Oak*; however, individual political opinions sometimes left marks on their critical formulations. Unable to deny its artistic value, some called it "a hostile masterpiece," "a distorting and unfavorable mirroring" of Romanian realities (Voda, 1992, 17). These represent the ever smaller segment of Romanian criticism still writing under the influence of old mentalities and nationalistic clichés. For them, only the "positive" aspects make up the true image of a country, some clear reminiscence of socialist realism. The liberal, enlightened critics grappled with the same problem in a different manner: "Only a lover can feed on the shortcomings and deformities of his love's object" (Liiceanu, 1992, 17). Consequently, they defined *The Oak* "a controversial film which aims at reconsidering the concept of normalcy" (Serban, 1992, 17); "an allegorical love story functioning as counter-balance to the grotesque, the mutilations and the calamities of a world born under a double zodiacal sign: Ceausescu and Caragiale" (Voda, 1992, 18), the greatest Romanian writer of satirical comedies; "a film devoted to the recent past but also to a present in which the Romanians are feverishly trying to redefine their own identity" (Duma, 1992, 6). These critics extensively commented upon basic characteristics of Pintilie's film—black humor, the grotesque with a cathartic value, the tragic constantly "tamed" by the therapeutics of the ridiculous—which together shape lively images of Romania in the 1980s. Finally, from the extreme right to the extreme left of the political spectrum, they all agreed that the film evinces a typically Romanian trait: the propensity toward loquacity, toward a "colorful" language. The characters swear passionately and ostentatiously, their rich repertory of swearwords being a special gift of the Romanian language itself. Hence, the difficulty, even the impossibility, of finding equally graphic equivalents when translating them in other languages. However, both the novel and the film use this foul language to excess in order to make a clear political statement: To swear and to snap the fingers at the others have long become a Romanian way of reacting to and/or resisting terror, privations, and interdictions of all kinds.

Most critics, both Romanian and foreign, treated *The Oak* as a *film d'auteur* because Pintilie also wrote the script. This approach is supported by the director himself: "In the end, the film represents an autonomous work and must be judged according to the newly set up laws" (Ciment and Tobin, 1992, 20). However, *The Oak* is no exception among his other scripts. All have literary works as a starting point, which Pintilie adapts and filters through his own creative personality. That is why it is but fair to pay due attention to the film's main source of inspiration, Ion Baiesu's novel.

Pintilie's choice of *The Balance* was not random. Ion Baiesu is primarily known as a successful playwright and only to a lesser degree as a journalist, a short story writer, or a novelist. Like Pintilie, who rejects the idea of "a rigorous boundary line that divides theatre from cinema" (1992b, 31), Baiesu also recognized the impact of his playwriting practice on his other works. In other words, the director and the writer both share a love for the theatre. Yet, a closer look into their work reveals deeper affinities: comic imagination, dexterity in contriving simple plots out of a microscopic examination of everyday life, an inclination toward a paradoxical amalgam of the broadest kind of humor with the most refined meditation upon the human condition and the most remarkable perception of social tragedy. Furthermore, they place at the core of their work devices such as excessive parody and caricature and call upon the extremity of absurdity to make their point—a risky game which they play successfully. These are but basic ingredients that help them create scenes of derision and the grotesque, of explosive, subversive, liberating anarchy of laughter, reminiscent of a long-established Romanian tradition brilliantly illustrated by Caragiale at the end of the last century and Ionesco after World War II. Considering these strong affinities, it seems particularly surprising and strange that the novel and the film have never been made the object of a comparative study.

The novel begins with "a Hitchcock-like scene" (Simion, 1992, xii), which narrates the heroine's strange dream: While she was lying naked basking in the sun, lots of sparrows "invade" her body. They pick at it, become restless, and start to tear it to very small pieces—a grotesque, cannibalistic scene foreshadowing death. And, indeed, when she gets up, she has a sudden revelation that fills her with horror: Her father, lying next to her in bed, had died. Pintilie's film begins with a series of visual images with a shock value. They are placed against an obsessive sound background based on Wagner's terrifying music in the scene of Isolda's death. Furthermore, it takes the spectators into a metarealm: "a film within a film." The heroine watches the shots taken at a party celebrating her birthday at Christmastime. These few, yet forceful images bring out, through graphic symbols, a most ferocious period in contemporary Romanian history, the totalitarian Stalinism of the 1950s.

It is a world whose values are turned upside down. The child's birthday party is attended only by grown-ups, whose behavior and clothes indicate that they occupy high positions in the Securitate (secret police) hierarchy. They stand for the privileged, the *nomenklatura* that propagated and imposed the Soviet ideology by force. Their attempt to play with the girl, to enter her world, looks very awkward, while that to play with sacred, religious values— the father disguises himself as Santa Claus—is undoubtedly grotesque. Yet, they seem to enjoy "the performance" because impersonation/travesty and enactment were part and parcel of the "real" tricks they used in the "class struggle" of the period. The child cries and refuses to enter "their" game. She calms down only when she is given her father's unloaded revolver. She points it to each of them and takes a great delight in shooting them. In other words, she "acts" what those grown-ups are really doing; she enjoys "imitating" their reality. The adults enter "her" game and unwillingly play the victim's part by simply dropping dead to the floor. This is as much to say that these images "challenge reality with a carnivalesque blasphemy. Everything is carnivalesque: the massacre, the revolver" (Ciment and Tobin, 1992, 22). Nevertheless, the child's "deed" and its consequences also disclose the wish-fulfillment of many Romanians then and later because these few people "simulating" death metonymically stand for the system which they have hated all along. This feeling of gratification is but short lived. These adults unexpectedly stand up and leave the game world behind once they hear the doorbell ring. Their fearful gaze, the last image of the film-within-the-film, suggests that they, in their turn, are part of a mechanism that deprived the individual of any certainty.

The sound of the doorbell in the metaworld is simultaneous with the one in the reality of the film itself. It is a jarring sound that most appropriately links the past of the former to the present of the latter, memory to reality. In the film-within-the-film, the ring seems to have summoned the father to go out. It is an action with obvious symbolic meanings: It signifies his "exit" from the political arena and from life that has just occurred while his daughter has been watching and reliving scenes from her "golden" childhood. In the film, nobody is at the door, except two envelopes squeezed under it. This time, the bell ring reinforces a climate of suspicion and reminds the heroine that everybody is under surveillance, that the Securitate has a long, though invisible, hand. This image represents the beginning of the film's descent into the grotesque dimension of the Romanian socialism in the 1980s, "a unique monstrosity . . . a mad world in which any trace of normalcy was abolished when it was not made a parody of, a mad, mad, unforseeable world in which anything was possible" (Ciment and Tobin, 1992, 18).

The initial setting, kept rather ambiguous in the novel, is drawn in masterly naturalistic, raw images in the film. The director emphasizes the sordidness and dilapidation of a studio in a working-class apartment building. It is a single room with a corner used as both kitchen and toilet. These images are in sharp contrast with the party shots on the 8 mm film. The opposition clearly suggests the father's downfall. He, like all the "old comrades," the party hard-liners, fell in disgrace in the 1960s. Furthermore, the studio is at the end of a narrow corridor with doors on either side. Thus, both the inside of the room, full of old, broken pieces of furniture, and its outside strongly suggest a claustrophobic, stifling atmosphere.

The film-within-the-film is also relevant to the penultimate episode, one of Pintilie's few meaningful additions to the novel. They are in a counterbalance, which enhances the coherence of the film as a whole. The mass murder in the 8-mm film is but part of a game in which the killer is an innocent child, while the victims are the professional executioners of real life. The roles of victim and executioner will be reversed in Pintilie's ending. The ending first shows a bus full of children in the middle of a very dusty country road. Next, we see some young men with guns slamming the bus door. The spectator immediately infers that they have taken the children hostage. Yet, paradoxically enough, the men do not look like and are not "terrorists," as might have been the case in most Western countries. They are but a few "desperados" playing their last card, which might miraculously set them free from a regime obstinately refusing to grant them the permission to leave the country. They want to use the children as the exchange for a plane or a helicopter ready to take them abroad. This whole fuss is over something which, in the civilized world, stands for the individual's normal and indefeasible right to travel or leave his own country to settle down somewhere else if he wants to. Thus, the whole episode is but a telling example of the strange type of normalcy the Romanians had to put up with in that period.

Further series of close-ups bring into stronger relief the display of forces surrounding the bus: young soldiers, Securitate officers, local Communist Party officials, military cars and trucks. Everybody seems to be in a Beckettian waiting. The appearance of the party first secretary "brings the moment to its crisis," as T. S. Eliot would put it. He seems to have received a very important call because suddenly, portable telephone sets are taken out of a car. His gestures of deference while simply listening suggest that the person on the other end of the line must be Ceausescu himself. The order given is short and, as usual, nobody is supposed to question or oppose it. However, the party secretary has a glimpse of humanity and dares remind his interlocutor in a very polite manner that "there are children in the bus. I may not have made myself clear. I repeat once again that there are children between ages six and nine." It is the only attempt made to save those innocent lives. As it was but expected, that is, normal within that regime, the warning had no effect whatsoever. On the other hand, the young soldiers, who had been placed in firing positions long before, seem to be unaware of the monstrous cruelty of their impending action. Some of their attitudes—such as the attempt to surreptitiously take a watermelon—offer a comic relief, a "counterbalance" to the tension of the moment.

Under these circumstances, the massacre itself is but "a paroxistic climax of stupidity and ferocity, springing out of an extremely animalic fear" (Pintilie, 1992a, 391). Yet, the soldiers go on shooting long after those in the bus had already been killed—the very act of firing becomes a means of releasing deep-seated anxieties. The episode as a whole, based on a real, similar incident that took place near Timişoara airport, is an ironic comment on the discrepancy between the rulers' deeds and their words, the party propaganda. The daily slogans—man's welfare is our major concern, the children are our country's future—were completely disregarded in front of the slightest deviation from the official conception of normalcy. Refusing to take any risks, the ones in power usually resorted to exemplary punishment. To carry it out, they did not hesitate to sacrifice the life of innocent people. The children in the bus, so mercilessly killed, joined the innumerable victims of a regime that, though totalitarian in deeds, pretended to be for the people and by the people in words.

The episode is also the last in a series of short vignettes Pintilie contrived in order to raise a delicate question: the role of the army. It is known that, in the 1989 revolution, the army obeyed the orders and killed innocent civilians. Yet, this has remained a taboo topic. And so have all its crimes committed in the former regime, of which the film's "The Massacre of the Innocents" is but a sample. On the other hand, a new slogan was coined in the first days after Ceausescu's fall: "The army is with us." Though effectively reassuring at that time, it has become a cliché ever since. In 1992, Pintilie already mocks it. In a comic sketch, a paratrooper falls with his parachute over a greenhouse. He destroys it, while the noise of the fall interrupts the feast taking place in the house. The drunken men go out, surround him, and greet him with "The army is with us." In those circumstances, the cliché sounded affectionately ironic. Only the housewife, sober enough to evaluate the damage, begins to swear.

The noise of the helicopters flying up in the sky dominates parts of the film. Both sound and visual image reinforce an important detail of the setting: The action takes place in an area where the army does tactical exercises. At the hospital windows, in the street, or in cars, people usually look up, wave at the pilots, and, quite often, express their admiration in another cliché: "Our boys!" The soldiers are all very young, enlisted in a training program which does not exclude mistakes. That is why people sympathize with them, have a parental attitude toward them.

These vignettes construct an image of the army which counterbalances the end of the film. It is a contrast that enhances a tragic and sad paradox of socialism: The inexperienced soldier, once he becomes part of the army as a repressive institution, ends up obeying sometimes the most absurd order, that of killing those who love him most. The film emphasizes what has become most terrifying and thought provoking: the cold blood in which they accomplish it, an epitome of indifference and abnormal humanism.

The frequent references to "balance" and "counterbalance" concern the importance of the film's title as an element which mediates the spectator's admittance in the process of artistic communication. *The Balance*, the title of the novel and of the film's Romanian version, is most appropriate to unravel the events, the situations, and the characters, building up a world in which "perpetual catastrophe has become part of daily existence" (Pintilie, 1993). The title of the English version, *The Oak*, as well as of the French one, *Le Chêne*, strengthen a symbolic dimension of the film's ending. The type of tree matters the least, though both the novel and the script speak of a nut tree. Anyway, in both of them, the heroine buries the tin with her father's ashes at its foot. The act itself has a double meaning: an attempt to part with a certain, individual past and a warning that this separation will never be complete—the tin is placed at the root of what usually stands for a life evolving in a time span that necessarily encompasses past, present, and future. Pintilie also makes his heroine bury the pictures of her "supergifted" pupils close to the ashes. It is a gesture that strongly connotes the failure of her endeavor to be "different" as a teacher but not an end of her struggle with the official views on a "normal" education process. Furthermore, the last line of the film, identical with that of the novel, is uttered in this very setting, Pintilie thus placing greater emphasis on the optimistic connotations of the tree in the background. This last image is both graphic and symbolic: the top of a tree, a "he" and a "she" under it—the beginning of any world and, consequently, some hope for the future. Yet, the woman gives the man a revolver rather than the forbidden fruit, as might have been expected. Even their conversation about a possible heir ends abruptly with a striking remark: "If he's normal, I'll strangle him." While uttering it, the man points the revolver toward the audience. It is clear that his concluding cue rejects "the normalcy" the entire film was about and against which he fought all along. His gesture, however, might be interpreted either as a threat to all those who still believe in that "normalcy" or as a drastic way of opposing it, also reinforced by one of the film's subtitles: "Wake up, Romanian!"

Reminding people of their past can often stimulate them to bring about change. This is what Pintilie envisaged when he decided to adapt The Balance, a novel whose very structure lends itself quite easily to such a process. He believed that the film's "cool, critical reexamination of the Romanians' near past and of their own image" (Voda, 1992, 17) might help them to really want this change.

Ion Baiesu's novel does not raise special construction problems. The novelist narrates what happens to the protagonists; gives accounts of their lives at the right moment; places them in short, dramatic situations; makes them explain things in a confessional manner; and has them tell all kinds of exciting, fantastic incidents and listen to the others' similar stories, all the time using the technique of the traditional short story transposed into behaviorist prose. The novel as such is filled with facts that shape a panorama of Romanian society of the 1980s, from its institutions to its people, but the sensational and the all-embracing irony is only the facade of an interesting political novel interspersed with penetrating moral observations.

Pintile followed the major outlines of the novel's plot. However, he had to make it cinematic. Consequently, cutting became an inevitable operation. He extensively cut the confessions, the stories told by the characters. Powerful visual images often succeed in making up for these omissions while the characters' behavior and actions have precedence over their ideas and discourse. With Pintilie this emphasis on the paraverbal elements is more than something substantive for the film as an art; it is often meant to reinforce a characteristic of Communism in its last stage: "a minimal language as the outcome of chain catastrophes, a language of survival" (Ciment and Tobin, 1992, 23).

To press this point even further, Pintilie devised a significant plot stratagem: the heroine has a special fondness for taking photographs of all the things and people she finds interesting and surprising. Taken with her Polaroid camera, they are, quite often, miniature versions of the slices of life the film camera displayed in close-ups. On the other hand, it is also obvious that the grotesque is not only "the destiny of the director's gaze" (Ciment and Tobin, 1992, 24) but also that of his heroine's. In Pintilie's film, derision is indeed a powerful weapon, a brilliant illustration of a French wise saying: "*Le ridicule tue.*" In other words, catharsis may also occur by means of the wild anarchy of humor.

With the help of the two protagonists, both the novel and the film effect the radiography of a world turned upside down by natural calamities, massacres, and the shipwreck of values. They are modern "picaros," having roots nowhere yet passing through life with the urge to study its mechanism, its hidden, impelling motives (Bakhtin, 1981, 124). To be marginalized yet to oppose society temperamentally is part and parcel of their fate as picaros. Furthermore, they can give verdicts on that cancerous society precisely because they are not dominated by it. Nela and Mitica's wanderings—a feverish mobility that defines their condition of picaros—are a descent into progressive layers of abjection. They react to them both orally, through an insolent tone, and physically, through violent conduct (e.g., Mitica uses his fists quite often). In an environment where everybody is silent, they are the only ones who speak out loud. They represent the exception to the rule, whom the others know to be right yet whom they want defeated so that they could peacefully continue their sleep. The film strongly suggests that this need for tranquility in abjection and this rage against all those who are "different" have not been completely forgotten after 1989. Consequently, those audiences who still regard Nela and Mitica as a couple of eccentrics will undoubtedly continue to adhere to the normalcy the film satirized all along. Who are these two characters? How can we explain their relative freedom?

Nela is brought up in an "ivory tower," far from the reality her father substantially contributed to set up at that time. The outcome is a maladjusted young woman, fully living the paranoid illusion of absolute justice. Nela is not used to humiliation and duplicity, a behavior that has helped "the others" to become part of the "normal" society. Refusing to join it, she has no other option but to struggle with the world created by her own father. This can also be viewed as "a sign of divine justice: the daughter pays for the father's sins" (Iaru, 1992, 17). Though she does not win, she never experiences the despair of complete defeat. In fact, her being bad tempered and insolent was never severely punished. There are at least two reasons at hand to account for this rather paradoxical situation: the high position occupied by her father in the past and the fact that her behavior was judged as foolishness or strangeness rather than opposition or resistance. These are the most obvious explanations for their refusal to treat her as a "case" or a "potential threat" and, consequently, for letting her enjoy her relative freedom.

Though patterned on the character in the novel, Mitica is felt as being highly autobiographical in Pintilie's film: "I have to make a Flaubertian confession: Mitica, *c'est moi*" (Ciment and Tobin, 1992, 23). His is, like the director's, a privileged dissidence. Even when he is imprisoned, the jailkeepers and the policemen treat him with respect, try to ease his situation by advising him on what to say when confronted with the judge and the prosecutor ,and surreptitiously bring him extra food from the outside. His courage to defy everybody else in order to impose his will or his views on certain matters springs out of a personal realization: He enjoys the immunity granted to him by his position as the best surgeon in town. In other words, he is not a true dissident; he is only clever enough to take full advantage of his professional competence, which renders him indispensable, in order to establish "his justice."

Duplicity is the defining trait of the others' behavior toward him. They try to hold him within the limits of rules and hierarchies—he must use the operation room only according to the schedule; he is given the worst ward because he is the youngest doctor in the hospital; he is arrested when he punches a prosecutor in a fit of anger. Yet, the constraints are not absolute. These very people tacitly allow him to operate whenever he wants, to turn a storage room into a ward, to be given a minimal penalty for the offense committed, and so on. This loyalty-duplicity was operative at all levels as a unique feature of the Romanian Communist society. Pintilie represents it in a very brief, yet telling, image. Two Securitate officers, those supposed to have been devoted body and soul to the regime, are in "mission," closely watching the protagonists from a car. They are listening to the "Free Europe" radio broadcasts, while admiring the mountain landscape. The discrepancy between their behavior and their words, a basic source for the comic, reinforces the quasi-original relationship mentioned above. They do something forbidden—to listen to this radio station was considered treacherous, anti-Romanian, punishable—but in words they voice the clichés of the official, patriotic propaganda: "What a beautiful country we have!" It is this very loyalty-duplicity that allowed Nela, Mitica, and others like them to enjoy a certain freedom that became absolute in December 1989. These few marginalized, rebellious spirits were the spark of the Romanian revolution. And, indeed, this is what the film lets a Romanian postrevolutionary spectator infer.

Mikhail Bakhtin's insistence on the centrality of the chronotope to the artistic work invites an application of this concept to film as well. In his remarks he ascribes an all-encompassing function to the chronotope: "All the abstract elements—philosophical and social generalizations, ideas, analyses of cause and effect—gravitate toward the chronotope and through it take on flesh and blood permitting the imaging power of art to do its work" (Bakhtin, 1981, 250). Bakhtin adapts the chronotope—which literally means time-space, that is, "the intrinsic connectedness of temporal and spatial relation-ships" (84)—to his own purposes using it almost (but not entirely) as a metaphor to express the inseparability of time and space (time as the fourth dimension of space). "In the literary, artistic chronotope," Bakhtin writes, "time, as it were, thickens, takes on flesh, becomes artistically visible; like-wise, space becomes charged and responsive to the movements of time, plot, and history. This intersection of axes and fusion of indicators characterize the artistic chronotope" (84). In the light of these definitions, it is quite obvious that the chronotopes to be examined shape the action and frame the issues of both the novel and the film.

The road is the major chronotope, which focuses the issues and functions as signifier. It is especially fruitful when applied to the film because, as the di-rector states in the script, its main concern is "to uncover successive infernal circles—a catastrophe after another" (Pintilie, 1992a, 276). The analysis of space in this chronotope should emphasize its concreteness, its indispensable connection with the heroine and her destiny. In the turmoil of everyday life on the road, time seems to be threefold: an individual, fragmented time com-prised in the sketchy biographies of the people she meets by chance during her journey; a historical time, whose indicators strongly shape a certain pe-riod, the 1980s; a mythical time, connoted by the apocalyptic vision of the real floods, tightly woven with the historical time. The road is charged with the flowing of the historical time, primarily with the marks of that era. More-over, the road crosses the country and discloses a large, natural environment; as the point in time and space where the life paths of all kinds of people in-tersect, it also uncovers a social diversity.

Nela travels from Bucharest to Copsa Mica, one of the most polluted towns, by a night train. Darkness outside, darkness inside: No light is switched on in the whole train. For a Romanian, this is no accident. It was part of a tacitly accepted absurd order—to cut down, by all means, the ex-penditure of electric energy—which became a clear mark of the period. The train is overcrowded: in Nela's compartment, ten people on eight seats, pieces of luggage everywhere. Most of them are bags full of food products, an-other telling indicator for those times: The shortage of such products made people grab whatever they found whenever the opportunity presented itself. The outer landscape is "fantastic, grotesque, oneiric" (Pintilie, 1992a, 276), worthy of an E. T. A. Hoffmann: a full yellow moon throwing a macabre light over the boundless mirrorlike waters that had flooded the fields. The human beings in the compartment call to one's mind expressionistic paintings: tired, distorted figures "flickering" in the dim light of cigarette butts.

To wile away the time, the travelers engage either in telling implausible stories of survival and death at the time of previous floods or in discussing the politics decided by the great powers. In other words, they take refuge either in a past able to strengthen them morally or in topics of interest for the whole mankind—the nuclear war—they minimize by expounding in very simplistic terms. It is a conversation that shrewdly avoids the desperate situation of the moment, a wise defense mechanism as part of a more comprehensive strategy of survival. Pintilie shortens this episode to a minimum by resorting to a clever trick: Nela, the outsider, prefers to listen to the tape in her walkman so that the film retains only what she overhears as a fragmented dialogue that still makes sense.

The train stops with a jar; the waters had already torn down the embankment ahead. The passengers are urged on like cattle to leave the train and shift to another one supposed to come on another track. The images are almost Dickensian in their gloomy, dreary atmosphere: mud and waters everywhere, people losing their foothold and quite often slipping or falling down, pieces of luggage "floating" on the water surface. Nela, who has been different all along, refuses to join the others; she wants to return to Bucharest by the same train. However, the railway people, like the policemen, are used to obeying orders. No wonder that one of them takes her in his arms by force, while another grabs her two suitcases. Though they make a mess of the whole job—a suitcase gets lost in the waters, Nela is thrown into the dirty waters when the man carrying her falls down—they ask to be rewarded with a tip. Both the novel and the film refer to tipping as a widely spread custom. Yet, they also let the characters distinguish between giving and receiving a tip, generally accepted as something "normal," and begging for it, considered gypsylike and, consequently, shameful and degrading. This clear-cut distinction indirectly points to a strong nationalistic mentality.

To pass the time and warm up, the women huddle together and begin to sing a folk song. Pintilie adds this image as a parody of those women's choirs that used to take part in "Romania's Song" national competition. They surround Nela to keep her away from men's view while she is changing her wet clothes. However, the moment they hear the train whistle, they leave her, though she is almost naked, and start to make room for themselves jostling one another. The scene vividly describes a mob's reaction, its survival instinct when confronted with an ultimate situation. It is "the dress rehearsal" for "the commuters' scene" to follow. Though the train is already over-crowded, the commuters, workers at a chemical plant, believe that they have "the right" to get on it: "it's our train!" They trample on the others' toes, they push with their elbows, they break windows. It is the very picture of extreme collective violence unleashed in apocalyptic situations. To render cinematic this nightmarish scene, worthy of a Hieronymus Bosch painting, Pintilie found a valuable source of inspiration, not in art, but in a traumatic post-revolutionary reality that works as a successful "objective correlative": the violent destructive actions performed by the miners who "spontaneously" came to Bucharest "to defend" the legitimate power in the summer of 1990.

With Nela's arrival in Copsa Mica, a town where "the dust of death" is like a thin layer covering everything, a new chronotope—a strange world in a time of adventure/initiation—shapes the heroine's image. In such a chrono-tope, the accident governs the "simultaneity" and the "countertime" of the events or phenomena. The attempt made by some hoodlums to rape Nela is this very accident-initiative that stimulates the unfolding of the plot. Yet, this evolution is not under the auspices of the malefic forces but of the bene-factor that saves her in the nick of time. In other words, the meeting between Nela and Mitica, her savior, also functions as motif with chronotopic values and enhances the coherence of the novel/the film as a whole. Henceforward, the two protagonists come in contact with a variety of social spaces par-ticularized through references to sociopolitical institutions. The confronta-tion with them puts to test the constancy of their character, beliefs, and affections.

Nela, the fresh graduate of psychology, starts her teaching career in a slums high school. From the very beginning, the other teachers, mostly women, dislike her. She is young, eccentric, independent, full of idealistic projects to put in practice. In a word, she is different, she is "the other" they must "naturalize" to their routine "normalcy." However, they do not dare confront her openly, in a fruitful exchange of ideas. Theirs are the diffuse tac-tics of innuendoes and distortions to attack her in terms of both her private life—her "affair" with Mitica—and her proficiency as a teacher—her exper-iment with a class of gifted pupils to be trained "differently." They succeed in convincing some of the parents to take their children away from her class. This is an opportunity, primarily for the novelist, to draw sensational biogra-phies of couples who, in their youth, defied the norms and conventions, both written and unwritten, of the Communist regime, that is, they were a kind of dissidents in their own way. Surprisingly enough, these former rebels refuse to give a chance to their children to be well-individualized entities. What they prefer to envisage for their children is the quiet life of citizens completely adjusted to the aberrant normalcy of the overwhelming majority. This is a telling reference to how most of the dissidents of the 1950s and 1960s ended up. This is also as much to say that the ideal of any totalitarian regime—the new man, the man as product of and subject to all possible alienating norms—was successfully "implemented" in Communist Romania. Furthermore, it is a well-known fact that the school system was an efficient tool in having carried out that task. That is why both the novel and the film take those who serve it, the teachers, as main target of their satire. They pinpoint parodically traits such as self-sufficiency, narrow-mindedness due to excessive indoctrination, fear of assuming the responsibility of any initiative, blind submission to the directives from above, refusal to even think of possible changes, "revolutionary vigilance" in crushing any deviation from the status quo.

Mitica takes us to other spaces—the hospital, the prison, the courts, behind the scenes of local authorities: police, judicial officers, party officials. They represent a microcosm of what was happening on a large scale in the country as a whole. However, both the novel and the film present them indirectly through the individual destinies of those appointed to serve them.

The hospital is virtually run by the vice manager, whose stunning biography is typical for those who were in power at that time. A very young soldier during the war, he is seriously wounded and is made a hero overnight. After World War II, his heroic behavior is proof enough to view him as a trustworthy young man. Consequently, he climbs the party scale of ranks until they finally find out that he is illiterate. Eliminated from the race for a position in the party upper hierarchy, he is given this safe job in the hospital. He performs it imitating the local party dictators. In other words, it is not his professionalism that commands the others' respect. It is his many abuses of power that impose him and make both the medical staff and the patients fear him. Moreover, he feels his position secure because he is well connected; he is one of those who pull the strings at the lower levels of the local power. To do favors for one another is what keeps them together. Each represents for the others the reliable person in the right place. Thus, after the rape, the head of the municipal police sends Nela to him to get the medical certificate more quickly; he, in his turn, makes sure that the prosecutor will arrest Mitica on the spot, and so on.

While in prison, Mitica discovers another horrifying truth: Hierarchy as a concept is operative among the prisoners as well as among the policemen and the jailkeepers, not to mention its strong, traditional relevance for the relationships between the two parties represented by victims and persecutors. It usually gave these people the satisfaction of a double-standard behavior: arrogant and autocratic with those inferior, flattering and submissive toward those above them. It is this very balance between the two attitudes that made people become, consciously or unconsciously, part of the infernal mechanism that supported the system.

While still in prison Mitica experiences another shocking reality: The local party highest official rules with absolute powers in his own county. It is in his power to order that Mitica's case should be reexamined and the prisoner acquitted on the spot. Furthermore, this simulacrum of a trial takes place while Mitica is fast asleep in his cell. This is as much to say that the separation of the powers in the state was but a simple slogan in that period. Yet, it is for the first time that the hero's view on the matter differs considerably from that of the reader/the spectator. If Mitica clearly regards it as an abuse and raises against it, the latter judges it with a certain sympathy and understanding. In the complicated web of the sensational plot, he or she paradoxically perceives it as gratifying his or her sense of justice.

Other individual types—the corrupt prosecutor, mad after women yet under the thumb of his wife and mother-in-law; the opportunistic, alcohol addict mayor of a village; the country priest, more conversant with the worldly things than with the sacred ones; incompetent doctors; impudent street vendors; simple people with a disposition to philosophize, from the messianism with a nationalistic even fascist tinge (Titi) to the apocalyptic, disillusioned vision of the near future (Miletineanu)—further define the period down to its grotesque variegated details. In fact, they are the ones who shape the daily social and political conventions with which the protagonists are constantly confronted. Brutally initiated into this world, they viscerally oppose it, remaining true to their own identity of nonconformists and rebels.

In the film, Pintilie brings to the foreground the theme of death, a personal obsession that he exorcises by treating it in a grotesque and derisive manner. It is an approach that places him in Rabelais's tradition: death in the proximity of laughter, eating, and drinking. It is also a very Romanian treatment. The Romanians are the only people to have a "merry" cemetery. The images on most of the stones are blasphemous, while the epitaphs are humorous rhymed versions of the dead person's life story. In a word, an iconoclastic, carnivallike cemetery. In Pintilie's film, there are at least three or four scenes vividly illustrating this view; they are quite terrifying in their macabre concreteness.

The inside of the Bucharest crematorium, close to the opening of the film, is such an episode ingeniously added by the director. Close-ups point to the wall with the square canisters of ashes and to the raised bier in the middle of the mortuary chapel. Here Nela brings her father's body for the "traditional" funeral reserved to "former" underground Communist fighters, mostly Comintern members in power in the 1950s and 1960s. Yet, no pomp or public funeral is attached to it, a telling sign that the deceased had completely fallen out of favor. In the immense empty hall, resembling a dark, grotesque cave, in the sounds of "L'Internationale" vibrating unevenly from loudspeakers, the barrel cylinder is closed and the coffin begins to go down while fire blades invade the screen. This shot is also a telling symbol of the death/end of a part of Communist history in Romania. Like the old man's ashes, that past is but a sad memory.

However, in most cases, it is the outrageousness of the situation that makes death appear as an object of ridicule. A few close-ups show Nela and a friend drinking beer in a bar. Suddenly, she takes out a Nescafe tin from a plastic bag with an advertisement for the Marlboro cigarettes printed on it. When asked what is inside the tin, she answers coldly, "It's my father." Her friend bursts out laughing. This is the only possible reaction to the enormity of the situation and to Nela's complete, impenitent passivity. Death, rendered concrete through the ashes, finds itself in the proximity of laughter and drinking. Yet, the grotesque of the whole scene deepens once we corroborate it with the meaning of the dead man's life. First, these are the ashes of a man for whom Communism remained an ideal up to the end. Ironically enough, they are wrapped in the most obvious signs of capitalism. It is a stunning association that enhances the futility of his struggles and beliefs. Second, the man was, at least for a time, a tyrant whom the others respected out of fear. Dead, his ashes are treated with an outrageous irreverence even by his own daughter. The contrast proves once more that Pintilie is a master of shock and paradox of the highest order.

A memorable episode is the feast given by the priest after Titi's burial. The custom of eating and drinking for the dead man's soul brings together, at the same table, people of different backgrounds: the mayor, that is, the representative of the Communist Party in the territory; the priest; a couple of local notabilities; two Securitate officers, a comic pair, the counterbalance of the railway people at the beginning of the film; Mitica; and Nela. However, instead of talking about the deceased, as it is but usual, they start a heated debate on the condition of the Romanian peasant and of the agricultural economy in general. The discussion has its own rules, is like "a game." Once they decide that the speaker has started to speak in earnest, they interrupt him with "that's politics." It is a solidarity in cowardice that prevents them from slipping toward the dangerous zones. Moreover, this attitude also alludes to their distrust in each other, to their fear not only of the others but also of themselves. The only topic that is not considered taboo is the other as foreigner. The mayor's diatribe against the American as "the most stupid man on earth" is in line with the party's official policy as well as a way of discharging with a vengeance, through language, his long-repressed hatred. All the others, including Mitica, applaud him approvingly. It is only Nela, the outsider all along, who watches them with a large, cynical smile on her lips.

The feast unites around the same table both the victims and the persecutors. Pintilie has magnificently translated in the specific language of the film their sophisticated complicity. In other words, what the director renders as horrifying in this society is the potential of the upside-down world pattern to blur the clear-cut distinction between these two conflicting roles, even to make them interchangeable. These shots, though impeccable in their concreteness, are, at the same time, abstract, that is, ideas. Hence, their being open to interpretation, to more than one meaning. In fact, both Baiesu and Pintilie have the intelligence and the skill of not making their symbols explicit.

The film, clearly an after-1989 work, elicits, to a higher degree than the novel, a bitter, bilious laugh because it mocks at the Romanians' predicament as men and women caught in the trap of history. "History is crafty," Lenin declared. Indeed, it is, when shaped by shrewd and unprincipled leaders. That is why the film provides a strong warning for the Romanian spectators: They may laugh, but they must not laugh their fears away. Leaving aside the allusive and elusive vocabulary forged by most dissident artists in Eastern Europe, Pintilie rises, in the straightforward language of his medium, against all those who have placed historical amnesia on their political agenda.

Works Cited

Baiesu, Ion. 1985. *Balanţa* [The Balance]. Bucharest: Cartea Romaneasca. Second edition (uncensored). 1990. Bucharest: Minerva.

Bakhtin, M. M. 1981. *The Dialogic Imagination: Four Essays*. Trans. Caryl Emerson and Michael Holquist. Ed. Michael Holquist. Austin, TX/London: University of Texas Press.

Ciment, Michel, and Jann Tobin. 1992. "23 Questions pour Lucian Pintilie." *Positif* 379 (September): 18–24.

Duma, Dana. 1992. "Balanta" (*Balanţa*, "The balance"). *Cinema* (November).

Iaru, Florin. 1992. "In cumpana 'balantei'" ("In the Balance of 'The Balance'"). *Romania literara* (Literary Romania), 9–15 December.

Liiceanu, Gabriel. 1992. Speech at *The Oak*'s opening night in Bucharest. 26 October.

Ostria, Vincent. 1992. "Réactions en Chaine" (review of *Le Chêne*). *Cahiers du Cinéma* 459 (September): 27–28.

Pintilie, Lucian. 1992a. *Four Scripts*. Bucharest: The Albatros.

———. 1992b. "Interview," with Camille Nevers. *Cahiers du Cinema* 459 (September): 29–31, 33, 35.

———. 1993. Interview on Romanian television.

Serban, Alex Leo. 1992. "Balanta etica" ("The ethical balance"). *Romania literara* (Literary Romania), 9–15 December.

Simion, Eugen. 1992. Preface. *The Balance*, by Ion Baiesu. Bucharest: Minerva.

Voda, Eugenia. 1992. "Romania, cosmarul meu iubit" ("Romania, my beloved nightmare"). *Romania literara* (Literary Romania), 4–10 November.

CHAPTER SIXTEEN

~

Adaptation and the Cold War: Mankiewicz's *The Quiet American*

Brian Neve

It was in 1956 that Joseph L. Mankiewicz decided that his second independent production, for his own company Figaro, would be an adaptation of Graham Greene's novel of the previous year, *The Quiet American* (1955). Given the political resonance of the book's reception, the process of translation into the film medium was always likely to be problematic. Neither Greene nor Mankiewicz could have anticipated at the time the future salience of events in Vietnam to America and the world, and even today the director's use of his source material raises strong political feelings.

The controversy owes something to the way Greene's novel came to encode a powerful (and for some defining) notion of American foreign policy, but it also relates to Mankiewicz's own background and work. Hollywood has been well known for its cavalier use of the literary properties that it purchased, either to trade on a successful and or respected name or to avoid dangers of litigation. Mankiewicz, however, even before he moved to New York in 1951, had been associated with sophisticated, talky, adult dramas, usually written by him. As a producer at Metro-Goldwyn-Mayer (MGM), he was responsible for *Fury* (1936) and *The Philadelphia Story* (1940), while after the war he had established a strong reputation, both in America and among European cineastes, as the director of a series of films at Twentieth

Century Fox. Among his writing and directing credits were one of the studio's most uncompromising contributions to the postwar Hollywood cycle on racial themes, No Way Out (1950), together with the celebrated All about Eve, released the same year. Few critics have queried the liberties taken with Shakespeare in his MGM production of Julius Caesar (1953) because of something of a cause célèbre in relation to The Quiet American.

In terms of politics Mankiewicz had voted for the Republican Wendell Wilkie in 1940 and was described by his fellow East Coast–based director Elia Kazan as a "classic nonjoiner" (Geist, 1978, 175; Kazan, 1988, 388). Yet he had been closely involved in the controversy concerning the Hollywood blacklist and made critical comment on it in his People Will Talk (1951). It was in 1950 that the director, as president of the Screen Director's Guild, had successfully fought off the efforts of a conservative faction in the guild to introduce a loyalty oath for members. He had the same year stood up for what he saw as the beleaguered position of liberals in the United States, seeing them as under attack "by an organized enemy as evil in practice, purpose—and indistinguishable from—the Communist menace that fosters and encourages that destruction" (Mankiewicz, 1950, 6). Mankiewicz here attacked McCarthyism while also making clear his anti-Communism.

Certainly the specter of an internal and an external Communist threat was to make social and political themes very much the exception in the Hollywood of the 1950s. In 1953 the CIA monitored the social content of movies, indicating the U.S. government's concern with the way film influenced foreign perceptions of America (Eldridge, 2000). Darryl F. Zanuck, for whom Mankiewicz had made No Way Out at the end of the previous decade, was particularly worried by themes that looked like political propaganda and felt that audiences were no longer attracted by serious political themes. Political fears, for example, contributed to the unwillingness of any of the studios to back the project that Kazan and Budd Schulberg were seeking to finance about the New York waterfront. Yet by 1956, with movie audiences at the bottom of their postwar decline, directors such as Mankiewicz were convinced of the need to break away from the blandness of much of Hollywood fare if the perceived threat of television was to be challenged. He talked in 1956 of the need for more adult themes and linked his own decision to purchase rights to Greene's novel to his friend Kazan's forthcoming work with Tennessee Williams, Baby Doll (1956) (Mankiewicz, 1956).

Graham Greene had based his 1955 novel on his experiences as a journalist in Saigon in the early fifties, during a time when American policy was shifting away from notions of self-determination for previously colonized states and toward support for European and other allies in an American-led fight against Communism. Ho Chi Minh's nationalist and Communist forces were bearing down on the French-backed government in the north in the period leading to the French military defeat at Dien Bien Phu. By the time the book was published, Vietnam had been divided, and America was beginning to see South Vietnam was a democratic bulwark against Communist advance in Southeast Asia.

Greene's book is an extended confession, a story told by the main protagonist, Thomas Fowler, a British journalist in Saigon who clings both to his Vietnamese mistress, Phuong, and his cynical reluctance to take sides. To the north, the French fight the Viet Minh, while locally the pressman is much occupied by the way that an American acquaintance, a younger man called Pyle who works for the local Economic Legation, is becoming a rival suitor to Phuong. Fowler also gradually suspects that the American, the quiet American, is involved in some way with a so-called Third Force in Vietnam, an anti-French and anti-Communist movement that has links with forces that are perpetrating terrorist bombings in the city. After a particularly destructive explosion, Fowler moves toward a feeling that he must take sides. Although the balance of personal and political factors in his action is never clear, he acts against what he sees as an American who, however well intentioned, is meddling dangerously in affairs that (unlike veterans of human fallibility like himself) he does not understand. Following his decision to aid the Communists to assassinate the American, Fowler contemplates a renewed life with Phuong but also guilt about his behavior. The mix of motives is seen as characteristic of Greene; as one admiring critic has said, there is "no real way to be good in Greene, there are simply a million ways to be more or less bad." To the same commentator, Greene's great achievement in his novel is to "allow a cynic like Fowler to champion the cause of life by insisting on the authenticity of those deaths Pyle considers to be merely symbolic" (Smith, 2004, 4–5).

Greene's book had outraged the American intelligence community, as well as anti-Communist liberals who were associated with the American Committee for Cultural Freedom (Saunders, 1999). To the critic Philip Rahv, who reviewed Greene's book in *Commentary*, it was a "thriller with political complications" that was a "clever attack on the United States, its policies and methods, values, and ideals" (Rahv, 1956, 488, 489). Yet Rahv's "wry tolerance" of the new book prompted one of the more passionately pro-American and anti-Communist writers, Diana Trilling, to a furious rejoinder in the same journal. To Trilling, Greene's novel was "an entirely orthodox statement of the neutralist position," a position that she felt was actually nonneutral and in fact masked a stance of "pro-Communism." She felt that too many liberals at the time feared to take an unequivocal stand on the Communist threat because of a fear of allying themselves with reactionaries (Trilling and Rahv, 1956).

Mankiewicz shared much of this feeling, and his screenplay, while drawing extensively on Greene's dialogue, included a crucial structural change to the story that altered the political thrust of the material. Fowler's motivation for conspiring with the Communist assassination squad is made more clearly personal, overriding the political disgust of the American's presumed behavior that Fowler feels in the novel. The most important change, however, concerns the introduction by the director of a new ending scene that has no basis in the book. This is a prolonged conversation between Fowler and the French police inspector Vigot (Claude Dauphin). Vigot, one world-weary old colonialist to another, reveals to Fowler that the American had in no way been connected with the bombings and that instead the Englishman had been tricked by Communists into betraying the man who had saved his life on the road to Saigon.

There is clear evidence of Mankiewicz's political intentions in the production history of the project. Before location shooting began in Saigon in January 1957, the writer-director talked of how his film would show an intellectual "being led around the nose by the Commies" [sic] (Mankiewicz, 1956, 24). An early appointment to the project also indicated the change in political line. Mankiewicz appointed Vinh Noan as an advisor and associate producer and as the only Vietnamese-speaking member of the production team. Noan had directed *We Want to Live*, a film that had been well received at the Asian Film Festival in 1955 and was highly critical of the Hanoi Communists and their intimidatory methods (Russo, 2001). Mankiewicz was also helped by career diplomat Angier Biddle Duke, a diplomat who was president of the International Rescue Committee (IRC; Mankiewicz was a board member) and who had formed a subsidiary group of the IRC called American Friends of Vietnam (Lewis, 1998). There is also evidence of a meeting in Washington between Figaro's vice president, Robert Lantz, and Allen Dulles, the head of the Central Intelligence Agency (Russo, 2001), to clear the way for the proposed eight-week stay in Vietnam. When the film was completed, an early version was previewed for the Vietnam ambassador and State Department officials, while the premiere in early 1958 was for the IRC (Russo, 2001; Lewis, 1998).

Perhaps the most interesting clue to the politics of the project was an exchange between the director and the key American intelligence figure, Colonel Edward Lansdale. Lansdale, who is seen as the country's leading expert in counterguerilla warfare, had been sent secretly to Vietnam in 1954 to begin operations against the Viet Minh (Sheehan et al., 1971). It was Lansdale who advised the director on the circumstances of the actual bombing in Saigon in 1952 that Greene had used in the climax of his novel. Greene had believed that there was American complicity in the bombing, by a renegade general, General Thé, who claimed responsibility at the time. Lewis cites Lansdale, in a letter to Mankiewicz in early 1956, as agreeing that it would be sensible and acceptable to him for the filmmaker to make the Communists responsible, and not the general, in the forthcoming production (Greene, 1980; Lewis, 1998; West, 1997).

The film also contains several references to President Ngo Dinh Diem, the great hope for supporters of postcolonial anti-Communist nationalism in Vietnam in the late fifties. The "American" in the film (no longer Pyle) refers to him as a prominent Vietnamese living in New Jersey: "If all goes well," he tells Fowler, "if Vietnam becomes an independent republic, this man will be its leader." In addition a title card at the conclusion of the film thanks the people of the Republic of Vietnam and "their chosen president and administration." In fact he had decided, with his allies, against the holding of elections in the south, following the Geneva agreement to this effect in 1955. In the film there is also a reference to the "Friends of Free Asia," a reference to the real Friends of Vietnam whose supporters included Arthur Schlesinger Jr., key figure in "vital center liberalism," and Robert Kennedy. Diem had banned Greene's book but was clearly happy for the film to be made (Whitfield, 1996, 74).

It is doubtful if Mankiewicz could, even had he wanted to, have made a film that more faithfully conveyed Greene's political point. The script was as usual submitted to the Production Code Administration, and Geoffrey Sherlock, in a letter to Mankiewicz, indicated that there were clear constraints, even on independent filmmakers with their own companies. Sherlock was concerned that "the American" not be portrayed in a way that might make the film be "open to the criticism that it represents unfairly a prominent institution such as the Foreign Service of the United States, or any branch of it" (MPAA Production Code Administration Records, 1956). Contemporary industry mores also limited Mankiewicz's thinking on the casting of the one prominent Vietnamese character, Phuong. The choice of the Italian actress, Giorgia Moll, reflected the industry prejudice against the use of Asian actors for leading roles.

Visually the film is distinguished mainly by Robert Krasker's location photography, particularly in the scenes set against the celebrations of the Chinese New Year. Krasker had also worked on Carol Reed's *The Third Man*

(1949), a film made from a Greene script that contains some parallels with his Vietnam novel. Jean Luc-Godard saw *The Quiet American* as a film that confirmed the director's reputation as "the most intelligent man in all contemporary cinema," praising the constant play on words and languages. Yet he admitted that the shooting added little to the script, and that overall what was missing from the film was "cinema." (Godard, 22 July 1958, in Narboni and Milne, 1986, 81).

There are other elements of the novel that have no equivalents in Mankiewicz's film. In the novel Fowler's stance is informed by a sense of the appalling nature of warfare. Greene shows Fowler joining a patrol of men who come across a canal full of bodies, the "human clay" that results from war, an "Irish stew containing too much meat." Later, in an account that directly reflects the novelist's own experience, the correspondent reports on a French pilot's mission to destroy a human target on the ground. Both passages present striking images of the human consequences of warfare but have no equivalents in the film. Although Robert Aldrich and Stanley Kubrick dealt in their own ways with this theme (in *Attack*, 1956, and *Paths of Glory*, 1957), for Mankiewicz the notion that war was hell did not fit easily with the confident, late-fifties perspective on Vietnam under Diem.

The fifty-year-old British actor Michael Redgrave, selected when Laurence Olivier turned down the role, deepened Greene's sense of Fowler as a tired, rather desperate man of empire, clinging to his hopes of marriage to his Vietnamese mistress despite the refusal of his wife to grant him a divorce. In contrast the thirty-two-year-old Audie Murphy (again a replacement for the original choice of Montgomery Clift), brings quite different associations. Murphy had been the most decorated G.I. of World War II and had been the hero of a series of undistinguished Westerns, as well as John Huston's ambitious and ill-fated adaptation, *The Red Badge of Courage* (1951). Far from the dangerous figure of the novel, the American is presented as a rather ineffectual do-gooder, an importer of plastic for the local toy industry. Mankiewicz had intended more location shooting, which might have deepened the American's film role and his film relationship with Phuong, but Murphy's sudden illness in the first week of February led to a suspension of shooting and the culling of some of these scenes. Other scenes shot to indicate the younger man's relationship to Phuong were also cut at a late stage, further enhancing the film's concentration on the life and thoughts of the older man (Russo, 2001).

The opening, posttitle sequence shows the New Year's celebrations in Saigon and establishes the murder of the American, leading into the long flashback, making up the bulk of the film, in which Fowler recounts his story.

The film follows the novel early on in placing the emphasis is on the threat that the "quiet American," a man apparently involved with charitable and economic organizations, poses to Fowler's relationship to Phuong. The politics at this stage is largely restricted to debates about what the Vietnamese want from life, and the relevance to them of what the American wants, and America's ideas about "national democracy" and a "third force." Only late in the story does Fowler become so suspicious of his American friend, the man who saved his life on the road to Saigon, that he becomes willing to take sides.

In place of Greene's political point about America's "meddling" in Indo-China and his study of moral complexity, Mankiewicz introduces a theme that is very much his own, but which also owes much to liberal anti-Communist thinking of the time. In the novel, at the point where Fowler has made his melodramatic sign to the Communists waiting outside his apartment, making him complicit in the assassination of the American, he says, "I was suddenly very tired. I wanted him to go away quickly and die. Then I could start life again—at the point before he comes in." In the film, Fowler's line states, "I was very tired. Suddenly I wanted him to go away and die, so that Phuong and I, and the world, would be as we were, before he came in." The line is not without grace, a reflection of the old world, fearing the energy and meddling of the new. But the inclusion of Phuong's name is part of a new theme, the emotional immaturity of intellectuals and "fellow travelers" such as Fowler. The change also highlights Fowler's personal reasons for betraying his friend. This theme is made explicit in Mankiewicz's extended exposition scene at the end, in which the French inspector Vigot confronts his fellow European with his understanding of how the American died. The inspector tells Fowler that Communism appeals in particular when "the mentally advanced are also emotionally retarded." He adds, before being interrupted, that so often "one finds brilliant, sensitive minds inwardly tortured by unexplained fears and hatreds who find temporary peace of mind in devoted lip-service."

By the later 1950s, after events in Hungary and the Khrushchev speech, the American Communist Party was of minor significance. Yet the theme that Mankiewicz overlays on Greene's story during this extended exchange between Fowler and Vigot reflects the liberal anti-Communist view of the continued susceptibility of many of the Left, perhaps including literary figures such as Greene, to political positions that derive from heart rather than head. The director made his theme explicit at the time, arguing that he had often "wanted to do a picture about one of those ice-blooded intellectuals whose intellectualism is really just a mask for completely irrational passion" (Knight, 1958, 27). The theme seems to reflect something of contemporary liberal analyses of the appeals of Communism in the West, including notions of "neurotic susceptibility" and Arthur Schlesinger's idea of the attraction to "lonely and frustrated people, craving social, intellectual and even sexual fulfilment they cannot obtain in existing society" (Schlesinger, 1949, 104; Almond, 1954, 258). Fowler is seen as a fool, a dupe, and as someone whose "taking sides" is based not—at least in part—on his understanding of events as a journalist but on a misunderstanding of them prompted by his emotional needs. The film then "punishes" the journalist for his sins in a way that is more typical of traditional Hollywood thinking by having Phuong rejects Fowler's final advance. (Although at a symbolic level, the film version does allow a belatedly strong response by the key Vietnamese character to the key colonial one; in a sense this can be seen as consistent with the director's confidence in an independent, postcolonial Vietnam.) The film thus ends with the journalist as a lonely and defeated figure, confronting, as he saw life without his Vietnamese love, the "beginning of death." Mankiewicz famously cuts the beginning of Fowler's last line, to Vigot: "Everything had gone right with me since he had died, but now I wish there existed someone to whom I could say that I was sorry."

The American in the film becomes merely an idealist, a "boy scout." Mankiewicz makes him reveal to the journalist at their last meeting that he had only a very limited contact with the mysterious General Thé, approaching him only about his receptivity to a possible return to Vietnam of a figure such as Diem. When Fowler asks his friend about his association with the man apparently responsible for the bomb blast, the American replies, "What makes you think it was his bomb?" This is where the film leaves the question of responsibility for the bombing, which in real life General Thé claimed responsibility for. Fowler's warning, that "your country mustn't trust men like Thé," seemed logical at the time but viewers of the film are later told by Vigot, a kind of father confessor to Fowler's unrepentant sinner, that the Briton had been tricked by the Communists Heng and Dominquez. Using fictitious drums marked "Dialacton" and drawing on a confusion between American plastic and the explosive with a similar French name, we are told that Fowler was merely a dupe (Geist, 1978, 269). Although the film does not make this clear, the implication is that the bomb blast might have been a further part of the Communists' efforts to engage the support of Fowler in the assassination. Why the Communists should wish to kill the American shown to be an ineffective do-gooder (about to be sent home by his government, he tells us) is not explained.

Mankiewicz, while drawing on Greene's language, sometimes effectively as in the watchtower debate between the two principals, too often conveys information through dialogue. There are exceptions, notably the point-of-view shots that accompany Fowler's realization, as he returns to his apartment, that his mistress has left him. But the notion that the American's relationship with Phuong was more genuine, more loving, more democratic, is rather clumsily demonstrated by a tape of the two together that Vigot plays to Fowler. Even the bomb blast, well staged as it is, is in the film disconnected from the meaning of the film. In the book it raised political questions, while in the film Fowler's final, existential decision is both linked to his emotions (i.e., it is not a decision at all) and is then shown to be based on a delusion. The bombing, and the Vietnamese lives lost in it, is separated from the themes of the film, as ultimately is the politics of Vietnam.

What is performed is a kind of late-1950s negation of the promise of anti-fascism that invades the privacy of isolationist Americans in the forties —Humphrey Bogart, for example, in *Casablanca* (1942) or *Key Largo* (1948). Instead, by the late fifties, the rhetoric of national democracy and anti-Communism have taken over. The breaking up of the Popular Front progressive alliance and the growth of liberal anti-Communism are mirrored at the level of foreign policy by the change from Roosevelt's anti-colonialism in 1945 to the support for the French and the counterinsurgency policies of the Cold War. The American's idealism and "meddling" is purged of the malignant consequences examined by Greene, but Mankiewicz's restructuring leaves the American as a weak figure, betrayed by the man whose life he saved and duped and then killed by the Communists. Even the U.S. government, he tells Fowler in their last encounter, has asked him to withdraw, something that at the same time hints at a political role (denied in Inspector Vigot's "voice of God" exposition at the end) and also suggests his ineffectiveness.

With the Murphy character revealed as an innocent, the whole of the drama revolves around and within Fowler, the burnt-out case. Fowler's narration, the point-of-view shots, the cuts in the action and love scenes all reinforce our concern with the moral and political dilemmas of the Redgrave character. From being the naïve but dangerous interloper, taking to foreign lands an arrogant belief in native support for U.S.-backed "national democracy," the American becomes simply a competitor for Fowler's woman. The political theme, as applicable, some might say, to Iraq in 2004 as to 1950s Vietnam, is left as a ghost in the film, in part a residue of the use of so much of Greene's dialogue and characterization and in part a product of the way audiences are tempted to interpret the film against the meaning that fitted the Cold War politics of the time.

Works Cited

Almond, Gabriel A. 1954. *The Appeals of Communism.* Princeton, NJ: Princeton University Press.

Eldridge, David N. 2000. "'Dear Owen': The CIA, Luigi Luraschi, and Hollywood, 1953." *Historical Journal of Film, Radio and Television* 20 (2): 155.

Geist, Kenneth L. 1978. *Pictures Will Talk, The Life and Films of Joseph L. Mankiewicz.* New York: Charles Scribner's Sons.

Greene, Graham. 1955. *The Quiet American.* London: Heinemann.

———. 1980. *Ways of Escape.* London: Bodley Head.

Kazan, Elia. 1988. *A Life.* New York: Knopf.

Knight, Arthur. 1958. "SR Goes to the Movies." *Saturday Review of Literature*, 25 January, 27.

Lewis, Kevin. 1998. "The Third Force: Graham Greene and Joseph L. Mankiewicz's *The Quiet American.*" *Film History* 10: 477–91.

Mankiewicz, Joseph L. 1950. "Mankiewicz Pleads the Cause of the Liberal in the U.S." *Daily Variety*, 15 September, 6.

———. 1956. "Mankiewicz Hails Shortage." *Variety*, 12 December, 3, 24.

MPAA Production Code Administration Records. 1956. Margaret Herrick Library, Center for Motion Picture Study, Los Angeles, January 5.

Narboni, Jean, and Tom Milne, eds. 1986. *Godard on Godard: Critical Writings by Jean-Luc Godard.* New York: Da Capo Press.

Rahv, Philip. 1956. "Wicked American Innocence." *Commentary* 21 (May): 488–90.

Russo, William. 2001. *A Thinker's Damn: Audie Murphy, Vietnam, and the Making of The Quiet American.* Carson City, NV: Lukeion Press.

Saunders, Frances Stonor. 1999. *Who Paid the Piper? The CIA and the Cultural Cold War.* London: Granta Books.

Schlesinger, Arthur. 1949. *The Vital Center: The Politics of Freedom.* Boston: Houghton Mifflin.

Sheehan, Neil, et al. 1971. *The Pentagon Papers, as Published by the* New York Times. New York: Bantam Books.

Smith, Zadie. 2004. "Shades of Greene." *Guardian Review*, 18 October, 4–5.

Trilling, Diana, and Philip Rahv. 1956. "America and *The Quiet American.*" *Commentary* 22 (July): 66–71.

West, W. J. 1997. *The Quest for Graham Greene.* New York: St. Martin's Press.

Whitfield, Stephen J. 1996. "Limited Engagement: *The Quiet American* as History." *Journal of American Studies* 30 (April): 65–86.

~

CHAPTER SEVENTEEN

All the Quiet Americans

C. Kenneth Pellow

The history of transformations of *The Quiet American* provides an excellent opportunity to use transformation as a critical tool. When we compare the "versions" of this story—Graham Greene's 1955/1956 novel, Joseph Mankiewicz's 1958 film, and Philip Noyce's 2002 remake[1]—we gain greater insight into each of them. One film captures some of the novel's best achievements but badly distorts others; the other restores what the first one missed but downplays or disregards other salient aspects of the novel. At the end of our comparing, we see more clearly the novel's entire moral/political composition, if only by observing what has been missed or altered elsewhere. At the same time, this process of "triangulation" lends us better comprehension of each of the films, not only in regard to intent, but to content. This kind of outcome is the real use of examining alterations in "texts." Those who see transformation studies as a disappearing species—and who applaud that prospect—are inclined to observe that we who perform such studies search for difference only for the purpose of being annoyed by it. In that view, the person juxtaposing any novel with the film "based upon" it is outraged by difference per se, since he or she sees the "ur-text," the novel, that is, as a sacred entity which must not be defiled by any alteration. This is a shortsighted view at best. The fact is that those of us who are committed to such examinations see the differences between a novel and "its" film in much the same way as we see textual variants by a single author—as an opportunity to gain critical insight on the basis of those changes. The varying "versions" of *The Quiet American* provide just such an opportunity.

Some of Greene's most intriguing accomplishments in this novel reside in the character of the protagonist/narrator, Thomas Fowler. A somewhat typical Greene protagonist, and in several ways not unlike Greene himself, Fowler is a war correspondent (he prefers "reporter") in Vietnam for a London newspaper and has been covering Indo-China, especially Saigon, for some years. Over the course of the plot, he sets up Alden Pyle (the title character) to be executed by Viet Minh functionaries. The reader is well aware that Fowler has several defensible motives for the set-up. Pyle is ostensibly attached to the American "economic mission" but is more likely an agent for the CIA. He has made connections to one Colonel (later he promotes himself to general) Thé as part of the American search for a "third force" to take over the French war against Communist insurgents. Pyle is, in effect, a dangerous killer; by the time Fowler becomes aware of what the young American is really doing, Pyle is already responsible for the deaths of 50 to 100 innocent citizens, including women, children, the aged, and the infirm. There is no telling how many more he will take out—or what other harm he will cause—if he is not stopped. Fowler's decision, however, is greatly complicated by some other compelling facts: He has always been genuinely fond of Pyle, and recently Pyle saved Fowler's life, at some considerable risk to his own. It would not be Graham Greene, however, if the complexities stopped there. The reader is also well aware, as is Fowler of course, that Pyle has "stolen" Fowler's Vietnamese mistress, Phuong; and Fowler has expressed his willingness to do almost anything to get her back. This is the central dilemma in the novel, and most of this story line is pursued in both films, with such deviations as we shall see.

Because Brian Neve has (in chapter 16 of this volume) written thoroughly about Mankiewicz's film, I will not concentrate long upon it but merely summarize what I see as its strong and weak points in order that we may get a context for examining Noyce's later revision.

As Mankiewicz does the story, Fowler does not have an accurate read upon Pyle, and Pyle clearly has not committed the atrocious acts Fowler believes he has—and that clearly he does commit in Greene's novel. Nor is Pyle's demeanor anywhere near the same. Mankiewicz gives us an angelically innocent, boyish—indeed, puerile—Pyle, the only kind he was likely to get once he had cast Audie Murphy in the role. Greene's Pyle certainly appears earnest, but he is not as innocent as he pretends to be, and he demonstrates, late in the novel, a cold efficiency. The crucial change is that Mankiewicz's (unnamed) version of Pyle is not guilty, even from Fowler's final perspective, let alone ours. The "plastic" that is imported, in this version, is beneficial; "the American" is precisely what he represents himself as being. It is only Fowler who is duplicitous in this version. Moreover, Pyle is not, as in Greene's novel, a dupe of American foreign policy and of "York Harding," his favorite writer. Rather, Fowler has been duped by Heng and other Viet Minh operatives. The evidence that Fowler clearly assembles against Pyle in the novel has, in this film, been faked by Heng's people. Why Fowler has leaped at a motive that is so bogus is because it covers up for him his real reason to want Pyle dead.

Now, this is not, potentially, an altogether bad story. That it is a wretched version of Greene's story need not trouble us overmuch. Mankiewicz, as he himself has argued, has some license to do his "own" story. But it would necessarily be extremely difficult to make the story credible once one has chosen to begin with and to remain anywhere close to Greene's story. Once Mankiewicz, following Greene this far at least, has created such a naïve, sweet, young "American" as Audie Murphy portrays and such a crafty, wily, experienced coverer of the Saigon beat as Michael Redgrave's Fowler, it will hardly do to make an eleventh-hour effort to switch their capacities, make Fowler a gullible dupe and establish "the American" as a more savvy guy than the old-timer. Worse than this, however, is Mankiewicz's oversimplification of Greene's admirable moral complexity. In this film, right and wrong turn out to be just about as simplistic as "the American," in all his adolescence, has thought them to be. If one is going to throw away Greene's justly achieved moral ambivalence, then one would do better to choose another source to transform or to write one's own script from scratch. One of the most jarring examples of this reduction to the simplistic is when Mankiewicz's "American" challenges Fowler with "Why don't you belong to a church?" It is perfectly clear that he thinks that this would solve everything. More disturbingly, it is not clear that the film does not want us to believe the same. Toying with Greene's political framework is one thing; these constant reductions are quite another. In any Graham Greene story, guilt and innocence are never this simple.

Not everything in Mankiewicz's film is a weakening of the original version. This adaptation does capture the sense of guilt that wracks Fowler at the finish (albeit giving him too much genuine reason to feel guilty and making him guilty on a "wrong" basis). It also brings in more of Greene's use of religion than Noyce's film does, even though here, too, there are good points and bad: That Police Inspector Vigot is, as Greene made him, a devotee of

Pascal is fine; that Pyle is a crusading advocate of church going is not as good. Perhaps best of all, Mankiewicz's *Quiet American* comes near to Greene's inconclusive ending—"inconclusive" here, at least, in terms of nobody's having won. At the end of Noyce's film, as we shall see, Fowler is somewhat triumphant, albeit—again!—for wrong reasons.

When we look carefully at Noyce's *Quiet American*, we might be led to conclude that Joseph Mankiewicz was a deconstructionist ahead of his time. That is, he did not so much work from the text of Greene's novel, or with that material, as he did *against* the text. More than forty years later, Noyce reverses the process; he works from Greene's version but also against the version by Mankiewicz. In the words of Pico Iyer, he "reverses the revisionism" of Mankiewicz (Iyer, 2003, 19). The result is certainly an improvement over the earlier film, but while much of Greene is restored, much is still ignored.

Noyce, along with his screenplay writers, Christopher Hampton and Robert Schenkkan, does his best to resurrect Greene's story from the harm dealt it by Mankiewicz in several ways. First of all, the prophetic political quality of Greene's novel is put back in. Greene always possessed an uncanny penchant for political prophesy. He seemed always to be in a place—and to write a novel in and about that place—just on the eve of that place's becoming the world's latest hot spot. Thus we find him writing from Saigon in the early 1950s, from Kenya in 1954, Havana in 1957, Algeria in 1962, Haiti in 1964, Chile in 1971, and so on and so on.

The truths that Greene told us from Saigon in 1955—we know now—were these:

- Americans *were* interested in locating (and even sponsoring) a "third force."
- Various potential third forces *were* being "auditioned."
- Instruction and supplying of such forces *were* underway.
- American media *were* being "fed" misleading information.
- We were heading toward a disaster that could have been—ought to have been—avoided.

As early as 1951, Congressman John F. Kennedy, having visited Vietnam, returned home to report that "the French cannot succeed in Indochina without giving concessions necessary to make the native army a reliable and crusading force" (Sherry, 1989, 422). Meanwhile, Emperor Bao Dai was convinced that if the Vietnamese army were expanded into a nationalist force, it would defect in toto to the Viet Minh. We know, now, of course, to our regret, that Bao Dai's fears were perfectly well founded.

In January of 1952, the *New York Times* reported that in Saigon on the 21st of that month, "Seven plastic time bombs, all of them attached to bicycles, by Communist terrorists, exploded in the crowded streets . . . injuring twenty-four persons, eight of them seriously" (Durdin, 1952, 3). Four days later, a correspondent for the *Times* sent home word that that first report was of suspect authenticity. By now we know—from American legation and State Department memos, then classified but now made public—that Caodaists in the employ of Colonel Thé were responsible for the explosions, very much as Greene depicts it in the novel. Colonel (later General) Thé was, of course, one of the earliest American designees to head that "third force."

Noyce's film redeems Greene as a political prophet. To be sure, Noyce has the great advantage of hindsight, as Mankiewicz filming in 1958 did not; but keep in mind that neither did Graham Greene writing in 1955. Better than this, however, Noyce also restores much of Greene's ambiguity, much of his artistry, much of the truly compelling drama of his novel.

The central ambiguity to the novel, of course, is this: Does Fowler set up Pyle for execution by the Viet Minh because Pyle is a danger to many people, primarily but not exclusively Vietnamese people, many of whom Fowler is fond of? Or does Fowler set up Pyle because Pyle has "stolen" Fowler's mistress? The answer is *yes* to both; he does it for both reasons. Fowler hopes that the former reason—Pyle is dangerous, deceptive, and efficient in a misguided way—is not only primary but dominant. And we as readers mostly agree— Pyle has already, after all, been responsible for scores of deaths, and he clearly does not intend to stop. He has absolutely no remorse and hardly any second thought. On the other hand, always in the back of Fowler's mind, and the reader's, there are questions regarding how much of his motive is protective of others and how much is sheerly self-serving. It is this that makes the ending of Greene's novel so intriguing—and it is mainly this that Mankiewicz threw away. While Noyce recaptures much of this ambiguity, he does not quite get it all. What we want most to examine here is

1. what one can say in Fowler's defense;
2. the other side—how he is not so clearly justified; and
3. the complexities that Greene creates to "muddle" the matter.

We will notice as we go along that Noyce excellently recaptures number 1, is almost as restorative of number 2, but lacked either the time or the inclination to solidly restore number 3.

Fowler's main justification for stopping Pyle is that Pyle is dangerous. While the "knowledge" he has arrived at regarding what is best for Vietnam is recognized as thoroughly naïve by the much more experienced and thoughtful Fowler, Pyle is no less thoroughly committed to it. Not only that, but there is no way to gauge how deceptive he is: He is not some underling functionary as he has led Fowler and others to believe; he is considerably more closely linked to General Thé than could at first be discerned; and he can be highly, coldly efficient. We are made aware of this last quality in the scene in which he saves Fowler's life. When they are trapped in a lookout tower with two young members of the Vietnamese army while a prowling Viet Minh patrol threatens to blow them all up, Pyle quickly seizes a sten gun in the tower, covers the two guards while he and Fowler escape, carries the injured Fowler to cover, then leaves—with the sten gun—to return later with rescuers. Before they leave the tower, he asks of Fowler, "And these? . . . Shall I shoot them?" (106).[2] As does Fowler, we regard Pyle differently hereafter. Nor has he, ever, any remorse regarding the role he plays in recruiting a third force and in staging explosions to look like the work of "Communist terror-ists." As Fowler once observes, Pyle is "impregnably armoured by his good in-tentions and his ignorance" (163). Following the huge explosion in the Place Garnier, the final turning point in Fowler's deciding to do something to stop Pyle, there is one last bit of wavering on Fowler's part, a moment when he still might not go through with the setting-up of Pyle, for as Fowler tells him-self, he is "not made to be a judge." But then when he quizzes Pyle on whether the young man's views have been changed by that morning's explo-sion and the deaths of all those innocent bystanders, many of them aged per-sons, women, and children, Pyle's response is "They were only war casualties. . . . It was a pity, but you can't always hit your target. Anyway they died in the right cause" (179).

Noyce's film keeps most of this justification and in fact adds some of its own. Early in the film, Pyle specifically tells Phuong that he knows almost no Vietnamese—he can say, he mumbles, "Beer, haircut. . . ." But in the explo-sion scene in the Place Garnier, he speaks perfectly fluent Vietnamese to a Saigon policeman; moreover, he not only directs that policeman where to go and what to do, he bullies the policeman. As in the novel, he shows no re-morse; indeed, here he displays cynicism that Greene never suggested. Hav-ing come to Fowler's apartment, he not only lights up a cigarette but agrees to have a drink: "Whiskey'd be fine." Because both of these contradict the "boy scout" image he has so carefully cultivated, Fowler expresses surprise, to which Pyle responds, "People change." When Fowler pursues that, asking, "Or maybe they just never were what we thought they were, hmm?" Pyle's re-tort is "Who of us is, Thomas? Who of us is?" Furthermore, we learn in this same scene that Pyle had very nearly set up Fowler to be killed. Fowler is making one last attempt to dissuade Pyle, insisting to him again that Thé is not controllable, that he even tried to get Pyle himself killed; Pyle answers, "No, he tried to kill *you*." "And you knew?" Fowler asks. "Well," says Pyle, "I suspected he'd try something." There is not only a complete reversal here of the guiltless American that Joseph Mankiewicz tried to create, but there is an even more dangerous, unprincipled killer than Graham Greene created.

Regardless of how dangerous Pyle might be, or how evil, or how necessary it is that he be stopped, Fowler does have another reason for wanting him removed. Fowler is not only in love with Phuong, but has grown quite dependent—in several ways—upon her. This is clear to us in the earliest pages of the novel, as Fowler shuts his eyes and reflects upon all that she is to him: "The hiss of steam, the clink of a cup, she was a certain hour of the night and the promise of rest" (12; that this last is essential to him we shall see later). When Pyle is in the process of winning her away, Fowler warns him that he would do almost anything to keep her: "You shouldn't trust any-one when there's a woman in the case" (131). Once she has gone to live with Pyle, Fowler is aware that he is behaving like "the cuckold who mustn't show his pain" (21). And at the end of the novel, this causes much of Fowler's sense of guilt, this is the center of his misgivings—he is not perfectly certain that he has not marked Pyle for removal so that Phuong will be his again. Again, here is that moral complexity for which Greene is famous.

Noyce's film keeps a good bit of this amvibalence, none of which had been retained in the earlier film. In fact, once again, Noyce (and/or the Hampton/Schenkkan writing team) adds elements to the mix. In the novel, when Fowler leaves Saigon, headed north to cover the war, it is because he is in danger of being called back to England by his employers. So it is in this film, but here he expresses in a voice-over that he does so because he "fears losing Phuong." And directly to Pyle later, he claims that "If I were to lose her . . . that would be the beginning of death." The film adds a scene not included by Greene at all, in which Fowler loiters on the street outside Pyle's apart-ment, looking longingly at the window of the room he knows well that Phuong is in. In the last bit of dialogue within the film, he apologizes to Phuong for the fact that Pyle is permanently gone. The equivalent "apology" in the novel is, as we shall see, considerably different from this.

So this later film has much more of the novel's mature moral complexity than does the simplistic "not-nice-fellow-makes-mistaken-choice-that-kills-well-intentioned-hero" that Mankiewicz filmed. However, there is still a good bit of Greene's adult complexity that eludes this film as well. The novel's Fowler, to begin with, is not a thoroughly pleasant or attractive per-son, not just because he lies in his attempt to hold on to Phuong—that's quite forgivable—but he is weak. In a moment of self-revelation (one of his redeeming characteristics), he admits as much: "I couldn't [he says] resist the temptation to tease Pyle—it is, after all, the weapon of weakness and I was weak" (87). This weakness shows up in his main craving, which is for "rest"; recall that we have seen that before when he speaks of Phuong. Much later, he catches himself veering toward apparent generosity, and he stops to explain the "depth" of his "selfishness": "I cannot be at ease," he says, "if someone else is in pain," and that is extremely important to him, for "to be at ease is my chief wish" (114). Whether it is related to this craving or not, he resists commitment of any kind but particularly moral commitment. To Vigot, the Saigon police detective investigating Pyle's murder, Fowler says,

> "You can rule me out. . . . I'm not involved. Not involved," I repeated. It had been an article of my creed. The human condition being what it was, let them fight, let them love, let them murder, I would not be involved. My fellow journalists called themselves correspondents; I preferred the title of reporter. I wrote what I saw. I took no action—even an opinion is a kind of action. (28)

(The Noyce film includes that attitude, but not quite that speech.) Greene's Fowler is sometimes the attractively "hard-bitten" realist; more frequently, though, he is unattractively cynical. Thus, we freely grant him—indeed, we are amused by—such skeptical bon mots as this one, on the novel's very first page: "Phuong . . . means Phoenix, but nothing nowadays is fabulous and nothing rises from its ashes" (11). Less appealing are those moments when this same strain runs to cheap nihilism: "One never knows another human being" (133–34), for instance. Such a "philosophy" threatens to become tiresome when repeated: "No human being will ever understand another, not a wife a husband, a lover a mistress, nor a parent a child." (60). Nor are his politics attractive to most of us, whether on large international issues or domestic ones that are nearer to him. At one point, in attempting to defend the French presence in Vietnam, he lures himself into a spirited argument—to Pyle, no less—*for* imperialism: "I've been in India, Pyle, and I know the harm liberals do. We haven't a liberal party any more—liberalism's infected all the other parties. We are all either liberal conservatives or liberal socialists: we all have a good conscience. I'd rather be an exploiter who fights for what he exploits, and dies with it" (96). And at times he speaks so condescendingly of Vietnamese people that it is as embarrassing as it is insulting: "It's a cliché to call them children—but there's one thing which is childish. They love you in return for kindness, security, the presents you give them—they hate you for a blow or an injustice" (104). Fowler's studied noncommittal attitude is retained by Noyce; the weakness, the cynicism, and the condescension with which he sometimes speaks of Asian people are not.

At no time does Noyce's film take us into the most typical "muddle" of any Graham Greene novel: the protagonist's religious outlook. In this regard, Fowler is Greene's prototypical character. He does not believe in God, but he is keenly in tune with Vigot's readings of Pascal. Twice he observes that Vigot would have made a good priest and the second time inquires, "What is it about you that would make it so easy to confess—if there were anything to confess?" (139). Several times in the midst of a dilemma he comes close to what can only be called praying, and in the novel's final pages, he attempts to use the nonexistent God to ease his own dilemma. He has engaged Pyle to meet him for dinner at the Vieux Moulin; by Fowler's prior agreement with the Viet Minh agent Mr. Heng, this is where Heng's people will intercept Pyle. Now, Fowler tries to believe that there is "no harm in giving [Pyle] that one chance," and he makes a contingency plan in case anything comes up that will prevent Pyle's making it to the Vieux Moulin. In doing so, he tells himself,

> I handed back the decision to that Somebody in whom I didn't believe: You can intervene if You want to: a telegram on his desk: a message from the Minister. You cannot exist unless you have the power to alter the future. (180; the capitalization is, significantly, Greene's)

To be sure, this is a pure piece of evasion, particularly because Fowler has already gone to his window to signal Mr. Heng's lookout that the dinner engagement is on; but then, much of what Fowler thinks regarding religion is pure evasion. With him, it has not so much to do with belief or disbelief as it does with his devout avoidance of commitment. Probably it is this as much as anything that bothered Evelyn Waugh, who, in a letter to Greene expressed strong disapproval of Fowler, noting at one point, "What a shit he is!" Religion, of course, is one thing that Waugh and Greene had in common. Each famously converted to Roman Catholicism, and each attempted determinedly to cling to the conversion—with variant success and variant consequences. In any case, Fowler returns one more time to his having "handed back" his decision: In the novel's concluding sentence, he tells us "How I wished there existed someone to whom I could say that I was sorry" (189). This is extremely different from Noyce's ending, in which, as we have previously noticed, Fowler does apologize—but *to Phuong!* Not to any "Somebody" who does not exist.

In Greene's story, more than in Noyce's, Fowler's psychological makeup is intriguing, with or without the religion—albeit more intriguing with the religious dimension added. At the center of that interest is his oft-repeated death wish. Death attracts him because it is the only kind of certainty, the only kind of permanence he can think of. As he tells us once, "I had never believed in permanence, and yet I had longed for it" (44). On the other hand, death also frightens him: "Even though my reason wanted the state of death, I was afraid like a virgin of the act" (52). This dilemma brought him to Vietnam: "I wanted to get death over. . . . Then I came east" (103). Or, as he even more blatantly tells Pyle when the latter is trying to rescue him, "Who the hell asked you to save my life? I came east to be killed" (110). This part of his psychological construct is not separable from his religious outlook, as we see when he is first planning the trip to Phat Diem:

> Death was the only absolute value in my world. Lose life and one would lose nothing again forever. I envied those who could believe in a God and I distrusted them. I felt they were keeping their courage up with a fable of the changeless and the permanent. Death was far more certain than God. (44)

This, combined with the use of "religion" as evasion that we have just seen, explains Fowler's need, expressed to Vigot, to be shriven. Or is it a need to be blamed? Convicted? Or even damned?

Noyce comes close to making up for missing this moral/theological complexity. He includes a late scene which is one of Greene's best; while at first it might seem to us digressive, it is crucial to understanding Fowler's complicated feelings of guilt. However, Noyce "throws away" the scene by upstaging it with concurrent activity. In both versions, while Fowler awaits Pyle at the Vieux Moulin, knowing all the while that he will not come, and wonders whether Heng's men will kill him or spare him, the obnoxious American journalist, Granger, approaches his table. In the novel, he invites Fowler to come outside, and Fowler, thinking Granger plans to beat him up, almost welcomes the prospect. But, in either version, he instead hears Granger tell of a son back home who has polio and may be dying. Not only has Fowler, in Greene's story, never liked him, thinking him "like an emblematic statue" of all that Fowler "thought" he "hated in America" (184), but Granger is in fact innately dislikeable. There has been an embarrassing scene earlier involving his drunkenness and (in the novel) some apish behavior on his part at a press conference; moreover, when the novel's Fowler says, upon hearing of the son's polio, "I'm sorry," Granger's rude answer is, "You needn't be. It's not your kid." Now, however, Fowler finds that he at least shares this much with him: "Do you believe in a God, then?" Fowler asks; "I wish I did," Granger replies (185). Not only does Granger have genuine grief, but for the first time in Fowler's experience, Granger displays something like genuine ethics. His assistant, Connolly, has given out that he is sick, although he is actually pursuing an assignation in Singapore, and Granger has "got to cover for him" (185). Fowler has yet another epiphany: "Was I so different from Pyle, I wondered? Must I too have my foot thrust in the mess of life before I saw the pain?" (185–86). In this spirit, he divulges a new attitude toward Granger: "I don't dislike you. . . . I've been blind to a lot of things."[3] And he offers to do Granger's story for him and to pretend that it has been written by Connolly (185). This is the only such kindness that we have seen him extend—with no hope of reciprocity—in the entire novel. It's enough to change our agreement with Evelyn Waugh. However, while Noyce includes this scene, he runs it concurrently, alternately, with the murder of Pyle, thus undercutting it almost completely; also, he excludes all of Fowler's response to Granger— most notably Fowler's comparison of himself to Pyle.

Yet, as Tennyson says, if much has been taken, much abides. Noyce has restored most of what the novel attempted. We who know how hellish our involvement in Vietnam became see an entirely different and more accurate story from the one woven by Mankiewicz. Even though the newer version omits most of those compelling moral/theological dilemmas that are vintage Graham Greene, it is far superior to the 1958 oddity. So while cinema has not entirely patched up its quarrel with Graham Greene, it has come close.

Notes

1. Noyce's film was reportedly completed in 2001; release was delayed by the events of 11 September 2001.

2. Unless otherwise indicated, parenthetical page citations are from the 1997 Penguin Books edition of The Quiet American.

3. Not the least part of what makes this an important scene in the novel is its relating Fowler to Pyle again, this time on the basis of egocentrism.

Works Cited

Durdin, Tillman. 1952. "Saigon Blasts." New York Times. 25 January 3.

Greene, Graham. 1955. The Quiet American. London: Heinemann, 1955; New York: Viking Press, 1956. Citations here are to the Penguin Books paperback published in 1997.

Iyer, Pico. 2003. "The Unquiet Englishman." Review of The Quiet American. New York Review of Books, 13 February, 19–20.

Sherry, Norman. 1989. The Life of Graham Greene. Vol. 3. New York: Viking Press.

PART IV

HISTORY, BIOGRAPHY, AND MEMOIR

CHAPTER EIGHTEEN

~

Camille Claudel:
Biography Constructed as Melodrama

Joan Driscoll Lynch

Bruno Nuytten's film *Camille Claudel* (1988) presents itself as biography. At a historical moment when we are increasingly sensitive to the effects on history of the demands of art and to the relationship between genre and ideology, this film offers itself as a case study, an exemplary instance of layered representation. Beneath the apparent melodrama—a love story in which a historical figure, a brilliant woman, degenerates into madness—is the story of self-interested biographies and the subordination of women's history to the complicity of patriarchal interests and generic requirements.

It makes a good story, the great Rodin's fame at the price of his beloved's sanity. And it serves the purposes of Camille's own family in transferring personal responsibility onto Rodin, who meets the requirements of cliché: cruel man to exploited lover. Sacrificed by this plot—which of course has elements of truth—is Camille Claudel herself, the complexity of her own life circumstances and the fair apportionment of blame on her family origin and the historical time and place in which she found herself.

The film *Camille Claudel* is based on the biography *Camille: The Life of Camille Claudel, Rodin's Muse and Mistress* (1984) by Reine-Marie Paris. Paris is herself the great granddaughter of Camille's brother, Paul Claudel. Paul, French diplomat and famed poet, with his mother, committed Camille to an insane asylum in 1913 at age forty-nine, where she remained until her death in 1943. Paris's 1984 biography, like Paul Claudel's 1951 memoir of his sister before it, blames the sculptor Auguste Rodin for Camille's mental disintegration. Paul Claudel writes, "At thirty, when she realized that Rodin did not want to marry her, everything collapsed around her and her mind was unable to bear the strain" (Grunfeld, 1987, 235). He omits the fact that Camille lived and worked alone for fifteen years before he put her in an insane asylum. Reine-Marie Paris sustains the family myth by ignoring the role Camille's family played in incarcerating and abandoning her. By casting the lover as the villain of the piece, the biography set the stage for a biopic that would be constructed as a melodrama.

In this chapter, the story will be recast by offering another version, beginning with an overview of Camille Claudel's life set in the sociocultural milieu in which she lived. This reading interrogates the evidence of the published biography and produced film by imagining what a feminist film dealing with the same life might have looked like. The properties of the family melodrama, the particular genre the filmmakers chose in which to construct her story, are defined. These concepts are illustrated by the thematic and formal analysis of five scenes between her and her brother Paul, which imply an incestuous relationship and serve as good examples of the formal properties of the melodrama. Finally the position of women artists in the late nineteenth century will be explored because it is this larger historical construct that meaningfully resituates the life of Camille Claudel and reveals the ideological implications of these other versions of her life.

Virginia Woolf in *A Room of One's Own* (1929) asks her readers to imagine what life would have been like for Shakespeare's hypothetical sister had she had comparable talents. Camille Claudel's story illustrates what life was like for a nineteenth-century female artist who wanted to be a sculptor and who did have comparable talents to her famous male counterpart.

Camille Claudel, who was born in 1864 in Fère, France, to middle-class parents, began sculpting at age thirteen. Her work came to the attention of a noted sculptor, Alfred Boucher, who began tutoring her. M. Claudel moved the family to Paris in 1881 so that his children, Paul, Louise, and Camille, could have the finest education available. Because of M. Claudel's job, the move to Paris meant that the husband and wife were separated six days a week. This exacerbated the tension between Camille and her mother, who is said to have resented her because a brother one year younger than Camille died in infancy and Camille survived (Delbée, 1992).

In 1884, at age twenty, Camille chose to apprentice with Auguste Rodin, thus beginning a professional and personal relationship that was to last fourteen years. During that time, the two artists influenced one another enormously. Rodin was twenty years her senior and his work had become austere and predictable. The time he spent with Camille was the most artistically fertile in his career; she in turn absorbed from him his "revolutionary beliefs concerning anatomical realism, spontaneity of handling and emotional expressiveness" (McGee, 1989, H15).

They may have influenced one another equally, but there was no equality in what they gave to each other. It is documented that she sculpted the hands and feet on Rodin's "Burghers of Calais." It is suspected that a number of pieces that he signed in that period were in fact Camille's; his "Galatea" is almost identical with her "Young Woman with a Sheaf" (Paris, 1984, 17). Some of the figures in "The Gates of Hell" are thought to be her work (Higonnet, 1993, 18). Adding to this belief is the fact that the number of her own signed works in this period is uncharacteristically scant.

Rodin's professional exploitation of Camille was echoed in their personal life. Among the unpalatable facts of Camille and Rodin's life was the possibility that she had as many as five pregnancies during their relationship. They were either aborted or the infants were given to others to raise, a practice that was not uncommon at that time when the children of artisans were sent to the country to be wet nursed, thereby freeing the mother to work. Nor was permanently abandoning children unusual among artists of the day who felt that the demands of artistic creation superseded those of parenthood (Grunfeld, 1987). A new historicist reading of the practice recognizes that so much that we think of as natural, for example, the love of parents for their children and the attendant caring that this implies, is indeed cultural. It is interesting to note that the film represents only one of these pregnancies, thereby eliminating the possibility that audiences would judge her harshly. In melodrama the woman must be a sympathetic victim.

In what is arguably the best and most economical scene in the film, one in which Camille is given a voice, the filmmakers allude to the impact of the loss of these children on the pair's relationship. Rodin visits Camille in her studio; as they argue about the differences that separate them, the camera moves around them, keeping at the center of the mise-en-scène Camille's sculpture "The Little Chatelaine," an innocent child that looks questioningly at them.

Rodin felt that marriage was out of the question for him; he had a common-law wife and even his major biographer, Grunfeld (1987), quoted from a letter which described him as a satyr. It was understood that his models would sleep with him. As he became increasingly famous, the opportunities for liaisons included middle-class and upper-class women. Indeed, he gained a reputation as "an erotique, a serious collector of interesting women" (Grunfeld, 1987, 227).

Though her father continued to support her, the relationship with Rodin horrified her mother. Conduct books at the time described the Victorian lady as "pure, modest, delicate, civil, complacent, reticent, chaste, affable and polite" (Gilbert and Gubar, 1979, 23). Louise, her sister, who lived a conventional life, may have fit this description. Camille, who lived to create her art and who flagrantly sustained a relationship with Rodin, most certainly did not. Her unconventional morals added to her interest as a heroine in 1988.

When Camille went out on her own in 1898, she faced the economic problems of sculpting at that time. Rodin, the entrepreneur, had three studios and countless apprentices and technicians to execute his work. Camille, with few resources, needed to find and pay models, buy and transport clay, bake the clay, and enlarge the model, which working alone could take five years. As an alternative, if she had the money, she could hire technicians and pay a foundry to cast the model in bronze or shape directly in stone or marble.

In addition to the economic problems of sculpting, she confronted the patriarchal views of the time, which associated creative women with monsters. Women who rejected the submissive silence of domesticity were seen as terrible objects—gorgons or sirens. Literary women at this period who didn't apologize for their efforts "were defined as mad and monstrous; freakish because 'unsexed' or freakish because sexually 'fallen'" (Gilbert and Gubar, 1979, 63). As if to record how her unconventional femininity was demonized by society, in 1899 Camille portrayed herself as a monster when she chose to make Medusa in her "Perseus and the Gorgon" a self-portrait. In this sculpture Perseus triumphantly holds aloft the head of Medusa. Medusa, in particular, embodies a castrating threat. In Freud's analysis of this myth, the multiple snakes of Medusa's head represent the threat of castration. Looking at the Medusa produces a reassuring suffering and reaffirms male invulnerability (Higonnet, 1993). Camille's self-representations may have reflected her anxieties about male responses to her work. While attempting to make her way in the world of men who held these attitudes, she inevitably had difficulty with those who had commissions to grant, with technicians and suppliers.

Compared to Rodin with his sculpting factories, her output was slim. She was, however, well regarded by the most prominent critics of her day. In 1893, Octave Mirabeau called her "one of the most interesting artists of our time" (Delbée, 1992, 220). In 1898, Mathias Morhardt proclaimed "The Gossips" "a prodigious masterpiece" (Delbée, 1992, 351). In 1905, Gustave

Kahn placed her next to Berthe Morisot as "the authentic representative of the female genius" (Paris, 1984, 221). At the same time, more generally, female artists of the period were looked on, in Woolf's words, "like a dog walking on his hind legs—you are surprised to find it done at all" (1929, 54). It is not surprising, then, even given her critical acclaim, that her work wasn't bought and she failed to get many commissions. As Rodin became increasingly wealthy, Camille became poorer.

In 1913, the week after her father died, Camille's mother and brother had her committed to an insane asylum where she remained until her death thirty years later. At this period the majority of inmates of insane asylums were women. Families had the right to commit their most troublesome members without recourse. Because a desire on the part of women for independence and the free exercise of their own sexuality were regarded as insane during the period (Showalter, 1985), these were grounds enough for Camille's incarceration. Added to these liberties she took, she was poor, paranoid, eccentric, slovenly, and kept an unconventionally large number of cats. The protests of the artistic community, Camille's lucid appeals in letters, and the asylum director's assurance of her sanity all failed to move the Claudel family. She was a nuisance and an embarrassment to them, and they wanted her to stay where they wouldn't have to deal with her.

This is the material the filmmakers had at their disposal in creating their film. A feminist representation of her life would need to explore the restrictions of the period on women, the fact that ideologically they were cast as either angels or monsters. The angels fulfilled the roles of Victorian wives and mothers: docile, helpful, nurturing, caring for others rather than for themselves. Creative women devoted to the expression of their own ideas and talents were viewed as aberrations, monsters. A filmmaker would need to explore the difficulties a nineteenth-century female sculptor would have in doing the physical aspects of her work, as well as the effect that the biases of the men she dealt with had in the process of selling pieces and getting commissions.

A filmmaker could give voice to the nineteenth-century female sensibility by modeling the film on Anne Delbée's excellent novelized biography, *Camille Claudel: Une Femme* (1982, English trans. 1992), the first work to bring her to widespread attention. Delbée told her story from the point of view of Camille herself, making the reader privy to her thoughts as well as allowing her to voice her private opinions and feelings. Interspersed with the narrative were her actual letters, pictures of her sculptures, and reviews from the critics of the day.[1] Filmmakers interested in pursuing a feminist interpretation of Camille could have gone one step further and given the film a documentary cast or, perhaps, by employing Brechtian distanciation, might have interrupted the narrative with sociocultural explanation.

Instead, Nuytten and Marilyn Goldin, the screenwriters of *Camille Claudel*, constructed her story as a melodrama, the genre most closely associated with women, the one genre that puts a woman at the center of the narrative, with her role as victim paramount. Thus Camille was twice victimized, first in the nineteenth century by the circumstances of her tragic life and then again in the late twentieth century by filmmakers purporting to resuscitate her reputation.

According to Ann Kaplan (1983), melodrama is a "genre concerned explicitly with Oedipal issues—illicit love relationships (overtly or incipiently incestuous), parent–child relationships, husband–wife relationships—all of which are excluded from the dominant, male genres. Women are central in the melodrama, cast in the role of recipient of male desire, the victim, passively appearing rather than acting" (25).

Thomas Elsaesser (1987) finds the dictionary definition of *melodrama* as a "dramatic narrative in which musical accompaniment marks the emotional effects" most useful in describing the genre's style "because it allows melodramatic elements to be seen as constituents of a system of punctuation, giving expressive color and chromatic contrast to the story line by orchestrating the emotional ups and downs of the intrigue" (50). Elements such as montage, lighting, framing, close-ups, oblique angles, visual rhythm, blocking, decor, and style of acting become functional and integral elements in the construction of meaning (Elsaesser, 1987).

In terms of theme, then, family melodrama concentrates on generational and gender conflict, frequently with heavy Freudian overtones. In terms of style, excessive mise-en-scène is what makes a work melodramatic. Thus melodrama exteriorizes conflict and psychic structures (Gledhill, 1987). In the melodrama everyday actions take on symbolic meaning; ordinary gesture is heightened, and setting and decor are used to reflect the characters' psychological fixations. Violent feelings are often vented on symbolic objects (Elsaesser, 1987). Feeling states are signaled by elements, such as the composition of the frame, and "subliminally and unobtrusively transmitted to the spectator" (Elsaesser, 1987, 59).

Camille Claudel's biography provided the filmmakers with ample melodramatic material. She was most unusual for a woman of that time in that she had a father who supported her ambitions emotionally and financially. Her mother, on the other hand, was unsettled by her choice of profession and outraged by her personal life choices. This dichotomy in parental attitude served the filmmakers well as the stuff of melodrama, as they implied jealousy between the two women. Her affair with Rodin with his many mistresses and a common-law wife also provided intense emotional material, which became the central focus in the portrayal of their relationship. The artistic bonds that Camille and Rodin shared and the successes she enjoyed were diminished accordingly.

The filmmakers transformed the relationship between Camille and her brother, Paul, into an incestuous one in which they implied Paul's life choices were dictated by Camille's rejection of him in favor of Rodin. The implication is that Paul's interest in religion is a displacement of his passion for Camille. The film is structured with Paul and Rodin as rivals for Camille's affections. The reputation of Paul Claudel, considered the most important Catholic dramatist of the twentieth century, has also been done a disservice by this representation, implying as it does that his spiritual motivations are suspect. This is ironic given the filmmakers' close relationship with the Claudel family.

Although there are many fruitful areas of investigation in this text when dealing with melodrama (e.g., the relationship between Rodin and Camille and that of Camille and her mother), the following analysis of five scenes played between Paul and Camille succinctly demonstrates the melodramatic structure of this particular biography. The purpose in doing the analysis is threefold: to describe the way in which the character of Camille and her relationship with Paul were constructed, to point out the sociocultural omissions in the text, and finally to highlight the film's formal elements that make it a traditional melodrama using Elsaesser's definition (1987).

Scene 1: At the opening of the film, Paul is searching for Camille—he is constructed as rational and conventional. In a privileged shot, accompanied by the music that will play throughout the film, the spectators find what Paul is searching for: Camille standing in a pit, digging for clay with her bare hands. She has what Boucher, her teacher, had called "the madness of the mud," a madness for which she will eventually be incarcerated. Her crime is that she must create. The clay is her life, but the filmmakers suggest through the imagery of the grave in which Camille is standing that it will also be her death. The pit has been dug for the new Parisian sewer system, one of the many images of modernity in the film. Camille, herself, is caught between the old ways and the new. Women who opted for professional self-fulfillment in the nineteenth century were caught in a double bind. Elaine Showalter writes in *The Female Malady* (1985),

> At the same time that new opportunities for self-cultivation and self-fulfillment in education and work were offered to women, doctors warned them that

pursuit of such opportunities would lead to sickness, sterility and race suicide. They explicitly linked the epidemic of nervous disorders—anorexia nervosa, hysteria, and neurasthenia—which marked the *fin de siecle* to women's ambition. (121)

Camille is linked also to the workers whom she passes on the way to her studio, for she, like them, will labor for little reward. Rodin, on the other hand, the capitalistic entrepreneur who succeeds by harnessing the labor of others, including Camille's, will prosper. When she returns to her studio, Giganti, her model, is waiting for her. In using a male model who poses nude, Camille breaks with the tradition that a lady should not look at the male body. If women did use an unclothed male model at that period he was required to wear boxer shorts (Nochlin, 1988). For the rest of the film, the bust of Giganti will stand for Camille's period of independent creation, a period in which she radically broke with female tradition by acquiring her own studio and by daring to sculpt a male nude. This at a time when she as a woman was barred from attending the best art schools. Most twentieth-century audience members, however, do not have the background to recognize her audacity in doing this and there is no commentary to guide them. The lack of contextualizing on the part of the filmmakers obscures numerous sociocultural codes.

Scene 2: Camille and Paul are in bed together; iconographically, the mise-en-scène evokes the classic image of lovers in bed. The shot is a tightly framed close-up of their faces, implying their intimacy. They speak of art, Hugo, and Rimbaud, but the tone of their voices and the dialogue in which Camille asks if her love for him is a sin suggest that the relationship has erotic overtones.

Scene 3: Paul and Camille are outside the Claudel apartment. Camille is seen leaning against the house in an oblique angle shot from Paul's point of view. The suggestion is that her developed relationship with Rodin has seriously disturbed Paul's world. He explains his need to leave, the proxemic distance between the two is intimate, the tone much more that of a lover than a brother. The scene ends with Paul saying, "At least now you remember that I exist." Both this scene and the one of Camille and Paul in bed with their overt implications of brother/sister incest succeed in shifting the spectator's attention away from any larger critique of patriarchy to these forbidden scenes of love—a staple of melodrama.

Scene 4: Paul visits Rodin at his studio, La Folie Neufbourg, to ask his help in launching a diplomatic career. The scene opens with a point-of-view shot of the crumbling stairway leading to the interior of the decaying mansion, which is now where his sister lives, a reflection of his view of the dissolution of her life. He uncovers the busts for which Camille has modeled and lovingly runs his hand over a nude, a good example of the way in which feelings are vented on symbolic objects in the melodrama. The scene ends with the two men having a box lunch prepared by Rose Beuret, Rodin's common-law wife. In the competition between the two men, Rodin has won Camille completely on his own terms. She will serve him artistically, just as Rose serves him domestically. While he has the comforts of a traditional home, Camille will be subjected to the rigors of life in this inhospitable place.

Juxtaposed to this scene is one in which Camille discovers she is pregnant. As she leaves the doctor's office, the half-finished Eiffel tower rises in the background. Another image of modernity, it suggests that Camille's work is unfinished and is jeopardized by her pregnancy. The music that has been recurrent throughout the film plays, a reminder that in the melodrama the musical accompaniment marks the emotional effects.

Scene 5: The final scene of the five is played in the shadowed semidarkness of Paul's apartment. The blocking in the scene is a pas de deux of intimacy and estrangement, a good example of the notion that the mise-en-scène in melodrama exteriorizes conflict and psychic structures. Brother and sister move close together to share secrets, secrets that will estrange them further as the film progresses. Camille confides that she has had an abortion; he tells her of his conversion to Catholicism. There is an implication that Paul turned to the church because he wanted to be a successful writer in Catholic France. He tells her he needs faith to be a great artist; she says she will do it on her own. The scene ends with a voice-over of him praying for her while she hides under the bed sheets in another room. He believes that he is saved and she has fallen. His embrace of the dominant ideology coupled with his growing stature as a representative of his nation in both diplomacy and art will make him ever more embarrassed by her. His writings will justify her as a great artist while excoriating Rodin. His actions will be those of an ashamed relative, and he will relegate her struggle as a female artist permanently to absence and silence, not unlike the ways in which this film also claiming to extol Camille chooses to ignore her historical struggle in favor of the emotional draw of melodrama.

In her *Women, Art, and Power*, Linda Nochlin describes the characteristics of women who achieved preeminence as artists in the nineteenth and twentieth centuries: Each had a close personal connection with a strong male artist, fathers who were encouraging, the personal strength to rebel against the current traditions and attitudes, and the psychic fortitude to adopt the attributes associated with masculinity that lead to success—"single-mindedness, concentration, tenaciousness and absorption in ideas and craftsmanship for their own sake" (1988, 168–70). Camille Claudel had all of these qualities and was able to achieve distinction, but she paid a terrible price. In order to be mentored, she was exploited. A century later, the price she paid for cinematic fame as the heroine of a box-office and critical success, winner of five Caesars and an Academy Award nomination, was exploitation once again.

The film *Camille Claudel* is an excellent case study of the many levels in which Laura Mulvey's statement that "the unconscious of patriarchal society has structured film form" is played out (1977, 412). First, there is the reality of life for a female artist in the late nineteenth/early twentieth century, a life that is structured by the demands of a patriarchal society. Second, there is the representation of that life in the late twentieth century, structured in order to afford an audience visual pleasure. The pleasure is in sadomasochistic expectations fulfilled: two powerful, successful men and a beautiful, victimized, rejected woman. Patterns of dominance and submission are at the heart of the pleasure of the melodrama and indeed most Hollywood cinema, with males identifying with the power position and women with the suffering of the beautiful victim. This is yet another one of our operative cultural myths, "a crucial part of both male and female sexuality as constructed in western civilization" (Kaplan, 1983, 27).

Camille Claudel masquerades as a feminist film because it shows Camille's victimization and grants that she is an excellent artist. This chapter has deconstructed the film by exposing the fact that beneath the surface there lies a familiar and oft-repeated story and by demonstrating that the formal preoccupations of the film "reflect the psychical obsessions of the society that produced it" (Mulvey, 1977, 414). By structuring the biography of Camille Claudel as melodrama, the emphasis by generic convention shifted from the sociohistoric to the personal, thus disallowing any far-reaching critique of patriarchy.

Note

1. Anne Delbée wished to make a film based on her book. According to Guy Austin, "This project was scuppered by the Claudels, who granted access to personal documents and letters to Nuytten and Adjani instead, since their version was based on a much more favorable biography by Camille's grandniece, Reine-Marie Paris" (1996, 156).

Works Cited

Austin, Guy. 1996. *Contemporary French Cinema*. Manchester, UK: Manchester University Press.

Camille Claudel. 1988. Dir. Bruno Nuytten. Perf. Isabelle Adjani, Gérard Depardieu, and Laurent Grévill. Orion Classics.

Delbée, Anne. 1992. *Camille Claudel: Une Femme*. Trans. Carol Cosman. San Francisco: Mercury House. Original French version published in 1982.

Elsaesser, Thomas. 1987. "Tales of Sound and Fury." In *Home Is Where the Heart Is: Studies in Melodrama and the Women's Film*, ed. Christine Gledhill, 43–69. London: BFI.

Gilbert, Sandra M., and Susan Gubar. 1979. *The Madwoman in the Attic: The Woman Writer and the Nineteenth-Century Literary Imagination*. New Haven, CT: Yale University Press.

Gledhill, Christine. 1987. "The Melodramatic Field: An Investigation." In *Home Is Where the Heart Is: Studies in Melodrama and the Women's Film*, ed. Christine Gledhill, 5–39. London: BFI.

Grunfeld, Frederick V. 1987. *Rodin: A Biography*. New York: Henry Holt.

Higonnet, Anne. 1993. "Myths of Creation: Camille Claudel and Auguste Rodin." In *Significant Others: Creativity and Intimate Partnership*, ed. Whitney Chadwick and Isabelle de Courtivron, 15–29. London: Thames and Hudson.

Kaplan, E. Ann. 1983. *Women and Film: Both Sides of the Camera*. New York: Methuen.

McGee, Celia. 1989. "Camille Claudel, Passion Reborn." *New York Times*, 17 December, national edition, H15.

Mulvey, Laura. 1977. "Visual Pleasure and Narrative Cinema." In *Women and the Cinema*, ed. Karyn Kay and Gerald Peary, 412–28. New York: E. P. Dutton.

Nochlin, Linda. 1988. *Women, Art, and Power and Other Essays*. New York: Harper and Row.

Paris, Reine-Marie. 1984. *Camille: The Life of Camille Claudel, Rodin's Muse and Mistress*. New York: Arcade Publishing.

Showalter, Elaine. 1985. *The Female Malady: Women, Madness and English Culture*. New York: Harcourt, Brace, Jovanovich.

Woolf, Virginia. 1929. *A Room of One's Own*. New York: Harcourt, Brace, Jovanovich.

~

CHAPTER NINETEEN

W. C. Handy Goes Uptown: Hollywood Constructs the American Blues Musician

John C. Tibbetts

When does a man cease just to be a songwriter and become a composer? When does a man cease just to write hit songs and become part of the music and a nation. You've graduated from Tin Pan Alley! I want to see you in Carnegie Hall. I want to hear your music at its peak. I want a symphony orchestra to play it.

—Lillian Harris to Sigmund Romberg in *Deep in My Heart* (1954)

St. Louis Blues, released by Paramount in 1958 and starring Nat King Cole as blues composer W. C. Handy, was but one of dozens of biopics released during Hollywood's so-called classical studio period (roughly 1930–1960) that dramatized the lives of the great American songwriters, ranging from America's first professional songwriter, Stephen Foster, to the tunesmiths of Tin Pan Alley and the Broadway musical show.[1] However, only *St. Louis Blues* was about a black composer. Released in observance of Handy's recent death and featuring an actor whose own biography and abilities rather resembled Handy's, the film might have been presumed to constitute a landmark in the history of screen's depiction of African American identity and performance in American popular culture. Moreover, it boasts an all-black cast, including, in addition to Cole, Eartha Kitt, Pearl Bailey, Ruby Dee, Juano Hernandez, and Ella Fitzgerald and Cab Calloway in cameo roles.

But the film proved to be nothing of the sort. That the characters were black seemed incidental to the story. There was little indication that Handy and his music arose from and reflected the conditions of oppressed African Americans in the racist society of the South. While most critics acknowledged the earnestness of the film, they did not fail to note these sins of omission and, as a result, condemned the film as a stiff, stodgy, and bloodless affair. For example, William R. Weaver in *Motion Picture Daily* noted that "the life, times and music of the late W. C. Handy, from age ten to forty, are dealt with carefully, respectfully, and more slowly than is good for the project" (Weaver, 1958, n.p.). *Harrison's Reports* described it "as a rather listless and disappointing entertainment that does not do justice to either the man or his music" (Anon, 1958, n.p.). More to the point of this chapter is the damning assessment from Powe in *Variety* (1958), which I quote at length:

> The story . . . is unconvincing; the music is seldom seen or heard to advantage. . . . But in the end the reaction is to wonder what there was about the man and his music that was so great. . . . A real and successful effort has been made to avoid any possible charge of "Uncle Tom" in the characters. But for this reason or others, the result is such a genteel portrayal of life in Memphis in the early years of this century that you might wonder why the Negroes ever sang the blues. . . . A clumsy effort is made to show Handy getting inspiration from watching Negro laborers load a wagon. The blues certainly came in part out of the spirituals that expressed the deep and justified melancholy of the Negro, but they also came from the honkytonks, the bordellos, and the bistros, and this is barely indicated. (n.p.)

Indeed, *St. Louis Blues* privileged instead a melodramatic story—Handy's struggle against blindness, his attempts to reconcile with his estranged and disapproving Baptist preacher father, and his search for the legitimacy and approval of the uptown musical establishment—only tangentially related to Handy's biography.[2] It is not my intention here to trace the film's tenuous relationship to the historical record, a matter of only secondary interest; rather, I propose to examine the film as a case study in the Hollywood practice of "whitening" its source text—the racial ethnicity of the composer and his music—and the adaptation of that text to the conventions of the standard biopic paradigm common to mainstream films at the time and targeted to predominantly white middle-class audiences.

Most of the action of *St. Louis Blues* takes place in Memphis, Tennessee, which, contrary to the historical record, is depicted as his lifelong home (a suggestion doubtlessly welcomed and endorsed by the Memphis Chamber of Commerce!). Young William's interest in secular music is indeed violently discouraged by his Baptist minister father, who angrily brands jazz and blues as "the Devil's music." So obdurate is the good reverend that Handy has to pursue his interests in secret, signing on to perform his songs with a fictitious singer named Go Go Germaine (Eartha Kitt) at a notorious (and likewise fictitious) local nightspot called the Big Rooster Club. Handy is smitten with Germaine, much to the chagrin of his girlfriend (Ruby Dee), but his marriage proposal is turned down. Germaine is convinced of Handy's genius, if not his romantic attractions, and decides to take his songs to New York City. The disconsolate Handy remains behind in Memphis.

Suddenly, without warning, Handy suffers an inexplicable attack of blindness. He turns to composing church hymns for what he intends as penance for betraying his father's religion. One day while performing one of his new hymns at a church service, he miraculously regains his sight. Feeling redeemed, armed with a new song that he's been toying with throughout the story, "St. Louis Blues," and newly determined to pursue a career as a blues composer and musician, he leaves Memphis and goes on the road, performing his music from town to town.

Back in Memphis news reaches Handy's family that his "St. Louis Blues" is scheduled on a concert program in the prestigious Aeolian Hall in New York City (site of the legendary, self-proclaimed Experiment in Modern Music concert on 12 February 1924, that introduced George Gershwin's *Rhapsody in Blue*). It is a glittering, upscale affair, featuring the all-white New York Symphony Orchestra in evening dress conducted by that presumably esteemed European artist, Constantin Bakaleinikoff (an amusing detail, considering that in real life Bakaleinikoff was a studio composer for Paramount Studios[3]). "This is Aeolian Hall," whispers Go Go Germaine to the arriving Handy family. "No dancing, no drinking. People pay three dollars and thirty cents a seat and listen to great music." After concluding Mendelssohn's Third Symphony, Bakaleinikoff steps forward to make an announcement.

Ladies and gentlemen, you ask why the Symphony Orchestra would play the blues . . . the only pure art form to originate in America. Only in the art of a new folk music is America pre-eminent. One man, more than any others, is responsible for that fact, W. C. Handy.

Whereupon the orchestra launches into a full-blown symphonic arrangement of "St. Louis Blues," with blaring brass and crashing cymbals, as Go Go Germaine steps forward to sing the song. By this time Handy himself has arrived; and he now finds himself rather reluctantly on stage, dapper and trim in his tuxedo, for the grand finale. It is a triumphant occasion, even if the only African Americans present are Handy, his family, and his girlfriend, who are relegated to a backstage peek at the proceedings. Fade-out. "[The Father] is won over," dryly remarks historian Krin Gabbard in *Jammin' at the Margins*, "at least in part by the majesty of the symphony hall and the spectacle of white men in tuxedos playing violins" (1996, 60).

As already noted, it is striking that Handy's racial identity as an African American living and working in a black community in the racist, segregationist South is scarcely apparent. There is nary a hint of bigotry and oppression—a striking departure from the oppressive social milieu and numerous racist incidents described in Handy's autobiography. In the film, apart from overhearing as a child some work songs, Handy seems unaware of the painful origins of blues music. Indeed, the only moment when he acknowledges it as a distinctly black expression comes in a brief and vague declaration he makes to his father: "The music I play is the music of our people. It's not mine, it's theirs. Are our people evil because they sing other songs besides hymns? I was born with this music in me." Oddly, there is no mention in the film of Handy's business endeavors, of his publishing firm, and of his indefatigable labors on behalf of the popularization of blues music. His passive genius is privileged rather than his more masculine, activist industry.

The W. C. Handy depicted in *St. Louis Blues* is cut from the same cloth as the subjects of other Hollywood songwriter biopics about American gentile and Jewish composers alike, such as Stephen Foster (*Swanee River*, 1939); Paul Dresser (*My Gal Sal*, 1942); George Gershwin (*Rhapsody in Blue*, 1946); Jerome Kern (*Till the Clouds Roll By*, 1948); and Sigmund Romberg (*Deep in My Heart*, 1954), as well as their "classical" counterparts, the European "canonical" composers Johann Strauss Jr. (*The Great Waltz*, 1938); Franz Schubert (*The Melody Master*, 1941); Frederic Chopin (*A Song to Remember*, 1945); Richard Wagner (*Magic Fire*, 1954); Ludwig van Beethoven (*The Magnificent Rebel*, 1960); and so forth. Their success, fame, and celebrated music made them ideal subjects for a prestige-hungry Hollywood. At the same time, however, as historians George F. Custen, Thomas Elsaesser, and Jolanta T. Pekacz have pointed out in their discussions of the formulas of Hollywood biopics, and composer biopics in particular, these subjects must be "contained" and "normalized" according to prevailing studio story agendas and the strictures of the Hollywood Production Code, the chief censoring organ in the industry.[4] Putting it another way, while a composer may be depicted as a somewhat marginalized individual struggling against stifling societal conformism, there must be a compensatory view of the artist as a citizen striving to compose a "song of the people" that reflects, confirms, and celebrates the community's own commonly held experiences. (Here was a neat balancing act, summed up best in a dialogue exchange in the Chopin biopic *A Song to Remember*, 1945, wherein Chopin is advised by his mentor, "A man worthy of his gifts should grow closer to those people as he grows more great. Fight harder for them with that same genius.")

Other agendas dictated that these "lives" must cater to Hollywood's star system and be congruent with the stars' faces, personalities, and public images. Even the musical texts, like the composers themselves, must be transformed, removed from their specific historical contexts, stripped of their autonomy, and redeployed on the soundtrack as a supplement to the narrative discourse. This last item, suggests historian Carol Flinn (1990), is particularly ironic in that some of the greatest music ever written should not draw attention to itself qua music; no matter how distinguished it might be, "it is not successful unless it is secondary to the story being told on the screen" (38).

Absent from these agendas is any examination of the particulars of sexual orientation, ethnicity, and race. To understand this we have only to look to that generation of Jewish immigrants who guided the establishment and operation of the big Hollywood studios in the first half of the century. As has been argued in numerous histories of the period, most especially in Neal Gabler's *An Empire of Their Own*, most of the studio moguls—Carl Laemmle, Adolph Zukor, Louis B. Mayer, Jack Warner, and the rest—were immigrants who effectively turned their backs on their Jewishness and the America that discriminated against them. They Americanized themselves and projected that collective identity onto America's screens: "They would create its values and myths," wrote Gabler (1988), "its traditions and archetypes" and proclaim in their movies "an empire of their own," the imaginary America they wished to inhabit, an America of "whitened," or indeterminate, cultural, sexual, and racial definition (5–6).

One film more than any other, argue Gabbard and Michael Rogin, mirrors this process and provides the paradigm for films like *St. Louis Blues*. "The Jazz Singer," writes Rogin (1996), "displays the history of the men who made Hollywood" (84).[5] Regarded in its purest incarnation, the popular 1927 part-talkie starring Al Jolson tells the story of a cantor's son torn between his Old World Jewish heritage and the New World jazz music. Its themes are peculiar to the American experience—the conflicts between Old World tradition and New World expression, ethnic identity and "melting pot" assimilation, elitist art and populist expression, the sacred and the profane, father and son.

A brief review is in order. *The Jazz Singer* is, of course, about the path a young man takes from cantor's son to jazz singer. Jakie Rabinowitz, a boy from a working-class Jewish family, wants to sing popular songs, or "jazz" (his father dismisses them as "raggy songs"), at a sleazy joint called Coffee Dan's under the blackface stage personna of "Jack Robin," much to the chagrin of his cantor father, who insists that his son follow in his footsteps.[6] When Jakie finally receives his father's deathbed forgiveness and blessing, he declares, "You taught me that music is the voice of God. My songs mean as much to my audience as yours to your congregation." Jakie promptly repairs to the synagogue where, in white robe and skull cap, he replaces his father on Yom Kippur and sings a rather jazzy "Kol Nidre" ("a jazz singer singing to his God," says the intertitle). Later, wearing a wool cap and donning burnt cork makeup, he appears as "Jack" on the stage of the prestigious Winter Garden Theater singing "My Mammy" as his adoring Jewish mother and gentile girlfriend look on. The traditional blackface makeup, writes Gabbard (1996), "eases his path to assimilation by concealing his Jewishness" (38). Moreover, by donning the blackface and by singing jazz, argues Rogin (1996), Jakie achieves upward mobility, transforming from Hebraic particularism to American universalism.

It seems clear to me that St. Louis Blues is The Jazz Singer in "white face"; and Nat King Cole's Handy is the obverse to Jolson's "Jakie Rabinowitz." Just as Jakie dons blackface and a new name, "Jack Robin," on the way from ghetto and synagogue to Broadway, the black musician William Handy acquires the "white face" of a prestigious composer, "W. C. Handy," as he leaves the Memphis back street and his father's church on the way to the uptown concert hall. Both men derive their music from an instinctive response to the everyday world around them, not from formal training and Old World conventions.[7] Defiance of the pleas of their sternly traditionalist and religious-minded fathers to abandon the pursuit of this "Devil's music" leads to their expulsion from home and community (and, in Handy's case, to a temporary attack of blindness). Anti-Semitism and race discrimination play no part in their problems. The apparent shift from ethnocultural to generational conflict in both indicates that Jakie's and William's problems appear to be only with their parents and their own culture and not with racist society at large.

Jakie and William find themselves temporarily suspended, helplessly torn between Old World traditions, which have deflected them away from "the people," and the siren call of the New World, which has uprooted and displaced them from the nourishing soil of tradition and respectability. Their great song, whether it's "Toot Toot Tootsie" or "St. Louis Blues," on which they have been laboring all this time, must for now remain silent. Sympathetically looking on, meanwhile, is the great love, a good woman (a gentile, in Jakie's case, an African American in William's case), who loyally stands by her man. It is only when Jakie and William return to synagogue and church and receive the blessings of their fathers (and William regains his sight) that they are newly empowered to pursue their career ambitions and bring their great song to the whole wide world. Immigrant Jakie is Americanized by his imaginary blackness as jazz singer Jack Robin, and African American William is legitimated by his imaginary whiteness as blues composer W. C. Handy.

To be sure, this is no easy and harmonious reconciliation. You assume that neither Jakie nor William will return to the Lower East Side or the Memphis back streets. Their American identity, whatever it is, is at best an uneasy assimilation of their ethnic past and their American future, leaving them no longer specifically Jewish or African. And their music, moreover—whatever *that* is—has relinquished its ethnic specificity: Jack Robin's "jazz" and W. C. Handy's "blues" now share in common a fusion of minstrel tune, jazz riff, Hebraic chant, and sentimental song—a new soundtrack of contemporary America.[8]

The casting of Nat King Cole as W. C. Handy, ironically, played a crucial role in the "whitening" agenda of the composer and his music. That the film was made at all proves how crucial the casting was in conceiving and executing a black subject at a time when Hollywood was notoriously reluctant to pursue such ventures. To begin with, obvious similarities were perceived between Cole's and Handy's backgrounds. Cole claimed that, like Handy, the issue of religious music versus popular music was one that he had confronted in his own life. "Both of us were the sons of ministers," Cole explained at the time in material quoted in the film's pressbook, "and both our fathers firmly disapproved of our playing jazz. It took a long time before my father became reconciled to my singing, as it did with Mr. Handy" (*St. Louis Blues* pressbook, 1958, n.p.). And, like the Handy of the film, Cole was known as the composer and singer of many of his own songs (his "Straighten Up and Fly Right" was for him the "breakthrough" equivalent of Handy's "St. Louis Blues"). Thus, he, too, played a significant role in bringing jazz and the image of the black artist into the mainstream of American entertainment.

What cannot be ignored, however, is that Hollywood was also exploiting another aspect of Cole's popularity, that is, his acceptance in the popular mainstream as a performer of a blurred and indeterminate racial identity. As Krin Gabbard (1996) notes, "Cole functioned as a healthy alternative to the unsavory image of the drug-crazed, psyched-up black jazz artist that had been thoroughly inscribed on the American mind by the late 1950s" (99). A comfortable, familiar, nonconfrontational presence, viewers knew him either from his television variety series that had premiered the year before (a breakthrough in network television), his career in the early 1940s as an es-teemed jazz artist, his previous appearances in the films *The Blue Gardenia* (1953) and *China Gate* (1957), among others, or as a popular singer identi-fied with such mainstream classics as "The Christmas Song." As a result, Cole's Handy is the inverse of Elvis Presley in another Paramount release in 1958, *King Creole*. Cole is "a restrained black man acting 'white,'" concludes Gabbard, "rather than a shameless white man acting 'black'" (1996, 246).

By now we are not surprised that what Handy's music really *is* and what re-lation it bears to the milieu in which Handy lived and what it contributed to the American songwriting "melting pot" known as Tin Pan Alley is largely ir-relevant to Hollywood. A review of the historical record tells us that Handy was forty years old and living in Memphis when he composed "St. Louis Blues" in 1914. Up to that time, with only the moderately successful "Memphis Blues" to his credit, he was known more as a bandleader, arranger, and publisher than as a songwriter. His new song changed all that. Handy claimed that he was in-fluenced by the "crude singing of the 'Negro'" while living in Mississippi and in his hometown, Florence, Alabama (Tracy, 2001, 91–92). Within the next five years, hit recordings and sheet music sales made "St. Louis Blues" the most famous blues song in the world—and the best-selling song in any medium.[9] The lyrics, reports David A. Jasen and Gene Jones in *Spreadin' Rhythm Around* (1998), were in dialect but not "coon" or minstrel speech. "The words do not convey ignorance, helplessness, or foolishness. The song is the plaint of some-one who is hurting, but there is a frankness and toughness in the telling about it. . . . This dual package of pain and strength is the essence of the blues" (Jasen and Jones, 1998, 236–37). As for its musical vocabulary, continues Jasen and Jones, "Its harmonies literally put new notes into the pop music scale, and its structure showed writers a new way to build popular songs . . . like giving painters a new set of primary colors and showing them shapes they had never seen before." African song dealt in quarter-tones that hovered between major and minor, more proper to the voice or the guitar but not a piano. Handy found a way to approximate those tones in band instrumentation. He approximated the major/minor sound by flatting the third note in the major scale; moreover by occasionally flatting the fifth and seventh tones he could deepen the minor, or "blue note," effect without changing the "major" sound of the melody. "Blue notes had occurred in popular music before," conclude Jasen and Jones, "—as syncopation had occurred before ragtime—but Handy was the first to use the blue-noted scale as a basis for a body of composition" (Jasen and Jones, 1998, 236–37).

However, with the exception of a brief, charmingly simple rendition of a fragment of the song by Pearl Bailey midway through the film, *St. Louis Blues* is determined to sanitize and clothe its eponymous song in symphonic garb for the edification of white musicians and the white folks in the audience of the hallowed precincts of Aeolian Hall. Thus, its rough edges and gritty vernacular are smoothed out and rendered acceptable to the predominantly white middle-class audiences of the American movie-going public. I hasten to add that this was not just a Hollywood conceit but a reflection of real-life events. In his own lifetime, many of Handy's songs did indeed achieve symphonic orchestrations and performances in major American concert halls.[10]

In any case, the havoc wreaked upon Handy's song is lamentable, in my opinion, if all too predictable. True, the tune had gotten off to a noble start in the movies in 1929 with Bessie Smith's stark and grittily definitive reading in Dudley Murphy's independently made and released film of that name.[11] But six years later it ran aground in Nunnally Johnson's *Banjo on My Knee*, wherein a black cast of professionally trained voices subjected it to an operatic treatment, replete with solos, chorus, recitatives, and elaborately choreographed formations of dock workers bearing their burdens in a painfully self-conscious lock step against rear-screened riverfront settings. Arguably, this sort of thing is even more deplorable than the "apotheosis in white" at the end of *St. Louis Blues*. Instead, this "apotheosis in black" is mired in its own dreadful, self-indulgent sincerity.

This sort of fate can be seen in countless other films. Three examples will suffice. In *New Orleans*, for example, a 1947 film directed by Arthur Lubin for United Artists, another blues song, "If You Know What It Means to Miss New Orleans," travels from the cabarets and gambling halls of Basin Street to the celebrated Manhattan Symphony Hall in New York City, acquiring ever more polish and pretentiousness along the way. When we first hear the song, it is performed with great charm and intimacy in a humble cafe by Louis Armstrong (playing himself) and Billie Holiday (playing a maid named "Endie"). But after about an hour of screen time, and a furious montage showing Louis and his band touring Europe with their music, the song ends up in New York City, where it is warbled in a preposterously ineptly inappropriate performance by a white opera singer (Dorothy Patrick) and given full concert dress and a swing orchestral arrangement by an all-white complement of symphonic and swing musicians (Woody Herman's band, no less). Armstrong and Holliday, meanwhile, have disappeared without a trace. In *A Song Is Born* (1948), Danny Kaye conducts a radio broadcast that traces the history of jazz, wherein the faux-spiritual, "Goin' Home," is subjected to a series of musical "tests," including an a capella rendition by a black vocal quartet, a jazzy rendition by Louis Armstrong and Benny Goodman, and a pop song warbled by Virginia Mayo.[12] And the fate awaiting Jerome Kern's "Old

Man River" in the Jerome Kern biopic, *Till the Clouds Roll By*, is especially gruesome. Heard initially in something approximating its original stage setting with a black cast, "Old Man River" is heard again at the end of the film, transformed now into a swing peroration performed by none other than a slim, white-tuxedo-clad Frank Sinatra perched atop a tall white marble column and warbling his tonsils out. James Agee greeted this catastrophe with the remark that he would prefer to hear a zither solo played by W. C. Fields. Mercifully, Jerome Kern died just before the film's release and was spared the ordeal.

It's worth noting that a similar process happens in reverse with the popularization of classical music. A particularly cogent example is found in a 1943 Oscar-winning MGM short, *Heavenly Music*, in which a group of celestial classical musicians, including Beethoven, Schubert, Paganini, Bach, Johann Strauss, Chopin, and others haughtily audition a swing composer's bid for entry into Heaven's Hall of Composers. However, before the audition is through, the classical guys literally step down from their pedestals and join the upstart composer in a swing version of his music (accompanied by Gabriel's horn, no less).

The music heard in these examples is, like the ethnicity of the composer, whitened and indeterminate in character and expression. It's a paradox best expressed by the character of Sigmund Romberg in the biopic *Deep in My Heart* (1954), "This music isn't highbrow music and it isn't lowbrow music. Perhaps it might be called 'middlebrow' music. It belongs in the heart."

In sum, Hollywood was determined in films like *St. Louis Blues* to bring the "respectable" composer and the popular songwriter, the Old World and the New, together in a *juste-milieu* synergy, or equilibrium. There were ethical and moral lessons here: As we have seen, the classical composer must bow to the dictates of "the people"; and the popular composer must strive for the legitimacy of the "classics." The extraordinary individual must not overreach himself because success has a price; and the humble artist must strive for social and cultural improvement, lest he sink into frustration and mediocrity. In other words, those creative geniuses of the Old World European classical canon must climb out of their ivory tower and industriously pursue the American work ethic, relinquish their autonomy, and blend their voices with those of "The People." On the other hand, the unschooled, vernacular artists of the New World must not content themselves with their humble lot but strive to connect with Old World traditions and prestige. These antimonies must meet, as it were, somewhere in between. "America is a mixture of things that are very old with more that is new," a classically trained teacher tells George Gershwin (Robert Alda) in *Rhapsody in Blue* (1946). "Your nature has the same contradictions, ideals and material ambition. If you can make them both serve, you will give America a voice."

Thus, the resemblances in these films between Hollywood's constructions of classical and popular artists—between, for example, Franz Schubert and W. C. Handy, between Franz Liszt and George Gershwin—are not accidental. Their similarities border on identity. Their portraits are like the composite drawings found in police files, whose faces are collations of "types" of eyes, ears, noses, chins, and hairlines gathered together from sundry disparate sources. Composers, statesmen, inventors, athletes, artists, soldiers, and the like are not specific individuals existing at specific times but collective entities for all times that entertain while they function as catalysts of social, political, and cultural change and assimilation.

Notes

1. See my *Composers in the Movies: Studies in Musical Biography* (2005), 102–54, for an overview of the Tin Pan Alley biopic.

2. For the record, composer, bandleader, minstrel performer, and song publisher William Christopher Handy was born in 1873 in Florence, Alabama, the son of freed slaves. His interests in dance and folk music were discouraged by his conservative, hymn-singing parents, and beginning in his mid-teens, he hit the road with several minstrel shows. Years of struggle and near starvation paid off when he landed several successful gigs with show bands touring the South. He married Elizabeth Price in 1898 and continued his itinerant ways, despite her disapproval. Shortly after the turn of the century, while living in Memphis, his increasing interest in music arranging led to his first forays in song composing, resulting in his earliest blues successes, "Memphis Blues" in 1912 and "St. Louis Blues" in 1914. At this time he formed a partnership with Harry Pace, establishing the Pace and Handy Music Company, the third music publishing company by African Americans, with branch offices in Chicago and New York. Encouraged in New York by prominent black musicians like James Reece Europe, his career in publishing, editing, and entrepreneurship flourished, not just in blues but in jazz, spirituals, and popular songs. His blues music garnered "legitimate" status when it was performed in concert arrangements in several prestigious auditoriums in New York City, and he began to be referred to as the "Master" and "Father of the Blues," a claim vigorously disputed by other black musicians, notably Jelly Roll Morton. As the result of an accident that had damaged his eyes years before, his vision began to deteriorate at this time, and by the mid-1930s he was blind. Handy's autobiography, *Father of the Blues*, appeared in 1955. After the death of his wife in 1954, he remarried. A year later he suffered a stroke and was confined to a wheelchair for the rest of his life. He died on 29 March 1958 before the release of *St. Louis Blues*.

3. Constantin Bakaleinikoff and his brother Mischa both worked in the Hollywood studio system for many years: Mischa for Columbia and Constantin for MGM,

RKO, and Paramount. Constantin was born in Moscow in 1896, studied at the Moscow Conservatory, and came to America as a member of the Los Angeles Philharmonic. He became head of RKO's music department in 1941.

4. Extended discussions of biopic formulas include George F. Custen's pioneering *Bio/Pics: How Hollywood Constructed Public History* (1992); Thomas Elsaesser's "Film History as Social History: The Dieterle/Warner Brothers Bio-Pic" (1993); and Jolanta T. Pekacz's "Memory, History and Meaning: Musical Biography and Its Discontents" (2004).

5. See Michael Rogin, *Blackface, White Noise* (1996), particularly pages 81–120. See also Gabbard (1996, 35–65).

6. Whether or not Jack Robin's "jazz" satisfied our definitions of just what "jazz" is, is open to dispute. See conflicting opinions in Gabbard (1996) and Rogin (1996).

7. In *Father of the Blues* (1955), Handy suggests many times that his music came not from formal training but from an intuitive receptivity to the world around him. "As a child I had not heard of the Pipes of Pan," he writes, "but pastoral melody was nevertheless a very real thing to me. Whenever I heard the song of a bird and the answering call of its mate, I could visualize the notes in the scale. Robins carried a warm alto theme. Bobolinks sang contrapuntal melodies. Mocking birds trilled cadenzas. Altogether, as I fancied, they belonged to a great outdoor choir" (14). In another passage, he observes that he learned more about music from "those country black boys" he met in Cleveland, who "taught me something that could not possibly have been gained from books, something that would, however, cause books to be written. Art, in the high-brow sense, was not in my mind" (77). As for the idiosyncratic rhythms of ragtime, blues, and spirituals, he writes, "Negroes react rhythmically to everything. That's how the blues came to be. Sometimes I think that rhythm is our middle name. When the sweet good man packs his trunk and goes, that is occasion for some low moaning. When darktown puts on its new shoes and takes off the brakes, jazz steps in. If it's the New Jerusalem and the River Jordan we're studying, we make the spirituals. . . . In every case the songs come from down deep" (82).

8. In a remarkably prescient statement published during his New York sojourn, 1892–1895, Antonin Dvořák (1895) defined what he called the "the music of the people" as deriving from "all the races that are commingled in this great country." He cited "the Negro melodies, the songs of the Creoles, the red man's chant, the plaintive ditties of the German or Norwegian . . . the melodies of whistling boys, street singers and blind organ grinders." He seems to have anticipated the rise of the ragtime song and the Tin Pan Alley songwriters. (See Dvořák, 1895, 433.) For the full text of this and Dvořák's other writings about American music, see my *Dvořák in America* (1993, 355–84).

9. In *Spreadin' Rhythm Around* (1998), authors David A. Jasen and Gene Jones write that by 1930 "St. Louis Blues" was the best-selling song in any medium—sheet music, recordings, and piano rolls. A study conducted in 1950 concluded that it had had nearly a thousand recordings in America alone, making it the most recorded song up to that time (236).

10. The film was actually alluding to the numerous uptown, concert-dress performances of Handy's music held in his own lifetime. In *Spreadin' Rhythm Around* (1998), Jasen and Jones report that themes from Handy's "Harlem Blues" were presented by bandleader Vincent Lopez under the title *The Evolution of the Blues* at the Metropolitan Opera House on 23 November 1924 as a "rejoinder" to Paul Whiteman's famous jazz concert at Aeolian Hall. "St. Louis Blues" also received the symphonic treatment at Carnegie Hall 27 April 1928. The arrangements were purportedly Handy's own. And in his autobiography, *Father of the Blues* (1955), Handy reports that Paul Whiteman conducted "The St. Louis Blues" in concert arrangements several times, once at Carnegie Hall and again in 1936 at the Hippodrome. Introducing it was the well-known composer and writer, Deems Taylor, whose quoted words bear a similarity to the speech given by Bakaleinikoff in the Paramount film: "The next number on our program marks an epoch in musical history. There are two schools of thought regarding the invention of the blues. One regards it as an event equal in importance to Edison's invention of the incandescent light" (Taylor quoted in Handy, 1955, 217–18). As a result, "The public began to think of him as the channeler, the bringer of the most distinctive 'American' elements to American music. The construction of his lofty reputation was underway. Handy was beginning to be seen as someone above the workaday world of the pop music business, as someone serving a higher good" (Jasen and Jones, 1998, 248).

11. Bessie Smith first recorded "St. Louis Blues" in 1925 in Columbia's New York studio, accompanied by Louis Armstrong's cornet. Her first and only performance on film came four years later in *St. Louis Blues*, produced by RCA Photophone in the Astoria Studios on Long Island, to a scenario cowritten by Handy. She was supported by pianist James P. Johnson and members of the Fletcher Henderson orchestra.

12. The song, "Goin' Home," was based on the "Largo" theme from Antonin Dvořák's Ninth Symphony ("From the New World"), written in America in 1893. The 1922 popularization was by William Arms Fisher, and it was sung by Deanna Durbin in *It Started with Eve* (Universal, 1941). The version heard in *A Song Is Born* was written by lyricist Don Raye and composer Gene DePaul. The cue sheets from the Goldwyn Archives list the entire number as "Long Hair Jam Session Production Routine."

Works Cited

Anon. 1958. "St. Louis Blues," *Harrison's Reports*, 2 April.

Custen, George F. 1992. *Bio/Pics: How Hollywood Constructed Public History*. New Brunswick, NJ: Rutgers University Press.

Dvořák, Antonin. 1895. "Music in America." *Harper's New Monthly Magazine* 90 (537) (February): 429–34.

Elsaesser, Thomas. 1993. "Film History as Social History: The Dieterle/Warner Brothers Bio-Pic." *Wide Angle* 8 (2): 15–31.

Flinn, Carol. 1990. "The Most Romantic Art of All: Music in the Classical Hollywood Cinema." *Cinema Journal* 29 (Summer): 35–50.

Gabbard, Krin. 1996. *Jammin' at the Margins: Jazz and the American Cinema*. Chicago and London: University of Chicago Press.

Gabler, Neal. 1988. *An Empire of Their Own: How the Jews Invented Hollywood*. New York: Crown Publishers.

Handy, W. C. 1955. *Father of the Blues*. New York: Macmillan. [Originally published in 1941.]

Jasen, David A., and Gene Jones. 1998. *Spreadin' Rhythm Around: Black Popular Songwriters, 1880–1930*. New York: Schirmer Books.

Pekacz, Jolanta T. 2004. "Memory, History and Meaning: Musical Biography and Its Discontents." *Journal of Musicological Research* 23: 39–80.

Powe. 1958. "St. Louis Blues." 9 April. In *Variety's Film Reviews, 1954–1958*. New York: R. R. Bowker.

Rogin, Michael. 1996. *Blackface, White Noise: Jewish Immigrants in the Hollywood Melting Pot*. Berkley: University of California Press.

St. Louis Blues pressbook. 1958. Author's collection, n.p.

Tibbetts, John C. 1993. *Dvořàk in America*. Portland, OR: Amadeus Press.

———. 2005. *Composers in the Movies: Studies in Musical Biography*. New Haven, CT, and London: Yale University Press.

Tracy, Steven C. 2001. *Langston Hughes and the Blues*. Urbana: University of Illinois Press.

Weaver, William R. 1958. "St. Louis Blues." *Motion Picture Daily*, 8 April.

CHAPTER TWENTY

~

Memoir and the Limits of Adaptation
William Mooney

The problem of "adapting" written memoirs and other autobiography for film begins with the fact that the author of the book is rarely, if ever, the "author" of the film. A writer could conceivably also make a film memoir, and perhaps someone has created such parallel works in the two media. But generally speaking, when a filmmaker or movie producer becomes interested in an auto-biographical book—whatever his or her motive—the movie is a collabora-tive effort. And even where the film has an identifiable "author," this author will *not* be the same person as the film's protagonist. Yet in the case of auto-biography, identity among author, narrator, and protagonist defines the genre. In memoirs, the author, narrator, and protagonist are one and the same; the name on the book's cover and the voice of the narrator implicitly represent the protagonist later in life. On the one hand, this produces a re-flexive work where a figure in the present engages his or her memories of the past; on the other hand, it produces a work which readers judge according to the apparent good faith and the success of the author in revealing what he or she knows from his or her privileged, subjective perspective.

Altering the relationship between author, narrator, and protagonist, then, brings about—in addition to all other inevitable differences between film and literature—a generic transformation of one kind of work into another, of autobiography into biography, at the very least, though the films made from recent memoirs rarely seem like biography and certainly not like biopics devoted to the lives of the famous. A filmmaker's adapting someone else's written memoir is a little like Pierre Menard's authorship of *Don Quixote* in the Borges (1963) story: In order to adapt a memoir successfully, the nonauthor filmmaker would have to elaborate a film through a process of engaging memories that he or she never had. The filmmaker might then take the protagonist's name in order to encourage the audience to accept the film's confessional posture. Of course, if the imposture is discovered, the audience's feeling of betrayal will sour the experience of the film.

Any recent memoir/film pair will bear out that the generic shift described above takes place. Let us consider the film *This Boy's Life* (1993) and the 1989 memoir by Tobias Wolff that it was "based on." The film's story is about a wild, fatherless boy who is placed by his mother—a woman with "more courage than common sense"—under the tutelage of a man named Dwight in the hope of reforming her son. Unfortunately, Dwight is a rigid, intolerant bully because of his own insecurities and fears. Dwight is homophobic and desperate to control his world to the point of instructing Toby how "properly" to put the cap on the toothpaste. Before leaving the house, Dwight counts pieces of candy to control how many are eaten; when he returns home he checks the temperature of the TV with his hand to see if Toby has been watching too much. Dwight apparently needs Caroline, the boy's mother, because his view of himself includes being "loved." He wants to break Toby because, as Toby eventually tells him, "You just can't stand the fact that I exist." Everything in Dwight's narrow world is precise, clearly defined, and, ultimately, dishonest: He lies to the world and to himself about his abilities and his place in society, and all his energy during the period we witness goes toward sustaining the dishonest image of himself.

Dwight's rigid and narrow view of masculinity, which the movie pillories, depends on fending off all sensitivities: His attempts to indoctrinate Toby include giving him a military-style haircut, making him join the Boy Scouts, teaching him to fight, and encouraging him to bully the effeminate Arthur Gayle. Fighting means "dry gulching" the other guy when he least expects it. Dwight sets himself up as a great hunter, yet his only kill has been a deer that leaped in front of the car. When Toby wants an affectionate collie, Dwight buys—with Toby's money—a vicious bulldog. Dwight is abusive and emotionally closed to Caroline; he expects her to bow to his wishes in everything, including sex, which must be from behind: "I don't like to see the face," he generalizes. He uses the same childish argument here that he used about the cap on the toothpaste: "It's my house and I get to say."

Dwight is a veritable poster boy for all that has been exposed as wrong in our patriarchal tradition.

Escape from Dwight, therefore, means that Toby must resist conforming to Dwight's ideal of manliness, which is shared by most of the guys in the town of Concrete. The issue is partly one of socioeconomic class—Toby's friends are the children of janitors, auto mechanics, and other lowly blue-collar workers. Toby and his mother carry with them memories of the middle class, or even of the elite, because Toby's brother attended Choate before going on to Princeton, while their father attended Deerfield and is "rich," in Dwight's words. Caroline only consented to enter Dwight's world because of Toby; her first step away again is to work for the Kennedy campaign. She and Toby look middle class—their manners and reactions to their surroundings show a broader range of feelings and ideas than those of their Concrete neighbors. We might say that in this film the middle class is constructed as being more varied in experience and more flexible in manners than the rural working class.

Toby is a "performer," with the several meanings of someone who entertains, who puts on an act, and who is capable of taking action. Toby pretends to be a tough guy when he is not, and ultimately he takes the necessary steps to get out of the trap he is in. His abilities as an entertainer are seen in his mimicry of Dwight and in his Elvis act for the new family. Most significant, however, is his piano and singing duet with Arthur Gayle, for Toby's real difference from Dwight and from all of Concrete is most clearly marked by his friendship with Arthur, who "plays for the pink team" in Dwight's words. Toby works hard to be like his Concrete High School buddies, but we are allowed to see the effort it requires. Arthur, however, immediately identifies Toby as, like himself, an "alien" in this culture, and after an initial confrontation, Toby is clearly more relaxed with Arthur than with the other guys in their endless posturing over sex. An affectionate kiss from Arthur causes Toby no more than a surprised hesitation, and Arthur—apparently in love with Toby—is the one who provides Toby with the school stationary that allows him to escape by forging his way into Hill School.

Caroline is a "performer" too, attractive and expressive if largely incompetent. She wins the turkey shoot when Dwight can't even hit the target. She finally has the strength and courage to club Dwight with a baseball bat during his last assault on Toby: Dwight is rendered powerless, whimpering "but what about me," after Toby tells his mother that she can leave, too. According to Dwight, she has already been promised a job in Washington and plans to run off with a coworker, though these claims are difficult to evaluate because of

Dwight's jealous paranoia. The film opens with the voice of Frank Sinatra singing "Let's Get Away from It All," to which Toby's voice-over narration adds, "My mother had her own way of solving problems—she left them behind." At the end of the film she does this again. Even before they go to Concrete, Toby has commented that she has "lousy taste in boyfriends"; Roy, the most recent, has been controlling and abusive just as Dwight will be. The point we are not to miss is that Caroline repeats her mistakes. Any progress in the film is measured in Toby's learning, which is real if limited: A postscript informs us that he was later expelled from Hill School.

The film's handling of point of view is particularly important to the audience's understanding of this story. Toby's view and understanding of events could bring an audience closest to some emotional truth of the character's experience, yet staying too close to Toby's perspective would also limit what can be portrayed on screen—between Dwight and Caroline, for example. And it would deny us the perspective of others on Toby. Perhaps for these reasons the filmmakers chose a fluid, roaming point of view, sometimes that of Toby, sometimes of Caroline, occasionally of others, even Dwight, and often simply that of a fly on the wall, as in the kitchen with the family, in a car with Toby's buddies, or across the room as Arthur Gayle and Toby sing together. Although there is voice-over narration, it is barely differentiated from young Toby's point of view: The voice is Leonardo DiCaprio's, first heard in conjunction with a close shot on DiCaprio/Toby's face. The narration offers a summation of recently past events that carries only the barest hint of irony with the words "We were going to get rich and change our luck, which hadn't been so hot since our family broke up five years back." A narration more strongly identified with Toby, especially as an adult looking back after many years, would be inconsistent with the shifting perspectives, so the voice-over is reduced in significance to helping with transitions, such as the arrival in Salt Lake City or the move to Seattle.

The turkey shoot scene is a good example of the shifting point of view: Shots of Caroline in her red dress as she walks to her post and shoots are intercut with close-ups of Toby watching, of Dwight, and with medium shots of the crowd of admiring onlookers. As Caroline shoots, there is even a totally unattributable long shot which, while distancing us from the action, seems flatly without comment on the scene. Here, and throughout the film, the point of view remains largely in a public, social space, audience insight following the shot/reverse shot and eye line matches as characters read each other's countenances.

Even the point of view in the important scene where Toby rides alone with Dwight to Concrete—and finally gets to see what Dwight is really like—is handled coolly using lighting and a series of shot/reverse shots to encourage us to focus on Dwight without dwelling on any profound fears or uncertainties which might be stirring in Toby. The sequence actually begins from Caroline's perspective as she watches Dwight's car, in daylight, carry Toby away from her, a train pulling across between her and the departing car, separating her from her son. The following shots are of the car on the road at night, after which we are shown Toby and Dwight from a neutral frontal angle through the windshield. Toby is in shadow, as he is throughout the scene, while Dwight's face is illuminated, apparently by lights from outside the car. Two-shots in the interior of the car and angled toward Dwight dominate the scene, particularly as he drinks and talks. In the reverse interior two-shots angled toward Toby, who is already in half-darkness, a confining bar of shadow is cast across him: Toby is imprisoned. To Dwight's insistent invitation to mimic him, "Do your act," Toby responds, "I can't." At one point another neutral point-of-view shot through the windshield isolates Dwight, cutting Toby out entirely. There is no attempt in this scene to give us a window into Toby's feelings; rather we are shown Dwight, and Toby's erasure or confinement, from the perspective of an outside observer.

The film's period re-creation of the 1950s complements the sense of a public space established by the camera, lighting, and editing. The boys watch *Superman* on TV and "talk dirty" about Lois Lane, whereas Dwight watches Lawrence Welk and his Champagne Music Makers. For the young people, this is the epoch of Elvis, and the film's soundtrack is largely made up of popular songs, the lyrics often commenting on the action. Both the period references and constant extradiagetic intrusion are carried to the point that everything becomes generic, not about a particular boy's experience but rather a clichéd evocation of nostalgia for the fifties. Cars, clothes, hair styles, and especially the music all foreground popular culture of the time at the expense of detail to individualize Toby.

Following the drive to Concrete, which in the formulaic screenplay structure is the obvious transition into act II, we are given a few typical moments that represent the activities of Toby's life with Dwight. Dwight lists his preparations: he has bought horse chestnuts, enrolled Toby in the Boy Scouts, and signed him up for a paper route. The music rises—Nat King Cole singing "Smile though your heart is aching"—and a montage begins: shots of Toby's hair falling in slow motion to the barbershop floor followed by a series of dissolves to Toby delivering papers and to Toby shelling nuts. Toby is shown sneaking into the bathroom with pornographic photos while the song lyrics comment, "life is still worth living." Dwight in a dark room recites, "I believe that there *is* such a thing as a bad boy," his voice seeming to carry into Toby's thoughts. Then another series of the nut shelling and paper route shots, nuts, papers, nuts, papers, emphasizing the repetition until the montage ends with Dwight announcing he will buy Toby a Scout uniform (he gives Toby an oversized hand-me-down and buys the new one for himself).

In the driving scene, in the montage sequence described above, and throughout the film, all stylistic decisions serve to limit exposure of Toby's consciousness. Rather, the story becomes mostly about Dwight, a certain type of macho monster, and there is little room for narratorial comment, either retrospectively by the protagonist or even by the filmmaker as auteur. The audience is encouraged to look smugly back on this apparently simpler era of ridiculous hair styles and blatant gender inequality, just as we look smugly down on the rural, working-class male of which Dwight is a typical, if exaggerated, example. There is more to be said—about the impact of using stars like Robert De Niro, for example—but we can return to that after considering Wolff's memoir.

Among the most important of the differences between the film and the book is sense of doubleness, or perspective in time, that arises from an awareness of the book's author engaging his memories, a sense of an ongoing dialogue between a person's present and past selves which is absent from the film. The author discovers a pattern in the past and focuses attention on it from the beginning with an epigraph from Oscar Wilde: "The first duty in life is to assume a pose. What the second is, no one has yet discovered." Posing, here, is an existential process of creating new identities, often linked to Toby's desire to be other than the way he is, and there is no end to the series of identities that result. Toby's temporary name change to Jack, for example, is identified with the narrator's "dreams of transformation," in this case to a Jack London–like, Western, "taciturn self sufficiency"(Wolff, G., 1990, 8). Tobias's father is actually a famous impostor whose adventures are documented in *The Duke of Deception* by Tobias's brother Geoffrey. In *This Boy's Life*, the father gets briefer recognition: "'My family,' he told me, 'has always been Protestant. Episcopalian actually.' Actually his family had always been Jews" (9).[1]

A move across the country is an opportunity for Toby/Jack to recreate himself by adopting a new pose. Remembering his arrival in Dwight's house in Chinook (the names of localities are reversed in the film), the author/narrator writes: "I thought that in Chinook . . . I could be different. I could introduce myself as a scholar-athlete, a boy of dignity and consequence, and without any reason to doubt me people would believe I was that boy, and thus allow me to be that boy. I recognized no obstacle to miraculous change but the incredulity of others" (89). When Dwight, the evil stepparent of the story, assigns Toby the endless task of shucking inedible horse chestnuts, Toby takes on the role of "a kitchen boy in a spellbound castle" (96).

Toby's most elaborate pose, echoing the father about whom he knew little at the time, is the re-creation of himself as an "A" student fully involved in the life of his high school. To become this, Tobias forged not only his academic record but an entire portfolio of letters of recommendation, confecting an application essay full of lies and maintaining his new persona in an interview with an alumnus representing Hill School. Wolff remembers seeing through the false image of himself when he was being outfitted for the school: "The elegant stranger in the glass regarded me with a doubtful, almost haunted expression. Now that he had been called into existence, he seemed to be looking for some sign of what lay in store for him." The boy before him has "a dash of swagger in his pose, something of the stage cavalier, but his smile was friendly and hopeful" (276). The distance between the posture and reality, at this point, as well as the hunger to be other than what he is and a sense of self-satisfaction, reaches the extreme of Patricia Highsmith's sociopathic Tom Ripley (Highsmith, 1999).

The poses are not assumed in a void. Around Toby are models of how to live in the world, among them the absent father and brother, the mother and her various partners, the idealized image of the Boy Scout, Arthur Gayle, a downtrodden farmer who represents "failure," and Mr. Howard, who embodies the promise of the genteel world of elite prep schools. The models present themselves actively, impressing themselves on the unformed child. Of Sister James, a no-nonsense nun at Toby's school in Utah, we are told, "Being so close to so much robust identity made me feel the poverty of my own, the ludicrous aspect of my costume and props" (28). Ultimately Dwight is the principal model against whom Toby will define himself: "All of Dwight's complaints against me had the aim of giving me a definition of myself. They succeeded, but not in the way he wished. I defined myself by opposition to him" (134). Yet in the end, Wolff must write, "When I think of Chinook I have to search for the faces of my friends, their voices. . . . But I can always see Dwight's face and hear his voice in my own when I speak to my children in anger" (233). Years later, Wolff is aware that, even in opposition, he absorbed some of Dwight into himself.

Wherever one cuts into the book, the past remembered events are always firmly in the grasp of the present writer/narrator. The present is evident in the incisive vocabulary of the mature writer, as well as in overt references to retrospective understanding, as when he mentions how his father hides his Jewish heritage: "I had to wait another ten years before learning this" (9). In the present he parses what he knew and did not know at the time, as when recalling how he "yielded easily to the comradely tone" of the *Scout Handbook*, "forgetting while I did so that I was not the boy it supposed I was" (103). In linking present and past, the writer even acknowledges that, as suggested by the epigraph from Wilde, the assumption of new identities continues: "I recognized no obstacle to miraculous change but the incredulity of others. This was an idea that died hard, *if it every really died at all*" (89; my emphasis). The hungry child who creates alteregos with such facility has become the successful fiction writer.

Finally, the writer/narrator is present in moments of direct address to his reader:

> Knowing that everything comes to an end is a gift of experience, a consolation gift for knowing that we ourselves are coming to an end. Before we get it we live in a continuous present, and imagine the future as more of that present. Happiness is endless happiness, innocent of its own sure passing. Pain is endless pain. (230)

The "innocent" past is gone: The text retrieves traces of the past into an ongoing thought process in the present. This is the sense of a phrase of Rousseau's in his *Confessions* that underlines the importance of the writing as a dramatization of the writer's engagement with the past: the writing "fera lui-meme partie to mon histoire" (Olney, 1980, 81).

This double nature of autobiography—remembered events and the writer's understanding of the events in retrospect—is among its characteristics most recognized by critics.[2] A second is the tension that arises between factual truth and the discovered or imposed pattern of meaning, such as the repeated emphasis in *This Boy's Life* on the theme of posing.[3] The interaction of remembered event and pattern calls for selection, manipulation, and reorganization of material. Yet typically the memoirist is unwilling to push the remembered events too far. The title of Nabokov's memoir, *Speak Memory* (1966), is eloquent on this point, suggesting that the Proustian kind of memory that floods into the mind unbidden must be allowed to speak for itself, for its own sake. When this kind of event and detail are not present, we are suspicious.[4] Of course, the reduction of any book to a two-hour movie forces choices on a director, and the makers of *This Boy's Life* typically eliminated most of what does not pertain to the relationship with Dwight, the film's central character. The memoir, by contrast, is full of incidents and characters that teach no lesson, have no "value" beyond being curiosities witnessed along the way. For example, the basketball episode: Young Tobias was forced to play in street shoes. In retrospect, he remembers this as a full-fledged drama in which he evolved into a martyr, cheered by the crowd while a mad woman, set off by the spectacle and unable to stop shrieking, was escorted from the bleachers. The mad woman is the detail that has nothing to do with Toby's psychological postures. In the film there is only Toby's unsuccessful request of Dwight to be allowed to use his paper-route money to buy sneakers.

While such wanderings from the story or from main themes can cause readers of a novel to complain, in nonfiction, of which the memoir is one variety, details present for their own sake seem rather to authenticate the factual nature of the work, that aspect of life and the world which resists our will.

If a sense of truth to events as remembered is a second important characteristic of memoirs, the third and perhaps dominant characteristic is the reader's sense of being addressed directly, in good faith, by another person about his or her life. Philippe Lejeune is the critic most frequently cited for defining this implicit author/reader relationship which he calls the "pacte autobiographique":

C'est l'engagement que prend un auteur de raconter directement sa vie (ou une partie, ou un aspect de sa vie) dans un esprit de vérité. (2006, n.p.) [It is the commitment made by the author to recount his or her life (or a part or aspect of it) directly, in a spirit of truth.]

To the truth claims of all nonfiction, then, is added the confessional posture of the author, speaking about him or herself in an honest attempt to communicate from the privileged, subjective perspective. The audience's sense of being addressed directly is like the moment when a friend turns and, dropping the mask with which we shield ourselves from others most of the time, speaks openly about something that matters.

In *This Boy's Life*, the memoir, this sense of direct address by the author is typically strong. The film, by contrast, is without any comparable frame to establish Lejeune's autobiographical pact. In fact everything distances us from any sense of an author addressing us directly about his life. The camera offers us a third-person view of DiCaprio/Tobias instead of the first person, and I have already described the atrophied state of the voice-over narration which might attempt to reclaim the first-person. Furthermore, stars are introduced— Robert De Niro (as opposed to Dwight) was certainly not a part of Tobias Wolff's early years, and De Niro brings with him all his baggage from *Mean Streets* to *Analyze This* (whenever a film is viewed, at the time of release or years later, the accumulating complexity of a star's persona increases his or her difference from the autobiographical protagonist, further undercutting

Lejeune's "pact.") Ellen Barkin is not Caroline and Leonardo DiCaprio obviously not Tobias Wolff. The effect on the audience's sense of reality here is comparable, say, to suddenly seeing Robert De Niro in documentary footage from the 1930s. Credits for screenplay and direction further diminish any illusion of the film's having been made by the main character. The phrase *based on the book by Tobias Wolff* reiterates the fact that this is not the book, thus the film is not by Tobias Wolff. Film viewers who have read the book will also notice that facts have been changed—most obviously the switching of Chinook and Concrete but also changing the year from 1955 to 1957, Tobias's brother's name from Geoffrey to Gregory, and so forth.

Taken all together, the differences between the situations of the memoir and the film are so extreme that it is inaccurate to say the film techniques "undercut" any sense of the author addressing us directly about his life. Rather, no attempt is being made to establish any such illusion. The goal is entirely different—to create an interesting drama, characterize a period of life in a nostalgic fifties framework, from an essentially third-person point of view, essentially another fiction film with decorative "truth" claims like those of so many other fictions in the history of film and literature.

As this is true for *This Boys Life*, we will find that it is true generally for the use of memoirs by the film industry. If a filmmaker were to set out to make a film memoir, the product would have to be the story of his or her own life, elaborated by him or her, convincing us of its author's good faith in presenting him or herself to us. If the film memoir as a genre were to become popular and commercially successful as written memoirs have been for the publishing industry, then we might look for all the ways of focusing such works that have been explored so successfully in written memoirs—focus on a difficult childhood, an abusive parent, a minority experience, a disability, a gift, and so on.

There can be written memoirs, and there can be film memoirs. Yet the written memoir, because of its peculiar dependence on the interrelation of author and protagonist by way of the first-person narration, inherently resists adaptation into film by someone other than its author. As in the case of *This Boy's Life*, eliminating the "auto" from autobiography typically transforms the written memoir into a flat reenactment of past events, "based on a true story" yet presented from an entirely different perspective, to be viewed and evaluated as a completely different kind of work.

Notes

1. Unless otherwise indicated, parenthetical page citations are from *This Boy's Life* (Tobias Wolff, 1990).
2. Essays by Gustoff, Mandel, and Storobinsky in the Olney (1980) collection all develop aspects of the complex interactions between present self and memory of the past, as does Olney himself and much of the vast body of critical work on autobiography over the last thirty years.
3. Roy Pascal's *Design and Truth in Autobiography* (1960) is an early, important book devoted to this issue.
4. An example of this is *The Kiss* (1997) by Kathryn Harrison, a memoir sold on the basis of its story of incest yet unsatisfying because it lacks the detailed texture of recalled experience.

Works Cited

Borges, Jorge Luis. 1963. "Pierre Menard, Author of Don Quixote." In *Ficciones*, ed. Anthony Kerrigan, 45–55. New York: Grove Press.

Harrison, Katheryn. 1997. *The Kiss*. New York: Random.

Highsmith, Patricia. 1999. *The Talented Mr. Ripley; Ripley under Ground; Ripley's Game/Patricia Highsmith*. New York: Knopf.

Lejeune, Philippe. 2006. "Qu'est-ce que le pacte autobiographique?" http://www.autopacte.org/pacte_autobiographique.html

Nabokov, Vladimir. 1966. *Speak Memory: An Autobiography Revisited*. New York: Putnam.

Olney, James, ed. 1980. *Autobiography: Essays Theoretical and Critical*. Princeton, NJ: Princeton University Press.

Pascal, Roy. 1960. *Design and Truth in Autobiography*. Cambridge, MA: Harvard University Press.

Wolff, Geoffrey. 1990. *The Duke of Deception: Memoirs of My Father*. New York: Vintage.

Wolff, Tobias. 1990. *This Boy's Life: A Memoir*. New York: Harper.

CHAPTER TWENTY-ONE

~

Getting It Right: The Alamo on Film

Frank Thompson

In January 1910, the New York–based Star Film Company came to San Antonio, Texas, in search of sunny "winter quarters" in which to make moving pictures. The company, under the direction of Gaston Méliès, older brother of cinema pioneer Georges Méliès, came to San Antonio to populate their one-reel westerns, comedies, and melodramas with "real cowboys" and "real Mexicans." They stayed in the famous health resort Hot Wells Hotel and rented a house and barn on the banks of the San Antonio River. They called it the Star Film Ranch; it was the first moving-picture studio in Texas.

Given the location, it was inevitable that the company planned on bringing to the screen—for the first time—the tragic and inspiring story of the siege and fall of the Alamo. This was the famous battle of 6 March 1836, in which some 200 Texans were defeated by the Mexican army under General Antonio Lopez de Santa Anna. Every defender of the Alamo was slain in the final battle. Among the dead were two men who were already famous across the North American continent—knife fighter, land pirate, and slave trader James Bowie and former U.S. congressman David Crockett. Six weeks later, General Sam Houston defeated Santa Anna at San Jacinto. The vengeful Texans' battle cry was "Remember the Alamo!"

The Film Index (1910) reported that the company planned "a correct representation of the Alamo insurrection, famous in history, taken on the very ground where it took place. Many of the old houses which played an important part in the 'defense of the Alamo' are the scenes of the picture" (3).

The Alamo picture was among the first announced projects of the Star Film Company, but it took them a year to get around to it. When they did, director William Haddock stressed how hard they were working to fill the film with solid history. He told a *San Antonio Light* reporter in January 1911,

> Already the scenario is being prepared and has necessitated delving into the old archives to obtain the correct historical setting and the infinite number of details to be known. Of course it would be impossible to give the siege in its entirety, but the incidents of most historic interest will be faithfully portrayed. The Alamo as it now stands does not resemble its appearance at the time of the famous battle, so we are building an exact reproduction of the structure as it then looked.

In 1911, the siege of the Alamo was still within living memory, closer in history than, for example, we are to "Black Friday" of 1929. Many elderly citizens of San Antonio had witnessed the event. Indeed, at least one survivor of the battle—Enrique Esparza who, as an eight-year-old boy, had watched his father die in the Alamo—still lived in the city, not far from where the film was produced.

All of the information from these witnesses and the records found in the "old archives" certainly must have insured that *The Immortal Alamo* (1911) would be as accurate and authentic a reproduction as was possible to make.

But, of course, it wasn't.

The "exact reproduction" turned out to be a painted canvas backdrop. Cadets from nearby Peacock Military Academy were pressed into service because their uniforms were vaguely similar to those worn by the Mexicans in 1836. And the plot was pure fictional melodrama about a pretty Anglo wife who survives the battle only to be nearly forcibly "married" to a lustful and deceitful Mexican (portrayed by Francis Ford, older brother of director-to-be John Ford). Luckily for her, her husband, Lieutenant Dickinson (a historical character who actually perished in the Alamo) had been sent out for reinforcements. He and Sam Houston's army arrive just in the nick of time, like the cavalry, defeating the Mexican army and, more important, saving Mrs. Dickinson's honor.

The Immortal Alamo set the pattern for Alamo movies over the next nine decades. Claims of exhaustive research and rigorous attention to historical detail are always followed by cinematic depictions that are rarely anything other than pure fiction.

The pressbook for producer Anthony J. Xydias's *With Davy Crockett at the Fall of the Alamo* (1926) claims that the film bears "the stamp of authentic detail" and that the Alamo and San Antonio sets "are shown exactly as they were in those days," a lie made even odder by the fact that the city of San Antonio appears nowhere in the film, authentically or otherwise. And, needless to say, only the tiny snippets of history were allowed to seep into the action-packed movie.

John Wayne loudly touted how the sets for his *The Alamo* (1960) were based precisely on the "original blueprints" in Spain and that screenwriter James Edward Grant had read scores of books on the Alamo. Of course, there *are* no "original blueprints." If they existed, perhaps art director Al Ybarra's sets wouldn't be as fanciful and inauthentic as they are. And if Grant read even a single book on the Alamo, there is no evidence of it in his dreadful, entirely fictional screenplay. More interesting is the fact that Wayne hired two of Texas's leading historians, Lon Tinkle and J. Frank Dobie, to act as historical consultants on the film. Both men left the set in disgust at the historical liberties being taken and asked Wayne to remove their names from the credits.

And the IMAX production *Alamo . . . the Price of Freedom* (1988), which even Alamo historians believed would be the most scrupulous film of all, was compromised by the use of Wayne's inaccurate set (which still stands near Brackettville, Texas), the cast of primarily amateur actors, and the simplistic screenplay, written by one of the film's major financial backers. The creative forces behind the project crowed loudly about their scrupulous adherence to fact, but even these careful history buffs were not immune to the lures of myth. The screenwriter, the late George McAlister, told me during production of *Price of Freedom* that whenever his research yielded more than one version of any given event, "we came down on the side of heroism every time."

So do nearly all Alamo films come "down on the side of heroism." Although the filmmakers always want the public to believe they are witnessing precise reproductions of events as they actually happened, the story of the Alamo has always been particularly problematic on this score. First, and perhaps most important, the myth of the Alamo has always been more pervasive in the public's imagination than the facts of the matter. Before the smoke of battle had cleared, the event was already inspiring poetry. Soon would follow songs, novels, plays, toys, games, souvenirs, comic books, and, of course, movies. And in all of these media, the battle of the Alamo was portrayed as a pristine moment of heroism, an outnumbered band of patriots who stood bravely against an overwhelming gothic army led by a despot. That makes a shining legend, but it has little to do with the reality of the Alamo.

Still, as the newspaper editor in *The Man Who Shot Liberty Valance* says in one of the most oft-quoted lines in movie history, "When the legend becomes fact, print the legend."

In 1955, when Fess Parker went down swinging his rifle at the onrushing Mexicans in the *Davy Crockett at the Alamo* episode of Walt Disney's *Disneyland* TV series, the image was fixed in the minds of millions of impressionable youngsters. The "Crockett Craze" of that year was the big bang of the baby boom—more than 3,000 items of Crockett merchandize were sold; Crockett-related clothing accounted for a whopping 10 percent of all children's clothes sold during the period; and the theme song "The Ballad of Davy Crockett" sold millions of recordings by a score of artists. There was almost nothing of real historical value in the program. The sets and costumes are all wrong, nearly all of the characters are fictional, and there is no political context for what the fight is all about—just some vague lines about "freedom." But none of that mattered to the kids who became Crockett fiends overnight. If this isn't what the battle of the Alamo was like, it's what it *should* have been like.

This was only compounded five years later when John Wayne's epic *The Alamo* was released. This huge Todd-AO production was found wanting by many, but its homespun script, its outsized characters, and its colorful scenes of action were hugely attractive to those same kids who had so lately been converted to the secular religion of Alamoism by the Crockett Craze. The Wayne film—called *The Waynamo* by aficionados, of whom there are more than you'd think—contained not a word, character, costume, or event that corresponds to historical reality in any way. But in its heartfelt simplicity, it remains enormously entertaining and even moving. Its vast sets and location shooting even gave it a powerful aura of reality. Unfortunately, many have confused this aura with genuine authenticity, of which the film contains not a whit.

The second problem with getting the reality of the Alamo on film is that even historians are rarely in agreement as to what actually happened there. Here's what we know: In February and March of 1836, a band of "Texans" were besieged in an old mission-turned-fort called the Alamo by a Mexican army under General Antonio Lopez de Santa Anna. On the thirteenth day of that siege, the Mexican army attacked and, in short order, killed every defender of the Alamo. In terms of inarguable facts, the kind you could take into a court of law, that's about it.

Everything else, from motives to events to questions of character, has been debated, sometimes with enormous contention, ever since.

But even when some elements of the Alamo story have met with a certain level of consensus, the story itself is far too ragged and chaotic—like any real event—for a movie to fully grasp. In this sense, John Wayne and Walt Disney had the right idea—outnumbered heroes fighting for freedom is a much easier and more powerful concept to grasp than that of men swept by different, sometimes vague circumstances into a situation which they cannot control. And movie audiences want—and have always preferred—simple concepts and clear distinctions between good and bad.

The third problem with telling the Alamo story correctly on film is that while most Alamo films have been content to depict the Mexican army mostly as a faceless horde, a respect for the realities of history now demands that both sides of the story be told. In today's ever-more multicultural world, a film about good white men being massacred by bad brown ones would be offensive in addition to being, in the case of the Alamo, inaccurate. This isn't simply a case of that despicable phrase "political correctness" but an acknowledgment that there are two sides to every story. In the case of the Alamo, both sides had perfectly valid, if mutually exclusive, points. Unfortunately for all of them, the only way their argument could be settled was with blood.

Perhaps, in the wake of 11 September, when Disney head Michael Eisner put a long-dormant Alamo project on the fast track, he didn't quite understand what the implications were. Eisner believed that Disney was in a position to produce a sprawling patriotic epic that would serve as an inspiring tale of sacrifice and heroism, perfect for these troubling new times.

The original script by Les Bohem had been brought to Disney by director Ron Howard. From the beginning, Howard wasn't thinking in terms of patriotism but of telling the story of the Alamo with all the grimness and violence of *Saving Private Ryan* or *The Wild Bunch*. But even though Howard had his own dark take on the film, his first impulse was to make sure that it was the first Alamo film to be true to history. In May 2002 he assembled a group of eight Alamo historians (myself among them) in an Austin hotel for a day-long meeting. He soon realized what a complex task he had undertaken; often, in asking a question, he would receive subtly different answers from each historian. On some points, the authorities disagreed vehemently.

Howard left the project soon after and was replaced by John Lee Hancock. Happily, Hancock (a Texan) was even more determined to make the film as authentic as possible. He kept two noted Alamo historians, Stephen Hardin, PhD, and Alan Huffines, on the set with him nearly every day. Even so, he admitted to himself that "each of us who attempts to tell the story of the Alamo, whether in words or images, is doomed to some degree of failure. Seemingly, every source one finds defends itself against a counter source; every bit of data carries an asterisk that puts its relevance or veracity in question" (Thompson, 2004, 7). One day, in conversation with production designer Michael Corenblith, Hancock was reminded "that in any true story there exists both a factual and emotional truth. And that, to be faithful to the tale, you need a balance of both" (Thompson, 2004, 7).

Hancock's The Alamo was released on 9 April 2004. It was by far the most authentic and accurate Alamo film ever made. For the first time, all of the events were actually based on what we know—or, at least, what we think we know—about the historical reality of the time and place. Also for the first time, the costumes evoked the top hat and tailcoats fashion of 1836 rather than the generic "frontier" style of other films on the subject. Hancock took to calling the clothing style "Dirty Dickens."

And Michael Corenblith's sets, among the largest ever built at over fifty acres, are impeccable. The Alamo church—today, the only standing building and the structure that we now call "The Alamo"—was reproduced to its 1836 appearance in stunning detail. Indeed, each stone in the façade is the precise size and shape of those in the real thing.

And the characters, Bowie (Jason Patric), Travis (Patrick Wilson), Crockett (Billy Bob Thornton), and Santa Anna (Emilio Echevarría), are thoughtful and multidimensional creations, built solidly on what we know about the real men.

The film correctly depicts the climactic battle as a surprise attack under darkness of night and meticulously recreated according to Santa Anna's original battle plans and the eyewitness accounts of survivors.

But even with all this, The Alamo presents a curious dichotomy—it is by far the most accurate and authentic Alamo movie ever made yet, by its very nature, it can be neither accurate nor authentic; such a thing is simply beyond the capabilities of a single film, on any subject. Hence, the lovers of the myth may be offended by the distinctly human, and often fallible, portrayals of the Alamo heroes; the hero worshippers can be dismayed that the motives of the Mexican army are presented with respect and understanding; and the hardcore Alamo buffs, each of whom clings to his specific set of beliefs as though they were handed to him by the Angel Moroni, can endlessly nitpick each detail that differs from his own conception—and almost any detail of this particular moment in history can be nitpicked to death.

As an example of how impossible a task Hancock faced, let us consider a single character, arguably the most famous figure at the Alamo—David Crockett, bear hunter, Indian fighter, U.S. congressman.

Who was he? What was he really like? It depends on who is describing him. To his political enemies, Crockett was an illiterate buffoon, a figure to ridicule. To his followers, he was a shining symbol of the frontier—clean, virtuous, and canny. To readers of the ubiquitous Crockett almanacs, he was a devilish—and witty—trickster, violent, racist, crude, and exuberant—"a ring-tailed roarer, half horse, half alligator and a little tetched with snapping turtle." To baby boomers in 1955 and ever after, he was the perfect hero—kind, principled, and brave.

But no movie has the luxury of exploring every single aspect of a personality—especially one in which we have so relatively little to go on. John Lee Hancock had to do what any screenwriter must—create a character that is basically fiction but which would *seem* real, based as closely as possible on the historical record.

Billy Bob Thornton's portrayal of Crockett is the richest and most complex of that in any Alamo movie (mea culpa, Fess). It is a brilliant, nuanced performance which explores the duality of Crockett's life—"David" versus "Davy." There is plenty of evidence to support the idea that he did engage in such a struggle, that he felt limited, if not trapped, by the public's unrealistic perception of him.

One of the earliest scenes in the film depicts a true incident that speaks volumes about how the world viewed Crockett and how he viewed himself. In the scene, Congressman Crockett attends the performance of a play called *The Lion of the West*. The lead character, Nimrod Wildfire, was widely known to be a crude lampoon of Crockett, a buffoonish bull in a china shop constantly enraging or embarrassing the high society types on whom he imposes himself.

The real Crockett was not pleased by the portrayal, and when he showed up in the theatre in Washington that night in 1833 (1835 in the film), the actor, James Hackett, had every reason to be nervous; as far as he knew, the real Crockett may have been a violent bumpkin like Nimrod.

Before the play began, Hackett bowed to Crockett. As the audience applauded enthusiastically, Crockett stood and bowed back, a beautiful moment of the real man being introduced to his own legend.

Thornton's Crockett realizes the political power of this legend and when he shows up in Texas, where he hopes to begin a prosperous new phase in his political career, he is dressed in buckskins and fur hat—exactly as his constituents, or audience, expect to see him. Later, in the Alamo, when Bowie teases him about the hat, Crockett sheepishly admits, "I only started wearing that thing because of that play they did about me. People expect things."

Throughout the film, this tug of war between the man and the myth continues. Trapped behind the walls of the Alamo, Crockett confides to Bowie, "If it was just me, simple old David from Tennessee, I might jump over that wall one night and take my chances. But that Davy Crockett feller—they're all watchin' him."

The struggle is only resolved at the point of his death. Of course, the manner of Crockett's death is among the most hotly and bitterly contested Alamo topics, even though there is virtually no real evidence that supports any of the theories. But many historians take the word of one of Santa Anna's officers, Colonel José Enriques de la Peña, that Crockett was among the few Alamo defenders who survived the battle and were executed later.

The film's purely speculative solution to this conundrum is only slightly controversial but, dramatically, highly satisfying. As Crockett, on his knees before Santa Anna, faces death, he notices that one Mexican soldier is wearing his vest and another sports the coonskin cap. With a rueful laugh to himself, Crockett realizes that he now has to choose for good—David or Davy. And he chooses Davy, the hero. He grins at his attackers and takes as his last words a line from the stage production of The Lion of the West—"I'm a screamer!"

Did this actually happen? Certainly not. In fact, except for de la Peña's version, we have nothing reliable on which to base our guesses about Crockett's death. But this is a fictional moment that seeks to illuminate a truth about Crockett, one that embraces the "emotional truth" of the moment while respecting the "historical truth."

It is, in short, something that virtually no movie about the Alamo has ever attempted, preferring to look at Crockett and the others as men, not marble statues. This doesn't make the 2004 telling of The Alamo a documentary-style foray into unvarnished truth; it simply takes history seriously and tries its best to honor the reality of what those men and women in distant 1836 went through. This, finally, is probably the best we can ever ask of a movie with a historical subject. It's impossible to fully resurrect a time, a place, a people. But if those elements can be evoked with honesty, integrity, and sensitivity, the attempt can help ease us into a fuller appreciation and understanding of the subject. The result may be more emotional than historical, but when it comes right down to it, emotion is what the movies do best.

Works Cited

The Film Index. 1910. 26 February, 3.
San Antonio Light. 1911. No title available.
Thompson, Frank. 2004. *The Alamo: The Illustrated Story of the Epic Film.* New York: Newmarket Press.

~

CHAPTER TWENTY-TWO

"Plains" Speaking: Sound, Sense, and Sensibility in Ang Lee's *Ride with the Devil*

John C. Tibbetts

Here's a sigh to those who love me, And a smile to those who hate; And whatever sky's above me, Here's a heart for every fate.

—William Clarke Quantrill[1]

Ang Lee's *Ride with the Devil* (1998), based on Daniel Woodrell's novel, *Woe to Live On* (1987), chronicles the story of the Kansas–Missouri Border Wars in the early 1860s, culminating in William Clarke Quantrill's infamous dawn raid against the "free state" city of Lawrence, Kansas, on 21 August 1863.[2] In the ensuing massacre, an estimated 440 pro-Confederate guerillas surprised the town in its sleep, plundered and burned most of its buildings in a matter of hours, and killed an estimated 200 men and boys. The raid was the direct result of a prior series of bloody skirmishes between the so-called Missouri "bushwhackers"—the origins of the term remain obscure—and the pro-Union Kansas "jayhawkers," a name possibly derived at the time from the combination of a swooping hawk and the crafty bluejay.[3] Although, compared to Lee's other films, *Ride with the Devil* has suffered somewhat in popular and scholarly neglect, it commands our attention not only as a scrupulously detailed and rendered historical representation on film of the Kansas–Missouri Border Wars but as a masterly adaptation of Woodrell's novel. To that end it translates faithfully to the screen not only the book's themes, incidents, and characters but the distinctive "sound" of its Plains-inflected narrative voice.

Borders Wars Films

It is necessary first to review other screen depictions of the Kansas–Missouri Border Wars in order to gain the proper measure of *Ride with the Devil's* achievement. Hollywood films on the subject have largely ignored the political, personal, and social contexts (particularly the slavery debate) behind the conflict in order selectively to emphasize the exploits of William Clarke Quantrill and his bloody Lawrence raid. Appearing in 1914, the two-reel *Quantrell's Son* set the pattern for a spate of related pictures, including a series of films aligning Quantrill with the James brothers, such as *Jesse James: Under the Black Flag* (1921), *Jesse James as the Outlaw* (1921—in which Jesse James Jr. portrays his father), and *Jesse James* (1927).[4] Subsequent releases include Raoul Walsh's *Dark Command* (1940), Ray Enright's *Kansas Raiders* (1950), William Dieterle's *Red Mountain* (1951), William Witney's *Quantrill and His Raiders* (1954), Edward Bernds's *Quantrill's Raiders* (1958), Melvin Frank's *The Jayhawkers* (1959), and Clint Eastwood's *The Outlaw Josey Wales* (1976).[5]

Dark Command, Red Mountain, and *The Jayhawkers* privileged the mythic resonances surrounding the figure of Quantrill. Indeed, soon after his death in 1865, the former schoolteacher, surveyor, Confederate deserter, and bushwhacker had followed Jesse James and Allan Pinkerton into the fantasy regions of dime novels and movies, subsequently becoming a popular paradigm of the "good bad man," the prototype of so many western heroes to come. "Some of the guerilla-hero's gifts became hallmarks of the movie-cowboy and gunfighter," wrote historian Richard Slotkin in his classic *Gunfighter Nation* (1992), "including his superb horsemanship and love for a favored animal, and his almost fetishistic preference for the pistol as a weapon and his 'preternatural' skill with it." Like Jesse James, Slotkin continues, Quantrill was gradually transformed in the popular consciousness from a local hero into a figure of western and frontier mythology, "the hero of a *national* myth of resistance" (135–37). Thus, in the misleadingly titled *Kansas Raiders* (Quantrill was a *Missouri* raider by the time he attacked Lawrence), based on a story and screenplay by Robert L. Richards, Quantrill (Brian Donlevy) is driven by the desire to bring the Civil War to the western territories, where he will rule alongside Robert E. Lee. "When Lee eventually realizes the hopelessness of his present position, where's he gonna go?" asks Quantrill. "Here, to the

West. It may take months, even years, but here he can bide his time, gather his strength for that great counterattack that'll drive the Union Army into the sea." In *Dark Command*, adapted from a 1938 novel by W. R. Burnett, the Quantrill character—here renamed "Cantrell" (Walter Pidgeon)—assumes a more demonic aspect. His mother accuses him of "fighting for the hosts of Darkness [with] the Devil riding beside you."

At other times the Quantrill character is revealed to have no political or ideological loyalties whatever. In Burnett's (1938) novel, a character describes him as "a man of no principles whatever. . . . Our worst people are making a hero of him. . . . He likes chaos. It's his natural element" (113–14). In the film adaptation, in a speech to his raiders, he abandons any pretense of ideological loyalties:

> You're not fighting for the North, and you're not fighting for the South. But you're fighting to take what's coming to you. The fine gentlemen of Kansas and Missouri will be fighting each other in a war we don't want any part of. And the longer they keep each other busy, the better we're going to like it. We're going to live off the fat of the land; and what we don't want, we'll burn."

The historical record confirms Quantrill's opportunism, though not the self-awareness implied by this quote. According to historian Duane Schultz (1996), "William Clarke Quantrill was fighting only for his own greed and glory and his inherent love of cruelty and killing" (276).

Similarly, in *The Jayhawkers*, scripted by Melvin Frank, Joseph Petracca, Frank Fenton, and A. I. Bezzerides, and *Red Mountain*, scripted by John Meredyth Lucas and George F. Slavin, the guerillas are led by opportunistic adventurers, named Luke Darcy (Jeff Chandler) and Quantrell, respectively, who opportunistically ride as a bushwhacker or a Jayhawker, depending upon the given situation. Literate, articulate, and well versed in the classics, Darcy is a self-proclaimed "Napoleon of the Plains" who is determined to stand apart from the issues dividing North and South and devote his energies to conquering "the country of Kansas." His strategy is to pillage towns with troops disguised as Missouri guerillas, then to ride in as a Free-Stater to offer protection to the bewildered citizenry. "I take the little towns one by one and get the people to like me," he explains to his lieutenant, Cam Bleeker (Fess Parker). "I always make sure they need me. Before I come into a town, it's hit and hit hard by Missouri red legs [sic]. I make sure of that because they are my own men wearing different outfits. When I move in with my Jayhawkers, I'm a big strong daddy come to protect them against the nasty raiders. And believe me, I don't have to take their town; they hand it to me." In *Red*

Mountain "General Quantrell" has fled Kansas after the Lawrence massacre and come westward to Colorado Territory in 1865 with plans to recruit Native American tribes into what he calls a "Confederacy of Plains Indians." Clad in Union blue to allay the suspicions of any Union troops in the area, he declares, "The South is dead. When the war is over, the Union will be too exhausted to fight another. We have a whole western empire in our grasp if we have the vision to see it." The reality, however, as his lieutenant, Brent Sherwood (Alan Ladd), comes to learn, is a different matter. Quantrell is motivated purely by selfish greed. "The Confederacy is dead," he later admits. "We have loyalties only to the living."[6]

As for the infamous Lawrence raid, few films have depicted the massacre with anything approaching historical authenticity. A detailed examination of the historical circumstances of the raid lies well beyond the scope of this essay—see Thomas Goodrich's *Bloody Dawn: The Story of the Lawrence Massacre* (1991). Suffice to say that Quantrill's raid culminated a series of anti–Free State campaigns against the town. Lawrence represented to Quantrill everything the pro-Southern forces despised: It was a Free-State bastion, a center of Jayhawker activity, an important new home for contrabands fleeing their Missouri masters, a recruiting center for Union troops— and, not least, the home of the hated Senator Jim Lane, who in 1861 had led a raid on the town of Oceola, Missouri.[7] And it was precisely at this time that Quantrill gained badly needed support for the Lawrence raid from his guerrilla chieftains "Bloody Bill" Anderson and Coleman Younger, whose kin had been killed during their recent incarceration in a Kansas City jail on suspicion of collusion with the bushwhackers. First to fall under the onslaught of the raiders were a handful of inexperienced soldiers (none of whom had weapons) camped on the west side of New Hampshire Street. Next were the citizens who fell to the detachments of raiders patrolling Mount Oread, the roads leading to town, and the streets of Massachusetts, Vermont, and New Hampshire. Quantrill himself led the charge down Massachusetts and into the lobby of the Eldridge Hotel. "[Quantrill] was back doing what he did best," writes Schultz (1996). "He watched it all from his perch on the second-floor landing. It was the supreme moment of his life. He was back in the town that had wronged him, the place he hated more than any other, and at that moment, he owned it and everyone in it. One word from him and any man would die before he could open his mouth in protest" (172–73).

As might be expected, Hollywood has had its own way with the Lawrence massacre. Notable among these cinematic depictions was *Kansas Raiders*, which staged the raid by those redoubtable second-unit directors Yakima Canutt and Cliff Lyons. Wildly inaccurate, the sequence at least has considerable dramatic impact: At the report of Quantrill's revolver, the raiders charge down a hill in broad daylight into town where they meet the resistance of a few Union troops. After an exciting montage sequence of gunshots, plunging hoofs, and falling bodies, Jesse James relieves the Lawrence bank of its money—executing, the film implies, the first daylight bank robbery in American history.[8] Later, while an angry Jesse accuses Quantrill of allowing his men to shoot unarmed civilians, the sudden arrival of Union troops forces the gang to flee. Quantrill is blinded in a gunfight. Holed up in a cabin, surrounded by troops, he orders Jesse to leave him behind. Dressed in his military uniform, Quantrill defiantly marches out to confront his captors, who promptly shoot him dead. As Jesse and the Youngers and the Daltons ride away, a concluding title card informs us, "And so, into the pages of crime history rode five young men. . . . Five whose warped lives were to be a heritage from their teacher, William Clarke Quantrill." The outrageousness of this departure from history is matched by *Dark Command* and *Quantrill's Raiders*. In the first, the bushwhacker leader is shot dead by his mother during the raid; and in the second, he is killed *before* the raid even begins![9]

Of course, these films were made under the supervision of the watchdog Motion Picture Production Code, which, with many state censor boards and religious pressure groups like the Catholic Legion of Decency, held Hollywood in its thrall from 1934 to the mid-1960s.[10] What resulted was Hollywood history, a "celluloid 'seen,'" something so sanitized that, in the words of historian Mark C. Carnes (1994), "is so morally unambiguous, so devoid of tedious complexity, so *perfect*" (9). Thus, like all other films made at that time, these Border Wars films had to avoid radical political discussion; sidestep controversies in religion, race, and gender; and minimize graphic sex and violence. Under the circumstances, how could anybody reasonably expect the bloody Border Wars to reach the screen intact, with anything approaching its grim brutality and complexity? And who really cared how much of the historical record would have to be sacrificed in the process?

Critics knew this. Audiences knew this. They were complicit in regarding the screen with a kind of knowing wink—as if to say, *Yes, we know this is not an authentic document, but is it not a great story?!* This helps explains why the critical reception of these films seems astonishingly charitable to today's more jaundiced eyes. "Nobody cares about history when making—or seeing—a Western film," sardonically noted *New York Times* critic Bosley Crowther after viewing *Red Mountain*. Instead, he continued, "The question is how many Indians or cowboys or what-not are killed and how much muscular action takes place within a given length of time" ("Red Mountain," 1952, 2). The critic for *Variety* applauded *Kansas Raiders'* Technicolor photography and the exciting Lawrence raid while only mildly deploring its "whitewash" of Quantrill and Jesse James ("*Kansas Raiders*," 1950, vol. 8). Crowther (1940) chose to ignore the absurdities of the ending of *Dark Command*, praising instead its "fights and shootings, clashes of armed horsemen in the night, a bit of sweet loving in the cool of the evening, and a grand finale when Lawrence is burned by Cantrell's boys" (2). *The Jayhawkers*, according to *Variety*, reduces "an intriguing and little explored subject" into a "conventional narrative of love and revenge"; but at least it compensates with "handsome pictorial values" and "an amount of dynamic interest" in Jeff Chandler's portrayal of Luke Darcy ("*The Jayhawkers*," 1959, vol. 10) And after complaining about the distortions in the depiction of the Lawrence raid in *Quantrill's Raiders*—"The famous Quantrill raid on Lawrence, Kansas, when more than 400 towns-people were killed by many hundreds of the guerrilla's men, is reduced to a simple attack on the town by less than two dozen raiders, and instead of citizens meeting death, here it's Quantrill, who actually went on to further raiding"—the *Variety* critic goes on to praise the film as a "well plotted . . . tight, showmanly piece of filmmaking" that makes it "probably the best yet of films on this guerrilla leader." ("*Quantrill's Raiders*," 1958, vol. 9).

Adaptation as Sound, Sense, and Sensibility

In every respect *Ride with the Devil* departs from the precedents of the aforementioned Borders Wars films. According to *Ride with the Devil*'s producer-screenwriter, James Schamus, longtime friend and collaborator of Ang Lee, the director first encountered Dan Woodrell's book in 1994 while attending a screening in Deauville, France, of his recently completed *Eat Drink Man Woman*.[11] "Ang read it overnight," recalls Schamus. "In fact, he got so engrossed in it that it interrupted his reading of the script for *Sense and Sensibility*. He knew right away he had to make this movie."[12] Lee later confirmed that he had long wanted to do an "action story." He recalls, "At first I wanted to get away from a family drama and do something with more action and scope, but it turns out [Woodrell's novel] does both. Family values and the social system are tested by war. It's a family drama, but one where the characters represent a larger kind of 'family'—the warring factions of the Civil War and the divisions in the national character. I was especially attracted to the book's Midwestern dialects. I had never encountered anything like that. But it all seemed transferable to film. I felt you wouldn't have to destroy the book to make the movie. I told James [Schamus] to just copy the book, but make it shorter."[13]

Taking its cue from the Woodrell novel, Lee and screenwriter Schamus bring historical events, political contexts, and characters to the screen in a casual, seeming offhand manner as perceived from the periphery by the first-person narrator Jacob Roedel. Thus, the conflicts between the pro-Confederate "bushwhackers" and the Unionist "Jayhawkers" subtly underscore the more personal story of how Jake and his friends juggle their political and personal loyalties. Eighteen-year-old Roedel (Tobey Maguire) is a first-generation German American who, contrary to his father's Unionist political sympathies, rides with his Missouri guerilla friends. Daniel Holt (Jeffrey Wright) is a freed slave who, out of loyalty to the man who secured his freedom, also rides for the Southern cause. And the woman who enters their lives, Sue Lee (Jewel), exists outside of the political conflict entirely—she has concerns only for the fatherless child she must raise. In other words, issues dividing the North and the South are not what primarily motivate these three; it is their loyalty to one another and their fight to stay alive in a world gone mad.

Like Woodrell, Schamus and Lee have relegated the sensational Lawrence raid to a position of secondary importance. Out of 214 pages of text, Woodrell devotes only 15 pages to it, leaving the concluding quarter of the book to wrap up the stories of Jake, Holt, and Sue Lee. Likewise, on screen, the raid transpires in a mere eleven minutes of screen time, with fully a half hour left for what might seem at first the anticlimactic disposition of the three characters (but which, in actuality, constitutes the necessary culmination of the narrative). Yet, the raid, briefly dramatized as it is, has several important functions. On the one hand, it provides Quantrill with his one key moment, in which he delivers a speech alluding to an earlier historical event that played a key role in motivating the Lawrence raid, the deaths in a Kansas City jail of several bushwhacker sympathizers.[14]

> My boys, today I am a sad man. I am sad because I mourn for our sisters and mothers who slept in that Kansas City jail, who slept until the walls fell down around them, and they died. I am sad, boys, but I am vengeful. And I shall not sleep again until I stand upon Mount Oread and look down upon the abolitionists of Lawrence. . . . I will fight them all myself—unless there be any men among you who care to ride with me. So, I am asking—are there any men here who would ride with me? Then hell, boys! Ride with me to Lawrence!

On the other hand, the raid underscores the growing disillusionment and detachment of Jake and Holt from the brutal realities of a conflict gone insane. After tying themselves to their saddles lest they fall asleep during the nightlong march of forty miles to Lawrence, Jake and Holt are dismayed to find that the town is defended only by civilians and a handful of soldiers. "It's just bad-luck citizens, finding out just how bad luck can be," observes Jake. Carnage ensues as Quantrill orders no one be spared, except women and children. The raiders thunder down Massachusetts Street shooting and burning everyone and everything in their path, while Quantrill calmly observes the carnage from his headquarters at the Eldridge Hotel. Jake and Holt, meanwhile, already sickened by what has become senseless slaughter, repair to a boarding house in search of breakfast. What follows is a crucial turning point in their lives: When fellow raiders Pitt Mackeson and his gang burst into the room intent on killing the boarders, Jake intervenes. Pistol drawn, he faces down Mackeson. Blood oaths are sworn on both sides as Mackeson retires from the scene. Later, wounded, both Jake and Holt realize there's no cause to fight for, just the necessity of quitting the scene and staying alive. "It ain't right and it ain't wrong," declares Jake. "It just *is*."

"There are things about the Border Wars that might surprise some people," reported Daniel Woodrell at the time of the filming.[15]

> For many of those involved, on both sides of the state line, it was more a question of family more than ideology. Even a famous bushwhacker family, like the Youngers, who had started out pro-Union, turned against the Free-Staters when they were roughed up by Union militia. We forget that most of these guys were teenagers. They were coming of age at the wrong time. For another, German immigrants who came to America, like Jake's family, were 90 percent pro-Union, and they were not liked by the Southern side. Therefore, Jake's decision to ride with the bushwhackers is almost as strange, seemingly, as Holt's. Both Jake and Holt were outsiders in the cause, but they both acted on personal loyalties to their mutual friend, George Clyde. My research has revealed that, historically speaking, there really were such characters. It surprised me to find out that there were raiders with Quantrill who, like my character of Jake, actually tried to protect some of the Lawrence citizens during the massacre. But it was tricky, since they didn't want their comrades to catch them doing that. The violence that was committed was unspeakable, but understandable, in a way. In this and so many other ways, the Border Wars relate directly to some of the terrible events of more recent history, like Vietnam and Bosnia. While I was in the Marines I learned that there were guys who did horrible things and other guys who came down in choppers and tried to stop them. *Woe to Live On* is as much about those conflicts in our times as about the struggles between Missouri and Kansas during the Civil War.

On the page and on screen the characters of Jake and Holt and Sue Lee see history from eye level, from the ground up, as it were. They display not a trace of that self-conscious hindsight of events that all too often surfaces in Hollywood's history-based films. Their story blurs the lines dividing ideologies, reality and myth, frontier wilderness and domestic hearth, and history as pageant and history as personal story. Unlike the aforementioned films depicting the circumstances of the Kansas–Missouri Border Wars, *Ride with the Devil* concludes not with violence and bloodshed but with the promise of reconciliation and renewal. Even in the face of war and strife, the characters stubbornly insist on helping each other get on with their own lives. This is the sort of thing Lee has always privileged in his films, from *Pushing Hands* (1992) to *The Wedding Banquet* (1993), *Sense and Sensibility* (1995), *The Ice Storm* (1997), and now *Brokeback Mountain* (2005).

Thus, *Ride with the Devil* concludes with a lovely postscript. As Holt parts company with his friends and rides west, he turns in his saddle to lift his hat. It is the most beautiful valedictory salute in the history of the movies. Not since Henry Fonda doffed his Stetson in farewell to the eponymous school marm in John Ford's *My Darling Clementine* (1946) have we had such a graceful gesture. It is a benediction that rises above the flames of war.

Ride with the Devil is not only relatively faithful to both the historical record and to the plot and characters of Daniel Woodrell's *Woe to Live On* (1987), but it effectively captures the idiosyncratic speech and vernacular of the book's narrative voice and dialogue. This is a significant departure from other Border Wars films, which lack this presiding aural element. Indeed, few films come to mind that so completely bring to the screen the first-person "voice" of their literary sources (Philip Dunne's adaptation of the Welsh idioms in Richard Llewellyn's source novel for John Ford's 1941 *How Green Was My Valley* is one possibility[16]). Indeed, this aural aspect of adaptation, so prominent in *Ride with the Devil*, seems to have been rarely addressed in adaptation studies.

Woodrell derived the book's regional mid-nineteenth-century Missouri speech and diction—he refers to it as "plains speech"—from the many original source materials he found during his research at the Kansas University Spencer Research Library and the Lawrence Historical Society and Museum. "All the time I had been thinking and reading about the Border Wars," he explains,

> I realized I had a lot of feelings about it and wanted to write about it. The letters, diaries, and other first-person accounts I found at KU were particularly amazing. For instance, there was a hand-written letter from a black man who had ridden with the bushwhackers against Lawrence. That was odd, I thought at first—a black man riding with pro-slavery guerillas.[17] But I can understand

that. He wasn't thinking about the big political issues, he was thinking about his friends. Just as I had been doing in the Marines. To think of it, those various first-person writings are the closest we will ever come to "hearing" the sound of their speech, which is an integral part of their history. And that really helped my comprehension about what the Border Wars were really like.

Woodrell is particularly delighted that the filmmakers paid close attention to this "plains speech." "From the very beginning, James Schamus was calling me about the dialects. It was quite a challenge, making us *hear* what was on the page. He retained Jake's first-person narrative voice as a 'voice-over' on the soundtrack; and he retained some of the letters and a lot of the dialogue, just as it was on the page. Even the additional dialogue he wrote maintained those idioms and sounds. And when I read his first draft, I totally relaxed. I have no quarrels with his final script, either."

Jake Roedel's first-person narrative voice did indeed present the filmmakers with a rich vein of idiomatic language. To cite just a few examples, in the book's early pages, Jake's voice naïvely images the Border Wars as an opportunity for swashbuckling derring-do: "I can think of no more chilling a sight than that of myself, all astride my big bay horse, with six or eight pistols dangling from my saddle, my rebel locks aloft on the breeze and a whoopish yell on my lips" (Woodrell, 1987, 20). On the other hand, as the book progresses, Jake's tone darkens as he describes scenes of violence in a prose idiom that fairly smacks of a deadpan twang: In one brief scene Jake explains to Holt the benefits of losing a finger in a fight. In death, the missing finger would give him his identity:

> But eventually they would riddle me and hang me from a way tall limb like they do. No southern man would find me for weeks or months, and when they did I'd be bad meat. Pretty well rotted to a glob. I would be a glob of mysterious rot hanging in a way tall tree, and people would ask, "Who was that?" Surely, sometime somebody would look up there at my bones and see the telltale stump and reply, "It is nubbin-fingered Jake Roedel!" Then you could go and tell my mother I was clearly murdered and she wouldn't be tortured by uncertain wonders. Now do you see the tenderness of it all? (52–53)

The sights and sounds of randomly enacted violence elicit this comment: "Windy flab-grunts of the dying were a regular sound in our days" (72). When the bushwhackers discover men hanged in trees by Jayhawkers, Jake observes, "High in the branches, seasoned beyond recognition, there swung seven noosed rebels. It was macabre and altogether eerie. The bodies draped down through the leaves like rancid baubles in the locks of a horrible harlot" (158). Regarding the Lawrence Massacre, Jake notes, "Spurs dug into flanks and we came on, all as one, desperate and crazed, in terrible number, bent on revenge by bloody work. . . . With my throat choked, clotted by fear and rage, my eyes sprang leaks, and I looked about me, trembling with some sort of occult joy, for we were men and unapologetic, dashing down the slope, pistols primed" (166).

At the end, Jake's voice takes on a world-weary note when, sickened and disillusioned after Quantrill's raid, he and Holt and Sue Lee decide to forsake the struggle and strike out west: "I knew it to my bones that my world had shifted, as it always shifts, and that a better orbit had taken hold of me. I had us steered toward a new place to live, and we went for it, this brood of mine and my dark comrade, Holt. This new spot for life might be but a short journey as a winged creature covers it, that is often said, but oh, Lord, as you know, I had not the wings, and it is a hot, hard ride by road" (214).

Moreover, the letters that Jake reads to Holt bring other voices into the story. "When you read them mails out loud it is something the likes I never heard before," observes Holt (111). These letters, intercepted by the guerillas from the Union Mail, possess a still, sad music of their own. Among several examples is this letter from a homesteader:

Dear sons, no word of you in so long. Right past first frost of the year last. Father worries. His feet are bloated and he won't walk right on them. A fire hit the old church. Burned down. The new one was just ready so no great trouble was had of it. No pigs was lost. Margaret has married since the frost of this year last. You wouldn't know it for how could you. . . . This spring the dirt was turned over and the smell and deepness gave me heart. It is just black-rich and feels good in the hand. You boys know how that is. (63–64)

And there's this missive that Black John dictates to Jake, containing a threat to the citizens of a town holding several bushwhackers hostage:

Dear citizens: Mistakes are most common these days and deadly for it. The Federals are to hang two fine sons of Missouri named William Lloyd and Jim Curtin. They are good men, too brave to accept any injustice. The rule of Federals is one such depravity they would not endure passively. Me neither. By a provident cut of the cards four Federals have been dealt to me. . . . It is their hope that Lloyd and Curtin are not hanged, as they would provide the sequel to such murders. . . . All are young men with much promise before them, or else a short dance from a stout tree. (44)

These speeches and letters, quoted from Woodrell's book, reach the screen virtually intact.[18]

I cite these examples at length because they all resonate through Ang Lee's adaptation. Assisting in what is not so much an adaptation but a *translation* and transfer of these words on the page to the soundtrack of the film is its dialect and dialogue coach, Professor Paul Meier. Meier, a professor of the Department of Theatre and Film at the University of Kansas, specializes in dialect coaching and has written a system of teaching dialects of English to actors, *Accents and Dialects for Stage and Screen*. "I was on the set all the time," recalls Professor Meier.

> Ang Lee wanted me to be with him for most of the dialogue scenes. He would turn to me after a take to see if the things "sounded" right. There were seventy speaking roles. I coached all the cast members for six months, from February of 1998 to late July. We had a two-week "boot camp" for just the voice work. I would record their lines and play back the tapes for them. Then we would engage in impromptu discussions in which we would carry on with the dialects. I must say, among all the cast members, Tobey Maguire was the quickest study and came the closest to capturing what we wanted. Dan [Woodrell] was very concerned that the filmmakers capture on screen the words that he had put on the page. I don't mean just the sense of the dialogue and voice-overs, but the right rhythms and diction.[19]

Meier had to infer from the book's speech idioms and vernacular the proper sound inflection and rhythm of the actors' vocal performance. "You know, we rarely *listen* to how we and others talk. We have to remove ourselves from the *sense* of the everyday flow of speech to fully grasp it as a pure *sound*, as a kind of music." Meier thinks of the novel's speech patterns as "an 'Early Plains' dialect, or 'Early Midland.'" "To hear it spoken, it lacks chest resonance," he continues. "It has a flat intonation with no undue emphasis on the syllables. To our ears the diction is plain, yet rudely poetic, direct yet almost formal. There's a simple eloquence to it, and the occasional use of archaic words is reminiscent of the speech you might find in Shakespeare's time. The flow of words is moderate, even deliberate, what I call a polite use of time that doesn't rush the listener."

Further complicating these speech patterns, notes Meier, is the Woodrell–Lee observation of and sensitivity to the regional and multiethnic mix of the characters. "We have to remember that many of the characters came to Missouri in those days from all parts of the country, from the deep South, from the East, from Texas, etc. Remember, these were frontier times, so the people came from all over. It wasn't just a matter of Woodrell's regional dialect but of many other dialects from the other characters, like Jake's father, who was German. It was a smorgasbord of dialects, the full spectrum of mid-century American society, all the way from Virginia blue-bloods, to strong Missouri–Arkansas hill speech."

For his part, Ang Lee speaks admiringly of Meier's work on the voice coaching. He confirms that Meier was invaluable on the set during principal photography, annotating each take to assist in the selection of the best footage from the voice point of view. "You have to remember there were a number of non-American actors in the film," Lee says, "notably Tom Wilkinson, Simon Baker-Denny, Jonathan Rhys-Meyers (English, Australian, and Irish, respectively), all of whom needed Southern or Plains dialects. Under Paul's expert coaching they blended marvelously with the American members of the cast."[20]

Ride with the Devil demands that we consider the adaptation process as something that lies beyond the mere translation of a novel to the screen. It is also an adaptation of history itself, in all its visual and aural elements. Its pursuit of the "truth" of Woodrell's novel and of the historical record, as far as it may be ascertained, is not just the accumulation of data and the plausibility of dramatic invention but an interpretation of the very sound and speech of history. Before the invention of photography we had only the testimony of the hand-crafted image to supply history's visual aspect. And before the development of sound recording technologies, we had only the written word and musical notation to suggest history's aural dimension. *Ride with the Devil* strives, to quote Robert A. Rosenstone, to create on film the sense of the past as a "doubled vision" that plays "sound against image" (1995, 212). Few historical films and literary adaptations can claim to have given their stories and characters such a superbly persuasive *voice* as much as an *image*. History has a *sound* as well as a *sense* and *sensibility*.

Notes

1. Poem by William Clarke Quantrill presented to Ms. Nannie Dawson, 26 February 1865. Reprinted in Schultz (1996, 297).

2. See Michael Fellman (1989) for a useful overview of the subject.

3. Historian Stephen Starr (1973) alleges that the term *jayhawk* was first applied to Kansas raiders "whose sudden and unexpected incursions into Missouri were like the swoop of a hawk pouncing on an unsuspecting and less capably larcenous blue-jay." Jayhawkers were also referred to as "red legs" because of their red leggings they wore (31).

4. For a concise overview of Jesse James movies, see Pitts (1984, 176–79).

5. Edward E. Leslie (1996) reports that "Quantrell" was the preferred spelling of Quantrill's Missouri admirers (407). Quantrill first used the name "Charley Hart" in 1858 when he signed on at Fort Leavenworth as a teamster with a U.S. Army expedition headed for Utah. He continued to use the name while living in Lawrence in 1860.

6. Films about the Border Wars and Quantrill have received scant attention in extant writings about the representation of history and biography on film. The lone exception is Michael R. Pitts (1984), which briefly examines *Dark Command* and *Kansas Raiders*. For a more detailed account of films involving the character of Quantrill, see my "Riding with the Devil: The Movie Adventures of William Clarke Quantrill" (1999).

7. Senator Lane incurred the undying enmity of the bushwhackers when, on 22 September 1861, he and an army of 1,500 Jayhawkers attacked the town of Osceola, Missouri, scattering a tiny band of Rebels, looting its stores, and torching its buildings. Lane carried the plunder back to Lawrence.

8. Nice try, but Jesse's first daylight bank robbery actually transpired three years later in Liberty, Missouri, on 13 February 1866 at the Clay County Savings Association.

9. In *Dark Command* the bushwhackers meet stiff resistance from a heavily armed citizenry. As the raiders and defenders exchange fusillades, the guerilla leader decides he has better things to do and goes in search of his ex-girlfriend. Instead, he finds none other than the severe, black-clad figure of his mother (Marjorie Main in her pre-"Ma and Pa Kettle" days), rifle in hand, come to exterminate him like some vile pestilence. "I borned a dirty, murdering snake that's broke my heart to see it crawlin' along," she rages. "I curse the day I had you." But before she can fire, John Wayne comes forward to deliver the fatal shot. "You're at the end of the road," she whispers to her dying son, "and the Devil's beside you, waitin'." All the while, no one is apparently unduly alarmed that the town of Lawrence is burning to the ground. Viewing the devastation, John Wayne chirps, "We got a saying down in Texas that it takes a good fire to burn down the weeds. It lets the flowers grow." *Quantrill's Raiders* enjoys the dubious distinction of being the only Quantrill picture in which the city of Lawrence, Kansas, emerges completely unscathed from the raid. The historical record notwithstanding, the citizenry are so well prepared and so heavily armed that they turn away the small band of raiders with little effort. Quantrill's puny forces have been reduced from 400 riders to 25—doubtless a reflection of the film's limited budget. It's a distressing turn of events, not just because it's a breathtaking nose-thumbing at history, but because it defeats the reasonable expectation of any self-respecting movie fan to enjoy a "big finish." What we *do* have is decidedly anticlimactic—the sight of a twitching, cowardly Quantrill, cornered and shot dead in the Lawrence street by his nemesis, Westcott (Steve Cochran).

In reality, after weeks spent eluding his pursuers, Quantrill and his band moved on to Baxter Springs, where they slaughtered ninety-eight men of the personal escort and headquarters train of Major General James G. Blunt. After a disastrous sojourn in Texas, where he was deposed as the guerillas' leader, he ended up in Kentucky in early 1865, with vague plans to lead his remaining band of men to Washington and assassinate Abraham Lincoln. After a series of skirmishes and near-misses with federal authorities, he was ambushed at John Wakefield's farm by a detachment of Yankee guerillas under the command of Captain Edwin Terrill. He died from bullet wounds to the spine on 6 June 1865 at the age of twenty-seven. Or did he? Significantly, Quantrill's celebrity insured him a dubious kind of immortality. At various times in ensuing decades, he was reported to be hiding out in Chile, raising cattle in Mexico, teaching in Arizona, trapping in British Columbia, and investing in real estate on the island of Maui. One legend even held that he had become a Methodist minister in Alabama, where he concealed six guns under his coat and performed feats of marksmanship at church picnics!

10. Gregory Black (1994) has written a particularly valuable recent study of the Production Code.

11. Dan Woodrell's novel first appeared in short-story form in The Missouri Review in 1983 and was reprinted in George E. Murphy Jr., ed., The Editors' Choice: New American Stories, Vol. 1. The story was divided into three sections, "Coleman Younger, The Last Is Gone—1916"; "I Have Been Found in History Books"; and "Only for Them." The narrator is Jakob Roedel, a second-generation German American who lives with his son, Jefferson, and grandson, Karl, in Saint Bruno, Missouri. Jake has just learned that his old friend and comrade in arms, Coleman Younger, has passed away. Younger's demise triggers Jakes's memories of those bloody days of the early 1860s when conflicts between Missouri pro-Southern bushwhackers and Kansas Free-State Jayhawkers resulted in the slaughter of thousands of citizens and soldiers and divided the loyalties of many families. The subsequent novelization appeared in 1987. It expanded the central section of the story and confined the action to the years 1861–1863.

12. James Schamus, interview by author, 14 March 1998, Kansas City, MO. Unless otherwise indicated, all Schamus quotations are from this interview.

13. Ang Lee, interview by author, 24 March 1998, Kansas City, MO. Unless otherwise indicated, all Lee quotations are from this interview.

14. On 14 August several women were killed and many others were badly injured during the collapse of a Kansas City jail. Three of them were sisters of "Bloody Bill" Anderson and another was a cousin of Cole Younger. "The collapse of the building and the consequent injuries and deaths were just what Quantrill needed to revive his flagging leadership of the guerillas and to give vent to his hatred of the Kansas town." (Schultz, 1996, 143).

15. Daniel Woodrell, interview by author, 24 March 1998, Kansas City, MO. Unless otherwise indicated, all Woodrell quotations are from this interview.

16. See Philip Dunne, "No Fence around Time" (1990).

17. Historian Edward E. Leslie (1996) mentions at least three African Americans who rode with Quantrill: John Lobb, Henry Wilson, and John Noland ("Noland was

especially well liked by his white fellow veterans and was described by them as a 'man among men'") (86).

18. The only changes are subtle ones. For example, here is the screen version of Jake's soliloquy about his missing finger:

> It was a fine finger. And I'd rather have it still, but it was took from me. It has been et by chickens for sure. Someday when some federals catch up with me and kill me in a thicket, they would riddle me and hang me and no Southern man would find me for weeks or months, and when they did I'd be bad meat, pretty well rotted to a glob, and people would ask, Who was that? And surely someone would look up and say, Why it's nubbin-fingered Jake Roedel. Then you could go and tell my father I was clearly murdered, and he wouldn't be tortured by uncertain wonders.

19. Professor Paul Meier, interview by author, 22 November 2005, Lawrence, KS. Unless otherwise indicated, all Meier quotations are from this interview. See also Meier's "Dialect Coaching for the Movies" (1998).

20. See Professor Meier's website: www.paulmeier.com/testimonials.html.

Works Cited

Black, Gregory D. 1994. *Hollywood Censored*. Cambridge, UK: Cambridge University Press.

Burnett, W. R. 1938. *Dark Command*. New York: Alfred A. Knopf.

Carnes, Mark. 1994. *Past Imperfect: History According to the Movies*. New York: Henry Holt.

Crowther, Bosley. 1940. "Dark Command." *New York Times*, 11 May, 2.

———. 1952. "Red Mountain." *New York Times*, 26 April, 2.

Dunne, Philip. 1990. "No Fence around time." In *How Green Was My Valley: The Screenplay for the John Ford Directed Film*. Santa Barbara, CA: Santa Teresa Press.

Fellman, Michael. 1989. *Inside War: The Guerilla Conflict in Missouri during the American Civil War*. New York: Oxford University Press.

Goodrich, Thomas. 1991. *Bloody Dawn: The Story of the Lawrence Massacre*. Kent, OH: Kent State University Press.

"The Jayhawkers." 1959. *Variety*, 21 October. In *Variety's Film Reviews*, vol. 10. New York: R. R. Bowker, 1983, n.p.

"Kansas Raiders." 1950. *Variety*, 7 November. In *Variety's Film Reviews*, vol. 8. New York: R. R. Bowker, 1983, n.p.

Leslie, Edward E. 1996. *The Devil Knows How to Ride*. New York: Random House.

Meier, Paul. 1998. "Dialect Coaching for the Movies." *VASTA Newsletter* 12 (Fall): 8–9.

Pitts, Michael R., ed. 1984. *Hollywood and American History*. Jefferson, NC: McFarland and Company.

"Quantrill's Raiders." 1958. *Variety*, 7 May. In *Variety's Film Reviews*, vol. 9. New York: R. R. Bowker, 1983, n.p.

Rosenstone, Robert A., ed. 1995. *Revisioning History: Film and the Construction of a New Past*. Princeton, NJ: Princeton University Press.

Schultz, Duane. 1996. *Quantrill's War: The Life and Times of William Clarke Quantrill*. New York: St. Martin's.

Slotkin, Richard. 1992. *Gunfighter Nation: The Myth of the Frontier in Twentieth-Century America*. New York: Antheneum.

Starr, Stephen Z. 1973. *Jennison's Jayhawkers: A Civil War Cavalry Regiment and Its Commander*. Baton Rouge: Louisiana State University Press.

Tibbetts, John. 1999. "*Riding with the Devil*: The Movie Adventures of William Clarke Quantrill." *Kansas History: A Journal of the Central Plains* 22 (Autumn): 182–99.

Woodrell, Daniel. 1987. *Woe to Live On*. New York: Henry Holt.

Works Consulted

Blake, Minnie E. n.d. *The Quantrill Raid with Introductory Poems*. Archives of the Douglas County Historical Society, Watkins Community Museum of History, Lawrence, KS.

Brant, Marley. 1992. *The Outlaw Youngers: A Confederate Brotherhood*. New York: Madison Books.

Cecil-Fronsman, Bill, ed. 1997. "'Advocate the Freedom of White Men, as Well as That of Negroes': The Kansas Free State and Antislavery Westerners in Territorial Kansas." *Kansas History* 20 (Summer): 102–15.

Cheatham, Gary L. 1991. "'Desperate Characters': The Development and Impact of the Confederate Guerillas in Kansas." *Kansas History* 14 (Autumn): 44–161.

Cohen, Todd. 1998. "Reliving Quantrill's Raid: KU Libraries Play Role in New Movie." *Oread* 22 (8 May): 1–2.

Dary, David, ed. n.d. *Hovey E. Lowman's Account of the Lawrence Massacre, August 21, 1863*. Lawrence, KS: Watkins Community Museum of History.

Dobak, William A. 1983–1984. "Civil War on the Kansas–Missouri Border: The Narrative of Former Slave Andrew Williams." *Kansas History* 6 (Winter): 236–42.

LaForte, Robert S. 1986–1987. "Cyrus Leland Jr. and the Lawrence Massacre: A Note and Document." *Kansas History* 9 (Winter): 175–81.

Lewis, Sinclair, and Lloyd Lewis. 1935. *Jayhawker: A Play in Three Acts*. Garden City, NY: Doubleday, Doran and Company.

Patrick, Jeffrey L. E. 1997. "'This Regiment Will Make a Mark': Letters from a Member of Jennison's Jayhawkers, 1861–1862." *Kansas History* 20 (Spring): 50–58.

Peterson, John M., ed. 1989. "Letters of Edward and Sarah Fitch, Lawrence, Kansas, 1855–1863 (Part II)." *Kansas History* 12 (Summer): 95.

"Reminiscences of Quantrell's Raid upon the City of Lawrence, Kas.: Thrilling Narratives by Living Eye Witnesses." n.d. Lawrence, KS: Watkins Community Museum of History (originally compiled and edited by John C. Shea and published in Kansas City, MO, in 1879).

Robertson, James I., Jr. 1963. *The Sack of Lawrence: What Price Glory?* Kansas Civil War Centennial Commission.

Scott, Emory Frank. 1979. "The Dark Command." In *One Hundred Years of Lawrence Theatres*, 92–93. Lawrence, KS: House of Usher.

Sheridan, Richard B., ed. 1995. *Quantrill and the Lawrence Massacre: A Reader.* Lawrence, KS: Douglas County Historical Society.

Woodrell, Daniel. 1985. "Woe to Live On." In *The Editors' Choice: New American Stories*, vol.1., ed. George E. Murphy Jr., 315–33. New York: Bantam Books.

PART V

EPILOGUE: THE FUTURE OF ADAPTATION STUDIES

~

CHAPTER TWENTY-THREE

Where Are We Going, Where Have We Been?

Thomas M. Leitch

Editors' Note: Thomas Leitch's chapter first appeared in the newsletter of the Literature/Film Association 1 (September 2003). The chapter is quoted by Donald M. Whaley ("Adaptation Studies and the History of Ideas: The Case for Apocalypse Now*") and David L. Kranz ("Trying Harder: Probability and Objectivity in Adaptation Studies") in part I of this anthology.*

Even if Jim Welsh, the presiding spirit of the Literature/Film Association (LFA) since its inception [circa 1978], were not asking the question, it would still be important to ask where LFA is and ought to be headed. But my predictions and my advice about the road ahead, and even my ideas about why the question is important, will carry more weight if I first consider how we got where we are.

Since its inception, the academic study of film has been an insurgent discipline. The banner of auteurism under which film studies first entered American universities in the 1960s was a reaction against the Tradition of Quality, an approach to filmmaking typified, according to *Cahiers du Cinéma* agitator François Truffaut (1954), by such films as Claude Autant-Lara's *Le Diable au Corps* (1947), which relied on adapting established literary classics to establish their own aesthetic cachet. The infant discipline of film studies, given radical impetus by the May 1968 revolution in France, championed film directors who succeeded in shaping material that lacked such a cachet, material that might seem neutral, unpromising, or downright sordid. In the terms of Andrew Sarris, whose *The American Cinema: Directors and Directions, 1929–1968* (1998) became the bible of the new discipline. Hollywood directors like Howard Hawks, Nicholas Ray, and Alfred Hitchcock and French directors like Truffaut, Jean-Luc Godard, and Claude Chabrol were important precisely because their defiantly antiliterary brand of cinema resisted assimilation into traditional canons of aesthetic value and existing departments of literature.

From its beginnings, however, auteurism contained the seeds of a counter-insurgency that treated film directors as auteurs whose work could be judged just as seriously, and by the same standards, as the work of the canonical authors the Tradition of Quality had enshrined. Hitchcock was the first beneficiary of this policy. The shift in approach from the special *Cahiers* number on Hitchcock in 1954 to Chabrol and Eric Rohmer's *Hitchcock: The First Forty-Five Films* three years later shows all the signs of a new canonicity in its search for the kinds of thematic consistency, moral gravitas, and authorized meanings that would make Hitchcock a figure worthy of comparison to literary classics like Dostoevsky. Auteurism made it possible and attractive for American academics who had been trained as literary scholars to turn to the study of film as narrative mode that had both the significance of literature and the allure and accessibility of popular culture.

A year or so after I came to the University of Delaware to direct the film studies program, my chair, in endorsing my application for a research grant, wrote that I adopted "a literary approach to film." At the time, the phrase baffled me; I could only conclude that it meant that my terminal degree was in English rather than in the newfangled discipline of film studies. Now I can see what he meant: that my background, like that of many of my peers, combined what James Naremore (2000) has called "a mixture of Kantian aesthetics and Arnoldian ideas about society" (2). Naremore identifies this mixture as "the submerged common sense of the average English department" (2) that forms the backdrop to its assumptions about the project of adapting literature to film, and this context of "a literary approach to film" was the matrix of the LFA.

Not just yet, however, for the association, reversing the natural order of things, was preceded by its conference, which in turn was preceded by its journal. Jim Welsh has explained how a conference on D. H. Lawrence and film spawned the collection of essays that composed the inaugural number of *Literature/Film Quarterly* (*LFQ*) in the winter of 1973, kicking off a journal that soon became the preeminent and indeed the only journal focusing on adaptation studies but that soon grew to accommodate thematic studies of individual filmmakers and genres, interviews with leading filmmakers, scholarly bibliographies, and production histories. In adverting to this early history, I want to emphasize two salient points: that *LFQ* was from its beginnings defined as counterinsurgent—the journal that was not *Cinema Journal*, that did not speak with the increasingly consensual voice of American film studies, preoccupied since the 1970s with apparatus theories rooted in the work of Jacques Lacan—and that its brief soon grew to encompass many acres well outside the boundaries of adaptation, areas best described as adopting a literary approach to film. In addition to analyzing cinematic adaptations of canonical (and eventually not so canonical) literary texts—most notably in its frequent issues devoted to Shakespeare on film—*LFQ* published studies of the careers and leading films of establishment filmmakers from Hitchcock to David Lynch, close readings of newly canonical and variously arcane films, thematic studies of directors and genres, interviews in which filmmakers discussed the creation of their most significant works, and scholarly tools designed to foster future research. Though its central mission remained adaptation study, *LFQ* soon came to represent more broadly those lit-crit values—belletristic focus, lucid prose, Kantian aesthetics, Arnoldian ideas about the place of art in society—that American film studies had largely abandoned.

It was in this context that I attended my first literature/film conference. I had received broadsides for at least two earlier conferences in Salisbury, but it was not until 1989 that I bestirred myself to see what was happening down the road. It was instantly obvious that this was not just another film conference. My paper on remakes, placed in a session titled "Film Theory," was immediately preceded by a paper whose author began by announcing, "I can't imagine why my paper was put into a session on film theory. I hate theory." By the end of the weekend, the foregathered group, most of whom also seemed to have little use for theory, answered a challenge laid down by Jim Welsh (Tom Erskine, who had been so active in launching *LFQ* and sustaining it for nearly twenty years, stood aside this time, leaving Jim to rouse the troops on his own). Led by Jim, the conference attendees decided to make their counterinsurgent defense of Kantian aesthetics and Arnoldian cultural criticism official—though nobody put it that way—by constituting the LFA, which would be to the Society for Cinema Studies (SCS) what *LFQ* was to *Cinema Journal*: a haven from prevailing theoretical and political trends in contemporary film studies organized around an implicit defense of an older tradition of belletristic critical exegesis and American liberalism, which by this time had come in an academic context to look dangerously right wing. LFA was where you could go to give papers SCS wouldn't accept, or papers you didn't want to give at SCS, or papers you didn't want to give so much that you were willing to sit through a weekend of apparatus theory, and Jim's biggest worry in those years was that graduate students secretly flying the colors of SCS would colonize the conference and make it a wholly owned subsidiary of the enemy.

Nothing like this ever happened. The annual conference accommodated a mixed population of old-guard liberals, conservatives, and time-servers; mid-career strivers willing to take a chance on finding a receptive audience; and young firebrands of every stripe who regarded their museum-piece elders (and vice versa) with polite bemusement or indifference but never open hostility or plans for subjugation. The only flaw in this idyll of wary coexistence was the anemic health of LFA itself. If SCS was a professional organization whose membership numbered well over 1,000 that incidentally sponsored an annual conference and published a quarterly journal, LFA was the offshoot of a highly successful quarterly that had spun off a much smaller conference and a professional organization whose list of active members was still smaller.

The main reason, then, that it is important to consider the future of LFA is that its core membership is small and getting smaller. Like Shakers, the pioneers who founded and supported *LFQ* in its earlier years have not succeeded in replacing themselves. Few Arnoldians and fewer Kantians complete PhDs every year, and the backbone of LFA, film scholars who were trained in English departments, is clearly an endangered species. For better or worse, the literary study of film is likely to continue declining. (*Editors' Note: Since 2003, LFA membership has increased and the leadership group has broadened.*) At the same time, adaptation studies, the core mission of this dwindling corps of crossover scholars, is itself in crisis. The field's focus on film adaptations' fidelity or freedom vis-à-vis their canonical literary source texts, established as central as far back as George Bluestone's 1957 *Novels into Film*, has maintained such a stranglehold on adaptation studies that even Brian McFarlane's *Novel to Film: An Introduction to the Theory of Adaptation* (1996), which everywhere decries the tyranny of fidelity as a criterion for evaluating and analyzing adaptation, situates itself willy-nilly within that same tradition. Given the declining numbers of film professors trained as literary scholars and the inability of adaptation studies to define a more compelling rationale than the question of movies' fidelity to their literary sources—a question that guarantees film second-class status—it might seem that adaptation studies, dismissed as provincial by both literary studies and film studies, is on the ropes.

Yet, the opposite seems true to me. I consider this a time of tremendous excitement and limitless potential for LFA and its core mission. One reason is that the academic establishment of American film studies is far less monolithic than it was a generation ago. The rise of David Bordwell and Noël Carroll's constructivism, a viewer-response theory that emphasizes conscious rhetorical constructions of meaning by filmmakers and audiences rather than the dictatorial unconscious mechanisms of Lacan, has demonstrated that the discipline's critical orthodoxy can be successfully challenged from within. As film scholars have considered a wider range of filmmaking practices and theories, Lacanian apparatus theory has become less compelling, and the work of Lacan's brilliant successor Slavoj Žižek has been too protean and too constantly in touch with the shifting sand of popular culture to establish the same doctrinaire influence. The declining weight of disciplinary orthodoxy has allowed a thousand flowers to bloom, some of them most unexpected. The most frequent sentence I heard at the SCS convention in March 2003 was "I know it's unfashionable to quote André Bazin, but . . ." If Bazin's humanist realism is once more under serious consideration, who knows what film studies may rediscover next?

In the meantime, there are signs that the logjam in adaptation studies may finally be breaking up. In introducing the collection of adaptation studies essays she coedited with Deborah Cartmell, Imelda Whelehan (1999) agrees with James Naremore that approaching adaptation "from an 'English lit.' perspective" tends to prejudice the field by "privilege[ing] the originary literary text above its adaptations," if only because "it is possibly the 'literariness' of the fictional text which itself appears to give credence to the study of adaptations at all" (17). By emphasizing the ways institutional contexts have shaped adaptation studies, Whelehan, like Naremore, makes it easier to sidestep the dead end of fidelity studies by envisioning different contexts that could generate a different set of questions. At the same time, the critical and commercial success of recent films like *Adaptation* and *The Hours*, and the widely remarked confusion that greeted the most recent Oscar nominations for screenwriting, have rekindled public discussion about the nature of cinematic adaptation. If this discussion has rarely been especially penetrating, many of the simplest questions it has raised—Did the notoriously freewheeling *Adaptation* really deserve consideration in the Best Adapted Screenplay category and *Far from Heaven*, *Gangs of New York*, and *My Big Fat Greek Wedding* in the Best Original Screenplay category? What makes one of these films an adaptation but not the other three? More generally still, because every text, including allegedly original sourcetexts, depends on numberless intertexts, why does it suit observers to elevate some intertexts to the status of sources and ignore others?—are remarkably provocative.

In an important series of recent essays and a forthcoming book (which in fact turned into three books: *Literature through Film: Realism, Magic, and the Art of Adaptation*, *Literature and Film: A Guide to the Theory and Practice of Film Adaptation*, and *A Companion to Literature and Film*, all published by Blackwell in 2004 and 2005), Robert Stam (2000) has adumbrated a Bakhtinian approach to adaptation, that contends that fidelity is only one of "a whole constellation of tropes [for adaptation]—translation, reading, dialogization, cannibalization, transmutation, transfiguration, and signifying—each of which sheds light on a different dimension of adaptation" (62). Critics who follow Stam (2000) in seeing "the source novel . . . as a situated utterance produced in one medium and in one historical context, then transformed into another equally situated utterance that is produced in a different context and in a different medium" (68), will recast adaptation studies as intertextual studies, in which every text is a rereading of earlier texts and every text, whether it poses as an original or an adaptation, has the same claims to aesthetic or ontological privilege as every other. Such a reconfigured discipline would replace adaptation study's leading question, How has a given adaptation succeeded or failed in capturing the leading textual features or its sourcetext? with a new series of questions: How has a given adaptation rewritten its sourcetext? Why has it chosen to select and rewrite the sourcetexts it has? How have the texts available to us inevitably been rewritten by the very act of reading? and How do we want to rewrite them anew?

Questions like these carry the potential, not simply to construct a theoretical model capable of bridging the gap between adaptation studies and film studies, but to shake literary studies to its very core in a way neither of its wayward offspring has yet succeeded in doing. Instead of supplementing literary studies with new texts or theoretical models to consider, as adaptation studies and film studies have done, intertextual studies seeks to dethrone English departments' traditional emphasis on *literature*, the existing canon that deserves close study and faithful adaptation, and replace it with *literacy*, the study of the ways texts have been, might be, and should be read and rewritten. This is a dauntingly ambitious project but one whose time has come. It replaces deadlocked debates about the literary canon, the place of writing in the curriculum, the relation between humanistic values and deconstructive critiques, and the relevance of literature and literary studies to contemporary citizenship with a single question: Living as we all do in culture marked by the traces of thousands of texts, how do we want to respond to those texts, and what kinds of skills do we need to do so?

Film theorists and English professors have ignored each other or quarreled fruitlessly with each other for long enough. It is time for the scholars of the LFA and the contributors to *LFQ*, practically the only people on earth conversant with the languages of both parties, to lead them both to focus on promoting the active literacy promised by intertextual studies as the logical successor not only to adaptation studies but to literary and film studies themselves.

Works Cited

Bluestone, George. 1957. *Novels into Film.* Baltimore: Johns Hopkins University Press.

McFarlane, Brian. 1996. *Novel to Film: An Introduction to the Theory of Adaptation.* New York: Oxford University Press.

Naremore, James. 2000. "Introduction: Film and the Reign of Adaptation." In *Film Adaptation*, ed. James Naremore, 1–16. New Brunswick, NJ: Rutgers University Press.

Sarris, Andrew. 1998. *The American Cinema: Directors and Directions, 1929–1968.* New York: Dutton.

Stam, Robert. 2000. "The Dialogics of Adaptation." In *Film Adaptation*, ed. James Naremore, 54–76. New Brunswick, NJ: Rutgers University Press.

———. 2005. *Literature through Film: Realism, Magic, and the Art of Adaptation.* Malden, MA: Blackwell.

Stam, Robert, and Alessandra Raengo, eds. 2004. *A Companion to Literature and Film.* Malden, MA: Blackwell.

———. 2005. *Literature and Film: A Guide to the Theory and Practice of Film Adaptation.* Malden, MA: Blackwell.

Truffaut, François. 1976. "A Certain Tendency of the French Cinema." Translator unknown. In *Movies and Methods*, ed. Bill Nichols, 225–37. Originally published in *Cahiers du Cinéma* 31 (January 1954).

Whelehan, Imelda. 1999. "Adaptations: The Contemporary Dilemma." In *Adaptations: From Text to Screen, Screen to Text*, ed. Deborah Cartmell and Imelda Whelehan, 3–19. London: Routledge.

~

CHAPTER TWENTY-FOUR

The Future of Adaptation Studies

Peter Lev

Editors' Note: Peter Lev's chapter is an expanded version of an article that first appeared in the Literature/Film Newsletter *1 (September 2003). The original version is quoted by Donald M. Whaley ("Adaptation Studies and the History of Ideas: The Case for* Apocalypse Now"*) in part I of this anthology.*

Let me begin with what has already been done. Adaptation study was a marginal venture in the early 1950s, when André Bazin (1967) broke with critical orthodoxy by praising "impure cinema" (films based on novels and plays). Then George Bluestone in 1957 began to establish a new orthodoxy of adaptation criticism with a volume on prestigious adaptations of classic novels. Since Bazin and Bluestone, the analysis of film adaptation has stretched out in several directions, including Shakespeare and film, modern language studies and film, cultural studies of various kinds, intertextuality, and postmodernism. Today, adaptation studies is an accepted part of the academy, the subject of innumerable courses, dissertations, conference papers, articles, and books. The thirty-five-year history of *Literature/Film Quarterly* (*LFQ*) is itself a demonstration of adaptation study's strength and scope.

I believe one important direction for the future is greater hybridity. Films are often based on multiple works, visual as well as textual. Paintings, photographs, news articles, historical events, films, television shows, and so on can be sources for films; one loses some of the richness of this impure art by limiting sources to novels and plays. For the much-studied *Blow-Up* (Michelangelo Antonioni, 1966), for example, a conventional adaptation study would link the film to its credited source, a short story by Julio Cortázar. The Cortázar story provides a conceptual key to the film but does not help with the time and space setting, which is London in the mid-1960s. To understand this aspect of *Blow-Up*, it helps to look at another, uncredited source—Francis Wyndham's piece on young photographers in the London *Sunday Times Magazine* of 10 May 1964. One could then supplement the textual sources by describing the work of David Bailey and other photographers of "swinging London." Further, the look, sound, and feel of London itself in the mid-1960s is clearly an intertext of the film, and *Blow-Up*'s director and writers were, among other things, observers.

Another film based on multiple sources would be Joseph Mankiewicz's legendarily troubled epic *Cleopatra* (1963). The film's credits list "histories by Plutarch, Suetonius, Appian, other ancient sources," plus Carlo Franzero's *The Life and Times of Cleopatra* (1957). Mankiewicz noted in interviews that Plutarch was the primary source—not surprising, since Plutarch's "The Life of Julius Caesar" and "The Life of Antony" have been the basis for all later tellings of the Cleopatra story. Mankiewicz, as a great aficionado of the theatre, was also influenced by Shaw's *Caesar and Cleopatra*, Shakespeare's *Julius Caesar*, and Shakespeare's *Antony and Cleopatra*. The film's character of Julius Caesar seems strongly influenced by Shaw, for example, whereas the montage sequence of Caesar's assassination seems to carefully avoid Shakespeare's version of the same event (this might be called a "negative influence"). Mankiewicz's *Cleopatra* additionally was influenced by Hollywood's Greek, Roman, and biblical epics of the 1950s and early 1960s, which imposed ideas of visual style, narrative, costume, treatment of sexuality, and so forth. And the planning, writing, and production of *Cleopatra* took into account at least three previous motion picture versions of the story: Fox's 1917 *Cleopatra*, starring Theda Bara and directed by J. Gordon Edwards; Paramount's 1934 *Cleopatra*, starring Claudette Colbert and directed by Cecil B. DeMille; and Eagle Lion's 1945 *Caesar and Cleopatra*, starring Vivien Leigh and Claude Rains, screenplay by George Bernard Shaw (based on his play), directed by Gabriel Pascal.

A second area deserving attention is detailed study of the screenplay. Many adaptation scholars omit discussion of screenplays altogether, contenting themselves with a comparison between literary source and finished film. But screenplays can provide important insights into how and why a literary work was adapted, even if (perhaps especially if) a screenplay draft differs markedly from the finished motion picture. Screenplay study also brings up a fascinating theoretical issue: Is the screenplay a work of art in itself or simply a transitional stage between literary work and film?[1] There are two problems with screenplay research: (1) Screenplays are often difficult to access, requiring travel to faraway archives; and (2) understanding the connections between screenplays (often multiple drafts), literary sources, and finished films involves lengthy, painstaking research. However, these problems are not so different from archive-based research in many branches of the humanities, and they are certainly not insoluble. I therefore think we will see an increasing number of dissertations, books, and articles based on screenplay research.

Cleopatra can provide an example of the advantages and difficulties of screenplay study. At least nine screenwriters labored over *Cleopatra*, producing thousands of pages of screenplay drafts, and a more or less complete record of their work is available in the Twentieth Century Fox script collection, accessible via the UCLA Arts Special Collections Library. Reading through this voluminous material is a daunting task, yet one can learn a great deal from the effort. For example, the screenplay drafts would be crucial to any scholar seeking to understand what Rouben Mamoulian's version of *Cleopatra* would have been like (this production, starring Elizabeth Taylor, Stephen Boyd, and Peter Finch, was cancelled in 1961 because of Taylor's illness; Mankiewicz's version starring Taylor, Rex Harrison, and Richard Burton was a second attempt by Twentieth Century Fox to make the film). The *Cleopatra* file at UCLA also provides access to the work of three important, though very different, writers: Nunnally Johnson, Lawrence Durrell, and Joseph Mankiewicz. Though Durrell thought himself a very bad screenwriter, one of his scenes presents the lives and ideas of the ordinary people of Rome, thus correcting the Hollywood epic's focus on celebrities only. This kind of material can enhance our understanding of not only one film but also a whole period, and it would surely interest Durrell scholars as well. Mankiewicz's script drafts speak to other questions: how much was written at various stages of the film's production (*Cleopatra* started filming without a final script) and whether Fox's parsimony and Darryl F. Zanuck's brutal cutting destroyed a masterpiece (as Mankiewicz and others claimed). I believe scholars should and must get involved in screenplay research; discussing literary source and finished film while omitting the screenplay leaves out a crucial step in the creative process.

Finally, I think the next several years will see a blurring of the boundaries between media scholar and media producer. DVD and other computer-based technologies make it possible to add a great deal of related material (scripts, photographs, commentaries, advertisements, literary sources, illustrated critiques, etc.) to a home video release. Most projects of this type limit themselves to commentary by directors and actors, but on occasion classic films include commentary by literary and/or film scholars. For example, the commentary track on the DVD of *The Grapes of Wrath* features Steinbeck expert Susan Shillinglaw and film scholar Joseph McBride. There are certainly limitations to this sort of collaboration—for example, media companies are for-profit entities, and copyright law greatly limits what scholars can do on their own. But one can at least imagine a more flexible and open-ended version of the scholarly commentary. Suppose media texts such as films were available on the Internet (as some already are) and scholars could append multimedia commentary to them—for example, text, music, still images, links to other films. Many commentaries could be made for the same film, and they could link to each other as well as to the film itself. Such a system might be far more sophisticated and more specific than the print-based film scholarship that is now the norm. Or it might regress into multimedia cacophony.

The above three areas for further research suggest a very bright future for adaptation studies. We should await the intertextual, multimedia future with optimism.

Note

1. This issue was eloquently discussed by William Horne in "See Shooting Script" (1992).

Works Cited

Bazin, André. 1967. "In Defense of Mixed Cinema." In *What Is Cinema?*, trans. Hugh Gray. Berkeley: University of California Press. This essay was first published in 1952.

Bluestone, George. 1957. *Novels into Film*. Berkeley: University of California Press.

Horne, William. 1992. "See Shooting Script: Reflections on the Ontology of the Screenplay." *LFQ* 20 (1) : 48–54.

Index

339

About the Editors

James M. Welsh was the editor of *Literature/Film Quarterly* for thirty-two years. He is the author, editor, or series editor of numerous books, including *The Encyclopedia of Filmmakers* (coedited with John Tibbetts, 2002) and *The Cinema of Tony Richardson* (coedited with John Tibbetts, 1999). Welsh is professor emeritus of English at Salisbury University, Salisbury, Maryland. He founded the Literature/Film Association in 1989.

Peter Lev is professor of electronic media and film at Towson University, Towson, Maryland. His books include *Transforming the Screen: History of the American Cinema vol. 7, the Fifties* (2003), *American Films of the 1970s: Conflicting Visions* (2000), *The Euro-American Cinema* (1993), and *Claude Lelouch Film Director* (1983). He is working on a history of Twentieth Century Fox.

~

About the Contributors

Linda Costanzo Cahir is an assistant professor at Kean University and a contributing editor to *Literature/Film Quarterly*. Her publications include numerous articles and the books *Solitude and Society in the Works of Herman Melville and Edith Wharton* (1999) and *Literature into Film: Theory and Practical Approaches* (2006).

Sarah Cardwell is senior lecturer in film and television at the University of Kent, England, where she teaches, among other things, courses on adaptation. She is author of *Andrew Davies* (2005) and *Adaptation Revisited: Television and the Classic Novel* (2002), as well as numerous articles on the topics of adaptation, film, and television.

Odette Caufman-Blumenfeld chairs the English Department at the Alexander Ion Cuza University in Iaşi, Romania, where, at the turn of the last century, the Yiddish Theatre originated before migrating to New York City. She is the author of *Studies in Feminist Drama* (1998). In 1994–1995 she held an American Council of Learned Societies (ACLS) grant to study theatre at the Graduate Center of the City University of New York. She has taught the course Contemporary Women Playwrights at the University of Siegen in Germany.

Wendy Everett is reader in film studies and French at the University of Bath, England. She is author or editor of several books, including *European Identity in Cinema*, second ed. (2005), *Terence Davies* (2004), *Revisiting Space: Space and Place in European Cinema* (coedited with Axel Goodbody, 2005), and *Cultures of Exile: Images of Displacement* (coedited with Peter Wagstaff, 2004).

David L. Kranz is professor of English and film studies at Dickinson College, Carlisle, Pennsylvania, where he has taught many different courses on Shakespeare, Renaissance literature, composition, and film. He is also the author of numerous articles on Shakespeare and on film adaptation. A former president of the Literature/Film Association, he is coediting a book of essays arguing for a plurality of approaches to the criticism of cinematic adaptation.

Yong Li Lan is associate professor and coordinator of the Theatre Studies Programme in the Department of English Language and Literature, National University of Singapore, where she teaches modern drama, theatre internship, intercultural theatre, and Shakespeare studies across different mediums. She is interested in exploring the implications that intercultural, cross-media, and globalized performance in the East/Southeast Asian region have for the development of Shakespeare and performance studies and has published essays in *Theatre Journal, Theatre Research International,* and the *Blackwell Companion to Shakespeare and Performance* on the formal and cultural interstices in Shakespeare film, theatre, and the Internet, as well as in Singapore theatre.

Thomas M. Leitch teaches English and directs the Film Studies Program at the University of Delaware. His most recent books are *Film Adaptation and Its Discontents: From* Gone with the Wind *to* The Passion of the Christ (2007), *Perry Mason* (2005), and *Crime Films* (2002).

Joan Driscoll Lynch is professor emeritus and former chair of the Communications Department at Villanova University. She is the author of *Film Education in Secondary Schools* and has published articles in the *Journal of Popular Culture,* the *Journal of Film and Video, Literature/Film Quarterly, Millennium Film Journal,* the *Drama Review,* and others. Three of her articles have been reprinted in anthologies, one of them twice. She founded and for twenty-one years directed the Villanova University Film and Lecture Series. She is currently writing screenplays and serving on the editorial board of the *Journal of Film and Video.*

Brian McFarlane is honorary associate professor at Monash University, Melbourne, and visiting professor at the University of Hull. He taught literature and film for many years and is author of many articles and books. His recent books include *New Australian Cinema: Sources and Parallels in American and British Film* (1992 [coauthored]), *Novel to Film: An Introduction to the Theory of Adaptation* (1996), *An Autobiography of British Cinema* (1997), *Lance Comfort* (1999), *The Oxford Companion to Australian Film* (1999 [coedited]), *The Encyclopedia of British Film* (2003 [editor, compiler, and chief author]), *The Cinema of Britain and Ireland* (2005 [editor]), and *Great Expectations* (2007).

Walter C. Metz is interim department head in media and theatre arts at Montana State University–Bozeman, where he teaches the history, theory, and criticism of film, theatre, and television. He is the author of *Bewitched* (2007) and *Engaging Film Criticism: Film History and Contemporary American Cinema* (2004). His previous publications involve cinema and intertextuality for such journals as *Film Criticism*, the *Journal of Film and Video*, and *Literature/Film Quarterly*. In 2003–2004, he was Fulbright Guest Professor in American studies at the John F. Kennedy Institute at the Free University in Berlin.

William Mooney is associate professor of English and assistant dean for liberal arts at the Fashion Institute of Technology, SUNY, in New York City. He has taught screenwriting and film studies courses and is currently working with faculty from FIT's School of Art and Design to develop a digital film production and design BFA program.

Brian Neve is a senior lecturer in politics at the University of Bath and teaches on the University's cinema MA program. He is the author of *Film and Politics in America* (1992) and *The Cinema of Elia Kazan: An American Outsider* (2007) and editor (with Steve Neale, Frank Krutnik, and Peter Stansfield) of *Un-American Cinema: Film and Politics in the Blacklist Era* (2007).

C. Kenneth Pellow is professor of English at the University of Colorado at Colorado Springs, where he has taught for nearly forty years. Presently, he teaches classes on twentieth-century British literature, critical theory and writing, contemporary novels, and film and fiction. He is author of *Films as Critiques of Novels* (1994) and has just finished a book on Joyce's *Dubliners*.

J. P. Telotte is a professor of film studies at Georgia Institute of Technology. He coedits the journal *Post Script* and has published widely on film and literature, with a special emphasis on science fiction. His most recent books are *The Mouse Machine: Disney and Technology* (2007) and *Disney TV* (2004).

Frank Thompson is an author, filmmaker, and movie historian. He served as associate producer and historical consultant and appears onscreen in *Wild Bill: Hollywood Maverick* (1996), a biography of director William A. Wellman, and wrote and directed *The Great Christmas Movies* (1998). Thompson has to date published thirty-six books, including *Lost: Signs of Life* (2006), *King Arthur: A Novel* (2004), *The Alamo: The Illustrated Story of the Epic Film* (2004), *I Was That Masked Man* (1998 [coauthor with Clayton Moore]), *Lost Films* (1996), *Henry King* (1995), *Robert Wise: A Bio-Bibliography* (1995), *Tim Burton's* The Nightmare before Christmas (1993), and *William A. Wellman* (1983).

John C. Tibbetts is associate professor in the Department of Theatre and Film at the University of Kansas. His books include *His Majesty the American: The Films of Douglas Fairbanks, Sr.* (1977), *Introduction to the Photoplay* (1977), *The American Theatrical Film* (1985), *Dvořák in America* (1993), *The Encyclopedia of Novels into Film* (1998), and, with coeditor James M. Welsh, *The Cinema of Tony Richardson* (1999), *The Encyclopedia of Stage Plays into Film* (2001), and *The Encyclopedia of Novels into Film* (2002). His most recent book is *Composers in the Movies: Studies in Musical Biography* (2005). He is currently involved in the production of "The World of Robert Schumann" for Kansas Public Radio and WMFT in Chicago.

Elsie Walker is assistant professor at Salisbury University, Salisbury, Maryland, where she coruns the cinema studies program. She is coeditor of *Literature/Film Quarterly* and has published articles on adaptations of Shakespeare and the cinema of Ingmar Bergman. Her current research is on soundtracks.

Tom Whalen has published criticism, fiction, and poetry in *AGNI, Bookforum, Critique, Film Quarterly, The Georgia Review, The Idaho Review, The Iowa Review, Literary Review, The Missouri Review, Northwest Review, Ploughshares, The Quarterly, The Review of Contemporary Fiction, Seattle Review, The Southern Review, Studies in Short Fiction, The Wallace Stevens Journal*, and in several anthologies. He has published articles on films by Buster Keaton, Godard, Truffaut, Malick, Coppola, Carpenter, Tykwer, and others. His books include *An Exchange of Letters* (2007, stories), *Roithamer's Universe* (1996, novel),

Winter Coat (1998, poetry), and *Dolls* (2007, prose poems). He lives in Stuttgart, Germany.

Donald M. Whaley teaches American cultural history and coordinates the American studies program at Salisbury University, Salisbury, Maryland. He is a contributing editor of *Literature/Film Quarterly* and has guest edited a special issue of that journal on Vietnam War movies. His essays on American culture have covered such topics as jazz, soul music, rockabilly, the history of anarchism, the writings of Gore Vidal, the work of southern documentary filmmaker Ross Spears, and the films of Oliver Stone. He was one of the authors who contributed essays to *Hollywood's White House: The American Presidency in Film and History*, a book that won the Popular Culture Association's Ray and Pat Browne Award in 2004.